A Century of Recorded Music

A Century of Recorded Music

Listening to Musical History

Timothy Day

Yale University Press
New Haven and London

Set in FF Scala by Best-set Typesetter Ltd., Hong Kong
Printed in Great Britain by St Edmundsbury Press Ltd

Library of Congress Cataloging in Publication Data

Day, Timothy.
A century of recorded music: listening to musical history/Timothy Day.
p.   cm.
Includes bibliographical references and indexes.
ISBN 0–300–08442–0 (cloth)
1. Sound recordings – History.   2. Sound – Recording and reproducing – History.
3. Sound recording industry – History.   4. Music – 20th century – History and
criticism.   I. Title.
ML1055.D37 2000   780'.26'6 – dc21   00–043490

A catalogue record for this book is available from the British Library.

2 4 6 8 10 9 7 5 3 1

For Kate and Ruth

Contents

Preface

A century of recording has changed the way we listen to music and the way music is performed – as well as what we listen to – to an extent that we are only just beginning to grasp. Everyone acknowledges this and yet music historians, classically trained musicologists studying the concert traditions and opera and liturgical music of Western Europe, are reluctant to investigate discs and tapes and to study these phenomena. Why this should be is itself not an unimportant question and one which this book addresses.

Recordings offer new fields of enquiry, which will require the development of new techniques of research and the acquisition of knowledge and expertise about the artefacts themselves. But the study of recordings also prompts the formulation of fundamental questions about musical performance, and about the nature of musical experience. These questions in turn suggest new kinds of historical writing – very different from, for example, the analysis of compositional styles through concentration on the inner coherence of notes in musical notation – new styles of 'thick' historical analysis and description which touch on intellectual history and economic forces and the creation of markets, and on aesthetics and the history of taste.

The book attempts to give guidance to the scholar but it is not a comprehensive account of the history of recorded music. Such an account is hardly possible until much more information is unearthed and analysed. The outlines that I have provided may seem too boldly drawn. This straightforwardness, however, arises not from unshakable confidence in the validity of my own judgements, but from the hunch that such clarity will better assist and encourage others to expand,

revise, contradict and supersede my own work in a neglected field notoriously difficult to cultivate.

Ultimately the history of western art music in the twentieth century
cannot be isolated from the histories of other kinds of music; it is undeniable that classical music has been affected, especially in the second
half of the century, by recordings of popular music and jazz and the
musics of other traditions. But the classical traditions of Europe have
retained a high degree of autonomy and, leaving aside the limitations
imposed by my own ignorance, I considered it important, even in an
introductory text of this nature, to use space to illustrate particular historical points in considerable detail in order to suggest the rich possibilities that the study of recordings offers. The history of recording
has included both national and international elements and this too I
have tried to suggest; that many of my examples are drawn from developments in Britain is simply the result of the limitations in what I know
about best.

It gives me much pleasure to thank Malcolm Gerratt, whose idea this
book was, and my other editor at Yale, Robert Baldock, for their belief
in this book, and in me, and for their many kindnesses, and for their
patience. I should also like to thank my students at the University of
Southampton with whom I discussed some of the ideas in this essay
when I taught for a semester as a visiting lecturer in 1996, and Dr
William Drabkin for inviting me. Two conferences helped me to crys-
tallize my thoughts at a later stage, one at the Jerusalem Music Centre
in May 1998 on different aspects of recording and music, and one in
Stockholm in September that year on performance traditions in the
nineteenth-century keyboard repertory, and I should like to thank the
organizers, Hed Sella in Jerusalem and Professor Erik Kjellberg of
the University of Uppsala in Stockholm, and my fellow speakers on
those occasions. I am grateful particularly to my colleagues in the
sound archive of the British Library who have helped me with many
details, and especially to Jonathan Summers, who was my assistant
during the months the book was being written and was very generous
in sharing his expertise.

I
Making Recordings

The earliest cylinders and discs

There are very few recordings of classical music that survive from the nineteenth century. The first classical recordings were probably made by the pianist Josef Hofmann in 1887.[1] This was at Orange, in the suburbs of Newark, New Jersey, in the laboratory of Thomas Alva Edison, the man who had first succeeded in recording and reproducing sounds ten years earlier. Hofmann was an eleven-year-old prodigy and seems to have enjoyed the experience – later he was to loathe making recordings and as an adult made comparatively few[2] – and on New Year's Day 1890 Edison presented him with a cylinder phonograph which he used to make further recordings for himself at home in Berlin. He was very impressed and told Edison that a cylinder of his own playing was 'indeed wonderful'.[3] The German pianist and conductor Hans von Bülow (1830–94) is supposed to have visited the laboratory too and to have recorded a Chopin mazurka for Edison, though he is said to have almost fainted when he heard himself playing.[4] There are reports that Edison also recorded von Bülow conducting a complete performance of Beethoven's 'Eroica' Symphony, among other orchestral works, at the Metropolitan Opera House in New York.[5] But none of these have survived. Fragments do exist from a performance of Handel's *Israel in Egypt* conducted by August Manns at the Crystal Palace in south-east London on 29 June 1888 with a chorus of 3,025 voices,[6] and there is a recording of Brahms playing part of his Hungarian Dance no. 1 in G minor, which was probably made in Vienna in November 1889.[7] The original quality of this Brahms cylinder recording is not known; by the time it came to be copied decades later it was badly worn and very little can be made out behind the swish and hiss of surface noise.[8]

The first cylinder recordings issued commercially in any quantities went on sale in America in 1890.[9] They were expensive, each at least fifty cents, and were bought mainly for coin-in-the-slot machines in drugstores and saloons and hotels. If recordings were to become widely available and so generate enough capital to sustain a buoyant commercial operation, a means had to be found of duplicating the originals. To begin with, no duplication at all was possible; the sounds of a little band of perhaps six or eight players could be captured by ten cylinder recorders, each one equipped with a gigantic horn. So after three hours the band might have given thirty performances of the same march and there would be three hundred cylinders ready for sale. Had the musicians had the heart and the patience to carry on repeating 'Marching through Georgia', the recording company wouldn't have been able to pay them, even if they could sell the cylinders – as they would try to do – at a dollar each. It was worse for a solo singer, for the voice could be captured by only three recording horns at a time. By the late 1890s a method had been developed which allowed the duplication of at least twenty-five cylinders before the original wax impression had worn out. So a single performance might generate 125 cylinders. Even this meant that if a recording was to be a success, in commercial terms and in enhancing an artist's reputation, the performer had to return again and again to the studio. The first gramophone records appeared on the market in 1894, issued by the US Gramophone Company of Emile Berliner, for sale to begin with just in Washington, D.C., and one of the reasons for the record's early success was that by 1893 Berliner had devised a method of creating a metal master from the original wax recording which could then be used to stamp copies, first on to hard rubber, later on to shellac. Successful duplication was one of the chief reasons for the eventual supremacy of discs over cylinders, which were also more cumbersome and fragile and more difficult to store, though the Edison Company in fact went on producing cylinders until 1929.

What could be heard on these earliest cylinders and discs? There were marches by Sousa, there were polkas and waltzes, national anthems, instrumental arrangements of operatic arias and popular songs, clarinet and cornet solos with piano accompaniment, songs and ballads like 'Drink to me only' and 'Ta-Ra-Ra-Boom-De-Ay' and 'The Star Spangled Banner'. In the 1898 catalogue of Columbia cylinders there was only one classical performer, a French baritone called Bernard Bégué, who sang minor roles at the Paris Opéra and at the Metropolitan Opera in New York. On the cylinders produced by the Edison Company before the First World War were dozens of popular songs, arrangements of the Hallelujah Chorus and Handel's 'Largo' and the Grand March from *Tannhäuser* and the Coronation March from *Le Prophète*, and marches by Sousa and by Strauss, and arrangements of national anthems, and close harmony songs and hymns, the British Military Band playing an arrangement of Mozart's overture from *The Magic Flute*, Madame Pasquali singing the Jewel Song from Gounod's *Faust*, songs by Balfe like 'I dreamt that I dwelt in marble halls', as well as Miss Maud Dewey making imitations of the blackbird, nightingale and thrush. Among the most popular of Berliner's discs in the 1890s were arrangements of songs by Stephen Foster like 'My Old Kentucky Home' and Stephen Adams's 'The Holy City', and the 'Miserere' from Verdi's *Il trovatore* and the Intermezzo from Mascagni's *Cavalleria rusticana*.

In the first decade of the twentieth century the Gramophone Company in London did issue abridgements on perhaps twelve or fifteen sides of popular Italian operas sung by La Scala forces; and there were extracts from *Messiah* issued in 1906 on twenty-five single-sided discs.[10] But mainly the Company was issuing dozens of arrangements played by The Coldstream Guards Band – overtures by Flotow and Sullivan and Rossini and Auber, Beethoven's *Egmont* Overture, Sibelius's *Valse triste*, 'Norwegian Dance' by Grieg, Chopin's 'Funeral March', Berlioz's *Marche hongroise*. There were a great many banjo solos, a few bagpipe records, and the odd cornet, flute, harp, ocarina and 'clarionet' solo, and there were a few solo violin records: Herr Kubelik playing Bazzini's 'La ronde des Lutins', and the Habanera from Bizet's *Carmen*, Herr Fritz Kreisler playing Tchaikovsky's 'Chanson sans paroles' and 'Air' by J. S. Bach, and Lady Speyer playing Sinigaglia's 'Cappriccio All' Antica'. There were a few piano solos: Miss Janotha, 'Court Pianiste to H.I.M. The German Emperor', playing 'Fugue' by Chopin, Herr Vladimir de Pachmann playing Raff's 'La Fileuse' op. 157 no. 2, and Mendelssohn's *Rondo capriccioso* op. 14, Herr Wilhelm Backhaus playing Handel's 'Harmonious Blacksmith' and Liszt's *Liebestraum* and 'Prelude' by Rachmaninoff. The biggest category of all was formed by 'ballads and other concert music'; there was Mr John McCormack singing 'The Minstrel Boy', and 'I hear you calling', and Mr Thorpe Bates singing Stephen Adams's 'The Midshipmite' and Pinsuti's 'The Bedouin Love Song', and Mr Peter Dawson singing 'Rule, Britannia', and 'O star of Eve' from *Tannhäuser*, and Emilie Clarke's 'Sincerity'.

The ten operatic arias Caruso recorded for the Gramophone & Typewriter Company in Milan on one afternoon in April 1902, including 'Questa o quella' from *Rigoletto*, 'Celeste Aida' from *Aida*, 'Una furtiva lagrima' from Donizetti's *L'elisir d'amore*, and 'E lucevan le stelle' from Puccini's *Tosca* (which had had its première in January 1900), did mark a turning-point in the history of recorded music.[11] The singer was twenty-eight. He had made his debut in 1894 and by 1902 had triumphed at La Scala. Even before the discs went on sale in London the news that Caruso had made them was enough to convince seven of the leading international opera singers who were to appear with him that season at Covent Garden that they should sign contracts with the Gramophone Company; they included the French bass Pol Plançon, the baritones Anton van Rooy, David Bispham and Antonio Scotti, the American soprano Suzanne Adams, and the French dramatic soprano Emma Calvé.[12] It was important that such prestigious artists made discs and soon other renowned singers did too: like the English baritone Charles Santley, born in 1834 and a pupil of one of the greatest singing teachers in nineteenth-century Europe, Manuel Garcia, whose father, also Manuel, created a number of Rossini's tenor roles; like the Italian 'tenore robusto' Francesco Tamagno (for whom Verdi had written the title-role of Otello), whose voice caused the great chandelier at Covent Garden to vibrate as if in terror; like the Russian Chaliapin, who ranks with Caruso and Callas as one of the most influential operatic singers of the twentieth century; and like the Australian soprano Nellie Melba, who from the 1890s on 'Melba Nights' at Covent Garden brought high society to the opera. The records of these singers did something to convince the public that the gramophone and the phonograph were more than raucous entertainers in rather dubious taste. But it is an exaggeration to claim, as is often done, that these early discs of Caruso marked the gramophone's coming of age. For one thing the English at any rate were highly suspicious of opera singers, 'undoubtedly the most capricious and the most childish representatives of the whole profession', as *The Musical Times* had put it in 1889, 'the most injudiciously flattered performers in the world'.[13] Not many English men and women were devotees of Italian opera in the 1900s. Caruso's disc of 'Vesti la giubba' with its famous emotional sob was played soon after it came out at a demonstration of the gramophone to a group of ladies in a Mayfair drawing-room. They made no reaction while it played; there was a long silence at the end until one old lady looked up from her crochet and remarked: 'It seemed to me that the man was quite hysterical. . . .'[14]

The record catalogues were mostly filled with a succession of operatic potboilers and popular salon pieces and hackneyed ballads, as they would be considered by many serious musicians at the time.[15] Why should this be? It was, after all, an epoch of intense musical creativity, one of the richest periods in the history of western music. These pre-First World War years saw the first performances of Mahler's symphonies four to nine, and *Das Lied von der Erde*, Schoenberg's *Verklärte Nacht* and *Gurrelieder*, Webern's *Passacaglia* and Six Pieces op. 6, of Stravinsky's three early ballet scores, and Debussy's *Pelléas et Mélisande* and *La mer*, Elgar's *The Dream of Gerontius*, his *Introduction and Allegro for String Orchestra and String Quartet*, his Violin Concerto and his first two symphonies, and Vaughan Williams's *Fantasia on a theme of Thomas Tallis*. For many musicians were enthusiastic about recording almost from the first: Tchaikovsky considered recording 'the most surprising, the most beautiful, and the most interesting among all inventions that have turned up in the nineteenth century', and Anton Rubinstein saluted Edison as the 'saviour' of all performing artists.[16] Fauré thought that a performance 'recorded by the composer himself . . . will be able to cut across all previous debates . . . there will be an indisputable guide for future generations'.[17] Debussy in 1904 thought that this new apparatus would assure music 'a complete and meticulous immortality'.[18] In fact a number of these enthusiastic responses were testimonials solicited by recording people; no doubt the musicians wished to be generous to the 'celebrated electrician', as the newspapers called Edison, whose best-known invention was the incandescent lamp. And Josef Hofmann's excitement at going to Edison's laboratory probably derived as much from his interest in gadgets as in music; it was Hofmann after all who later invented the windscreen wiper.[19] It was not hard to perceive the enormous potential of recording, but for the time being some of the claims for it seemed rather extravagant.

Recordings were expensive to produce and from the beginning mass markets had to be created. So in the first decade of the century there was no Stravinsky or Schoenberg in the disc and cylinder catalogues. But in fact there was very little Mozart: there was Adelina Patti singing 'Voi che sapete',[20] Tetrazzini singing the same aria,[21] there was Pauline Donalda singing 'Vedrai carino' from *Don Giovanni*,[22] and Selma Kurz singing 'Königin der Nacht' from *Zauberflöte*.[23] There was very little Bach: Wilhelm Backhaus playing the Prelude and Fugue in C sharp major from Book I of *Das wohltemperierte Clavier*.[24] There was very little Beethoven: there was Mark Hambourg playing the second and third movements of the 'Moonlight' Sonata,[25] and the Renard Trio playing the Adagio from Beethoven's Piano Trio op. 11.[26] Why should this have been so?

The first piece Elgar recorded – this was in January 1914 – was *Carissima*;[27] it was in fact the work's first performance and the idea was to have the record in the shops before the music was published to create a demand for the sheet music versions. For as well as the orchestral version there were versions published in 1914 for solo piano, solo organ, violin and piano, cello and piano, in 1920 one for piano and strings, and then in 1924 arrangements for brass and reed and military band. It is a delightful piece of light music and it probably sold reasonably well; there was a big enough market for it. But there was no mass market for *The Rite of Spring* or *Gurrelieder*. What was selling very well and gladdening a gramophone record company man's heart was Mr Harry Lauder telling football anecdotes with 'exceptionally pretty and well played' introductory music, as prospective purchasers were assured.

Acoustic recording

But just as important as the absence of a mass market for most classical music – serious music, 'permanent music' is how *The World's Encyclopedia of Recorded Music* designated it in 1952, 'music of permanent interest' was a phrase used up to the middle of the century – were the technological limitations. The playing time of both single-sided discs and cylinders in the early 1900s was about two minutes. From the late 1920s a disc side could last up to about four and a half minutes, a ten-inch disc up to two and three-quarter minutes. Very occasionally twelve-inch discs were issued with sides lasting more than five minutes. A side lasting practically five and a half minutes as side one of HMV DB 192[28] does – the first movement and part of the second movement of Haydn's String Quartet in D major op. 33 no. 6 played by the Pro Arte Quartet – is entirely exceptional. And these limitations were to remain right up to the end of the shellac era, to the middle of the century.

Elgar's *Carissima* easily fitted within the four-minute compass of a twelve-inch disc. Hofmann recorded Chopin's Scherzo no. 1 in B minor op. 20 in April 1923 and it lasts four minutes thirty seconds;[29] when he made a piano roll of the same piece which was released in 1926 – many makes of piano roll could last up to about fifteen minutes – the performance took eight minutes and six seconds.[30] In other words, works constantly had to be abbreviated for the disc. The Chopin Scherzo could have been accommodated on two sides of a twelve-inch disc but no doubt the record company thought that an abbreviated Scherzo together with a complete Nocturne in F sharp major op. 15 no. 2 stood more chance of doing well at 8s. (40p) than if they tried to sell the Scherzo alone with repeats and uncut. Extended works were issued occasionally: Verdi's *Ernani* was recorded in 1903 by the Italian branch of the Gramophone Company HMV, but even in an abbreviated form it took up forty single-sided discs; Beethoven's Fifth Symphony recorded in November 1913 by the Berlin Philharmonic Orchestra conducted by Arthur Nikisch occupied eight single-sided discs.[31] But in England the complete set cost about £2 at a time when the average weekly wage was £1 6s. 8d. (£1.33). Sir Henry Wood's 1922 recording of Beethoven's 'Eroica' Symphony, the first of this work, omits almost half the music.[32] Elgar's 1916 recording of his Violin Concerto lasts about a quarter of an hour, about a third the time of the work's actual length, appearing on four sides with the fourth side for the accompanied cadenza, which could almost be recorded complete. In 1917 he reduced the *Cockaigne* overture, which lasts about a quarter of an hour, to fit onto a single-sided twelve-inch disc lasting just over four minutes. Joe Batten, the conductor of the recording of *The Dream of Gerontius* released in 1924 – he was at that time a house conductor for the Edison Bell Company who had been appointed after the First War to build up a catalogue of 'good' music – thought the cutting of the work for recording a 'cruel task. . . . But it had to be done, otherwise my directors would never have been convinced that what I had in mind was a saleable proposition.'[33] It was issued on the Velvet Face label on eight double-sided twelve-inch records, each costing 5s. 6d. (27½p) or all the discs in an album £2 5s. (£2.25). *The Gramophone* described it as 'this very liberal selection'.[34]

In the earliest days – up to the end of acoustic recording – it seems that decisions about cutting, at least when a soloist was involved, would frequently be made in the studio just before the actual recording was engraved. 'They wanted the Faust waltz (which lasts a good ten minutes) *but it was only to take four minutes!*' Busoni lamented to his wife after a day of 'suffering' in the studio in November 1919. 'That meant quickly cutting, patching and improvising, so that there should still be some sense left in it. . . .'[35] And Rosa Ponselle remembered cutting out a bar or two here, a bar or two there, 'to save a second or two'.[36] She hated even more the way the time limit could destroy the whole meaning and emotional impact of an aria: in 'Casta diva', for instance, recorded in 1928, only one of the aria's two verses could be put onto disc; in the opera house she sang the second verse, she said, entirely differently, louder in volume and darker in colour and tone and timbre. All that was missing on the record.[37] No doubt many conductors during the first half of the century would take charge in deciding exactly where stops should occur at the end of each side, working this out meticulously in advance of the recording sessions. Ormandy would continue up to the very moment of cut-off as if he were going on, without, that is, the slightest hint of a rallentando. Stokowski, though, insisted on a ritardando at the close of every section: 'You must finish each record off gracefully', he would say. But this enraged Josef Hofmann, who was contemptuous of Rachmaninoff for agreeing to do it when he recorded with Stokowski.[38]

Just occasionally life imitated technological limitation: one of the first important records made by the cellist Janos Starker – it was released in 1948 – was of Kodály's unaccompanied solo Sonata op. 8.[39] One of the cuts Starker made for this recording he thought improved the piece and he followed it in concert performances ever afterwards; the composer was extremely angry to begin with, though eventually, Starker thought, perhaps even he agreed with him.[40]

So recordings of short songs and arias and instrumental movements made better artistic as well as economic sense. That these very early catalogues contain more songs and arias than piano or violin solos and

even fewer short orchestral works is an indication of other technological limitations.

In the process of acoustic recording, which lasted until 1925 when a
system of electrical amplification was devised, sound vibrations themselves caused a sapphire cutter to gouge out a groove in a disc of wax.
This was an inefficient and ineffective way of capturing sound since
only a very small amount of energy could be employed in actuating
the cutting stylus. The sound waves – the acoustical energy – from a
solo singing voice could be concentrated crudely by means of a
horn, but the sound from the resonating strings of a grand piano, still
less the spread-out sound sources of a body of orchestral players, could
be caught much less successfully.[41] Very quiet sounds could not be
captured at all. But in addition the acoustic process was only able to
reproduce a limited frequency range. The human ear can encompass
frequencies between 20 and 20,000 cycles per second; the acoustic
recording process was limited to a range between 168 and 2,000 cycles,
which means that it was unable to reproduce all the frequencies of
notes below the E below middle C and of notes higher than the C
three octaves above middle C. This does not mean that notes whose
fundamentals lie outside that range were inaudible, but it does mean
that the characteristic timbres and qualities of all sounds were
distorted.

Singers recorded best, which explains the predominance of vocal
recordings in the acoustic catalogues, and bright-edged tenors recorded
best of all. The effect of the loss of harmonics meant that a clear and
pure soprano voice could sometimes sound plaintive or even ethereal,
often intriguingly distant, more often distressingly weak. A rich bass
might sound hollow or wooden, a rich contralto plummy, without edge
at all.[42] Sibilants could only be reproduced with difficulty; it was often
the music-hall artists who had had years of practice articulating for the
back row of the Hackney Empire on a Saturday night who were best at
registering clearly in the recording horn and then cutting through the
surface noise of the cylinder or disc. The singer was obviously able to
perform very close to the recording horn, often in fact he would have
his head actually inside it, though this manner of performing would
immediately cause difficulties for accompanists. How could he communicate with the singer, one of them pointed out, if all he could see,

as frequently happened, were his buttocks?[43] But things weren't so simple for the singer either. An English folk singer who recorded for Percy Grainger thought performing for the horn was like singing 'with a muzzle on'.[44] The recording needle was extremely sensitive and when the singer projected very loud or forceful passages – when, as Edison himself put it, the recording apparatus had to deal with the sort of sound an Italian makes when he falls in love[45] – the needle would jump and chip out a piece from the wax of the master. A dramatic soprano had to remember to retreat three feet for her 'chest tones', and five or six feet for her 'medium-high register'.[46] Singers certainly found this dancing about difficult and inhibiting, even with chalk marks on the floor.[47] According to the recording 'expert' who recorded her, Adelina Patti, '[w]ith her natural Italian temperament . . . was given to flashing movement and to acting her parts' and found it difficult to stand still when this was required.[48] The expert feared for the recording diaphragm when Chaliapin was standing ten yards away from the recording horn, his chest stripped bare like a prize-fighter.[49]

The piano recorded much less well than the singing voice. Mark Hambourg described the tone of the acoustically recorded piano as 'thin and tinny, like the plucked string of a banjo or guitar. . . . Loud pieces reproduced better than soft ones', he remembered, 'and slow legato movements were unobtainable'.[50] Rachmaninoff thought that the piano in his first recordings made for the Edison Company in New York in April 1919 sounded exactly like a Russian balalaika.[51] Often the piano itself was modified in some way in an attempt to make it reproduce more clearly; in the studio of the Musiphone Company in London in 1900 the piano was an upright mounted on a five-foot rostrum, its front and back removed, leaving only the action and the sound board, which meant that someone had to stand next to the pianist holding the music.[52] Mark Hambourg described the piano he recorded on for HMV between 1909 and 1925 as an 'old tin kettle of a piano . . . quite the worst-toned one that it has ever been my lot to play on'.[53] Gerald Moore first recorded for HMV in 1921 and described the tone of the piano he used – it might have been the same one as Hambourg – as having all 'the splendour of a brass spittoon'. He noticed that its tone had been modified for recording by filing down the felts on the hammers.[54]

String instruments were also difficult to record acoustically since they had less carrying power and required much more room to play

than an oboe or a clarinet. It was not possible to contemplate recording more than a handful of string instruments and even these could
easily become a 'ghostly murmur'.[55] In order to overcome the difficulty
with the violin, a German inventor called Augustus Stroh, who worked
for the British Post Office, devised a violin which for the sound box
substituted a diaphragm and a small metal horn or trumpet; this could
be raised or lowered to project the sound straight at the recording horn.
The Stroh violin was widely used for about ten years from 1904 and
its first commercial use was probably in April of that year, when
Charles d'Alamine played Léonard's *Fantaisie militaire* op. 15 for violin
and piano.[56] But the Stroh apparatus certainly distorted the tone of the
instrument. A newspaper notice of a new disc in December 1904 reas-
sured listeners: 'Kubelik has made two records with his own Stradi-
varius, *not a Stroh*.'[57]

The acoustic process of recording therefore limited what music could
be attempted, it affected how the musicians performed in various ways,
and it seriously distorted the sounds they actually made. Large
numbers of performing musicians could not be recorded at all. When
a record label or catalogue announced an orchestra it was always an
ensemble abbreviated in some way. Certain orchestral music could not
be appropriately abbreviated – because the harmony was too involved,
or the scoring too rich or subtle or attenuated – and so recordings of
it could not be contemplated: even had a record company decided that
it could have sold sufficient copies of a recording of Bartók's *Duke Bluebeard's Castle* or Scriabin's *Poem of Ecstasy*, it would never have been
attempted with the acoustic recording process, nor would Schoenberg's
Pierrot Lunaire, nor would Debussy's *L'après-midi d'un faune*. In the
earlier years of acoustic recording an 'orchestra' might consist of a
flute, two clarinets, two cornets, two trombones, solo Stroh first and
second violins, and a viola, with a bassoon playing the cello part. In
'orchestral' arrangements for the gramophone most of the instruments
played all the time and while the sound might be 'overwhelming in the
studio, little of it got through to the wax'.[58] Nearest to the recording
horn would be the strings, the cello sometimes mounted on a move-
able platform, with flutes, oboes and clarinets almost poking their
instruments into the string players' necks; bassoons often sat opposite
the violins and beneath the recording horn; the French horns would
be further away with their backs turned so that the bells of their instruments were directed towards the horn, using mirrors to see the

conductor, with the other brass instruments ranged as convenient further back. Any dynamic contrasts were difficult to achieve; if a wood-wind instrument had a solo he had to stand up and lean forward or even scurry round and make obeisance to the horn at a distance of a couple of inches.[59] When Fritz Kreisler and Efrem Zimbalist recorded Bach's Double Violin Concerto BWV 1043 in 1915 they were accompanied by a string quartet,[60] and when the Gramophone Company recorded music for Mattins and Evensong in a studio in October 1924 the 'Choir of St George's Chapel, Windsor' consisted of just three men, a solo alto, tenor and bass; for some of the pieces four boys were used, and for others either five, six or seven.[61]

Elgar rescored the Violin Concerto for recording, bringing in a harp – there was no harp in the original score – to replace the rest of the accompaniment where softness and lightness were needed.[62] When Joe Batten recorded Elgar's *Dream of Gerontius* he used nine strings instead of the complement of between forty and sixty that he would have wished for in a public performance, a choir of eight voices instead of one of between sixty and three hundred voices, and instead of a grand organ the 'convincing substitute', as he considered it, of a bass concertina. The recording sessions were spread over a week in a studio measuring thirty feet by eight.[63] Gustav Holst found the strain of recording *The Planets* with members of the London Symphony Orchestra in 1923 in such cramped conditions more exhausting than anything he had ever done before; the first horn on that occasion was Aubrey Brain, known for his astonishing technical mastery, and yet even he broke down thirteen times at the opening of *Venus* 'as a result of the almost unbearable physical discomfort'.[64]

The reproducing piano

For pianists there was an alternative to the horror of playing against the clock on an inferior instrument whose tone had been made nastier for the recording horn. A pianist could make a roll for a so-called reproducing piano. He played a special piano and completed an electric circuit by means of contacts just beneath each key; in this way, a set of pencils was activated to make marks on a player piano paper roll which was revolved at a standard speed, and the length and spacing of the pencil markings would exactly correspond to the performer's strokes on the keys. The pedalling could be similarly recorded. The roll was made by cutting out these pencil marks and it was possible to record the dynamic shading by measuring the speed of each hammer and by registering this by different kinds of perforation. To play the rolls back a special reproducing piano was required that was powered by an electric motor generating suction. The motor was piped to a tracker bar, pierced with a note for each piano key, and the bar transmitted the variations in air pressure to the tiny bellows operating each key. Unlike the pianola, which was powered by pedals like a harmonium, the reproducing piano presented not just the notes of works, but performances by actual artists; its rolls, in other words, encoded the original performer's dynamics and types of articulation.

The first reproducing pianos went on sale in Germany in 1904 and their popularity reached a peak in 1925, in which year the Aeolian Company in the United States manufactured more than 192,000 instruments. There were many competing systems, but three companies dominated the production of piano rolls, 'Welte-Mignon', Aeolian's 'Duo-Art' and the American Piano Company's 'Ampico'; the three companies' systems were not interchangeable. Nearly all the world's leading pianists made rolls in the first three decades of the century, and all the best piano manufacturers incorporated the reproducing piano mechanism into some of their instruments.[65] There were public concerts, concerto performances, lieder recitals with reproducing pianos, and recitals for two reproducing pianos playing duets. The instruments themselves were expensive, with the grand piano version costing in the 1920s about £2,000, and they disappeared within a few years with the American economic depression of the 1930s and with the rise of radio and the gramophone, both cheaper and both presenting a wide repertory of music.

But in recent years a number of reproducing pianos have been built and series of recordings of these have been issued.[66] These aroused immense controversy. The Welte-Mignon catalogues boast that the 'recording mechanism *phototones* [the pianist's] playing note for note – *instantly*. His touch, shading, accentuation, expression – everything that characterizes the individuality of the artist is faithfully reproduced. . . .'[67] Eugen d'Albert saluted the Welte-Mignon Reproducing Records as a means which could 'transmit [his] art to posterity'; it was 'astonishing and deeply affecting' for him to listen to his own playing, he said in the Company's catalogue.[68] Darius Milhaud thought that Welte-

Mignon rolls reproduced 'with the same accuracy the most minute details and manners of the artist . . . his personal interpretation'.[69] Josef Lhévinne thought that a Welte-Mignon roll reproduced his 'exact interpretation . . . with absolute accuracy as to tempo, touch and tone quality'.[70] Mark Hambourg considered that a Welte-Mignon roll of himself performing was 'the perfect reproduction of the touch, even to the finest shadings'.[71] Arthur Nikisch thought that it was difficult to believe that 'the artist himself is not present and performing perfectly'.[72] At least, these are what the company claimed they said. But in recent decades there has been energetic debate about the faithfulness of the original rolls, the extent to which the rolls could be edited and corrected, the extent to which different makes of roll could reproduce interpretational nuances, the seriousness with which players' endorsements printed in manufacturers' catalogues should be taken, the circumstances in which comments judging the fidelity of their rolls were made by pianists many years later – were their remarks made from memory or had they been listening to recent recordings of inadequately processed rolls? – and about the skill and expertise of the technicians and engineers who constructed or restored the reproducing pianos on which recent recordings have been made.

In 1974 Abram Chasins remembered making rolls for Duo-Art in 1926. At the time, he said, he regarded them with great distaste. He 'really hated them; they were stiff and unnatural and unrepresentative'. The rolls of his teacher Hofmann 'are almost the most distressing, because they lack his individuality', whereas the electrical discs Hofmann made in London in 1931 he considered entirely 'faithful reproductions' of his playing.[73] Artur Rubinstein idolized Busoni and knew his playing very well: he played 'more mysteriously' than other pianists, with 'such ease, such elegance, such mastery',[74] 'a towering personality', he described him as, 'a shining example to all musicians'.[75] In 1964 Rubinstein listened to an LP reissue of Busoni playing on rolls Chopin's Prelude in D flat op. 28 no. 15 and the Verdi-Liszt *Rigoletto* Paraphrase: 'This is a caricature. A distortion', he thought, 'a falsification of his playing'.[76] An expert on reproducing pianos, though one who is sceptical about the extravagant claims sometimes made for them, commented on a set of modern recordings of Duo-Art rolls that they could be made to 'sound much more sensitive and . . . be reproduced far more accurately': and he summed them up as '. . . insensitive distortions of the noble playing of the individual pianists presented, replete with a catalogue of bizarre, inhuman effects including jerky phrasing and inappropriate pedalling'. The fault in his opinion lay with those who had 'presented' the rolls for this modern recording.[77]

In 1962 Benno Moiseiwitsch was played four tape recordings of Ampico player piano rolls he made in the late 1920s. He did not claim too much. The rolls were good, he thought, 'in parts'. In his performances of the Schubert-Liszt *Hark, hark, the lark* S.558/9 ('Ständchen') and Brahms's *Capriccio* in B minor op. 76 no. 2 he was not convinced that some of the tempo changes were quite genuine. At times he thought aspects of the performance he disliked intensely were probably faithful reproductions: 'How could I be so stupid', was his simple explanation. But at other times he was 'really astonished' at the recordings' fidelity to his interpretative subtleties. If you were patient enough and careful enough in making piano rolls it was certainly possible, he believed, to reproduce faithfully the performer's intentions. Recording for the gramophone was unreal and nerve-racking; but when he made piano rolls he sat back in a chair and smoked and had a drink and would say: 'No, no, I want more crescendo there, too much accelerando' and the technician would punch the holes as Moiseiwitsch directed. He found it very agreeable.[78]

These conflicting opinions probably can't be reconciled. So much depends upon the expectations of the contemporary listener and on the state of mind of the pronouncer and upon his motives that it would be unwise to rely too heavily on piano rolls as sources of information about performance practices. But then it would be unwise to rely uncritically on acoustic discs for such information. Given the sound quality of gramophone records of the time it is certainly startling to hear the actual sounds of a piano being played by Debussy or Mahler through the reproducing mechanism. And it is perhaps also important to remember that most performers have always received an unpleasant shock on hearing themselves for the first time. 'Was I, after years of public playing, actually making mistakes that I would be the first to condemn in any one of my own pupils?' Max Pauer exclaimed in anguish when he listened to a record in 1913. 'I could hardly believe my ears, and yet the unrelenting machine showed that in some places I had failed to play both hands exactly together. . . .'[79] Acoustic recording was incapable of capturing piano tone faithfully, as was early electrical recording; and 78 rpm discs suffered the limitation of four-and-a-half-minute side lengths. Certainly the reproducing piano recordings can provide useful supplements to the evidence of performing styles captured on gramophone records.[80]

Electrical recording

The unsatisfactoriness of acoustic recording arose chiefly from its inefficiency in capturing acoustic energy. The solution, it had long been realized, would lie in the conversion of acoustic energy – sound waves – into electrical impulses, which could then be enlarged or boosted, that is amplified. It was research in radio, or 'wireless telegraphy', during the Great War that resulted in the first workable microphones and amplifiers and in part it was the threat to business, the competition that the record companies perceived in radio – a realization that 'machine-made music need not sound tinny and muffled and scratchy'[81] – that led the companies to pursue the possibilities of electrical recording. Electrical recording[82] could capture an enlarged frequency range, at the beginning from 100 to about 5,000 cycles, and by 1934 a frequency range up to 8,000 Hz could reliably be recorded. Bass frequencies not before heard from records gave weight and body to the sound, and treble frequencies introduced a definition and detail previously missing, with sibilants much more clearly and realistically reproduced. And an electrically amplified microphone system was able to capture sounds from sources ranged over a wide area so there was no longer need for performing musicians to be huddled together in cramped conditions.

The musical director of the Vocalion Company welcomed with relief the 'feeling of ease and realism which is now apparent at any orchestral sessions and which, before the advent of the microphone, was entirely lacking in the recording studio . . .'.[83] In April 1929 Rachmaninoff recorded his Piano Concerto no. 2 with the one hundred and ten members of the Philadelphia Orchestra and Leopold Stokowski in the Academy of Music in Philadelphia,[84] the nineteenth-century hall modelled on La Scala and seating almost 3,000, and the musicians played according to Rachmaninoff 'exactly as though we were giving a public performance'. And he thought it a 'thrilling' experience.[85] The new conditions probably struck Rachmaninoff all the more forcibly as he had made an acoustic recording of the same work with members of the Philadelphia Orchestra and Stokowski only five years earlier.[86] Electrical recording was felt as a liberation by nearly all recording musicians. Just a few, though, seem to have regretted the passing of the acoustic recording process; the baritone Roy Henderson remembered the disappointment he felt when he recorded electrically for the first time, the deadness of the Columbia recording studio, like the BBC studios of the time he sang in, and how he missed the resonance of the recording horn, which was 'rather like singing in a bathroom, or even better than a bathroom'.[87]

Some early orchestral recordings exploited the potentialities for orchestral freedom and for recording realism. Victor's first electrically recorded issue, released in July 1925, was of Saint-Saëns's *Danse macabre* in a performance by the Philadelphia Orchestra under Stokowski, a piece of 'orchestral acrobatics', as Roland Gelatt describes it, 'with its clattering xylophone obbligato and dynamic percussive effects', in which the potentialities of the new system 'were heard to exciting effect'.[88] The same performers recorded Tchaikovsky's *Marche slave*, and at the end of the year HMV issued the first symphonic electrical recording, of Tchaikovsky's Fourth Symphony, played by the Royal Albert Hall Orchestra conducted by Landon Ronald. During 1926 there appeared records of a complete *Symphonie fantastique*, the *Magic Fire Music* and *Siegfried's Rhine Journey*, the Nocturne and Scherzo from Mendelssohn's *Midsummer Night's Dream* music, Dvořák's *New World* Symphony, Brahms's First Symphony, Beethoven's Seventh, Franck's D minor Symphony, Rimsky-Korsakoff's *Scheherazade*, Stravinsky's *Firebird* Suite, and Stokowski's transcription of Bach's D minor Toccata, all these demonstrating early electrical recording 'at its most powerful, luminous and enveloping'.[89]

Attention was usually not drawn to the new technology by the manufacturers; the engineers were learning how best to use the microphone, and the tone of some of the earliest electrical records was certainly tinny and strident. And most listeners did not immediately buy new electrical gramophones to play the new records but kept on using their old acoustic machines. The machine mattered: one listener described how a disc on a friend's old machine sounded 'like a complicated cat fight in a mustard mill' whereas on his own new electrical gramophone the sound 'overwhelmed' him.[90] As with all subsequent major technological developments in recording history, this one caused much head-shaking: 'The exaggeration of sibilants by the new method is abominable, and there is often a harshness which recalls some of the worst excesses of the past. . . . Mellowness and reality have given place to screaming . . . the marvellous music is completely spoiled by the atrocious and squeaky tone. . . .'[91] But the highly influential music critic Ernest Newman saluted electrical recording as 'an enormous step forward'; 'at last', he said in July 1926, 'an orchestra really sounds like an orchestra . . . [the sounds] come to us with the sensuous excitement of actuality'. From electrical recordings he received 'the physical delight of passionate music'.[92]

Not only could large numbers of musicians, spread over wide areas, be recorded but the acoustic of the recording location could now be captured, or so it was claimed. Fred Gaisberg, who made the very famous recording of the Temple Church Choir singing Mendelssohn's *Hear My Prayer*, attributed its success to the 'silver voice' of the treble, the discipline of the choir, and 'the soft acoustic resonance of the church'.[93] In fact not very much of the particular quality of such an acoustic could usually be reproduced on record, the surface noise of the shellac disc being an important obscuring factor, but at least recordings in very distinctive acoustical settings could be attempted; HMV in the summer of 1927 were proudly boasting of their electrical recordings 'actually made in historic buildings' like York Minster, St John's College, Cambridge, New College, Oxford, and Liverpool and Salisbury cathedrals.[94]

The Royal Choral Society choir of 800 strong was recorded during a *Messiah* performance in the Albert Hall, *The Dream of Gerontius* in Worcester Cathedral during a Three Choirs Festival performance, and massed bands of 1,000 players at the Crystal Palace; recordings during performances were made at the Covent Garden Opera, at the Staatsoper in Berlin, at La Scala in Milan, and at the Paris Opéra. And many of these recording ventures were successful and issued as commercial discs.[95] In the 1930s Mozart's operas *Figaro*, *Così fan tutte* and *Don Giovanni* were recorded at Glyndebourne, not during actual performances, but at the end of the Festival Opera's season, using the theatre as a recording studio.[96] The disappearance of the horn, the introduction of the microphone, the liberation from physical constraints, of these all recording musicians were immediately aware. But some of the changes in studio practice which electrical recording effected, of revolutionary significance, musicians were only dimly aware of, and were to understand their implications only very gradually.

Post-Second World War technological developments

After the war Decca produced recordings which extended the frequency range to 14,000 Hz, almost to the limit of human hearing. This development was the result of war work undertaken by a Decca engineer for RAF Coastal Command whose officers needed this response when listening to sonar buoys in order to distinguish between Allied and German submarines. Decca provided a set of training records for this work and then developed a microphone to catch airborne sounds. It was first publicized in June 1945 and became 'ffrr', full frequency-range recording; because it could accommodate overtones previously reduced or eliminated on disc, the recorded sound was much richer and critics commented particularly on the improvement in string sound. Among the earliest 'ffrr' recordings which attracted most attention because of their vivid sound qualities were discs of the ballet music from Holst's *The Perfect Fool* with *The Ride of the Valkyries*,[97] Dukas's *L'Apprenti sorcier*,[98] Strauss's *Don Juan* op. 20,[99] Stravinsky's *Petrushka* played by the London Philharmonic Orchestra conducted by Ernest Ansermet,[100] and 'one of the most brilliant specimens of Decca's "*ffrr*" technique', according to Desmond Shawe-Taylor, Falla's *Noches en los jardines de España* played by the National Symphony Orchestra under Enrique Jorda with Clifford Curzon as the soloist.[101]

Shellac, the principal component used in making all discs between about 1896 and 1948, is a resinous compound secreted by tree insects native to India; supplies dried up during the Second World War and a replacement was found in vinyl, whose basic component is PVC, a much higher quality material. Vinyl allowed the reduction in the width of the grooves on discs – called 'fine-groove' or 'microgroove' discs – which required the development of new styluses, pickup cartridges and tone-arms, and a slower turntable running at 33⅓ rpm instead of at 78 rpm. The surface noise on shellac discs, the 'continuous frying noise' as it's been described, was the result of the addition of abrasive fillers like emery powder which were used to provide resistance to wear from heavy pickups. With the light and soft vinyl discs and extremely hard-tipped diamond or sapphire styluses no such fillers were necessary; there was a great reduction in background noise from the disc itself and quiet passages could be appreciated which on shellac discs would have been all but inaudible. But the possibility of more than twenty minutes on each side of the disc could not be contemplated by performing musicians with unalloyed pleasure. It was difficult enough to avoid split notes or small slips when recording for four and a half minutes. If executants were required to sustain concentration over twenty or twenty-five minutes, and to pay the kind of inhibiting attention to tiny details that recording necessitated, while at the same time attempting to invest a performance with intensity and élan, most, even the most transcendentally gifted virtuosos, would surely be found wanting.

Fortunately musicians were to escape this fate. The kinds of recording tapes developed in the 1930s did not give better quality than 78 rpm discs but it was clear from wartime broadcasts that the Germans had perfected a new kind of magnetic tape and the equipment was discovered when the Allies captured Radio Luxembourg in 1944. Within three years American broadcasters and record companies were using tape to create masters and by the early 1950s everyone was using tape.

Magnetic tape, which had been used for film sound since the early 1930s, allowed sounds to be captured without breaks, and long uninterrupted durations of recording were possible: pairs of tape machines could go on recording non-stop. Unlike recording waxes, tape could be set up very quickly and started at the touch of a button. And tape could be edited: unwanted material could be removed and preferred material, from another performance, could be substituted.

Stereophonic recording, stereo – the first commercial recording in stereo was made by RCA in February 1954, but it came into general use in both the UK and America in the summer of 1958 – imitated the human binaural hearing mechanism, recording two signals from the same sound source and producing on playback the impression of an arc of sound between two loudspeakers. In monaural sound it made no difference whether the two lovers' intimate exchanges were recorded with the singers far apart, with the tenor stage right and the soprano stage left, but in stereo the listener could locate them.[102] It was not in such simple antiphonies that the value of stereo lay, though. In creating the illusion of space and depth, stereo brought recorded music closer and more vividly to life and paradoxically allowed the listener to be less aware of the medium.

The introduction of cassette tapes in 1963 initially offered listeners a low-fi but convenient alternative to discs; cassettes were compact, they wore much better and they did not become afflicted with clicks as record surfaces tended to, however carefully they were played. Tape 'hiss' was a drawback and it was clearly discernible from the master-tape on LPs and especially on stereo LPs, but the Dolby noise-reduction system on tape was introduced at the British Decca studios in 1966 and was gradually adopted universally for tapes and cassettes, and it added another ten decibels to the potential dynamic range. By the late 1970s many of the best cassettes rivalled the quality obtainable on the best LPs, though one difficulty that remained that was never addressed by the manufacturers was the locating of the inner contents of the tape.[103]

Not all genuine developments and improvements in recorded sound have become widely adopted. Quadraphony (or quadrophony, or quadrasonic sound, and later 'surround' sound) is a four-channel sound reproduction system which aims to re-create, even more realis-tically than stereo, the impression of sound as experienced in the concert hall and to give the illusion that all four walls of the room in which the listener is sitting have dissolved away. The first quadraphonic discs were probably made by Acoustic Research, Inc., in Boston, Mass-achusetts, in 1968. The January 1972 edition of the *Schwann Record and Tape Guide* carried two pages of quadraphonic discs; the first batches of quadraphonic discs in the UK were released in 1972 and 1973. Many commentators felt that quadraphony did indeed give greater realism, richness, naturalness and vividness to the recorded sound,[104] but it required the purchase of four loudspeakers and asso-ciated decoding units, and the public were offered a number of com-peting and non-interchangeable systems simultaneously. The sales of four-channel discs were not large enough to persuade record compa-nies to continue manufacture.

The twelve-inch black vinyl disc playing at 33⅓ rpm gave at least twenty-three minutes on each side; it was rare for a side to exceed thirty minutes, though Britten's *Curlew River*, lasting around sixty-nine minutes, with each side well over thirty minutes, was accommodated on two sides because Decca judged that 'the sustained mood of the piece would be ruined by a second interruption'.[105] The twelve-inch long-playing disc was the principal carrier for classical music between the early 1950s – though EMI maintained production of 78 rpm discs for the UK market up to 1961 – and the mid 1980s. Cassette sales of classical music in the UK overtook LPs in 1983; by 1988 CDs had overtaken cassettes; in 1994 nearly 80 per cent of sales of classical music were CDs, 21 per cent were cassettes, and less than 1 per cent LPs.[106]

The long-playing record was a triumph of scientific knowledge and engineering skill but its drawbacks were clear to all who made records and some of them even to the music-lovers who bought them in such quantities. The tape-to-disc transfer – the mechanical etching of a master disc and electroplating to produce moulds or stampers – was a difficult process which demanded something of the skills of the old-fashioned watchmaker, and was prone to mishaps; the resulting black disc was easily scratched and liable to generate static electrical charges which themselves could be a source of unwanted noise in playing and which also attracted dust and fluff that could collect on the stylus and interfere with sound quality. In analogue recording the sound waves are inscribed as a continuous pattern, as a wave form which is an imitation, an 'analogue' of the changing air-pressures in the original sound waves. With analogue tape, tape hiss and the noise of the microphones and other parts of the recording system are mixed in with the musical information, and all kinds of flutter and distortion in the complex magnetic wave patterns will be preserved and reproduced on playback. All discrepancies in the replay speed, all imperfections and graininess in the tape, all scratches and dust particles will affect the elaborate tracery of the waves and will be reproduced as unwanted noise, as interference with the musical sound.

But from the late 1960s telephone companies and broadcasting organizations had been experimenting with digitizing sound. In digital recording the sound wave is not reproduced but sampled at regular intervals, about 50,000 times a second, and each sample is encoded as a series of pulses or 'digits' as used in computers. On playback the stream of pulses is scanned, simply read off without error, and the original wave forms reconstituted. Which means that digital sound is characterized by its cleanness, its definition, its brilliance and its clarity. In the recording studio this meant that recording equipment noise had to be reduced and as far as possible eliminated; creaky shoes and squeaking floorboards and clicking bassoon keys, which might have disappeared with analogue recording, with digital tape obstinately remain, sounding on playback much larger than life.[107] Even with the imperfections of the vinylite surfaces of the LP the improved quality and quiet background of digital masters can be detected, as they were when the first commercial digital recording was issued in the UK, of the Vienna Philharmonic's New Year's Day concert in 1979, actually drawing on four complete live performances of the programme on New Year's Eve and New Year's Day.[108] But the compact disc provided a digital carrier with all the advantages of a digital tape master: a completely silent background, a breadth of dynamic range, 96 dB, equal to that experienced at a live concert – the LP gave a range of 70 dB – a frequency range covering the complete audio spectrum discernible by the human ear, and an absence of pitch distortions. The mastering and pressing process of a CD cause no loss of quality or degradation: the CD in the shop sounds exactly like the master-tape in the studio. The disc is twelve centimetres, 4.75 inches in diameter; it can carry music on both sides but so far only one has been used, the upper surface carrying label details, and this allows up to about eighty minutes playing time. It rotates at between 300 and 500 rpm and is read by a laser beam which starts at the inner radius; it's moulded in clear PVC and covered in micro-thin aluminium with a protective coating of lacquer, and while a vinyl LP has suffered serious deterioration after twenty playings and after a hundred is badly worn, a CD does not deteriorate at all through normal use.

'Editing' and 'mixing' and musicians' attitudes to them

With the introduction of digital recording many of the everyday techniques of the recording engineer could be carried out electronically. It was no longer necessary to wield a razor-blade to cut or 'splice' a tape; this could be done electronically using a computer. But such techniques, editing, multitracking, mixing, have in essence remained the same for the past fifty years and some of the fundamental decisions to be taken by a sound engineer have required the same kind of approaches since the introduction of microphones in the 1920s. What have these modern techniques made possible and how have they shaped the way musicians perform?

With the introduction of the microphone in 1925 the quality of the recording acoustic became important. In the beginning very little of its distinctiveness could be captured and what remained at the end of the disc manufacturing processes would mostly be obliterated by the surface noise of the record itself. But with improvements in microphone sensitivity and with the introduction of tape and the vinyl LP the acoustic became more and more a factor that coloured the recording quality. Now, in the 1950s, it made all the difference that there'd been a shower of rain during the lunch break between recording sessions and the orchestral players had returned and hung their macintoshes round the hall in which they were working; on the tape it sounded as if they'd moved location after the first movement of the symphony.[109] Large rooms or concert halls or the stages or auditoriums of opera houses, even recording studios, sound different from different positions. Some large resonant spaces create complicated wave formations which muddy the sound when it is captured by certain kinds of microphone. And different microphone placings can change the proportion of sounds striking the microphone straight from the sound source against sounds reflected from the walls and other sources. So the placing of microphones could be crucial in determining the quality of sound of the recording.

In the recording studio one microphone or a number of microphones might be used to catch the blend and balance that the musicians themselves, or their conductor, judged most satisfactory, or else the microphones used to adjust the balance, or to modify the balance in certain passages or just with certain instruments, to bring forward or give extra presence to a single, crucial stroke on the glockenspiel, for instance. Or close miking might be arranged to disregard or ignore the effect in the live acoustic, allowing the desired blend and balance to be obtained by mixing tracks after the recording sessions. Whatever microphone techniques and systems are employed in the studio sessions, the sounds might be fused or given extra sheen by the addition of echo or reverberation electronically. For most of the history of classical music, right up to the 1980s with the introduction of digital recording and the CD, the techniques employed to record classical music have been moulded and shaped by technical shortcomings, by attempts to compensate, for example, for the wide dynamic range of an orchestra or a large organ in a vast building which was formerly impossible to capture faithfully, or for the tape hiss and vinyl surface noise that would obscure details caught without difficulty on the tape master. In the early 1930s Eugene Ormandy's recordings with orchestra were done with one microphone, and those with the Minneapolis Orchestra and Chorus with one microphone for the orchestra and one for the chorus; Thomas Frost used between nine and thirteen microphones when he recorded with the Philadelphia Orchestra, in the

1970s; when he recorded quadraphonically with orchestra Ormandy was pretty sure eighteen were used;[110] when Michael Tilson Thomas recorded *Carmina Burana* quadraphonically with the Cleveland Orchestra and Chorus and soloists, Ray Moore used fifty microphones.[111] For CBS studio sessions with Horowitz in 1975 there were four microphones fifteen feet away from the piano and two more twenty-five feet away.[112]

Inevitably there have been a great many theories about sound quality, about the ways to change or to 'interpret' the sound heard in actual performances in the studio for listening in domestic settings, there have been fashions in sound quality, there have been 'philosophies' propagated by record companies, to use a single microphone, perhaps, or not to rely on edits, or to dispense with a mixing desk. Listeners in the 1990s were extremely sophisticated and alive to the subtleties of acoustical settings. One critic upbraided Harry Christophers and The Sixteen in 1996 for not having chosen different acoustics for the secular songs and the sacred settings in recordings of music from the Eton Choirbook. The songs like 'Afraid, alas, and why so suddenly?' and Robert Fayrfax's 'Most clear of colour', and Turges's 'From stormy windes and grievious weather', he contended, belonged to that category of 'poems, chronicles of kings, the wonders of the world and other recreations suitable to the clerical state'[113] as laid down by statute at Winchester and Eton and other colleges at Oxford and Cambridge which would have been sung on greater feasts and important college occasions after supper in the stone and brickwork hall of the College in the 1490s, and by only a handful of singers; the votive antiphons and Magnificats of the Eton Choirbook repertory would have been performed by the full choral resources in the chapel, built wholly of stone and of vaster proportions.[114] But then all these performances, like all recordings, are reinterpretations of the music for the disc, for the domestic setting in which they will be listened to; the whole series of *Music from the Eton Choirbook* was recorded not in Eton Chapel but in St Bartholomew's Church, Orford, in order, presumably, to allow the intricacies of the florid counterpoint to be heard more clearly.

But in the 1980s and 90s a general trend toward simplification in recording techniques was discernible, a tendency to ensure that the balance was right in the studio and to remove the necessity even to consider complex post-recording manipulation. This was partly the result of the clean sound of digital recording, which has meant that the process has to be 'purified' from the very beginning since the sound generated by more microphones and associated equipment will be captured and preserved by the digital technology. The clarity of sound preserved by modern recording equipment has tended to show up the artificiality of the kind of aural analysis of the music arrived at through multi-miking and remixing which analogue recording and vinyl surfaces sometimes benefited from.

Using tape meant that a recorded performance could have errors excised and insertions substituted from other performances, or a recording could be stitched together from several complete performances, from several 'takes', or built up from sections of a piece or a movement recorded separately. So a recorded performance may not be – since the middle of the century was usually not – a continuous performance that actually took place but 'a composite of takes and inserts recorded over a period of time and spliced together'.[115] It was not uncommon for the master-tape for an LP, lasting perhaps fifty or fifty-five minutes, to be the result of 150 splices.[116] Notes, phrases or sections could be inserted or copied, the pitch of out-of-tune notes or phrases changed, accents could be removed, the quality of harsh-sounding notes could be mellowed. Even in the days of analogue reel-to-reel tape the spliced master-tape would not itself be used to make the tape-to-disc transfer, but would be copied to create what was known as the 'production master' and unless the spliced master-tape had been preserved or all the edits had been incompetently carried out and so were audible, it is impossible ever to determine how many splices were made in a recording. No amount of technological detective work can ever uncover this aspect of the history of a recording.

Studio practices and the cooperative nature of recording

Most performers have said that they do not like recording in small sections, even though the technology has made this perfectly possible since the introduction of tape. 'I don't like splices, I don't like any falsehood,' Piatigorsky said, 'I don't like any perfection. . . . If the spirit is there, it's good enough for me.'[117] Eugen Jochum always wished to record in long stretches, 'a whole movement of a symphony, or at least the exposition in a single "take"'.[118] George Szell might go back and record small sections which contained little imperfections in the complete run-through, but he would never 'do a patch-cobbler's job to begin with'.[119] The American conductor Jascha Horenstein insisted, he said, on recording a movement whole, playing it perhaps three times right through and leaving the engineers simply with those three takes to select from;[120] this was the way the Guarneri String Quartet liked to record in the 1960s and 70s too, in whole movements, with maybe a splice here or there to make repairs, but not many of them, not many edits.[121] Fischer-Dieskau, according to his accompanist, would record a song two or three times for the microphone and then would declare that he had done his best and would refuse to go on repeating it.[122] Vladimir Ashkenazy too would attempt to record a Beethoven sonata movement whole – he started off his sessions on op. 109 by playing the complete sonata straight through.[123] But rarely would a movement be free from some imperfection or other and he would generally expect to play each movement through a few times. Anne-Sophie Mutter very much disliked cutting and would rather 'keep the string that doesn't speak or other minor imperfections than lose the spirit. Reality isn't perfect.'[124] André Previn believed in making 'very, very long takes, a movement at a time', and only redoing a section if someone had knocked over the cymbals, not for the sake of a split semiquaver, which he was perfectly willing to let go, for which reason, he thought, the London Symphony Orchestra liked to record with him.[125] Alicia de Larrocha didn't like splices and so, she explained, not being one of those performers who always play faultlessly, she had to 'play the whole piece through three, four, five, six times'.[126] Haitink too liked 'to record straight through' and then simply to re-record sections only where it was necessary to correct slips.[127] So did Pierre Boulez: 'I'd rather play a longish passage two or three times, and if something's really wrong . . . we make an insert later. . . .'[128]

Not surprisingly, few performers (or their record companies) have been eager to divulge that this particular disc was recorded in sections of no more than ten bars at a time, or that the master-tape of this particular work required 186 splices. 'Don't you wish *you* could play like that' is what cynical sound engineers are supposed to say to incompetent artists as they listen to immaculate, stitched-together tape masters. But the Czech conductor Jindrich Rohan was keen to explain in 1977 that he only ever recorded in sections, that in a symphony he would expect '80, 100, or even 120 stops and retakes', that he could not recollect ever having recorded a symphonic movement without a stop.

He did not think that the Czech record label Supraphon had ever recorded that way; it was essential for accuracy – for the kind of meticulous accuracy that he judged essential in recorded performances – but also, at least in Czechoslovakia in the 1960s and 1970s, because an orchestra would rarely have given a recent live performance of the work to be recorded before the studio sessions, and so would often be learning the piece, or an interpretation, or at least refreshing often distant memories of the piece in the studio. Supraphon would not attempt to co-ordinate their schedule with the orchestra in question's concert programme, which would be common practice in Western Europe and in the United States at that time. And so Jindrich Rohan found it essential to teach his students at the Prague Conservatoire the special disciplines and techniques that would enable such work to be undertaken efficiently, to learn to develop a 'perfect sense of tempo', to be able to wake up in the middle of the night and be shown a score open at page 32, bar 4, and to know without hesitation at exactly what speed you as conductor habitually took this passage; his aim was to teach his pupils to make music 'in a 100 per cent professional way', as he saw it. Rohan was depressed when he played again some of his early records, he said, because he had been carried away by his emotions and too little concerned with ensemble.[129]

According to a producer in 1971 such a method of working as Rohan's would have been 'economically insane' in the USA, where, so long as the work in question had been thoroughly rehearsed and recently given live performances, there would be a reasonable expectation of recording a forty-minute symphony in two hours, which by the union regulations and restrictions at that time represented eighty minutes of recording time, the ratio of recording time to master-tape material being then 2:1. In England, where it was commoner with Decca to record with an unrehearsed orchestra at that time, the conductor of the same work might require four three-hour sessions which would have given a working period of eleven hours. And so the ratio would become $16\frac{1}{2}$:1. If the conductor were willing to use just three sessions the ratio would become 'slightly more than 12:1', but even using the union minimum of two sessions for a work lasting up to forty minutes the ratio would turn out to be 8:1.[130]

A recorded performance might also be multi-layered, built up by combining recordings made at different times in different places. This happened occasionally before the use of magnetic tape: it was used to provide orchestral accompaniments to old acoustic recordings of Caruso;[131] in September 1935 Elisabeth Schumann recorded both parts of the Evening Prayer from Humperdinck's *Hänsel und Gretel;*[132] in October 1946 Jascha Heifetz recorded both parts of Bach's Concerto for two violins BWV 1043.[133] But with tape it was happening all the time. For the opening of Verdi's *Otello* a 64-foot pedal note on the organ of Liverpool Cathedral was recorded first and then mixed in with Karajan conducting the Vienna Philharmonic Orchestra in the Sofiensaal in Vienna,[134] and this because 'what was left of the Liverpool sound when our equipment was driven to its limits was better than any kind of lesser, complete sound which we could easily have accommodated by using an electronic machine or a smaller organ'.[135] It would not matter that Kurt Böhme, singing Fafner in *Siegfried* in Solti's *Ring* cycle for Decca, was not available in May when the opening scene of Act Two was to be recorded; his part could be recorded in the autumn when he would attend the next studio sessions, and then be added to the earlier recording.[136] Daniel Barenboim could conduct the Chicago Symphony Orchestra in their home city in a recorded performance of Saint-Saëns's Third Symphony and the recording incorporate Gaston Litaize playing the organ of Chartres Cathedral.[137] And when Barenboim recorded *Don Giovanni* for EMI half of the opera was recorded in August 1973 in Edinburgh, most of the remainder in Kingsway Hall in London in December 1973, and the rest recorded in May 1974 in order to superimpose Zerlina, the voice of Helen Donath, who had had laryngitis in December.[138]

It is almost impossible to imagine many in an audience ever hearing a concert performance of Bartók's Second Piano Concerto, for example, in which most of the details emerge clearly and a satisfactory balance is obtained between piano and orchestra, or in, say, Richard Strauss's Duo-Concertino for clarinet, bassoon, harp and strings. But unexceptional recording techniques in the second half of this century and the combined skills of producer and sound engineer could solve these intractable problems.[139]

A famous example of a recording adding distance and perspective and clarifying the composer's intentions was the set of discs of Benjamin Britten's *War Requiem,*[140] made in January 1963, the forces for which exceeded four hundred. The separate groups were positioned and miked to give different effects. The orchestra was placed on the floor of the Kingsway Hall. Behind the conductor were the tenor and baritone soloists and the instrumental ensemble with a comparatively dry acoustic to ensure verbal clarity and to emphasize the astringent harmony of their sections. All the other singers were up in the balcony: the large chorus and the soprano soloist were in the main part, with their own microphones, suggesting a large ecclesiastical space yet avoiding the confused effect such numbers would create in a genuine cathedral acoustic; the boys' choir was in a corner of the balcony without extra microphones, giving them a different perspective.[141] Rarely can live performances have realized the distinctive perspectives imagined by the composer as does this recording, the calm, distance, otherworldliness, unearthliness of the boys' voices singing the impersonal ritual of the liturgy – boys and organ – the unease and mix of emotions experienced by humanity at large, fearful, supplicatory, guilt-ridden – choir and soprano and the main orchestra – 'sometimes sublimated, rather than personalized, by the soprano soloist',[142] and then the outcry of two particular victims of war – the male soloists and the chamber orchestra: 'I am the enemy you killed, my friend.'

An even more famous example of the way a work was produced for disc was Solti's *Ring* cycle, recorded between 1958 and 1965. Great trouble was taken to obtain the precise sounds that Wagner called for, tone qualities that are not usually faithfully reproduced in live productions: the overwhelming noise of eighteen anvils of various sizes in *Rheingold*;[143] the steerhorns Wagner calls for in the second act of *Götterdämmerung* usually played by trombones but for this recording specially made by an elderly instrument maker near Bayreuth who remembered clearly the original instruments, the ones carried off by American soldiers at the end of the war;[144] the horn calls which announce Hunding's arrival at the end of Act Two of *Götterdämmerung*, for which the producer found the right sort of mountain horn capable of playing the required low C – it belonged to a Swiss farmer living near Geneva.[145] This was partly a question of economics: it would simply have been impossible for an opera producer to spend time searching out such instruments and having examples specially constructed. But there were also sounds especially created by technological means. In scene three of *Rheingold*, Alberich, armed with a whip, puts on the Tarnhelm, the magic helmet that makes him invisible, which allows him to pursue the terrified Mime round the cavern. Mime was kept very close to the main microphones in order to capture his frantic whispers, Alberich put into a box with a glass panel – 'something rather like a telephone booth' – and so in a wholly distinct acoustic with a special microphone which could distort and magnify his voice and move it back and forth round the stereo arc.[146] At the end of Act One of *Götterdämmerung* the drugged Siegfried goes back up the mountain wearing the Tarnhelm, imitating the manner and guise and the voice of Gunther, singing, as Wagner's direction has it, in a deeper, rougher voice. The timbre of Siegfried's voice was subtly changed at this point by modifying the overtones of his voice electronically, giving his tenor voice a baritone quality.[147]

Such 'special effects' could not be mechanically or crudely applied; the record producer John Culshaw worked out precisely where the door should be through which Peter Grimes makes his entrance in the pub scene of the opera, but he did not add the sound of breaking waves or the crying of seagulls; he did not create a church acoustic for the First Act of *Tosca* or attempt an impression of open-air music-making in Act Three.[148]

What then is such a recording presenting us with? No-one listening to a performance of Britten's *War Requiem* in a large reverberant cathedral or to a performance of the *Ring* cycle in the opera house will hear the music with the same clarity and balance. To some degree such recorded interpretations are *sui generis*, in some sense reinterpretations. John Culshaw, the producer of that first recorded *Ring* cycle, inscribed at the front of his account of the project a quotation of Ernest Newman written in 1914:

> Can we not imagine something like the second Act of *Tristan* with silent or only dimly visible actors, the music, helped by their gestures, telling us all that is in their souls, while they are too remote from us for the crude personality of the actors and the theatrical artificiality of the stage setting to jar upon us as they do at present? . . . Or, to go a step further, *cannot we dispense altogether with the stage and the visible actor*, such external coherence as the music needs being afforded by impersonal voices floating through a darkened auditorium?[149]

And many thought that this recording did succeed in offering a different kind of musical experience, and an entirely legitimate one: 'Listening to these records is not like going to the opera house without looking at the stage', wrote Andrew Porter. 'In some mysterious way they seem to catch you up in the work – not in a particular set of performers – more intimately than that.'[150]

The Canadian pianist Glenn Gould insisted the record should not be the reproduction of a creative act, something artificial, but itself a created object, in the same way that popular music in the 1960s was making new kinds of music from mixing processes and multitracking, the disc itself being 'the music' of which no score could be notated – or at least of which no score was ever made – and which could never be reproduced in a live performance. So Gould recorded his arrangement for piano of the Prelude to Wagner's *Meistersinger* – the last three minutes in effect for piano duet – by superimposing takes of himself;[151] for his recording of the three lyric pieces by Sibelius called *Kyllikki* he used one microphone inside the piano, another several feet away at a conventional distance, and another 'in the equivalent of a balcony seat', and then edited the tapes 'to give each passage its ideal acoustic perspective, like a movie camera shifting from long shots to closeups', 'acoustic orchestration', as the producer described it.[152] Gould was hailed by some as a brilliant prophet, as being in tune with and knowledgeable about technological developments as most musicians were not, technology which they still regarded as 'a compromising, dehumanizing intrusion into art', as he himself described the attitude.[153] But many wondered why he applied his knowledge of the possibilities offered by the technology to distort and simply make eccentric existing works of art rather than attempt to put the technology at the service of something new, to create something afresh. The magic devices of a modern recording studio may be used to make clear the 'meaning' of a Brahms symphony, but not to add dimensions or effects that Brahms would never have thought of, was André Previn's view.[154] Undoubtedly Gould's theories owed too much to his own quirky temperament and personality to be of much general significance, though his recorded performances are often of great beauty and imaginative insight and – even at their most eccentric – always of the greatest interest.[155]

Recording as a 'photograph' of a performance

Fred Gaisberg, the most renowned 'recording expert' of his day – he would later have been called a 'producer' – whose recording activities extended over the first half of the century, said his aim was to take 'sound photographs'[156] of musical performances. Acoustic recordings were extremely fuzzy snapshots, blurred round the edges, in parts indistinct and out of focus because of the limitations of technology in capturing the sounds, and because of the limitations in playing the sounds back. And these acoustically recorded performances also differed from live performances because the sounds themselves in the studio were in fact different, because instruments themselves had to be modified – the Stroh violin, the piano with the felts filed down – or the music rescored – the substitution of tuba for double-bass, the use of a string quartet instead of a string orchestra. And these performances in the recording studio during the first quarter of the twentieth century were different too because players had to modify their performing techniques, deliberately – perhaps by performing at a constant loudness and removing subtle dynamic nuances of any kind – but also by having to play in unaccustomed positions, by performing with other players while yet being unable to communicate in the usual way, by having to modify speeds because of the time limitation of the twelve-inch disc.

With electrical recording these 'sound photographs' were still fuzzy and still blurred because of the limitations in the technology of capturing sounds and in reproducing them. Generally speaking, though, there was now no need to modify instruments in any way and it was possible to adopt usual playing positions and layouts and to employ the appropriate number of musicians, to record full orchestras and not artificially reduced ensembles. But interpretations were certainly affected because of the time limitation, passages rushed or tempi adjusted simply to fit on to the four and a half minutes of the twelve-inch disc or the two and a half minutes of the ten-inch disc. And the recording process itself was still cumbersome and rather hit-or-miss and so inevitably nerve-racking to both the performers and the engineers. There might be accidents with the wax disc as it was moved from the small oven where it was kept warm on to the cutting lathe. If a player hit a wrong note, or if a microphone began emitting 'frying' noises as they were called, there was nothing to be done except to start all over again. Because during the factory processing many wax discs were damaged, it was no good making just one wax master; the performer would perform several times and the producer would decide which two of the four versions or three of the five versions should be sent off for processing.[157] If the soft wax master was played in the control room it would be destroyed; and so nobody could be quite sure until the test pressings came back two or three weeks later whether or not artistic truths had been successfully engraved or whether, as a result of a shaky hand or a sweaty palm or spilt oil or a sudden shout, they lay in little bits on the factory floor.

In 1985 the keyboard player and conductor Christopher Hogwood used the same metaphor as Gaisberg; he too thought a recording was 'a photograph of an event'. But now, in the 1980s, he extended and developed the metaphor. There could be many kinds of sound photographs: a recording might be 'candid, or posed, or superimposed, or retouched'; it might be 'anything you want from the most honest to the most, many people would say, dishonest'.[158] This was because of the differences that could result from decisions over which the musicians might have no control, from the choice of location and recording acoustic, and from procedures which they might not even know about or might not understand, from editing techniques, from microphone placing and post-production balancing and mixing procedures. Who was it then who was ultimately responsible for the precise nature and quality and character of the recording?

The function of record producers

In May 1933 the Russian bass Alexander Kipnis was in London recording Hugo Wolf's Michelangelo songs. He was taken aback listening in the control room to some of the test recordings and he became aware that the volume levels were being adjusted; he was possibly unaware up till then that now, with electrical recording, volume levels could be adjusted. ' "Why must you turn the knobs?" ' he said. ' "I want to have that tone *loud* and the other tone *soft*. And you're doing the opposite." ' And the engineers replied: ' "If you don't like the things we are doing, make your own record by yourself!" and they left the studio. I made the Michelangelo songs and *Grenzen der Menschheit* at that session, and I believe those are the best recordings I ever made – without engineers!'[159]

This perhaps isn't exactly how it happened. Someone must have been around at any rate to operate the recording equipment. But Kipnis's attitude is clear. In the earliest days of making records the performer certainly didn't feel he was master of his fate, but the distortions in his recorded performances largely arose from the inadequacies of the recording apparatus, its inability to capture the sounds the musicians were making. With electrical recording, and still more later with the use of magnetic tape, the more startling modifications to the actual performances given in the studio could be the result of decisions taken by engineers and producers, sometimes in consultation with the musicians, sometimes not, which modifications were made through technical processes that the performers probably did not understand and certainly themselves could not implement. In other words, recording gradually became a co-operative endeavour. The engineers who so upset Alexander Kipnis were 'taming' the performance of its wide dynamic range, so that the loudest passages would not overload the cutter – or give repeating grooves in the master-wax – and quiet passages would not get lost behind the surface noise.

In 1928 Stanley Chapple, who was the 'director of music' for the Vocalion company – he suggested repertoire to the company, chose artists, made musical arrangements, and conducted for the recordings – wondered whether most performers should ever hear wax test discs. If they did they might attempt to make adjustments themselves, particularly regarding balance, without realizing the limitations and distorting effects of the recording apparatus being used in the studio or of the different kinds of gramophones and domestic settings in which the records would be listened to, and in so doing they would thwart the efforts of the 'recording experts'. Most performers hadn't succeeded, he thought, in cultivating a 'gramophone ear'.[160]

By the 1960s John Culshaw was sure most musicians realized that making recordings could only be a co-operative venture. Even in the recent past there had been those conductors who 'could not, or would not, accept the difference between transcribing the notes of music on a record and an imaginative approach to the same operation, through which one re-studied the score with a view to presenting the music in a way that would especially appeal to the listener at home'. Now the technological means whereby this was accomplished were simply too complex for the performer to understand, and, mostly, artists realized this and let those who did understand recording techniques carry out their work without interference. At any rate, recording had become such a costly activity by that time that the 'whims and conceits' of performers could no longer be indulged.[161]

Who were these 'record producers' and what did they do exactly? In the 1930s the American pianist, composer, and writer on musical matters Abram Chasins was impressed with the musical knowledge and sensitivity of the sound engineers in London who had, somehow or other, acquired a musical education, and understood what the musicians were trying to do in the recording studio. In America at that time, he thought, most sound engineers 'had really encyclopedic ignorance about music', like most record company executives; it was only the A & R men in America – the artists and repertoire people, who would later be called the 'producers' – who could read music and understood music. In America in the 1930s the engineers 'watched dials and needles' whereas in London they 'were listening and feeling'; in the 1970s American engineers were 'as masterful and sophisticated as any'.[162]

Record producers and sound engineers – and those 'experts' of the earlier days – have all had individual and idiosyncratic methods of working, but at least since the middle of the century, since the early days of tape and the long-playing record, roles and functions can be identified which have remained more or less the same in most recording organizations. The producer usually selected repertoire and artists, by himself or in collaboration with other 'artists and repertoire' personnel of the record company, and in projects with soloists or in opera with the conductor. With the musicians too the producer would often discuss the location, especially if this was not a recording studio, with regard to the style and period of the music, to the performing style and character of the performers, to the taste and education of the producer, the acoustics being 'to a performance what a stage set is to a play', as one producer put it.[163] Simply because most opera houses are of similar design – most of them were after all built in the nineteenth century to present the repertory then current to best advantage – there was no need to arrange singers and orchestral musicians in the studio as if they were similarly constrained. The acoustical setting which might be appropriate for *Otello* would not be for *Aida*, or for *Elektra* or for *Pelléas*.[164] Producer or chief engineer or Tonmeister would choose the make and number of microphones to be used, with different makes having different colorations, and would suggest the placing and disposition of musicians and microphones.

The producer would have submitted costed proposals to the company and had to ensure that timetables and budgets were adhered to. If an orchestral session overran by half an hour in America in 1980 this would have added between four and five thousand dollars to a session budget of perhaps $25,000. The producer would have had to plan according to the permitted local union rates: in America in 1980 orchestral musicians could work only forty minutes in each hour and the record company could only use fifteen minutes of finished music for each hour of studio time.[165] Planning sessions would have to take into account all such rules and restrictions. The producer took charge of the engineers and would have discussed with them the aims and objectives in musical and acoustical terms; he might have taken them through the musical score indicating possible difficulties, maybe himself proposing technical solutions. Certainly in America and England many concerned themselves with sound quality and explained the musical effects they and the artists were hoping to achieve. They might say in mid-session to an engineer, after a playback, 'I don't like the sound, I want the microphones closer'.[166] But in some European centres there are different traditions. At Deutsche Grammophon the Tonmeister, the mixing engineer, was responsible for sound quality and would not expect the producer to give opinions on the quality of the microphones or the dryness or luxuriance of the acoustic; he would have expected the producer to comment on balance, to discuss repeating material with the musicians. Everywhere the most successful relationships between the producer and engineer were based on mutual respect since the closest co-operation was clearly essential, and the specialist skills of the sound technician very great; the producer hardly existed in the second half of the century who could perform the functions of the engineer if necessary. Diplomacy and tact were vital since engineers could be as prima donnish as prima donnas.[167] The musical prima donnas were of course also the responsibility of the producer, to whom the musicians looked for advice, support, criticism and inspiration.

After the studio sessions were over, the producer, armed with notes on the sessions, would usually work with an editing engineer in creating the master-tape. Some commentators have argued that in making records of pop music the producer is the primary creator, that his role is similar to that of a film director, that the star is simply part of a bigger design and purpose with the producer in overall command.[168] This has never been so in the making of classical records. Most performers would listen in the control room to most of the takes at least, and make comments about the quality of each, draw attention to errors or passages of which they didn't approve, and make suggestions for the master-tape. Especially in the 1960s and 70s, when multitracking was commoner than it later became, important, sometimes crucial, decisions relating to mixing and balance were sometimes made as the master-tape was finally produced. Yet it was rare for the musicians to be assisting at this stage. Glenn Gould was always present, so was Gunther Schuller,[169] and Anne-Sophie Mutter, though she worked with a trusted sound engineer, always sat in on mixing sessions.[170] But this was uncommon. Who then were these shadowy figures, these record producers who wielded such power?

Gaisberg, Legge, Culshaw, and the training of modern producers and engineers

In the very beginning, when the skills to be specially acquired for recording by performers were important though not sophisticated – to singers, for example, the advice would be to sing loud, spit out consonants and retreat from the horn on high notes; to pianists, you can't play below mezzo-forte – the diplomatic skills of the producer, his ability to entice musicians to record at all, and then to encourage them and smooth ruffled feathers in surroundings rarely glamorous, usually undignified, and sometimes squalid, were of overriding importance. The best-known record producer of the first half of the century, though never called by that name, was Fred Gaisberg. He made his first recordings as a piano accompanist for the Columbia Phonograph Company in Washington, D.C., in 1889 when he was sixteen, retired from EMI in 1939, and remained a consultant for the firm until his death in 1951.

In 1900 The Gramophone Company signed a contract with the conductor Landon Ronald as a middle-man to recruit musicians to record. Fred Gaisberg, who was then styled the Company's 'chief recorder and artist scout', was very impressed with him when he saw him conducting the musical comedy *Floradora* at the Lyric Theatre in Shaftesbury Avenue, one of the biggest hits at the turn of the century, with the stars Kate Cutler, Louis Bradfield, Sydney Barraclough, and the smash hit song 'Tell me Pretty Maiden, are there any more at home like you?';[171] Ronald was given a contract and a roving commission to bring in artists, which job he retained to the end of his life in 1938. Ronald had worked at Covent Garden as an accompanist and coach since 1892, he had conducted at Drury Lane and with a touring opera company, and he had regularly conducted musical comedy in London and at summer seasons in Blackpool. And in 1894 he had toured the USA as accompanist to Nellie Melba. So he knew a great number of singers performing a wide range of repertory and was in a position to assess not only their musical gifts but also their temperaments and to judge how they might react to the trying conditions under which they would have to work in the studio.

Fred Gaisberg himself was fairly soon on intimate terms with some of the greatest musicians he recorded; at the Sunday evening supper parties at his home in London between the wars you might have seen John Barbirolli, or Ria Ginster, the German lieder singer, back from teaching in Philadelphia, or the conductor Marek Weber, who always came when he was in London; Ina Souez used to come when she was making the Glyndebourne recordings, and Backhaus came several times, and Schnabel and Edwin Fischer. There would be informal music-making after the food and Gaisberg himself would join in, playing jazz, and Viennese waltzes, and accompanying operatic arias and lieder; he was an excellent sight-reader and he could improvise fluently. His musical professionalism and knowledge were clear to all the artists he worked with. Most performing artists, he realized, required devoted interest and attention, rather like children; he was forthright and treated famous musicians with respect and courtesy, but he was never fawning. He had the greatest respect also for the engineers and was always keen to ensure they received acknowledgement. Gaisberg was a shrewd businessman and was able to reconcile his great love of music with a constant awareness that making records was a business. If you were hard up and times were really bad he would say, 'Make a popular religious record with a tenor'. He was kindly and genial and calm but he could be extremely blunt; he was confident of his own abilities. He was a man of great psychological subtlety and perceptiveness; he could dissipate tension in a studio by clowning, or by sitting down at the piano himself; he could be extremely patient with artists who found the business of recording trying and nerve-racking, and with those who did not invariably play all the right notes every time. Friends he had all over the place, and perhaps lovers too, but also a devoted elder sister who fed him well, managed all his domestic arrangements, gave him a very comfortable home life, and did not worry him or pry or interfere. He was, his record-producer niece thought, a happy man.[172] He thought recordings important but was content to see them in a greater scheme of things; he quoted Bruno Walter, who thought ' "canned music" tastes a little of the metal that preserves it. It is not fresh fruit but, even so, it is a great blessing.'[173] Gaisberg agreed. He would never have become involved in recording at all in the 1890s if he had been too fastidious.

Walter Legge, who was born in 1905 and belonged to the next generation at EMI, rejected Gaisberg's declared aim of producing 'sound photographs' of musical performances, of simply reproducing what the artists habitually did in the opera house or on the concert platform. 'I was the first', he would claim, 'of what are called "producers" of records.'[174] He wanted to record on disc what the best artists could do under the best possible conditions, to make records which would allow the listener at home to hear a performance such as he would hear 'in the best seat in an acoustically perfect hall'.[175] Legge wanted to take advantage of the ability to splice and so to create the kind of performance the artist would aspire to but, being human, could practically never achieve. But though he wanted to take advantage of the technology to remove wrong notes and technical slips, his preoccupation was not with accuracy for its own sake. The kind of listening that recording and especially the long-playing record made possible required the elimination of errors that would be disturbing and irritating on repeated hearings. Accuracy must be taken for granted, and a wrong note which would matter not at all in a live performance must be removed on a record. But above all, he looked in a recorded performance for the same virtues that he hoped for in a live performance, life and vigour and intensity and individuality and character. To fulfil such aspirations required a thorough knowledge of the repertory and its demands, both technical and musical and theatrical, and a wide and detailed knowledge of musicians everywhere – since recording had become by the middle of the century a thoroughly international business – and their skills and accomplishments and their personalities and characters. It also required authority and leadership and the ability to inspire the confidence and the co-operation of musicians and sound engineers and the record company administrators and money men.

Legge had the ability to make sessions in the studio intense, exhilarating, sometimes exciting and nearly always memorable. His own enthusiasm for gramophone records and his convictions about their significance helped to convince musicians that they were engaged upon an important activity. Many of the older generation were still sceptical about the whole business, but in the 1950s most musicians were realizing the ways in which LPs were forming musical tastes and raising standards and creating competition and making careers. And they were also aware of the extent to which recording fees and royalties from making records were contributing or might contribute to their livelihoods. It was only in retrospect that Artur Rubinstein had realized that the most significant moment of his whole career was his first professional encounter with Fred Gaisberg in 1928.[176]

With Walter Legge the preparation for a recording would start months before the actual sessions matching artists to repertory and casting. Schedules would be planned so that in an opera, for example, each singer's load would be spread out over the sessions, mixing solos and ensembles, allowing time and opportunity for possible retakes, enabling the singers to pace themselves and sing out whenever they were required. Sometimes there would be preliminary rehearsals, often at Walter Legge's own house, and he would take an active, occasionally a dominating, role in these coaching sessions. Certainly in the studio he was without question the man in charge, often sitting on high in the control room, puffing on a cigar, giving orders in all directions. He would have discussed the music to be recorded with the engineers, and indicated to them possible problems – this passage in thirds for two sopranos may require positioning the singers further apart. He would welcome the artists, many as old friends, and discuss matters of balance and matters of interpretation with them after a take as an equal, with a minute knowledge of the music itself.

During the take he would follow a score minutely, even if it was one he knew backwards, with an assistant producer sitting nearby also following a score, to whom Legge would give instructions to note down – 'Check five after B' – while he himself also concentrated on the flow and pace and spirit of the performance.[177] His confidence and enthusiasm in the studio, his knowledge of the repertory and his absolute convictions about style and interpretation gave him the authority – sometimes the nerve – to propose solutions which most producers would never dare advance. Once when Maria Callas was getting bogged down and tired and discouraged recording one of the Massenet items on a recital record,[178] he suggested she try it just once more, a fraction faster. It worked beautifully. But it couldn't have been fitted with any of the earlier takes had editing been needed.[179]

Legge never learnt a musical instrument (though he apparently had a good bass-baritone voice and would sing after supper at Fred Gaisberg's *soirées musicales*);[180] in adult life he sometimes wondered why, but guessed he realized that he would never be a good pianist and he soon became acquainted with the interpretations of world-class players through recordings. Walter Legge attended concerts assiduously and as a young man learnt how to inveigle his way into rehearsals. He listened to recordings all the time; as a twelve-year-old he would walk from record shop to record shop in London listening to the four or five available versions of a desired aria before finally parting with his 7 s. 6 d.[181] He was self-taught in music and in most things – he left school at sixteen – and had the unshakable confidence in his own opinions of the autodidact. He loathed the breeziness of the English musical establishment and he liked to think of himself as a European, as a sophisticated cosmopolitan – he would call Vaughan Williams and the other English composers, sometimes referred to as the English pastoral school, 'agricultural' composers, with their 'market-day modalism'. He despised the 'gentlemanliness' of Parry and Stanford, and admired the 'professionalism' of Elgar and Walton. He disliked equally the tastes of 'Mus.Bac.'s' and 'farmhands'.[182] He admired the breadth and style and magisterial pronouncements of the music critic Ernest Newman, 'his independent and international outlook', and noted that he was self-taught and that he held British schools and colleges of music 'in pitying contempt all his life'.[183]

Schoenberg's scores Legge closely and patiently studied and came to the conclusion that his 'eccentricities' stemmed from the composer's own realization 'that he was incapable of writing a natural melodic and original line'.[184] He who was notorious for his rudeness and high-handedness and bullying manner and know-allness – he was proud, he said, of the jealousy and dislike shown to him by many of his colleagues in the recording industry[185] – explained how well he had got on with Szell, himself so widely disliked among musicians. But then, he added: 'We talked the same musical language – "der Komponist hat immer recht." '[186] Small people always had difficulty with great minds and big talents, with whom Legge certainly wished to identify himself.

And to surround himself with. The Mozart concert aria 'Ch'io mi scordi di te?' contains a small part for piano, for which, when he recorded it with his wife Elisabeth Schwarzkopf, Legge hired Alfred Brendel. Legge's success as a record producer, his creation of a new kind of record man, stemmed first of all from his love of recordings, from the important part they had played in his life from his earliest years. In his family it was said that he had learnt to read from record labels and then progressed on to record catalogues. He decided when he was seven that he wanted to spend his life in music, either making records or directing an opera house. This was a music-loving but not a music-making home. It was a time when many professional and amateur musicians had little time for the gramophone, when many considered it far better to become acquainted with the orchestral repertory by playing the music through as a piano duet and so really getting to know the music 'from the inside', as Vaughan Williams put it.[187] Perhaps if he had had a more conventional musical education, learning the piano and playing chamber music, he would never have become the force in the musical world that he did. He first worked in a studio in 1931, assisting Fred Gaisberg, and he resigned from EMI in 1964; he supervised some 3,500 recordings.[188] 'The world owes him a debt', was one critic's verdict, 'for having sought out, sifted, promulgated and preserved for posterity the best in mid-twentieth century musical performance.'[189]

John Culshaw (1924–1980) belonged to a slightly later generation of record producers, whose career began after the war. Like Walter Legge, Culshaw did not come from a home in which music-making was assiduously cultivated. He discovered music for himself in his teens, by attending concerts and listening to broadcasts and recordings; there was certainly no prejudice against gramophone records in his family. Recordings developed his passion for music, but at the same time listening to Cortot or Schnabel or Backhaus increased the dissatisfaction he felt with his own attempts to play the piano which he soon abandoned. Culshaw stressed the differences between live and recorded music. He believed that such differences should be creatively exploited, not minimized, that a recording was an interpretation of a musical performance, a musical object in its own right. By the 1950s it was possible for recordings, through the use of several microphones and because of the clarity of reproduction of playback equipment, to present a musical score to the ear with far greater faithfulness, or at least literalness, than the greatest performer in the most sympathetic concert hall acoustic could ever accomplish, to capture the minutest detail of a violinist's articulation or a singer's enunciation while at the same time preserving the bloom and the richness of a large space.

Like Walter Legge, John Culshaw would plan the sessions meticulously in order fully to exploit the possibilities offered by recording of giving each performer every opportunity to sing at his or her best all the time. The principal character in *Siegfried* is on stage for most of the opera; the first act requires of him consistently big, expansive, declamatory singing and ends with the vigorous forging scene; the second act involves a very different singing style, quiet and lyrical; the third act is extremely long. These heavy demands on Siegfried – himself on stage for most of the opera – necessitate nearly all tenors taking the part attempting to conserve the voice in certain passages. Proper planning of recording sessions would allow Siegfried to sing out without any need to restrain the voice.[190] Like Legge, Culshaw demanded piano rehearsals for his *Ring* cycle. Previously this had usually been thought completely unnecessary; the artists who were being hired for the recording had made their names on the world's operatic stages in performances of the part which they were to record; it would be a waste of time, and also an insult, to require them to attend special rehearsals. What Culshaw and other producers were now asking singers to do was to rethink their own interpretations, to assist the record men to reinterpret the roles for the microphone.[191] And stereo sound made it essential for movement and spacing to be worked out in great detail; Decca facilitated this with numbered chalk squares on the floor of the studio which the singers would pencil into their score. Culshaw started from first principles: that there was a world of difference between communication in an opera house or in a concert hall and communication through loudspeakers in a domestic setting, and that every element in the process of communication should take the differences into account. A recording is an illusion; much is lost with a recording, the visual element most obviously, but also the sense of occasion, and the intensity of a communal response. But recorded music – especially now with vinyl record surfaces so quiet, especially now with music in stereo – offered the possibility of better clarity, better balance than was ever possible when attending a live performance, and a much greater sense of intimacy.[192]

A number of well-known producers working in America had undertaken professional musical training. Goddard Lieberson (1911–77), who joined CBS Records in 1939 and sixteen years later became president of the company, studied music at the University of Washington and at the Eastman School of Music at Rochester, and his first aspiration was to become a composer.[193] John Pfeiffer, who worked from 1949 for RCA, studied music at the University of Arizona and then took a degree in electrical engineering.[194] Thomas Frost, who was director of artists and repertoire for Columbia Records in the 1960s and then for CBS Masterworks, was born in Vienna in 1925 and was a member of the Vienna Boys Choir. At the Yale School of Music he studied composition with Paul Hindemith and trained as a violinist and a pianist and he studied conducting with Leon Barzin and at the Accademia Chigiana at Siena in 1938.[195] Sam Parkins, who was born in 1926, studied composition at Cornell University and the New England Conservatory of Music and worked for twenty years as a jazz clarinettist, flautist and saxophonist in New York City before becoming a record producer, first with Columbia Masterworks and then as a freelance.[196]

At the end of the century those who aspired to be recording engineers and producers in England would typically take a degree, probably in music, and then follow a degree or diploma course in 'audio engineering', or 'music technology and sound recording techniques', or 'recording, music technology and music business studies', or 'advanced sound recording and production techniques',[197] which courses distil and codify the practices developed empirically by engineers and producers over the previous five decades. A hundred years earlier, the English record man Joe Batten, who spent fifty years working for at least thirty record companies,[198] began his career in gramophone records as a piano accompanist, earning fifteen shillings for six hours hammering out piano accompaniments for the tenor Montague Borwell, and for A. H. Gee, better known as 'The Australian Baritone', Principal Bass at the New Westminster Cathedral, the Odeon catalogue proclaimed, singing songs like 'Come into the garden, Maud' and 'The Soldiers of the Queen'; as a boy of twelve he had accompanied his father who sang ballads in London music-halls. He appeared as a ragtime pianist under the name of 'Joe Bolton', he produced records of variety and music-hall stars and Jack Payne and the Hotel Cecil Band and Beecham and Stravinsky and Hamilton Harty and Bruno Walter and Solomon and Albert Sammons and the Léner String

Quartet, he conducted military bands and brass bands and *The Dream of Gerontius* and the *Siegfried Idyll*, and he accompanied and 'produced' John McCormack. At the end of his career he looked back and was amused and astounded when he remembered his humble beginnings, his lack of formal education, and the painful and laborious acquisition of musical and technical knowledge.[199]

Musicians' attitudes towards making recordings

The acoustic recording process itself created particular difficulties and artificial performing conditions. Rosa Ponselle had less stage fright when she made her early recordings, she said, than when she made her debut at the Metropolitan Opera, but she thought the technique of acoustic recording 'dreadful', with that 'awful horn', and those chalk marks on the floor to show how far she should retreat for high notes.[200] Frieda Hempel, who was described by a recording man as 'a refined and brilliant German soprano', did not have the benefit of chalk marks on the floor, and it's not surprising that she did not have fond feelings for the engineer who, when she forgot that she must retreat from the recording horn for high notes, shoved her backwards and forwards 'without gentleness'.[201] Because the wax had to be kept soft it was always hot and airless in the small studios in which acoustic recordings were made, 'well over ninety degrees' one musician remembered when he sang for the Gramophone Company as a choirboy in 1924,[202] which caused not only physical discomfort but problems with instruments and tuning difficulties. For Ferruccio Busoni recording was 'stupid and a strain . . . a *via crucis* . . . watching the pedal (because it sounds bad); thinking of certain notes which had to be stronger or weaker in order to please this devilish machine: not letting oneself go for fear of inaccuracies and being conscious the whole time that every note was going to be there for eternity . . . this absurd gramophone business', he called it.[203] Paderewski, according to his producer, hated making records and considered it an ordeal, chiefly because he never believed that the recording machine could ever catch the subtleties of his art; and he was right, too, in the producer's opinion, since so much depended on his 'broad and unrestrained dynamics' which caused such problems to the primitive recording horn. He had to reduce the scale of his performances and the machine reduced them still further; his recordings presented a miniaturized version of his art.[204]

Those primitive conditions of acoustic recording, with everyone crammed as close as possible to the recording horn, with a percussion player attempting to strike a metal sheet but missing and knocking the singer unconscious,[205] not surprisingly many performers found difficult, uncongenial, unsatisfactory and inhibiting. Not quite all musicians disliked recording, though. After Percy Grainger's first studio session, in May 1908, when he played the cadenza to the first movement of Grieg's Piano Concerto, a truncated version of Liszt's *Hungarian Rhapsody no. 12* and his own arrangement of Stanford's *Irish March-Jig – Maguire's Kick*, he wrote to a friend: 'Tuesday at the Gramophone Co. was fun. I like making records.'[206]

In an attempt to impress the early recording artists, to encourage them to take seriously this unprepossessing medium which many laughed at and regarded as a toy, Fred Gaisberg would constantly remind them that they were recording *for posterity*. But this would make many of them even more ill-at-ease. For older generations, performers of the greatest expertise and artistry and experience, the very idea of permanence was inhibiting, the thought that they were setting down their work upon which posterity could pass judgement was itself profoundly unnerving. For Serkin and for Segovia, according to their producer, this made recording 'torture'.[207] Sir Walter Alcock, born in 1861 and renowned as one of the greatest English organ virtuosos of his day, who played at the coronations of three English kings, found the experience of recording Bach's Prelude and Fugue in D major BWV 542 in Salisbury Cathedral in 1928 extremely unnerving: 'Think of waiting to play the scale of D major on practically full organ with your boots, while with uplifted hand the man-in-charge awaits the signal from his brother conspirator in the studio!'[208]

Some performers have felt intimidated by the studio setting, or at least have been unable to assume the commanding authority that they were able to summon without effort on the concert platform or opera stage. Certainly the early studios were depressingly dingy. Gerald Moore, though he himself enjoyed the recording procedure – he described the atmosphere as happy-go-lucky – was immediately struck by the strangeness of the studio at Hayes in 1921, the unreality of the atmosphere, cut off from all natural sounds and from daylight, and

with no carpets or furnishings of any kind to soften the spartan surroundings. Gerald Moore's first studio was eerily resonant,[209] Louis
Kaufman's was small, like a stockroom, he said, and with a depressingly dead acoustic, and he was particularly inhibited by the studio
clock of which he would catch sight every time he was conscious of
wanting to draw out a phrase.[210]

Sviatoslav Richter said that he hated microphones, 'they frighten
me'.[211] Arthur Grumiaux was also scared, at least when he began
recording: 'The idea of that red light going on made me feel terrible.'[212]
Poulenc thought the French soprano Madeleine Gray was 'terrorized'
by the microphone, at least in certain kinds of music. But then, 'we are
all', he said, 'victims of the treachery of the "wax"'.[213] And Rachmaninoff too so hated the red light and the buzzer that preceded it at RCA's
orchestral sessions in the 1930s that red light signals were used that
were visible only to the conductor, Eugene Ormandy, the first instead
of the buzzer at which Ormandy would bring everyone to attention –
'Quiet, everybody, please' – and then, while he was pretending to be
watching the pianist, a second red light for him to begin conducting.[214]

No doubt for most young performers still the strangeness and unfa-
miliarity of the recording studio can be disconcerting, but the idea of
recording is at the end of the century so familiar, and some experience
of microphones and studios usually comes so early in a performer's
life that the fear of the microphone is perhaps less inhibiting, or at any
rate less difficult to overcome than it was early in the century. Certainly
the American opera singer Jan Peerce – he began life as a violinist –
thought so: 'Today' – he's talking in 1977 – 'recording's a cinch. You
walk into a studio, and who cares where the mikes are, who cares about
a red light? Who looks at the red light?'[215] André Previn assumed his
liking of making records and his lack of nerves in front of the microphone derived in part from his 'misspent youth' in studios recording
film music.[216]

The need for accuracy has been the bane of the lives of most recording musicians throughout recording history, and the subject of countless laments for the inhibitions this striving for technical perfection
causes. Poulenc detected a 'lack of joy' in the studio performances of
a favourite soprano, an absence of the vivaciousness and liveliness that
characterized the singer's performances in the recital hall.[217] The
British pianist Mark Hambourg, who began recording in 1909, compared the stimulus and inspiration, 'the support and warmth of con-

centrated attention' that the artist derives from an 'alive and sympathetic audience' whose enthusiasm 'buoys him up', with the 'cold, dispassionate, analytical' and 'sinister' presence of the microphone. He thought that the concern for accurate execution could easily result in dead, lifeless, what he called 'pianoloistic' playing.[218] Clifford Curzon encapsulated the difficulty in this way: 'if you can't risk a wrong note, your right notes are apt to mean less'.[219]

Rachmaninoff, who made recordings before the days of tape, liked the recording studio, he claimed, because of the possibilities it offered for performing a work over and over again and at least approaching 'artistic perfection'.[220] Many of Rachmaninoff's issued recordings were from the first or second or third take, but a considerable number were takes five or six or seven or even later ones. The recording of Guy Weitz playing the third movement, the *Andante cantabile*, from the Symphony IV for organ of Charles-Marie Widor, issued in 1927[221] – it lasts 3'50" – was the result of forty-five attempts. The published take was finally recorded at the third session, on 4 May 1927.[222] But there were rather special reasons for this. The cathedral authorities refused to close the building for the recording sessions, nor would they silence the cathedral clock, and the sacristans were allowed to empty the 'poor' boxes at the back of the church under the organ gallery. The administrator of the cathedral did not like Guy Weitz – he had been appointed by the Cardinal Archbishop as his own 'Honorary Organist' without reference to the cathedral chapter – and he decided to walk up and down the aisles wearing squeaky new shoes during recording.[223] Repeating takes over and over again because the engineers cannot achieve a satisfactory balance is likely to fray voices as well as tempers, as singers have gently pointed out.[224]

Successful performers in the studio, or at least those who seemed to enjoy the experience themselves and with whom other musicians enjoyed working, were those who treated the whole experience in a very business-like fashion; Kreisler, Chaliapin and Schnabel all respected Malcolm Sargent's 'modest and practical' way of working in front of the microphone,[225] perhaps the result, at least in part, of his very practical, down-to-earth training as an apprentice to an English cathedral organist. For some performers there was the comfortable feeling of working 'with a safety net', with the ability to record again or to correct small errors together with the excitement of striving to create 'a potentially flawless product'.[226]

Moiseiwitsch recalled with pleasure a productive and trouble-free session at Abbey Road in 1939 at the end of which he was asked to play something in order to use up spare time. If nothing came of it, it didn't matter, he was assured, but the engineer's time might as well not be wasted. But he didn't want to; he had been thinking of the meal of oysters he was planning to have as soon as he'd completed the scheduled work. But if it was a failure, the record men assured him, he could go off and have a drink and his meal of oysters just the same. The producer agreed that he need only do one take. What should he play? He'd been suggesting to the record company Rachmaninoff's arrangement of Mendelssohn's Scherzo from *A Midsummer Night's Dream* but they'd been unwilling because they had Rachmaninoff doing it and it was one of their best sellers. He hadn't practised it, though. He would try. It was, he thought, the best recording he ever made.[227]

But very few performing musicians seem never to have been intimidated by the microphone. John McCormack was one, and another, according to their accompanist, was Dietrich Fischer-Dieskau. When he wished to begin he would step in front of the microphone and announce to the engineer that he was ready to start, which he then did immediately; there was 'no fussing and delaying with buzzers and red light'.[228] At the end of the song he would have a short discussion with his accompanist and then announce into the microphone speaking to the producer: '"Two corrections. I would like to repeat from bar 24 to bar 40 and Mr Moore wishes to repeat his *Nachspiel*, after which we would like to hear the whole song and corrections played back to us."'[229] The producer for many of his earlier recordings was Walter Legge, who usually dictated every move in the recording studio. Legge admired 'most of his work', though they did not, he recalled, become friends. He did not know why. Perhaps it was the 'Prussian exaggeration of consonants' in Lieder that 'slightly irritated' him.[230] Casals, though he would say he suffered greatly, that it worried him sick, appeared fearless in the studio; he seemed simply to ignore the microphone. He knew nothing about the technicalities of the recording process; the use of tape and the possibilities offered by tape splicing came in late in his life and if a slip was drawn to his attention he would always want to play the whole piece again, which, as he never wished to play the same piece in the same way, would cause headaches for editors.[231] The recording studio seemed not to bother Artur Rubinstein in the slightest, but then he enjoyed playing the piano anywhere, any time, and would willingly go on and on through the night dazzling his friends at a party immediately after a full-length recital.

Frans Brüggen thought that while he knew nothing about the technicalities of what the engineers did, they knew 'a great deal' about what he could do with his instrument.[232] André Previn had 'total, utter, blind, childish faith in engineers', and in 1974 he had made about eighty LPs with the same engineer and producer with whom he discussed the work to be recorded in general terms and did indeed then leave nearly all decisions up to them. Usually he didn't even listen to the test pressings.[233] Jascha Horenstein claimed to be 'completely ignorant' about the technical aspects of recording, without any technical knowledge of acoustics at all.[234]

Eugene Ormandy worked as closely as possible with the four or five record company people in the studio, endeavouring to show them beforehand how he felt about the music. He would say nothing about microphone placement, though he would point out to them all the critical problems of balance in the work to be recorded, and mark up a score for the producer to use during the sessions. And he would listen very carefully to the test pressings and write down his impressions for the producer who would, where possible, consider them and usually act on them. He would also listen carefully to the final version sent him, though he had never once requested that a disc should not be issued – but he knew of 'colleagues', conductors presumably, who had done so at this stage.[235] Pierre Boulez and his producer determined together beforehand which extracts from the work to be recorded should be tested first for judging balance; Boulez listened to each long take immediately afterwards in the control room and most decisions about editing had been taken by the end of the studio sessions; afterwards there weren't 'too many questions'.[236]

But evidently some performers, at least some of the time, felt that they were controlled by producers and engineers, and manipulated. The Guarneri Quartet considered the sound quality on a take unnaturally 'brittle' or 'metallic' and wondered whether this might be mellowed in some way, but the engineer patiently explained to them that while it might sound rather harsh here in the studio on these professional machines, when played back on domestic hi-fi equipment it would emerge much softer and rounder, and that if they were to record it as they themselves suggested, it would lack all definition when played by the average buyer, it would just sound 'like mush'; and to this the

Quartet could make no response, they simply didn't know enough about recorded sound. And they didn't sit in on the editing: 'We're too lazy'. But perhaps this self-deprecation betrayed a certain disillusion, an acceptance that their views would be listened to but politely ignored.[237] Mistakes had occurred in their experience, a wrong take inserted – not the take they'd agreed to be used – a bar left out completely, but generally the producers and engineers they had worked with had been 'pretty reliable'.[238] Alfred Brendel regretted that in his recordings of the late Beethoven sonatas issued in 1963[239] the scrolls between movements had been of standard length, regardless of the musical context or the composer's instructions because, he was told, 'the customer liked it that way'.[240]

Some performers have resented the imposition on them of a characteristic sound quality arising from the whim of a particular record producer for a particular sound quality, or from changing fashions among sound engineers for a kind of sound, or from the desire of a record company for distinctiveness in the market regardless of artist or repertory – for clarity and dryness with close-miking, say, or for richness and resonance with the microphones capturing the sound in its acoustical setting – and disliked the way this could transform that personal ideal in tone quality that they had long striven to cultivate, 'the most important thing the artist has',[241] according to Alicia de Larrocha. A lot of the records she had made, de Larrocha said in 1976, sound beautiful, 'but they are not true', they did not capture the specific subtleties in tone quality she had worked to develop. She might try to protest to a producer or engineer, she said, 'but they are very strong and I am very weak'.[242] Which sentiments recall Lotte Lehmann's making acoustic recordings fifty years earlier, who felt, she said, like a 'babe in the woods'.[243]

Why do musicians record?

Record producers have tended to emphasize the differences between making music for a live audience and performing in front of the microphone. The record producer John Culshaw was unequivocal: communication with a live audience is 'an entirely different exercise from communication through a microphone to a domestic audience'. This was a lesson that all those who work in a studio, technicians and musicians, he thought, 'must sooner or later learn'.[244] Many musicians, though, have insisted that there is no difference between giving live performances and performing for the microphone, or at least maintain that they are consciously striving for the same qualities in the recording studio as on the concert platform and that they use the same means to communicate in both situations: 'I don't vary my interpretations consciously in the studio', said a singer, one of the most recorded performers in the second half of the twentieth century.[245] Eugene Ormandy insisted that a recorded performance must always sound 'as close . . . as possible' to the 'real performance', the live performance in the concert hall.[246] Vladimir Ashkenazy was sure that the only difference should be the absence of small inaccuracies on the recorded performance, but that this must not be obtained 'at the expense of spontaneity or communication'.[247] In the recording studio, Ashkenazy explains, he always imagines that he is playing in front of an audience, which after all is not so difficult since he very often 'practices performing', as it were, playing in his own practice room just as if he were playing in a public concert.[248]

But as early as 1929 an organist and conductor of choirs, who also achieved fame as a broadcaster of radio talks, was sure that singers will fail before a microphone if they perform as they would from a concert platform, just as an actor will fail if he 'puts in footlight sobs and other ejaculatory trimmings. . . . It sounds to the listening ear as absurd as it would look to the perceiving eye if they painted their faces in order to speak with a single fellow-man. . . .'[249] Singers, like actors, he thought, should strive to cultivate 'unaffected simplicity' and 'directness of utterance' and to banish 'every kind of affectation'.[250] This was a very hard lesson for all musicians, public speakers, and actors to learn: a journalist and broadcaster observed how Franklin Roosevelt learnt almost instinctively to cultivate 'the soaring public speech and the microphone talk', and, unlike most politicians between the wars, mastered 'wholly different techniques for the massed crowd at the Capitol and the family settled before a loudspeaker'.[251] The journalist realized that 'the microphone enables a speaker to talk to an audience of two thousand with the same ease of emphasis and timing he would use before an audience of two'.[252]

Some conductors have deliberately tried to 'restrain' the musicians they work with in the recording studio, not simply because accuracy is so important, but because 'wild risks' or 'a fantastic cadenza', which would come off and elicit cheers in a live performance, nearly always pall, in their opinion, on repeated hearings.[253] And one record producer was sure that performers do make subtle changes to their performing styles which happen 'automatically'.[254] The soprano Martina Arroyo noticed too how performers make adjustments as they become used to hearing themselves in playbacks, sometimes perhaps unconsciously. She was certainly aware of some of the modifications she herself made: when she sang 'affranto!' in *Aida* she rolled the 'r' violently on the stage of the Metropolitan Opera, but in a much less bloodthirsty fashion when she articulated the word before the microphone; or when she sang the line 'Not for Greeks to *slaughter*' in Samuel Barber's *Andromache's Farewell*, she would similarly temper in the studio the vehemence with which she enunciated that last word on the stage.[255] Lorin Maazel was sure that although he didn't consciously alter his interpretation in the studio, nonetheless he was unconsciously making tiny adjustments to achieve the same ends; he reduced the spacing between the chords at the end of Sibelius's Fifth Symphony for the microphone; in the concert hall the longer silences were undeniably powerful; on a recording they would have been simply mannered.[256] Janos Starker agreed that such modifications were necessary since tension can be created with rests in the concert hall but not in a recording.[257]

The violinist Louis Kaufman considered it important to strive to be 'better than life' on records, that recording was the most taxing aspect of a performer's work; certainly accuracy was crucial and the care required was itself exhausting, but there must also be 'added qualities of intensity and sensitivity', which would be impossible to sustain in public performances – 'it would burn you up'. The microphone did not deal well with extremes of loudness but it required at the same time a more intense, a faster vibrato.[258]

How accurate an impression recordings can give of a particular artist's live performances has inevitably depended, even in the second half of the century, in the eras of the LP and the CD, upon the particular qualities of the particular performer and the particular qualities most prized by the commentator and his background, education, temperament, character and personality, on his taste, in other words. For Neville Cardus, born in 1889, those musicians who were technically accomplished, who to him did not communicate a personality, a presence, did not seem to lose very much in their recordings. But the art of some of the greatest performers, some 'beautiful and rare spirits', eluded capture by the microphone – he cited Schnabel, Klemperer and Kathleen Ferrier – and the effect they made in the concert hall vanished with them for ever.[259]

Producers and engineers of classical music inevitably were aware of the skill and expertise exercised by their colleagues in other fields of musical recording and the temptation to experiment along similar lines must have been hard to resist. At any rate it was not always resisted. Recordings containing hundreds of splices, and mixing and balancing techniques which created 'unreal clarity and exaggerated detail', according to one of them, were later thought to have been a mistake. A violinist who began recording in the 1920s was intensely disturbed and irritated by the 'sharpness and edginess' of a solo violin on recordings made in the 1970s and by hearing the noise of the bow on the strings and all those extraneous sounds of which the player is always aware but a live audience never.[260] Whatever goes on in 'variety shows' – Boulez is referring to the mixing and multitrack layering of pop music – with 'serious' music 'what the microphone picks up has to be real. ... It's absolutely indispensable that you begin with a well-performed, real object. .... The recording must be as close to reality as possible.'[261] Boulez's comments, made in 1988, may also reflect the opinions widely expressed towards the end of the century that technological sophistication and the tendency of performers to imitate in their live performances, whether consciously or unconsciously, the analytical perfection of recordings was having a deadening effect on musical expression.[262]

John Culshaw thought in 1966 that recording live concerts was 'a lazy – and cheap – way to make records'. Only where an important artist was too old or ill or where there was no other chance to record him should a concert performance be preserved as a historical document. He doubted that anyone ever played better with an audience than without; the audience is swept away in the excitement of the moment but a cool examination of the tape the next day will reveal all the blemishes that passed unnoticed in the hall.[263] Up to the 1980s there were normally special reasons why live recordings were made of particular artists. Two discographers reported in 1983 that more than half of Sviatoslav Richter's recordings were taken from live performances.[264] There were several reasons for this: Richter had a very wide repertoire but as he disliked the recording studio intensely much went unrecorded in prepared sessions; his fame guaranteed high sales of every recording released so that many unofficial and pirated tapes were issued; for much of his life he lived behind the iron curtain – he did not appear in the West until he was forty-five – and was not free to give concerts anywhere; he was deeply introspective, volatile, and none of his interpretations were ever predictable, and so each performance, as those who admired his qualities thought, revealed new insights.

Alfred Brendel started out in the studio by thinking that the recording was something quite different from a live performance. But by 1972 he had concluded that the 'over-refinement'[265] of recording could often be a disadvantage. He did not try consciously to alter the details of a performance for the microphone except when he listened to a playback and heard exaggeration of any kind, when he judged a detail, a gesture, to be 'out of proportion' without a visual presence. And by 1983 he was sure that musicians, having learnt so much from the kind of close listening recordings had encouraged and from the discipline and attention to detail work in the recording studio had fostered, should now examine the quality of 'heightened intensity' discernible in recordings of live performances, and should be less reluctant to allow the release, in special circumstances, of some of their public performances. For the effect of recording on the player could, he thought, 'not only be purifying but also sterilising, not only concentrating and distilling but also petrifying. The interpreter who aims at accuracy risks less panache, lesser tempos, less self-oblivion.'[266]

Only a very few eminent performing artists have refused to record. For most of his life the Romanian conductor Sergiu Celibidache was one. The value of a musical performance lay in its uniqueness, he thought, and the particular qualities of a performance arise from the time and location of the performance and the particular audience with whom the music is experienced. Recording kills spontaneity in performance and encourages a dangerous passivity in listeners. He wished all musical experience to be participatory and intense and revelatory. His performances tended to be slower than other conductors and with great attention to detail; when eleven CDs of his live broadcasts were released in 1998 after his death with the blessing of his family, one critic thought he detected an interpretative formula in his performances of all styles and periods of music, the creation of a trance-like atmosphere, a concern with sonority rather than with musical argument.[267] The violinist Miha Pogacnik is another musician who does not make recordings; he will allow radio transmission of a live concert if this is stipulated in a contract, but not the release even of such a performance as a commercial disc. The microphone has indeed brought about 'fantastic progress' in instrumental technique, he is sure. But technical perfection has become the be-all and end-all; musicians should 'reach for the heavens', and this is only possible if the whole personality of the artist can be perceived by a listener, and this certainly requires the physical presence of the musician. Listening to music should be 'sweat, tears, and blood' and not the superficial 'entertainment' into which recordings have transformed it.[268]

The composer and conductor Oliver Knussen, though, likes making records very much and if a fairy godmother appeared and promised him enough gold to make conducting live performances unnecessary he would give them up immediately – he doesn't get 'an enormous buzz out of doing things in public' – and concentrate solely on recording, 'getting something right on records and creating something that lasts'.[269] But most performing musicians, at least most of those who have devoted themselves to repertory from Bach to, say, Strauss or Stravinsky, have wished to keep their live, concert or opera performances at the heart of their activities, however necessary recordings might have been to the development of their careers or the maintenance of meticulously high technical standards. Most would probably not have concurred with the implication of John Culshaw's remark that a recording constituted 'something much more than an ephemeral concert performance'.[270]

Why then do musicians record? 'For posterity. For my own satisfaction. For the world. Because everyone does.'[271] Because they are asked to; for publicity, to become known; to support themselves and their families. Because conductors of major symphony orchestras cannot refuse to. Because younger musicians might learn something from their performances. Because they wish to realize their intentions more exactly than they ever can in a live performance; to maintain high standards in accuracy and in the tiny details in their live performances; to leave something behind them: 'They are children of mine', one said, 'They'll live forever.'[272] Because, they say, 'We belong to this age.'[273]

II
The Repertory Recorded

The creation of mass audiences for classical music

The public, Thomas Alva Edison thought in 1923, was 'very primitive in its tastes'. There might be a few who liked 'the most advanced music' but they were 'very very few. . . . The Debussy fanatic thinks that because he likes Debussy, there must, of course, be thousands and thousands who do. He would be amazed if he knew on what a little musical island he is standing. You could hardly see it on the great musical map of the world. All the world wants music; but it does not want Debussy; nor does it want complicated operatic arias.'[1] Edison was not a cultured man, nor very knowledgeable musically, and with defective hearing, but even so at that time many would have agreed with him, certainly many among those who were manufacturing discs and cylinders. And yet numerous commentators during the twentieth century have recognized what some termed the 'democratization' of musical taste, the creation of a mass audience for west European art music, for a repertory of music from the Middle Ages to the beginning of the twentieth century, which, though small compared to the audience for popular music, is yet vast indeed when compared to the numbers who knew this repertory at the end of the nineteenth century. Seventy-five years after he spoke Edison could have walked into a shop in New York and chosen from nine complete performances of Debussy's *Pelléas et Mélisande*, or from ten complete versions of records of all the composer's piano music, or from sixty-four different discs of *La mer*, or from sixty-eight discs for the *Prélude à l'après-midi d'un faune*.[2]

When a sociologist interviewed a hundred Oxford undergraduates in 1962 half of them expressed a keen interest in music, and the greatest interest was in classical music: they would say 'I adore music', or 'Music means a great deal to me', or describe it as 'an abiding interest'; a number of them wished they had been gifted enough to have read for a degree in music.[3] Their knowledge of music had been acquired in large part through radio and probably most of all through recordings and through programme notes on record sleeves, and they accepted recorded music naturally as a part of the musical culture; they regarded listening to records as a complementary activity to concerts and live opera, not as a second-rate substitute for it. In the Oxford of the 1950s, it seemed to the conductor Colin Davis, 'the *cachet* formerly reserved for poetry now seemed to be accorded to opera'.[4]

Prejudices against music

It was not only that this enthusiasm for recordings was new; such intense and serious and widespread enthusiasm for music itself was a comparatively recent phenomenon, certainly among Oxford undergraduates. The transformation had been effected by means of the spread of general education, through the music appreciation movement, through broadcasting and recording themselves, through lower and lower prices of recordings, and through the growth of disposable income and increased leisure. At the end of the nineteenth century there were fierce prejudices against music, even, especially, among the well-off and the well-to-do, the men – these were essentially male prejudices – who were economically best placed to attend concerts and the opera and to hear chamber music played by their wives and daughters in their own homes. When, in Oxford a century before, Sir Frederick Ouseley, the son of a distinguished Oriental scholar who had been successively Minister Plenipotentiary to Russia and Persia, had proposed to enter for the Oxford Mus.Bac.degree, the Dean of Christ Church used every endeavour to persuade him against this unfortunate course of action, telling him it was utterly derogatory for a man in his social position even to contemplate this.[5]

The status of musicians at the turn of the century was very low; the cultural accomplishment of most musicians *was* very low. The question posed by a Birmingham organist in 1888 in seeking to establish a professional association, 'Is it too much to ask that the profession of music should have as honourable a status and recognition on equal terms with those of Law and Medicine?'[6] could only receive an unfortunate answer. The words 'artist' and 'musician' continued to hold particular resonances for a great many people in England for much of the twentieth century, of effeteness, of a disorganized, unreliable, Bohemian lifestyle, of a taste for absinthe, as Vaughan Williams once mischievously remarked, and a mistress in Montmartre.[7] Percy Dearmer, an Anglican priest who ended his career as a minor canon of Westminster Abbey in the 1930s, attempted to convince churchmen throughout his life of the importance of aesthetics in religion but he privately admitted that many of his English contemporaries regarded art as a 'harmless, private craze, like . . . stamp collecting, only not so innocent', and those interested in art as 'not quite normal, a little suspect'.[8] In 1889 the editor of *The Musical Times* had conceded that in England there were 'many excellent people with whom the term "artist" is simply a synonym for "Bohemian" or "black sheep"'.[9] Just as around the horse, the noblest of animals, collect 'all the most accomplished blackguards on the face of the earth', so with the noble art of music are associated a great many charlatans:

> There is the drawing-room *tenorino*, a mannikin who fully justifies in his own person Von Bülow's strictures . . . 'not a man, but a disease.' There are dusky warblers of erotic inanities, skilled in the use of the falsetto, whose fervid folly plays havoc with the heartstrings of gullible women. There are violinists who profane a beautiful instrument by imbecile buffoonery, and, if they ever condescend to play anything in the *cantabile* style, render their soapy tone still soapier by the constant use of the mute. And about these pests of the drawing-room congregates a swarm of pallid *dilettanti*, cosmopolitan in sentiment, destitute of any manly vigour or grit, who have never played cricket . . . in their lives. It is from contact with these nerveless and effeminate natures that the healthy average well-born Briton recoils in disgust and contempt. . . .[10]

There was certainly a surge of interest in music in England during the later decades of the nineteenth century, partly the result of technological and economic changes which lowered the cost of musical instruments. Good, cheap, reliable pianos became generally available

in Britain during the 1880s for the first time and by the early years of
the twentieth century there was at least one playable piano for every
twenty people in Britain, and perhaps one for every ten.[11] Underpinning the growing interest in music were legions of 'music teachers',
principally piano teachers, the number of which probably increased
threefold between 1870 and 1914, and may have quadrupled.[12] Most of
these teachers were self-employed women, without qualifications,
earning very little and most of their pupils were girls. Husbands and
fathers certainly wished to possess a piano, to demonstrate both their
affluence and their cultivated tastes, but most would not wish to learn
the instrument themselves: they were busy men. But then came the
pianola which gave them the opportunity to make music, as it were,
without the necessity of spending laborious hours practising. It was
modern and mechanical; it gave 'a spurious sense of artistic achievement'.[13] Pianolas and reproducing pianos were soon obliterated by the
radio and the gramophone, but these too provided similar opportunities to hint not only at affluence, cultural sophistication and musical
taste and discernment, but also at down-to-earth masculine practi-
cality and knowledge of technology. Practical, up-to-date scientific
gentlemen of taste and refinement could now engage in discussion
about the specifications of the latest models, whether of gramophones
or wirelesses or of motor-cars.

Reviews and advertisements of gramophones and loudspeakers and
needles and amplifiers provided them with the necessary jargon. A
reviewer would speak of a pickup as 'a precision-built instrument for
the connoisseur who demands supreme quality and fidelity of reproduction', of its 'double, self-aligning ball-bearings to take both radial
and thrust strain with absolute freedom of movement in vertical and
horizontal directions', of the 'adjustable counterweight and calibrated
scale in ounces to record exact needle presure', of a 'very specially
selected crystal cartridge with an output of approx. 1.9 volts with flat
response up to 4,800 cycles', and assure the prospective purchaser that
'resonance points at any frequency are entirely eliminated'.[14] It clearly
wasn't difficult to penetrate all this and in a short time to join the magic
circle of initiates, and explain to others the purpose of twiddling the
knobs:

Such is the amazing frequency range that the only time that full bass
response and full treble is required is when the volume control is

very low (somewhat below the normal listening position) when listening to speech . . . an ample margin of treble and bass augmenta-
tion is provided. . . . Once the appropriate adjustments have been
made to the bass and treble controls the quality of a . . . good recording is admirable; the treble is clean, bright and forward, and the
lower bands of frequencies have just the right characteristic to complete an exciting picture. Our criticism of prolonged bass notes made
in respect of the . . . 800 does not apply to the 801; the bass here
is firm and definite and still such instruments as the double bass,
'celli, etc., are reproduced with an excellent degree of natural
reverberation. . . .[15]

Men who collected records – collectors were always men – were generous in giving full accounts of their experiments: 'No record seems
too difficult – Caruso at his loudest, heavy Philadelphia performances
. . . the needles reproduce delicate recordings equally well . . .'; 'I have
played the whole of Rachmaninoff's 3rd Symphony – 12 sides – on one
point without resharpening or even turning the needle partially round
and the tone at the end of the last side – a very heavy one – was still
quite good. . . .'[16] This was all gently sent up in the late 1950s in a
song called 'Reproduction' in the satirical West End show *At the
Drop of a Hat*: the gramophone consultant summoned by the two
'faithful fans of hi-fidelity' dismisses the acoustic of the fans' sitting-
room and advises them that the only hope of improving the sound from
their gramophone would be to raise the ceiling by four feet and extend
the fireplace along the entire length of one wall; he recommends that
when they listen they should sit in the bottom of the cupboard, though
even then they won't be able to obtain the proper full stereophonic
effect. These hi-fi enthusiasts were always itching to demonstrate the
latest sonic possibilities – 'I've an opera here that you shan't escape' –
even though, as one of them confesses, 'I never did care for music
much'.[17]

Suspicions that those who were record enthusiasts loved hi-fi more
than high art have been harboured by all kinds of musicians and
serious music-lovers whose concern has been for 'the music' and
for whom the sonorous trappings of the music's 'message' have
appeared at times almost incidental. And the gender stereotypes have
been played upon by advertisers: a 1998 advertisement for a hi-fi
systems retailer shows a sophisticated, confident girl in a nonchalant

posture, her long hair swept back, a glass of wine in her hand, leaning proprietorially on her hi-fi: 'Not just Toys for the Boys'.[18] No doubt many men did indeed not progress beyond the experience of a boyish glee in gadgets; but for others a deep and perhaps sometimes unexpected love of music developed through an initial interest in gramophone gadgetry. A great number of them kept on buying gramophone records anyway.

The recorded repertory of the 1930s

In the introduction to *The Gramophone Shop Encyclopedia of Recorded Music*, published in New York in 1936 and listing electrical recordings then currently available in America,[19] Lawrence Gilman, the experienced critic of the New York *Herald Tribune*, pointed out that 'most of the greatest music in existence' had been recorded, that the whole field of musical art was being covered 'with breath-taking swiftness by the gramophone'.[20] In addition to the standard works, now virtually all available on record, he pointed out that many of the rarest works of the past, known only by name hitherto to many musicians and music-lovers, could now be studied on record, chansons by Dufay and Ockeghem, for example, organ music by Giovanni Gabrieli and Frescobaldi, 'the famous *Chant des Oyseaux*' by Clément Jannequin, and Monteverdi's madrigal-sestina *Lagrime d'amante al sepolcro dell'amata*, right up to 'such last words in musical modernity' as the new symphony by William Walton and his 'delectable setting' of *Façade*.[21]

So there can be found in the book details of recordings of ten piano concertos by Mozart, and seven symphonies – numbers 34, 35 and 36, and the last four; of a recorded performance of *Le nozze di Figaro*, more or less complete, and of a forthcoming *Così fan tutte*, both of these by the Glyndebourne Festival Opera Company, but only extracts from *Idomeneo*, *Don Giovanni*, *Die Zauberflöte*, *Die Entführung aus dem Serail*, and only the overture of *La clemenza di Tito*; there are recordings of nine symphonies by Haydn, numbers 45, 88, 92, 94, 95, 97, 100, 103 and 104, and twenty of his string quartets; there is a recording on seven twelve-inch discs of Purcell's *Dido and Aeneas*, two recordings of 'Nymphs and shepherds' from *The Libertine*, a handful of the string fantasias played by a string quartet or trio or quintet, the 'Golden' Sonata, a few of the songs from the theatre music, the anthems

Remember not, Lord, our offences and *Rejoice in the Lord alway*, the first keyboard suite, Z.660, complete, but only odd movements from some of the others, and the Hallé Orchestra under Hamilton Harty performing the spurious 'Trumpet Voluntary'. There is a complete recording of all Bach's Brandenburg Concertos, an abridged version of the St Matthew Passion on twelve twelve-inch discs, though only a handful of excerpts from the St John Passion; only a few movements of the Magnificat, but a more or less complete recording of the Mass in B minor, only the first two of the keyboard Partitas, only a handful of the organ works, the first three parts including the first thirty-four preludes and fugues of Book I of a complete set then being issued of performances on the piano of *Das wohltemperierte Clavier*; of Beethoven all the symphonies, twenty-four of the piano sonatas – part of a complete set in process of being released – at least one recording of each of the piano concertos, and at least a couple of recordings of each of the string quartets; of Handel's oratorios and operas only one more or less complete version of *Messiah*.

By the 'greatest music in existence' Gilman meant those musical masterworks of chamber music cultivated by a very small number of middle- and upper-middle-class amateurs in their salons and drawing-rooms, and those musical masterworks that formed the core repertory of the symphony orchestras and the opera houses of the day. Or even perhaps of yesterday. Gilman, a 'suave, sensitive . . . gentleman of extremely aesthetic appearance' according to Winthrop Sargeant, was after all at the end of his career – he died in 1939 – and was not among the most progressive of musical commentators. He hated the coarse sounds of the non-musical world of New York and had taken to wearing plugs of cotton in his ears, removing them – along with his fur-collared overcoat – only when he arrived in the concert hall.[22] A music teacher in an English public school confessed in 1935 that he found it extremely difficult to catch out his boys with any of the 'recognized greater works of the orchestra'. They pool their records, he explained, and although they can only rarely go to concerts they 'can hear Brahms no. 1, or *Ein Heldenleben*, or *Petrushka*, or Sibelius no. 5, several times a day for weeks' if they want to. Already, he was sure, they 'know nearly all the music there is'.[23]

The repertory mostly being recorded in the 1930s consisted of works heard regularly in performance, but it also reflected a particular view of music history widely held from the end of the nineteenth century to the middle of the twentieth which considered music an evolutionary art, and, unlike painting or sculpture or literature or architecture, a comparatively young art, or at any rate an art which had only recently acquired a degree of sophistication. Music composed three hundred years ago, with one or two exceptions, seemed to present-day audiences, or so it was claimed, crude and incomplete. Josquin Desprez, for example, seemed 'singularly unexciting and severe';[24] Palestrina undoubtedly created imperishable works of art, the result of 'two or three centuries of experiment in the development of contrapuntal processes',[25] and the quality of his achievement is made clear if his music is compared with the masses and motets of John Taverner and his contemporaries, just one generation earlier, whose music is 'stiff and formal both harmonically and emotionally, over-elaborate and lacking in the consummate ease of the later work. These are, of course, the normal faults of immaturity.'[26] And crudities disfigured even later composers, some of whose works are undoubtedly worthy of the attention of twentieth-century music-lovers; Lully, for example, who evidently took pains over his instrumentation. But the pains show, and his harmony is 'not always correct'.[27] There is a crucial difference between, say, Byrd's Mass for five voices and Bach's Mass in B minor, or a set of variations by John Bull and Beethoven's 'Diabelli' Variations; to appreciate the older works and to comprehend their superior qualities over other works of their time an audience must make a conscious attempt to understand theories of music and aesthetics which are obsolete. But Bach and Beethoven speak to our world directly. Byrd doesn't, Bull doesn't. Purcell does. This is a world created for us by the masters of the past two centuries.[28]

At the beginning of the century when a handful of fanatical eccentrics – 'feather-brained cranks', they were called , and 'tiresome highbrows'[29] – were attempting to reinstate music composed before 1600 into the repertory and were assumed to think that old works were good simply on account of their age, a number of influential musicians were sounding a note of caution. It was important to distinguish between the 'historico-archivist' approach to music history and the 'critical' approach. Performing artists and scholars – who must be gifted and learned and of wide and deep culture – had a duty to preserve only works of the greatest artistic value, and if they failed to do this, if they abrogated their responsibility and revived old works indiscriminately, they would mislead the public and corrupt musical taste.[30]

The great composers were comparatively few – most authorities would have included Palestrina, Bach, Handel, Mozart, Haydn, Beethoven, Schubert, Schumann, Wagner, Brahms – and these very greatest 'stand at an immeasurable height above all others both in power and imagination'.[31] They were great artists because they were great men with force of character and passionate integrity. Not that all the works of even these supreme creators are imperishable monuments. Haydn, for example, laboured many years to achieve symphonic mastery. Many of his symphonies are of interest to the historian and analyst for the light they shed on the development of technique and as good examples of eighteenth-century styles and idioms. But it is the last twelve that are artistically complete in imbuing a *lingua franca* with nobility of character and that stamp of personality that makes them alive and valuable for modern audiences.

Such a view of musical history was concerned to distinguish between works of merely historical interest and those which live in some kind of continual present; ignorance of Haydn's earlier symphonies 'is not in the least a matter to be ashamed of', according to Sir Hubert Parry writing in 1886; what is important is a knowledge of the 'artistically complete' Salomon symphonies.[32] So the core of the repertory consisted of a coherent body of masterpieces created by men who were considered not simply exceptional craftsmen, the possessors of consummate musicianly skills, but by geniuses inspired by God or by supernatural forces of some other kind, who had created masterworks that transcended the time and the place of their creation. For Debussy, for example, Bach was 'a benevolent god, to whom musicians should offer a prayer before setting to work so that they may be preserved from mediocrity'.[33]

There were of course a host of interesting figures besides the greatest masters, composers like Dvořák, Telemann, Berlioz, Vivaldi, Bizet, Gounod or Domenico Scarlatti. They could not be counted among the greatest because, perhaps, the number of masterpieces they left was too small, or their range was too limited; their works might too often be disfigured by sentimentality, like C. P. E. Bach,[34] or they might not always be able fully to assimilate their influences, like Mendelssohn,[35] or their view of art might be too theatrical, like Berlioz.[36] Chopin might not be considered among the very greatest since he restricted himself almost exclusively to piano pieces, but, perhaps more fundamental – certainly to the English – his works were rarely elevating: this was music more for 'highly cultivated and wealthy society, loving luxury and delicate excitements of sensibility, than for strong, energetic, and intellectual natures'.[37] Some composers too were held to have lived at unfortunate moments in the history of musical development; the 'divine genius' of Henry Purcell was held to have been largely frustrated by unfavourable circumstances since the 'forms which would have suited him best – Concerto Grosso, fully-composed opera, and the mature contrapuntal choral style – were either not yet consolidated or not yet acclimatised in England'.[38]

There was a feeling in the years before 1914 which became more widespread after the war that music – that art in general – had reached some sort of crisis, that a chapter had been concluded. Maybe Stravinsky, Bach and Beethoven were equally great figures, though 'as to Stravinsky', wrote one sympathetic and up-to-date educationist in 1919, 'nobody ought to pretend to decide yet nor for the next twenty years or so'.[39] To the eminent scholar and historian Alfred Einstein it seemed – and he said it with scarcely concealed bitterness – that at the close of the nineteenth century music had come to the end of 'her first, most youthful and loveliest phase of development'. In the work of Stravinsky, he thought, 'barbarism, triviality, and mechanism are all conjoined'; with Schoenberg music had become 'so abstract, so individual and so divorced from all relation to humanity as to be almost entirely unintelligible'.[40] If such music rarely found its way on to the concert platform it was little wonder that record companies, whose products were expressly designed for mass audiences, by and large left such music alone.

Lawrence Gilman was encouraged and startled to find so much of this repertory of living masterpieces documented by recordings since it had only been possible to record symphony orchestras and choirs at all and to reproduce many timbres with any degree of faithfulness after the development of electrical recording in 1925. In other words he was contemplating the result of just a decade's recording activity.

Early attempts at widening the repertory on record: the 'Society' issues

In an attempt to persuade record companies to be more adventurous in their choice of recorded repertory, and to convince them that a public existed for music currently being ignored – and particularly for chamber music and for twentieth-century works – the National Gramophonic Society was founded in 1924. The Editor of *The Gramophone* had suggested the idea in the September 1923 issue, the magazine's fourth number, and the first set of records appeared in October 1924, of Beethoven's Quartet op. 74 played by the Spencer Dyke Quartet. This was enthusiastically received; it was thought the Quartet had excelled themselves, perhaps because they were aware that they were playing to a select audience of devotees. Early releases included Debussy's Quartet, Brahms's Sextet op. 18 and Clarinet Quintet, Schubert's Piano Trio in E flat, Schoenberg's *Verklärte Nacht* and Mozart's Clarinet Quintet, and particularly noteworthy later repertoire included Bax's Oboe Quintet, his String Quartet in G major and Sonata for two pianos, Warlock's *The Curlew* and music by Matthew Locke and Corelli and Boccherini. It was possible partly because of 'the generosity and keenness of the various players and conductors who gave of their best for deplorably nominal fees'.[41] These performers included the International String Quartet, Constant Lambert, the pianist Kathleen Long, John Barbirolli, both as cellist and as conductor, the oboist Leon Goossens, the clarinettist Frederick Thurston, the horn player Aubrey Brain, the piano duo Ethel Bartlett and Rae Robertson. Membership of the Society involved buying records issued at the rate of 5s. for every twelve-inch double-sided disc up to a limit of £1 a month, and was 'strictly limited' to 1,000, 'thus adding to these unique records the distinction of rarity which will be as greatly appreciated by the discerning amateur as the possession of a piece of Wedgwood by the ardent collector'.[42] A complete set of the recordings in the National Gramophonic's catalogue was retained at the salons of a department store, Murdoch, Murdoch & Co., in Oxford Street, where ('in a special room upstairs') any of the records could be listened to,[43] and where members of the Society would gather to hear talks and lectures about the music to be released.

Though it was referred to repeatedly as a great success, and cited as an influential factor in emboldening the commercial companies to tackle new repertoire – this was certainly true – after three years only five hundred readers of *The Gramophone* had been willing to join the Society.[44] In reviewing its output after three years and praising its achievements, a commentator hoped that if the Society were to record Beethoven, it should be noble compositions like the cello sonatas –

great masterworks which, unlike most of Beethoven, he thought, were quite likely to remain neglected by the leading record companies, and if Mozart, not the slighter, earlier works, charming and exquisite though these undoubtedly were, but the many later masterpieces which remained unrecorded. He offered a great number of further suggestions including the octets by Schubert and Mendelssohn, the Bach cantata *Wachet auf,* and the solo cantatas, Chopin's two piano concertos, Brahms's last two symphonies, Delius's 'Dream of Paradise Garden' from his opera *A Village Romeo and Juliet,* Debussy's *La Mer* and his *Nuages* and *Sirènes* from the orchestral Nocturnes, Bax's *Garden of Fand,* Ravel's *Daphnis and Chloë* Suite, the violin and piano sonatas of Guillaume Lekeu and Mr B. J. Dale, and Mr Rutland Boughton's *Sir Galahad: A Christmas Mystery.* By the time the Society was wound up in 1935 it had issued 166 records, and already a number of the works which it had proudly presented to the world for the first time in recorded form had been 'recorded by the commercial companies under better conditions', the Society's secretary noted, not at all in sorrow but with quiet satisfaction. And while any stock lasted, he exhorted members, 'we *must* try to get the records into more homes where they will be treasured'.[45]

By then the Gramophone Company had devised a similar plan for 'Society' issues, for issuing discs in subscription sets whereby subscriptions would be collected in advance for recordings of previously unrecorded works, and only when the required number of subscribers had been enlisted to cover costs and to yield a reasonable profit to the Company would the recording sessions take place and the discs be pressed and issued. The idea was Walter Legge's, working at that time for the Gramophone Company writing album and analytical notes and sales copy for new records and editing HMV's monthly magazine for the record retailer, *The Voice.* The first such Society issue was devoted to the songs of Hugo Wolf. This too was Legge's idea. Certainly it was a bold step which undeniably brought to public attention a repertory which was very rarely heard in the concert hall. But why did HMV begin with Hugo Wolf instead of with those unrecorded works by Mozart, or Beethoven, or Brahms, of which there was still such a great number?

As a teenager in the early 1920s Walter Legge had been in the audience at a London recital given by Frieda Hempel which ended up with Wolf's *Ich hab' in Penna.* He'd then discovered two more songs, *Der*

Rattenfänger and *Der Feuerreiter*. He'd failed to find any records of Wolf songs, though in fact four songs had been recorded in 1907 by the mezzo-soprano Elena Gerhardt with Arthur Nikisch playing the piano. But shortly afterwards he had come upon a biography of the composer by his hero Ernest Newman, whom he was reading regularly as the magisterial music critic on the *Sunday Times*. Legge was already regarded as an arrogant and opinionated whippersnapper – he had been dismissed as 'unsuitable' four years earlier after three months with the Company, only to be reinstated less than a year later – and he admired in Newman particularly that 'independent and international outlook'.[46] It would have given Legge much satisfaction to be advancing the cause of a composer largely unknown at that time to the narrow-minded and provincial and parochial British musical establishment, as he himself considered it. Newman discussed the Hugo Wolf Society idea in an article in the *Sunday Times*, and he also promised that he would provide album notes if the discs appeared. This enabled Fred Gaisberg, the Gramophone's chief recording 'expert' and the man who personally wooed all its major artists, to approach Elena Gerhardt intimating that the idea was Ernest Newman's, and to persuade her to record for a much reduced fee.[47] But support was not overwhelming. For three months running, when HMV were in fact already committed to the project, Compton Mackenzie used his editorial in *The Gramophone* to persuade, cajole or bully his readers into giving the Hugo Wolf Society their support: 'It will really be grotesque if 500 people out of fifty million cannot manage to possess records of the greatest living singers singing some of the world's greatest songs. . . . He who smokes twenty gaspers a day, let him smoke eighteen and subscribe to ten songs by Hugo Wolf.'[48] If this venture were to fail, Compton Mackenzie warned, the record companies would certainly conclude that they had no justification for experimenting as regards repertory and would feel fully justified in issuing another performance of Handel's 'Largo', for which the record dealer was expected by his customers to have available a dozen different versions. In the end five hundred subscribers did come forward, including 111 from Japan,[49] each contributing thirty shillings, and the first volume, issued in April 1932, was 'an acknowledged triumph'.[50] Five more sets followed before the war, all issued with booklets providing texts, translations and notes and analysis by Ernest Newman.

The Society series explored the greatest composers' outputs with much greater comprehensiveness than had hitherto been attempted. The Beethoven Society series of all the piano sonatas played by Artur Schnabel appeared in twelve volumes between 1932 and 1939, with a further three volumes containing variations, bagatelles and various other miscellaneous pieces.[51] And this was a great success. Before long the plan limiting sales to the original subscribers was abandoned and EMI reported that customers worldwide had spent £80,000 on the first three volumes.[52] The scheme included volumes devoted to Beethoven's violin sonatas, Haydn's string quartets in eight volumes containing twenty-nine of these works played by the Pro Arte Quartet, and three of the piano trios in the single published volume of the Haydn Chamber Music Society. There were three volumes devoted to Casals's performances of Bach's unaccompanied cello suites; a separate Bach Goldberg Variations set was played on the harpsichord by Wanda Landowska, and an Art of Fugue set – the version by Roy Harris and M. D. Herter Norton – played by the Roth String Quartet. In the three volumes of the Bach Organ Society – there were seven twelve-inch records in each volume – Albert Schweitzer played some of the biggest preludes and fugues, the D minor Toccata and Fugue BWV 565 and the Fantasia and Fugue in G minor BWV 542, and one set was devoted to chorale preludes. The instruments used were the instrument in All Hallows Church, Barking-by-the-Tower, in London, probably built by Gerard Smith in 1720 (and destroyed by enemy action in 1941), and the Silbermann organ in the church of St Aurélie in Strasbourg. There were series devoted to keyboard music by Couperin and Scarlatti played by Wanda Landowska. There were three Delius Society volumes, each of three twelve-inch discs; there were six Sibelius Society volumes which included symphonies 3–7, the records accompanied by analytical notes by Ernest Newman, Cecil Gray and Constant Lambert; there was a set containing songs by the contemporary Finnish composer Yrjo Kilpinen (b.1892), sung by Gerhard Hüsch, who was a great admirer and advocate of the works; there were three in a Medtner Society series, which discs were in part subsidized by H.H. the Maharaja of Mysore, who had had to abandon his musical aspirations – he had been accepted as a pupil of Rachmaninoff – when he succeeded to the throne.[53] There were two volumes published in an English Music Society. A set of eight Columbia records, five twelve-inch and three ten-inch discs, were devoted to Purcell, including the four-part fantasias and the five-part Fantasia on One Note, the 'Golden' Sonata, two songs

– 'How Long, Great God?' and the second setting of 'If music be the food of love' – and two catches. The second set was devoted to three works by the Master of the King's Musick, Sir Arnold Bax, the Nonet, the Violin Sonata, and the motet *Mater ora Filium*. All these subscription societies guaranteed that particular projects would at least break even.

The Bach Society series contained *Das wohltemperierte Clavier* complete, played on the piano by Edwin Fischer in five volumes. This was an obvious choice, surely, for there never was a time when these pieces were not played and at least a few of them would have been known well to the hosts of amateur pianists that were flourishing in the early decades of the twentieth century. And yet though these pieces had long been a pillar of the repertory everywhere in Europe – the English organist and Master of the King's Musick, Walter Parratt, was playing all the Forty-Eight from memory as a boy of ten in 1851[54] – there were very few early recordings. The first recording was probably Wilhelm Backhaus's of the C sharp major Prelude and Fugue in Book I, issued in 1909,[55] and Irene Scharrer made a recording of the same prelude and fugue in July 1921.[56] Busoni in fact proposed recording all the Forty-Eight to the Columbia Graphophone Company in 1921, but they rejected his proposal. After all, the single prelude and fugue that he did record (the first of Book I with Chopin's E minor Study op. 25 no. 5 on the other side of the disc)[57] cost 10s. (50p) at a time when a professor at the Royal College of Music was earning 10s. for an hour's teaching. Which would have meant recordings of the Forty-Eight complete would have cost the better part of a professor's weekly earnings.

Seven years later Columbia began a recording of the complete set. Electrical recording meant that reproduction of piano timbre had improved, and in England the BBC had begun transmissions and was creating a new public for Bach's music. Even so, this Columbia project begun by Harriet Cohen and Howard-Jones was abandoned after the two sets, after the first seventeen preludes and fugues in Book I had been recorded. Almost certainly sales were poor. Columbia began issuing a proposed complete set in 1933 performed by Arnold Dolmetsch on the clavichord, the 'Forty-Eight Society'. To record them, 'the Columbian mountain went to Mahomet', as *The Gramophone* reported, and the records were made in the music room at Haslemere, which would give them a special interest for 'the votaries of the annual

Haslemere Festival'.[58] Yet though the specialists of a certain age and the *aficionados* were enthusiastic – Robert Donington, a pupil of Dolmetsch, called the recordings 'irreplaceable . . . the tone and character of the clavichord have been admirably reproduced', he thought, and the interpretation he considered 'authoritative and inspired'[59] – Dolmetsch was an old man and had never been a keyboard player of the greatest accomplishment, and those less sympathetic seem to have been less struck by musical insights and more irritated by the bungling and poor technique demonstrated. R. D. Darrell reported that the set 'proved to be something of a fiasco'.[60] The first issue was never followed up.

The Bach Society's discs of *Das Wohltemperierte Clavier* played by Edwin Fischer, which were recorded between April 1933 and June 1936,[61] were perhaps even more enterprising than it might appear since it was a difficult time for the recording industry. Markets were not at all buoyant and in America one result of the Depression was the abandonment of all classical music recording; records of classical music were imported from Europe. The gramophone companies, though, did have by now a natural and very powerful ally; during these years between the wars broadcasting was widening and changing the nature of musical experience.

Radio between the wars

In 1934 Adrian Boult, who had been appointed Music Director of the BBC four years earlier, considered that broadcasting had done 'more than anything else to improve the musical taste of Britain'. He was equally sure that it had 'literally revolutionized music itself'.[62] The BBC considered itself 'the great Democratiser of Music', maintaining that broadcasting was 'the greatest ally that the divine Muse has ever had on earth',[63] bringing 'good music' to 'the shepherd on the downs or the lonely crofter in the farthest Hebrides . . . the labourer in his squalid tenement . . . or the lonely invalid on her monotonous couch'.[64] A series which ran from 1927 to 1936, transmitted each evening except Sunday and lasting ten or fifteen minutes, was called 'Foundations' and aimed to play music by composers of the eighteenth and nineteenth centuries 'whose work may be regarded as classical, and constituting the true foundation of modern music'.[65]

There is a great deal of the music composed by the great masters which is never performed in public because it is not of an essentially popular character, or likely to attract the attention of people who go to concerts and recitals, but which nevertheless forms part of that body of written music on which the superstructure of modern music rests. . . . Most amateurs and students of music would like to hear everything that, for example, Bach or Beethoven has written; and so far as keyboard music goes, the BBC, in this daily transmission at 7.15, aims at going through the works of the great masters in their entirety. . . .[66]

So weeks were devoted to 'Brahms' songs', 'Mendelssohn's Organ Sonatas', 'Beethoven's Variations', 'Schumann's Songs', 'Elizabethan Keyboard Music' (played on the piano), 'Bach's Sonatas for Viola da Gamba and Cembalo' (on the cello and piano), 'Modern French Pianoforte Music 1880–1900', 'Songs by Sir Hubert Parry', 'Tchaikovsky's Songs', 'Chopin's Studies', 'Brahms' Violin and Piano Sonatas', 'Bach's Sonatas for Flute and Piano', 'Schubert's Pianoforte Sonatas', 'Madrigals from "The Triumphs of Oriana"', 'Songs by Lutenist composers', 'Piano Duets by Dvořák', 'Moussorgsky's Songs', 'Songs by Richard Strauss', 'Pianoforte Duets – Schubert'. In that composer's centenary year, 1928, thirteen weeks of 'Foundations' were devoted to Schubert including song cycles, duets and sonatas. Rachmaninoff admitted that year that he had not realized there were any piano sonatas at all by Schubert.[67]

A critic in the July 1927 issue of *The Musical Times* thought that '[o]ne of the best features of the musical policy of the BBC has been its valuable salvage work. Hardly a week passes without the performance of several compositions that in the ordinary way would never be heard in public. . . . Their neglect in the concert-room is due to a variety of causes: the composer may be out of fashion, or he may have been a good second-rate man overshadowed by a giant; there are many capital works, too, whose merit is admitted, but which somehow are not concert-room "winners," so to speak.'[68] There was a good deal of new music, much of it the result of the advocacy of Edward Clark, who was a 'programme builder' for the BBC's music department between 1924 and 1936 and also a house conductor. He had been a pupil of Schoenberg before the war and had deep knowledge of contemporary music and wide sympathies and was an enthusiastic battling crusader on its behalf. Clark arranged broadcasts of Webern conducting his Five Movements for String Orchestra, of Stravinsky playing his own piano concerto, and Hindemith his own viola concerto, and Bartók his piano music, and Strauss conducting his *Alpensinfonie*. He programmed the British premières of Schoenberg's *Gurrelieder* and *Erwartung*, and an evening which combined *Music to Accompany a Cinema Scene* with the Variations for Orchestra op. 31. It was Clark who achieved broadcast performances of nearly all Berg's large-scale works: Three Pieces from the Lyric Suite, the Chamber Concerto, the Violin Concerto, symphonic extracts from *Lulu* and, in March 1934, a complete performance of *Wozzeck*.[69]

At the time of that first *Gurrelieder* broadcast in 1928 there were several hours of music broadcast each day; in the actual week of that broadcast there were programmes of orchestral and chamber music and military band concerts, there was opera, there were piano and organ and song recitals, and some of the concerts and recitals included vocal solos. There was Beethoven's *Fidelio*, there was the ballad opera of 1737 *Damon and Phillida*, there was César Franck's Symphony, there was Beethoven's Second Symphony, there was Mozart's Bassoon Concerto K.191, there were violin concertos by Glazunov and Mendelssohn and Tchaikovsky's B flat minor Piano Concerto, there was Smetana's tone poem 'From Bohemia's Woods and Fields' and Liadov's 'Musical Picture (on a popular Russian tale) "Baba Yaga"', there was piano music by Chopin and Liszt, there was organ music by Wesley, Stanford and Widor, there was Mendelssohn's Third Organ Sonata, there was Bach's Prelude and Fugue in B minor BWV 544, the D minor Toccata BWV 565, the C major Trio Sonata BWV 529, there was Schubert's 'Trout' Quintet and Dvořák's 'Dumky' Trio, there were songs by Michael Head and John Ireland and Hubert Parry and Peter Warlock, and each evening in the 'Foundations' series there were some of Brahms's 'Magelone' Lieder. The *Gurrelieder* performance was given two cover-page feature articles in *The Radio Times*, for the week of the broadcast performance and the preceding week, and there were articles introducing the work and a synopsis. In December 1928 there was a programme to celebrate the fortieth anniversary of the Plainsong and Mediaeval Music Society during which plainsong sequences and antiphons and responsories were sung, and 'Pastime with good company' ascribed to Henry VIII, and the carol sung by Chaucer's Clerk of Oxenford in *The Miller's Tale*, 'Angelus ad virginem'. Those directing the singing included the scholars and authorities Dom Anselm Hughes and J. H. Arnold. There were two recitals of 'choice old music', as the programme billing described it – music mainly of the eighteenth century – played by the Société des Instruments Anciens, the ensemble from Paris founded in 1901 by Henri Casadesus.

Writing in *The Radio Times* in September 1928, the distinguished critic Edwin Evans thought that 'on present evidence' it was unlikely that broadcasting would turn into music-lovers those who had not been fired by live music-making; he found it difficult to believe 'that the musical mission of broadcasting is to the heathen'. But he did think it could play an important role 'in the direction of widening and filling-up the repertory of the ordinary music-lover', whose experience necessarily derived from 'the haphazard constitution of the concert world'.[70] Greater audiences than ever before, than had ever been conceived of before, were experiencing a wider range of music than even scholars and specialists had known in performance a few years earlier. There was a consensus about high art and the value of high art: 'What can Broadcasting do for Civilisation?' Gerald Heard asked in a *Radio Times* article in September 1928.[71] Walford Davies talked each week on 'Music and the Ordinary Listener', and there were at this time copious musical annotations in the programme pages of *The Radio Times*, information and explanations and explications about music and the works to be transmitted prepared by the most active and best-known and most persuasive advocate for what had become known as music appreciation, Percy A. Scholes.

Music appreciation and the gramophone

In a lecture to the Musical Association in London in 1895 a professor from the Hartford Theological Seminary in Connecticut, Waldo Selden Pratt, expressed the hope that more music teachers, rather than always aiming to cultivate 'executive brilliance' in their charges, would ensure that their pupils acquired the 'power to read music readily and copiously' and so would be able to gain 'sympathetic familiarity with large numbers of works by many masters'; and he was equally interested, he said, in 'the musical culture of the huge masses of people who will never be musicians in any technical sense, and in the creation of a popular sentiment about music that shall securely link it with the abiding interests of intellectual and spiritual life'.[72] Professor Pratt did not make it clear how a more knowledgeable and sensitive audience with wider tastes and greater powers of appreciation and discernment was to be developed; his assumption seemed to be that the broader and more humane education he advocated for musicians would be reflected in their programmes and in the way music was presented to the public. And H. G. Wells in 1903 advocated music-teaching 'that would aim, not at instrumentalisation' – he meant not at developing performing skills – but at 'intelligent appreciation'.[73] One of the aims of the Music Teachers' Association founded in London in 1908 was to impress upon the heads of schools that music was 'a literature' and, because of the difficulty which attends the acquisition of instrumental technique, the need to bring 'the average boy and girl . . . into touch with good music, well played, and simply commented on by the teacher'.[74]

Percy A. Scholes was one of the earliest in England to be convinced that the gramophone and radio could play an important part in developing a love of music and in forming musical taste. It was unnecessarily cramping to children's musical imaginations, he thought, to restrict them to the music they could play for themselves, or that a music teacher could play for them on the piano. Until now, Scholes thought the music of the world (he meant a certain kind of music in Western Europe) had been 'the private preserve of a little band of people who happened to live in the places where it could be heard, and who happened to have money enough to pay to hear it. Henceforth, it belongs to everybody.'[75] But why was this man so ready to welcome the pianola and reproducing piano and the gramophone when so many other musicians were antagonistic or at best lukewarm in their feelings towards these newfangled mechanisms? Scholes had largely found his own way musically; he had had little formal education and his passion for music seems to have been untainted by the prejudices of any musical establishment or faction. He had worked as an organist in London right at the beginning of his career, but spent most of his life as a writer, a tireless pedagogue and a journalist, with the *London Evening Standard* and *The Observer*; he was the BBC's 'Music Critic' from 1923 until 1929, between 1932 and 1936 music editor of *The Radio Times*, and from 1925 until 1930 editor of the Audiographic Series of Pianola and Duo Art Rolls.[76] He was an enthusiastic and committed music educator and the author of a great number of books with titles like *Everybody's Guide to Broadcast Music*, *The Listener's Guide to Music*, *The Listener's History of Music*, *The Appreciation of Music by means of the Pianola and 'Duo-Art'*, and *In Purcell's Time: A Brief Sketch of Politics, Society, Literature, and Religion*, and *The Life and Adventures of Sir John Hawkins: Musician, Magistrate and Friend of Johnson*. *The First Book of the Gramophone* gave suggestions of fifty-five records of music up to and including Beethoven. Perhaps his best-known work was *The Oxford Companion to Music*.

No doubt Scholes was sympathetic to the threat to musicians – as they perceived it – as music poured into people's homes through broadcasting and records and as standards rose and cinema orchestras were wiped out with the talkies. But his detachment enabled him to see matters in a longer perspective and to devote his own creative energies to pouring out vivid, stylish prose; he combined the scholar's passion for accuracy and for lucidity and at the same time the journalist's eye for the arresting metaphor and the illuminating anecdote. He was a Yorkshireman, plain-speaking, a mixture of 'grit and gumption', as his obituarist in *The Musical Times* put it. During the First World War he collected money and organized the despatch of musical instruments to the troops in France; Elgar sent his trombone and the consignments included 25,000 mouth-organs. The energy with which he took up the cause of music appreciation derived in part from his perception of its rightness and its righteousness; he worked just as tirelessly for the Welsh Folk-Song Society, the Vegetarian Society, and the League for the Prohibition of Cruel Sports.[77]

It's true that by the late 1920s, the attitudes of many musicians towards the gramophone were beginning to change. Scholes himself pointed out that the article on the gramophone in the great French *Encyclopédie de la musique*, of which the first volume appeared in 1914 and the last in 1929, is found only at the end of the very last volume where an explanation is given for this peculiarity; when the plan for these volumes was being drafted the 'talking machine' was merely a disagreeable toy from which musicians turned away in horror, 'un jouet désagréable, dont les musiciens se détournaient avec horreur; et c'était justice . . .'.[78] But all that had now changed; the gramophone was certainly worthy and respectable enough to find its way into these learned tomes. But attitudes were changing only very, very gradually. Chambers *Encyclopedia*, as late as the 1926 edition, spoke of it as employed for 'amusement purposes' and as 'an office adjunct'.[79]

'The Columbia History of Music Through Ear and Eye', '2000 Years of Music', 'L'Anthologie Sonore', L'Oiseau-Lyre

Scholes thought the history of music 'unintelligible' unless it took as its starting-point actual performances of the music. For him an example in notation is 'not an actual specimen of art . . . but the mere means out of which a trained intellect and vivid imagination may construct such a specimen'. 'Modern instruments of musical reproduction' remove this 'centuries-old bugbear'.[80] *The Columbia History of Music Through Ear and Eye* for which Scholes was responsible consisted of five albums each containing eight ten-inch records issued between 1930 and 1939, about five hours of music. Each album had an accompanying illustrated booklet of about fifty pages published by Oxford University Press. The aim of the series was an overtly didactic one – sections within albums had titles like 'Illustrating the Elizabethan Lute Song' and 'Exhibiting the Madrigal in Its Various Forms' – and was guided by Scholes's convictions about music as an evolutionary art, of musical forms as organisms which grow and come to maturity and are best understood in the developing context of their creation.

The repertory of the *Columbia History* ranged from organum of the tenth or early eleventh century to contemporary works by Stravinsky, Hindemith and Bartók. The choice was not narrowly doctrinaire or partisan and gave evidence of Scholes's wide sympathies. The pieces were all characteristic and memorable, some of them at least such as a listener would come across on a provincial cathedral's music lists, or in local concerts by amateur musicians, but others which would be much less familiar in performance even to specialists. There was Purcell's 'Bell Anthem', *Rejoice in the Lord alway*, but also the first harpsichord suite, a nocturne by Chopin but also one by Field and movements from keyboard sonatas by J. C. and C. P. E. Bach and Clementi, the first Prelude and Fugue from *Das Wohltemperierte Clavier* and the Rondeau and Badinerie from the Second Orchestral Suite, but also the Sinfonia to the Church Cantata 156. There was Elgar's *Sospiri* op. 70, the Kyrie from Vaughan Williams's Mass in G minor, and Staccato and Ostinato from Book Six of Bartók's *Mikrokosmos*, but also an excerpt from Stravinsky's *Les Noces*, two of the songs from Schoenberg's *Das Buch der hängenden Gärten* and the Finale to Varèse's *Octandre* and the first movement of the Duo in Sixth-tones for unaccompanied violins op. 49 by Alois Hába.

Trouble was taken too to present authoritative performances: Stravinsky, Hindemith and Bartók were all heard as performers in their own music; plainsong and Dufay and Palestrina were directed by Sir Richard Terry, and madrigals by E. H. Fellowes, two musicians who had been responsible for rediscovering these repertories and for developing idiomatic performance styles, and the Dolmetsch family in music for viols and keyboard instruments and recorders. A clavichord by Dolmetsch was used, and a harpsichord by Pleyel, at a time when most musicians would have considered the piano an acceptable substitute. Scholes wrote accompanying texts which combined musical analysis and portraits of the composers with remarks on the evolution of instruments, and texts and translations of songs and lists of editions of the music. The set was available throughout the British Empire and in America and the accompanying texts were translated into Japanese. '. . . as we alternately read and listen', said *The Times* reviewing the first album, 'what was once mere dream in us is clarified to experience, and we visit regions which before we knew only on the map',[81] and *The Daily Telegraph* thought it 'one of the most remarkable undertakings in gramophone history'.[82]

In 1931 Parlophone began issuing discs in a series called *2000 Years of Music*, which consisted of twelve ten-inch discs of music from Ancient Greece up to the time of Bach. They were issued with an accompanying booklet, sixteen pages long in English; the discs were 2s. 6d. (12½p) each, or complete in an album with a text-book, 36s. (£1.80). This series was devised and compiled by Curt Sachs, who was born in 1881, and who had begun his career as an art historian; in 1909 he began to devote himself wholly to music. Being Jewish he was deprived of all the academic positions he held in Berlin in 1933 and he then went to Paris to work at the ethnomusicological museum, the Musée de l'Homme, and in 1937 he emigrated to the United States. Curts Sachs was a polymath, an ethnomusicologist, a scholar and specialist as a founder of modern organology and as a writer on music of the ancient world and the history of dance, but also a generalist, a synthesizer, and a great teacher. Through his interest in European musical instruments he became interested in the music of non-western cultures, in which field recording had already demonstrated its usefulness.

Curt Sachs was the guiding light behind the biggest anthology of all which began before the war, the French *L'Anthologie sonore*. This series of discs was initiated in 1933 and pressed in Paris by Pathé-Marconi; it continued after the war and on LP into the fifties. It was an open-ended series, available by subscription, and the discs were issued in no particular sequence, though when the Haydn Society reissued them on LPs, they were methodically rearranged by period. *The World's Encyclopedia of Recorded Music* and its supplements list 169 twelve-inch double-sided records and four seven-inch 33⅓ rpm discs and four ten-inch 33⅓ rpm discs and seven twelve-inch 33⅓ rpm discs. The leaflet announcing the series in England and dated March 1935 considered that there existed 'a considerable number' who wished to explore the 'little known' and 'lesser frequented realms of recorded music', who regretted that 'hundreds of chefs-d'oeuvre of ancient music lie buried – ignored and forgotten amid the dust – in the archives of museums, libraries, conservatories and the great seats of learning; whilst still more of this ancient treasury awaits discovery in many private collections'. It was a cause for the greatest regret that there was 'no single recorded example of the art of François Couperin-le-Grand', for example. Aspirations were high as far as performing styles went: 'No rearrangement, no single artistic licence of any description, has been permitted, and l'Anthologie offers you the most absolute guarantees as to truth and fidelity. Each record is accompanied by an explanatory leaflet dealing with both the work and the composer. . . . The greatest possible care has been taken in the choice of recording artistes (having in mind the special knowledge and particular executive ability required) to render these works scrupulously faithful to the originals.' The intention was, the company explained, to issue twenty twelve-inch double-sided records each year 'comparable from every point of view with the very finest productions of the great recording organisations'. The repertory covered was from Gregorian chant to Beethoven. There was plainsong and there were Russian liturgical chants; there was keyboard music by Frescobaldi and Giovanni Gabrieli, Pachelbel and Scheidt and Byrd and Farnaby, Sweelinck, Kuhnau, Galuppi, Haydn, Couperin and Domenico Scarlatti, Dussek and Schobert, and C. P. E. Bach, and J. C. Bach, and W. F. Bach, and there was chamber music by Purcell, and Couperin and Rameau, and

Marais, and Telemann; there was a performance of Vivaldi's Concerto in D major op. 3 no. 9 and Bach's transcription of the piece for harpsichord; there were extracts from Bach cantatas, there was sacred music by Taverner, extracts from Machaut's Messe de Nostre Dame, from Dufay's Mass 'Se la face ay pale', and from Josquin's 'Hercules' Mass, and Lassus's Mass 'Bergier et bergière'; there were madrigals by Dowland and Morley, Costeley and Marenzio; there were airs from Rousseau's *Le devin du village*; there was Monteverdi's *Il combattimento di Tancredi e Clorinda*.

The 'association of eminent musicians and musical experts' who founded 'the society known as l'Anthologie Sonore' wished 'to assume the largely educational role that the great recording companies, for purely commercial reasons, are only able to indulge in – somewhat haphazardly – at long and frequent intervals'. They acknowledged that the appeal of this repertory was limited, and yet those likely to respond constituted a 'powerful and important minority, inasmuch as theirs is the influence which eventually formulates the public's taste . . .'. Which might have been true; to flatter prospective purchasers was certainly a very good advertising strategy. The French Ministry of Fine Arts ordered that the *Anthologie sonore* be placed in all the French national conservatoires;[83] in London Mr E. M. Ginn of Soho Square in London acted as agent for distribution throughout the British Empire.[84] And the editor of *The Gramophone* saluted 'this great musical achievement'. Among the earliest artists who recorded for the anthology were Marcel Dupré, who had established his credentials as a stylistic and sensitive interpreter of historical repertory with the first performance of Bach's organ music complete in a series of recitals at the Paris Conservatoire in 1920, the scholar, editor and choral conductor Henry Expert, at that time the greatest authority on French music of the fifteenth and sixteenth centuries, Paul Sacher, who directed his Basle Chamber Choir, Safford Cape and his Pro Musica Antiqua, Curt Sachs, who played the harpsichord and the viol and directed orchestral music of Bach and a brass ensemble in music by Melchior Franck and Schein, the clavichordist Erwin Bodky, the baritone Yves Tinayre, the lutenists Emilio Pujol and Herman Leeb, the gambist Eva Heinetz, and the American scholar and conductor William Devan, who in his enthusiasm for ancient French choral music had become Guillaume de Van and founded the Paraphonistes de St-Jean-des-Matines.

Louise Hanson-Dyer was born in Melbourne in 1884, the daughter of a Londoner who had trained as a doctor in England and then emigrated to Melbourne where he had made money from property speculation and as a medical man, as a writer about medical matters, and as the manufacturer of Dr L. L. Smith's Vegetable Pills; and he had made a reputation as a forceful politician.[85] As a girl she had studied the piano, the harp and singing and had then attended the Melbourne Conservatorium of Music. She had had her Anglophile and Francophile tendencies reinforced during her youth when her father took her to Europe on several occasions – she was presented at court in London in 1907 – and she effortlessly entered Melbourne high society. She was herself confident, stylish and flamboyant; she loved especially rather sensational hats and was known in London late in her life as 'the Australian cockatoo'. But she was surrounded by a culture of altruism, driven by high ideals of public service. In 1911 she married a rich businessman born in Scotland, James Dyer, and perhaps her energetic determination to make things happen was strengthened because of her inability to have children. In the 1920s she settled in Paris, where she admired the artistic patronage dispensed by such figures as Marie-Laure de Noailles, the descendant of the Marquis de Sade who commissioned and underwrote *L'âge d'or* of Buñuel and Dali, and Cocteau's first film, *Le sang d'un poète*, and Princesse Edmond de Polignac – Winnaretta Singer, the American heiress of a sewing-machine fortune – and another American, Elizabeth Sprague Coolidge, who made visits each year to Paris where in 1926 she presented Ravel's *Chansons madécasses*. Louise Hanson-Dyer founded a publishing house, the Éditions de l'Oiseau-Lyre, whose first publication – the first volumes appeared in 1932 – was the complete works of François Couperin. To celebrate the publication and the composer's bicentenary in 1933 she organized three concerts, one of them in a grey-panelled eighteenth-century music room in the arrondissement where Couperin had lived and worked; a harpsichord dated 1737 was used in the concert. The audience was small, only about a hundred or so, but Mrs Dyer had managed to attract Monsieur Lebrun, the President of the French Republic, the British Ambassador, the Military Governor of Paris and the Director of the Beaux-Arts, and Sir Edward Elgar, who happened to be passing through.

But why did this larger-than-life Australian *grande dame* then begin to publish records in 1938? For one thing, by now records had become rather smart, at least in a certain cosmopolitan set. Stravinsky, after all, though he had his reservations – he considered recordings *ersatz* rather than the genuine article – was pleased to give his own versions of his music to the world 'free from any distortion of my thought' by means of 'these redoubtable triumphs of modern science', the record and the radio.[86] Old music was smart, just as Stravinsky was stylish. And she rather liked exotic composers like the Russian Ivan Wyschnegradsky who wrote in quarter-tones. But also she was a democrat who firmly believed in music as a moral force. She was inspired by the social cohesion she was sure music-making encouraged: she loved Vaughan Williams's festival at Dorking and the way in England the lady of the manor conducted her choir of farm-hands and the way, she said, the chauffeur would slip out of his uniform and into mufti to sing in the choir alongside his employer, and how you heard Brahms and Schubert and Holst whistled along the lanes. And she had read Percy Scholes. Gramophones could educate. And she had a lot of money: 'I don't need to go to a committee, Mr Ware. I don't *need* dividends', she once tried to explain to a Decca official who was helpfully suggesting how she might plan a recording that would ensure some healthy profits.[87]

She knew everybody personally. She knew ambassadors and other patrons of the arts. She sought out E. H. Fellowes, and younger scholars like Anthony Lewis and Thurston Dart who both recorded and edited for her. She recorded many of the editions which she had also published, Lully and Couperin and Clérambault, the thirteenth-century Montpellier Codex which included both facsimile and transcription, Purcell's trio sonatas and Blow's *Venus and Adonis*, as well as contemporary composers like Stanley Bate and Peggy Glanville Hicks and Georges Auric. She died in 1962 at the age of seventy-eight, ill and weakened with operations, but still recalling her recording adventures and planning new ones with the greatest zest – thinking of Notre Dame in Paris in the middle of a winter's night and the torrent of sound from the organ and the eight-second reverberation, deciding that she and Neville Marriner must now do Mozart, remembering the sound of 'the Baker girl', and the aching intensity of Janet Baker's 'Remember me' in the *Dido and Aeneas* that Anthony Lewis had recorded for her.[88]

The problems of running a record company with only two at the helm, she and her husband, even if the captain was as formidable as Mrs Hanson-Dyer, led to an affiliation with Decca in 1953, and the company was finally taken over completely by Decca in 1971.[89] In that first decade and a half L'Oiseau-Lyre had created a very strong label profile and this was a progression that was to become common in the later days of recording history, a small independent label creating a name and a niche in the market by specialization, often by concentrating on less familiar repertory, and then being taken over by a large multinational company.

'The History of Music in Sound'

There was another series of considerable importance in developing the recorded repertory on 78 rpm discs. This was HMV's *History of Music in Sound*, planned to be used in conjunction with the ten volumes of *The New Oxford History of Music*. The *History* originated in a series of programmes of the same name which was broadcast by the BBC between 1948 and 1950. The discs were issued between 1953 and 1959 and ran to 228 78 rpm sides, about nineteen hours of playing time. It began with 'Ancient and Oriental Music' and then the survey went from 'Early Medieval Music from 1300' up to 'Modern Music (1890–1950)'. Even with those periods with which most music-lovers of the time would have considered themselves fairly familiar, there would have been discoveries for nearly everyone. The eighth volume, for example, aimed to present 'the age of Beethoven as Beethoven himself heard it', as the accompanying booklet put it, in other words to allow music-lovers to begin to discover long-forgotten repertory, repertory much played and talked about in its day, a great deal of which was rated as highly as the handful of works that had survived in regular performances. Nearly half of the music was from opera, including extracts from Cherubini's *Deux journées* based, like Beethoven's *Fidelio*, on a libretto by Bouilly, and an opera which had as much success in Germany as Paris and was greatly admired by Weber, and Beethoven too when he heard it in Vienna in 1803, from Méhul's famous *Joseph*, from Spohr's *Jessonda*, and from *La Vestale* of Gaspare Spontini, who was a favourite at various times of the Empress Joséphine, of Napoleon, and of Frederick William III of Russia. There were extracts too from the less-known works of very well-known composers: a scene from Rossini's *Otello* and the farewell scene from *Les Troyens*. There were songs, Schubert's *Nachtgesang* side by side with the setting of the same text by Johann Zumsteeg, whose songs, Schubert told a friend, he could 'wallow in' for days on end. There were two movements from Spohr's Octet; there was a movement from a piano quartet by Prince Louis Ferdinand, the dedicatee of Beethoven's C minor Concerto, who played, Beethoven said, 'not like a prince but like a real pianist'; there were piano pieces by Tomášek, and Dussek and Clementi, and the Allegro from the Sonata in F sharp minor op. 81 by Hummel which Schumann called 'a truly great, epic, Titan work'.

The series ran then on similar lines to Columbia's *History of Music Through Ear and Eye* issued twenty years earlier but on a grander scale. Alec Robertson used the recordings as the basis for lectures to students at the Royal College of Art, enthusiastic auditors who felt special affinities, they told him, between their own work and plainchant and early polyphony,[90] and from the end of 1959 EMI promoted similar lectures by him to general audiences all over the country, from Birmingham to Cardiff and from Edinburgh to Bristol. In Newcastle more than 700 turned up to listen and *The Gramophone* was sure that 'a new world of enjoyment' had been shown them.[91]

The series was generally welcomed and some of the music was hailed as a revelation; a fragment of Richard Davy's Passion according to St Matthew from the Eton Choirbook Alec Robertson considered 'quite extraordinarily moving',[92] the very same music which the Music Librarian of the British Museum half a century earlier had considered historically 'of infinite value and interest' but of little interest aesthetically: 'That this music would sound beautiful to our ears is extremely improbable.'[93] But Alec Robertson himself had some reservations, on the recorded sound – the muddled textures of the performances recorded at Montserrat, some bad balances and a lack of presence or atmosphere with the recording of singers, the result of placing the performers too close to the microphone – on the coarse tone in loud passages which could only be improved by playing the records at 'an unsatisfactorily low volume',[94] and on the standard of some of the performances. The men's voices of the choir of Brompton Oratory were assured and convincing in Gregorian chant, but their performances were less idiomatic in Byzantine music, or in Russian or Greek or Mozarabic liturgical chants. And younger critics were less enthusiastic and had more reservations: there were comments on 'constricted' sound quality and rough surfaces.[95] Several of the performances, thought one reviewing volumes V and VI, 'cannot be said to rise above

the serious-minded and well-meant, which for a scheme of this importance is frankly not good enough'. The choice of artists seemed unduly
restricted, giving the whole thing a faint air of a family party: 'I cannot
believe that no other performers exist capable of authentic-style readings.'[96] And another thought that 'some of the performances are no
more than routine, and a few are poor – particularly in the earlier
volumes. The list of performers has a rather parochial look about
it. . . .'[97] There were comments on the 'meagre' sound of St Paul's
Cathedral Choir and the 'undernourished tone' of the choir's trebles,[98]
on a 'clodhopping' orchestra,[99] on the stiffness and monotony of the
chanting of Brompton Oratory Choir, on the dry, unconvincing and
'plummy' English soloists on an excerpt from the *St John Passion* and
on the fact that German artists hadn't been engaged.[100] Why was the
whole of a Vivaldi concerto recorded when this composer was, by 1955,
well served by the record companies already, and why short excerpts
from the *St John Passion* when there were two complete versions of the
work now available? Hardly had one critic regretted that Stravinsky's
The Soldier's Tale, of which excerpts were given such a good performance, was not available complete[101] when that 'fairy godmother
HMV'[102] had obliged and released the whole work. The absence of any
music by Webern was criticized; within a few months the set of records
of Webern supervised by Robert Craft and issued by American Columbia would become available in Britain.

In many ways the enterprise seemed to these critics to belong to a
bygone era. Which in fact it did. Musicology was making rapid strides.
When the recordings were reissued on forty-eight twelve-inch LP sides,
a number of works in the second, third and fourth volumes were
remade to take into account the latest scholarship.[103] And at the same
time there were increased opportunities for listening to repertory
outside the great works frequently heard in live performances. There
was the BBC Third Programme.

Postwar radio

In 1947 *The Economist* had noted the burgeoning interest in serious
music among all sections of society; postmen were whistling the
opening of Beethoven's Fifth Symphony – they had learnt it as the
musical V for Victory sign during the war – typists combined

'lip-stick repairs' with discussions about their next purchase of concerto records, musical appreciation classes were overcrowded, concerts in the Albert Hall were sold out weeks in advance. The writer was sure that 'there is still a very much greater volume of musical activity in Britain than ever before', the fruit of the sapling of universal education that was planted in 1870, or perhaps more likely, of state-aided secondary education planted in 1902.[104]

One commentator had pointed to the growing interest in music which had been provoked by the visits of great orchestras from abroad in the 1930s, from Berlin, Budapest, Vienna, Amsterdam, Prague and New York, and to the appearance of two new English orchestras of first-rate quality, the BBC Symphony Orchestra in 1930 and the London Philharmonic Orchestra in 1932, to the Courtauld-Sargent Concerts Society, with its scheme of group subscriptions, which made classical music played by 'the world's greatest artists available to those who could not afford the usual West End prices, thereby swelling the ranks of music enthusiasts by many thousands'.[105] Certainly the stresses and strains of wartime had caused many to realize that music didn't just offer 'solace and consolation' but had become for them a necessity. During the war a number of orchestras, and particularly the Hallé, the Liverpool Philharmonic, the Scottish, and the City of Birmingham and the London Philharmonic, had played in smaller provincial towns which had never before been visited by a symphony orchestra.[106] This activity had been supported by funds provided by the Council for the Encouragement of Music and the Arts – after the war it became the Arts Council – which also had given grants or guarantees to local music clubs promoting concerts of chamber music played by professional performers; these music clubs all over the country had increased from eleven to eighty during the war years. The Arts Council assisted the festivals which were established after the war, at Cheltenham in 1945, at Edinburgh in 1947, and at Aldeburgh in 1948. And the National Gallery concerts during the war had made serious music 'a study and recreation for those who had never been to a concert before'; now it was not even necessary for the players to be artists of international repute for there to be full houses at chamber music concerts at the Wigmore Hall. The 1,687 wartime National Gallery concerts had educated thousands of men and women to whom chamber music had previously been completely unfamiliar. But the writer of this article pointed out that public taste was mostly for orchestral programmes of Beethoven or Tchaikovsky or 'the one really familiar Brahms symphony', and that audience figures dramatically dropped when Walton or Prokofiev or Shostakovich was played. Maybe, as several authorities were asserting, the peak of the music boom had passed. There was certainly a feeling in the years after the war that sections of the new audience for serious music would be drawn away as consumer goods became more easily available.[107] But such prophets left out of account developments in England in broadcasting.

Before the war the BBC had two national radio networks, each aiming to cater for all tastes. After the war the BBC established three national networks, each designed for a separate kind of audience. On the Light Programme, the Director-General of the BBC explained, he would expect to hear the waltz from *Der Rosenkavalier*, a week or ten days later on the Home Service one complete act – 'the most tuneful act' – of the opera, and then within the month the whole work, 'dialogue and all', on the Third Programme.[108] It never worked out quite like that in practice but the idea suggested the networks' profiles. The Third Programme was intended, as a 1943 internal BBC memo put it, for 'a highly intelligent minority audience' with an appetite for 'critical discussions of art, drama, music and literature; poetry and prose readings of the less popular type; experiments in radio drama; programmes in foreign languages etc'.[109]

The Third Programme began broadcasting on 29 September 1946, transmitting each evening between six and midnight, and a week later one music critic thought that it was likely the musical landscape would be 'transformed'; he agreed that there was 'an immense profusion' of music-making all over London, but most of it consisted of 'vain and endless repetition of a handful of works: I mean the Beethoven-Tchaikovsky-Grieg-Rachmaninoff concertos, the Beethoven-Brahms-Tchaikovsky symphonies, and so on'. From what he had seen of the schedules the new network would offer much to those whose tastes were more catholic and sophisticated and would allow listeners not just to catch up with the repertory being presented in concert hall and opera house but 'to shoot well ahead'.[110] Before the year was out the Third Programme listener could have heard the first English performance of Kodály's *Missa brevis* conducted by the composer, Hindemith's *Ludus tonalis* played by Noel Mewton-Wood, Eugene Goossens conducting the first performance of his Second Symphony, Poulenc's Sextet for piano and wind, Honegger's *Symphonie liturgique*, and Stravinsky's *Symphony in Three Movements*. The last three were first English performances. Berg could be heard quite frequently; there were seven programmes of Schoenberg; there was Michael Tippett's Third String Quartet. And there were talks, by Michael Tippett who 'gave a general survey of the contemporary music scene', introducing pieces by Bartók, Berg, Stravinsky, Hindemith and Gershwin; Mátyás Seiber spoke about Bartók's string quartets, Nadia Boulanger spoke on 'Stravinsky and Neo-Classicism', and on the same day she conducted her own ensemble in a concert of early and contemporary French music.

The sixteenth-century liturgical repertory that R. R. Terry had rediscovered and put into performance while he directed music at Westminster Cathedral during the first quarter of the century was largely uncultivated after he left, and by the war pre-Reformation masses had faded from view. The Third Programme provided a new kind of opportunity for performing this music and during the first decade of the network's existence there were frequent performances of the Latin music of Byrd and Tallis, including the Byrd masses and the Tallis Lamentations. *Spem in alium* was broadcast in March 1948 from the Central Hall, Westminster, sung by the Morley College Choir conducted by Michael Tippett, and in August 1950 from the chapel of King's College, Cambridge, sung by the Cambridge University Musical Society under Boris Ord. Increasingly, though, the pre-Reformation repertory was explored as well. During those years there were broadcast performances of Tye's Mass 'Euge bone', four Masses by Taverner – 'Christe Iesu', 'Western Wind', 'O Michael', 'Corona Spinea' – the motets *Christe Iesu*, *Pastor bone* and *Mater Christi sanctissima*, and the Te Deum, Lloyd's 'O Quam Suavis' Mass, Fayrfax's Masses 'Albanus' and 'Tecum Principium', his Magnificat and Mass 'O Bone Jesu', and the antiphons *Aeterna laudis lilium* and *Ave Dei Patris Filia*, the Mass 'Deus Creator Omnium' of Philip Ap Rhys, Carver's Mass 'Pater Creator Omnium' and the antiphons *Gaude Flore Virginali* and *O Bone Jesu*, Ludford's Magnificat and the Mass 'Videte Miraculum', and of Sheppard, the motets *Haec Dies quam fecit Dominus*, *In Pace in Idipsum*, and *Non Conturbetur Cor Vestrum*; and there were programmes of pre-Reformation carols.[III]

From September 1953 even more music was broadcast when the Third spread itself into Sunday afternoons. A week in November 1953 was typical and characteristic: there was piano music by Ravel, one in a series of thirteen programmes on 'A century of French Piano Music', and there were sonatas by Domenico Scarlatti; Manfred F. Bukofzer gave a talk introducing six programmes of music by Dunstable and the first of the series 'Works from Dunstable's Early Period', and there was choral music by Gilbert Banester and William Byrd; Puccini's *La Bohème* was transmitted and orchestral music by William Schuman, Aaron Copland and Karel Boleslav Jirák; Stravinsky's *Fireworks* was heard and Sibelius's Symphony no. 7, Rubbra's *Ode to the Queen* for voice and orchestra, Bartók's Viola Concerto, and Strauss's Suite *Der Rosenkavalier*; there were cantatas by Purcell, 'When night her purple veil had softly spread', and Arne, 'Bacchus and Ariadne', and Handel's Organ Concerto in F op. 4 no. 4; a programme of chamber music by Poulenc included the first broadcast performance in the UK of his Sonata for Two Pianos; the schedules also included the first performance in the UK of Milhaud's *Concertino d'Automne*; there was Dallapiccola's *Chaconne, Intermezzo and Adagio* for unaccompanied cello; there was William Wordsworth's Third Quartet, and the Third Quartet of Elizabeth Maconchy, and chamber music by Mátyás Seiber, William Busch, and Imogen Holst; there was Mozart's Flute Quartet in A major K.298 and Reger's Serenade in G for flute, violin and viola, and chamber music by C. P. E. Bach, Boccherini and Telemann; there was a programme in a series of twelve Schubert Lieder recitals; there were songs by Fauré, piano music by Brahms, orchestral music by Boccherini and the first of three recitals of Liszt's *Années de pèlerinage*; and there was a performance of Monteverdi's *L'incoronazione di Poppea*, with an introductory talk by the conductor Walter Goehr.[112]

The amount of old music scheduled during the first decade of the Third Programme is explained in part at least by the fact that the BBC's staff responsible included a number of musicians who were themselves both scholars and performers. In charge of the original organization of the Third Programme had been Anthony Lewis, as a conductor best known for his performances of Baroque music, who in 1947 was appointed professor of music at Birmingham University. Denis Stevens was a planner and producer for the BBC music department between 1949 and 1954, having spent several years as a professional violinist. He conducted choirs singing the Tudor repertory and broadcast and made records with them, he made editions and contributed scholarly articles and was to write books on Monteverdi and Tomkins and Tudor church music. Gerald Abraham, who had been director of the BBC's gramophone department and who had helped Lewis launch the Third Programme, was appointed professor at Liverpool in that same year, 1947. This was a decisive period for British musicology, and for the intertwining of performance and scholarship. And those who felt that interest in serious music had been fuelled by the artificial conditions of wartime, and that as soon as consumer goods appeared in the shops again this interest in music would melt away, also left out of account the appearance of a new consumer durable, the long-playing record.

The long-playing disc and the emergence of small labels

In December 1924, towards the end of the acoustic era of recording, the records reviewed in the pages of *The Gramophone* comprised two symphonies, Tchaikovsky's 'Pathétique' and Schubert's 'Unfinished', Mozart's Violin Concerto in A major K.219, Beethoven's Leonora Overture, excerpts from Vaughan Williams's opera *Hugh the Drover*, the 'Sistine Vatican Choir' singing short works by Marenzio, Victoria and Palestrina, a few songs – Schubert's 'Ave Maria', Gounod's 'Nazareth', Adams's 'The Holy City' – a handful of operatic arias – from Gounod's *Faust*, from Verdi's *Un ballo in maschera*, from Puccini's *Madame Butterfly* – a number of piano and violin solos and Mark Hambourg playing Leonard Borwick's piano arrangement of Debussy's *Prélude à l'Après-midi d'un faune*. The 78 rpm discs issued in June 1950, the month in which Decca published its first batch of some four dozen LPs, consisted of one symphony, Sibelius's Sixth, and one concerto, Brahms's Violin Concerto, Roussel's *Suite* op. 33, Wagner's *Siegfried Idyll*, Mozart's *Eine kleine Nachtmusik*, a few other short orchestral pieces, a Bach organ toccata and a prelude and fugue, three Études and a Waltz and a Scherzo by Chopin, a few other instrumental solos, a Bach cantata, *Ich habe genug*, a couple of dozen songs and one song-cycle, Fauré's *La bonne chanson*, and an album of church music. In April 1960 *The Gramophone* reviewed long-playing records of thirty-two symphonies, including six of Haydn's Salomon set, Brahms's First and Third, Berlioz's *Symphonie fantastique*, Liszt's *Faust* Symphony, Dvořák's 'New World', Mendelssohn's 'Italian', and Schumann's 'Rhenish'; there were thirty-three concertos, which included four Handel organ concertos, the six concerti grossi op. 3, three of the op. 6 set of concerti grossi, Chopin's Second Piano Concerto, Brahms's

Violin Concerto and both piano concertos, Bartók's second and third piano concertos, flute concertos by Michael Haydn, Telemann and Stamitz, fifty-two large orchestral works – including Bartók's *Music for String Instruments, Percussion and Celesta* – and ninety-one short ones, the complete music for Delibes's three-act ballet *Sylvia*, twenty-two major instrumental works – pieces like César Franck's *Trois Chorals* and Janáček's *On the overgrown path* – and seventy-two shorter instrumental solos, ten major choral works including four of Bach's motets and Haydn's *The Creation*, there were Falla's *Seven Spanish Popular Songs*, some of Schütz's *Kleine geistliche Konzerte*, sixteenth-century German songs by Melchior Franck and Staden, three complete operas – Strauss's *Arabella* and Novák's *The Storm* and Bartók's *Bluebeard's Castle* – and fifty-eight assorted operatic excerpts.[113]

On electrical 78 rpm discs there had been no commercial releases of Mahler's third, sixth, seventh and eighth symphonies at all and only one each of the others except for the Fourth Symphony, of which there were four recordings, two of which were issued in 1951 and one, recorded in 1930 and extremely rare, on Japanese Parlophone. Of the First Symphony there was just one on 78s, a 1941 recording of the Minneapolis Symphony Orchestra under Dimitri Mitropoulos. During the 1950s nine recordings were issued of just the First: one on Urania and Vanguard, one on Vox and Turnabout, one on Capitol, one on Columbia, one on Angel, one on Westminster, one on Royale, one on Pye, and one on Everest.[114] One of these, Columbia, is a major company, one of them, Pye, an English company; all the rest are small American labels. The dramatic expansion of the repertory was to a great extent the result of the creation of a multitude of new labels produced by a host of small companies.

In England there was Argo, registered as a limited company in 1952, whose founder's original intention was to specialize in British music played by British artists. There was Nixa, formed in October 1950, which in 1951 entered into contracts to release the issues of several American companies like Concert Hall Society, Period, Lyrichord, and Haydn Society, and made a similar agreement with Westminster which included embarking on a programme of jointly financed recordings; in 1955 the label issued overtures by Suppé with Sir Adrian Boult conducting the London Philharmonic Orchestra; they recorded the complete Sibelius tone poems with Boult and the complete Mozart symphonies with Erich Leinsdorf.[115] In March 1954, the first *Messiah* described as 'authentic' was released by Nixa in Great Britain and by Westminster in the United States conducted by Hermann Scherchen, billed as the 'original Dublin version (1742)'.

But in America there were literally dozens of small companies which began operations in the early 1950s, some, in the beginning at least, with only local distribution, some starting out as subscription mail order businesses and only later being made available to the general retail market.[116] Certainly some didn't last for long. Allegro Records of New York City, which began publishing recordings in 1948, seems to have ceased to trade by 1952, but it issued notable recordings of the organist Robert Noehren and the harpsichordist Fernando Valenti and a performance of Debussy's *Le Martyre de St Sébastien* by the Oklahoma City Symphony Orchestra. Or labels might draw on the resources of particular organizations: Cambridge Records of Cambridge, Massachusetts, issued choral works by Debussy, Palestrina, Byrd, Lassus and Victoria sung by the Harvard Glee Club; Festival Recordings Inc. of Boston put out performances by the Harvard University Choir and Radcliffe Choral Society; Boston Records concentrated on recitals and chamber music performed by members of the Boston Symphony Orchestra; Overtone Records of New Haven, Connecticut, used the forces available through the Yale University School of Music, where Hindemith was the moving force behind performing early music, and their records included Monteverdi's madrigal cycle *Lagrime d'amante al sepolcro dell'amata*, choral pieces and madrigals by Weelkes, Gesualdo, Pérotin, Lassus, Dufay and Giovanni Gabrieli, and a series of organ discs played by Luther Noss which include excerpts from Scheidt's *Tabulatura nova*.

Some of the labels did concentrate on particular artists or on particular instruments, but little-known or neglected repertory was usually a key element: the Kendall label was devoted to organ music and included performances of Reubke's Organ Sonata and Leo Sowerby's *Organ Symphony*; Classic Editions issued recordings of the organist Clarence Watters, including the complete works of César Franck; Philharmonia Records of New York City issued chiefly recordings by the Stuyvesant String Quartet playing Debussy, Ravel, Malipiero, and Boccherini's Quintet with guitar; the Oxford Recording Company of New York was established by the flautist Julius Baker and nearly all given over to flute music including works by Haydn, Mozart, Ibert and Hindemith. Stradivari Records of New York City made a speciality of chamber music including string quartets by Barber, Dohnányi, Janáček, Smetana, Dvořák, Wolf and Mendelssohn; Cetra, also in New York, issued dozens of recordings of Italian opera, virtually all Verdi and Puccini, a number of operas by Rossini and Donizetti, Vecchi's sixteenth-century madrigal comedy *Amfiparnaso* and a few non-operatic recordings which included Malipiero's Seventh Symphony. Some of these companies built up catalogues whose distinguishing feature seemed only to be that the repertory was little-known: EMS of New York issued a small number of recordings including music by Giles Farnaby and Edgard Varèse; the recordings of Polymusic of New York City included works by Charles Ives, chamber music by Fauré, string quartets by Milhaud and Turina and Franck, and Mozart's opera *Zaide*; Esoteric of New York City issued *Canzone* for brass by Gabrieli, Poulenc's *Le bal masqué* and Schoenberg's Serenade for Septet and Baritone; Oceanic Long Playing Records of New York issued Rimsky-Korsakov's *Mozart and Salieri*, Gluck's Flute Concerto, Ives's *Theatre Set*, Beethoven's 'Battle' Symphony, and some of Handel's Italian cantatas.[117]

How was all this activity possible? First because tape recorders, tape and microphones were all comparatively cheap; the major companies like Columbia and RCA were perfectly willing to make the tape-to-disc transfer at reasonable cost provided the repertory complemented and did not duplicate the material issued on their own records. And while the greatest, internationally known artists commanded fees which would have been prohibitive to these small labels, there were a great number of players and singers of undeniable authority without existing contracts who were eager to increase their audiences and further their reputations by recording. Shellac records were more often a reminder of musical experiences, souvenirs, like signed photographs or visiting cards; microgroove discs quickly came to be regarded as different in kind, as enshrining genuine musical experiences. Not a few of these labels were vanity publications. Certainly the ambition of performing artists and the desire to win prestige were among the animating forces behind the issue of some of such releases, but musical enthusiasms for particular repertories, a kind of proselytizing zeal, also played an undeniable part. If the founders of one label had not ploughed the profits back in order to undertake 'wildly expensive things' on behalf of their composer they could, one of them later explained, all have driven around in Buicks and Rolls-Royces.[118]

Numerous releases of many of the small companies which appeared in the 1950s were rough around the edges, marred by infelicities of various kinds, rough-and-ready documentation, low-quality pressings, poor balance, audible edits. The first review Argo received in a national newspaper commented more in sorrow than in anger that 'they conduct their education in full view of the public. No technical fault strikes them as too serious to preclude publication. . . . It is rather a shock, when listening to a modern sonata, to be obliged to make the sort of allowances which we make listening to Tamagno's *Esultate* or Patti's *Ah, non credea*. . . .'[119] But most of the ones that survived, like Argo, quickly improved, and there was a buoyant excitement in the air at the continual revelations of new recorded repertory which perhaps made listeners more forgiving. They were after all still marvelling at the numerous advantages that the long-playing disc had given them.

Many of the small American labels operated as non-profit organizations. The American Recording Society of New York, which supplied discs by mail order, drew on funds from the Alice M. Ditson Fund of Columbia University to record a wide range of American music, from Stephen Foster to Alexei Haieff and Howard Swanson and Charles Ives, Copland and Piston, Roy Harris and William Schuman and Samuel Barber. Many of the orchestral recordings issued by such labels could never have been contemplated – they would have been prohibitively expensive – if they had been recorded in America. Some of the discs were pressed from existing tape masters. A German music-lover approached the manufacturing subsidiary of Columbia Records in 1951 and suggested issuing records from tapes he had in his possession of performances by the Berlin and Dresden State Operas, the radio orchestras from Berlin, Dresden and Leipzig and the Leipzig Gewandhaus, and groups from Prague and Vienna. German radio stations had been using Magnetophon recorders and tape for recording music from the late 1930s and at the end of the war many tapes were discovered by the US army and duplicates sent to regional German radio stations and to stations like Radio Normandie in France and Radio Luxembourg. It seems likely that copies of such tapes provided the source for such releases on the Urania label as Werner Egk's *Geigenmusik*, Wolf's *Der Corregidor*, Gluck's *Frühlingsfeier*, and concertos by Spohr.[120] Subsequently an agreement seems to have been made with the State Broadcasting Committee of the German Democratic Republic, under which

Urania would pay $4 for each minute of tape used along with an undertaking to settle itself any arguments over royalty claims that might arise with performers. A later deal for $100,000 resulted in enough material for five hundred microgroove discs. Urania were successfully sued over wartime recordings by Gieseking and by Furtwängler – the company had argued that because 'the United States and Germany were at war at the time the tapes were made, and Dr Furtwängler an alien, the recordings could not be registered in any way that entitled him to copyright protection' and that this fact freed them 'from any obligation to pay Dr Furtwängler any royalties'[121] – and two Vox LPs of Furtwängler performances were quickly withdrawn.[122] But some of these American companies were themselves able to make new orchestral recordings in a perfectly legitimate way in Vienna.

There was in Vienna a large pool of orchestral players struggling to earn a decent living after the austerities of wartime in an uncertain postwar economy, and exchange rates for the US dollar at this time were particularly favourable. In an effort to try to generate work the Vienna Symphony Orchestra had established a recording studio at the Konzerthaus, and the rates of the sound engineers and technicians were, by American standards, 'rock-bottom'.[123] And for a time it worked. Hermann Scherchen made radio recordings of Bach and Mahler with the orchestra in June 1950 and described the orchestra's schedule: 'The orchestra worked from 8:00 to 11:00, 11:15 to 12:15, and 13:15 to 15:15 with me, from 15:30 to 18:30 with Clemens Krauss for a trip to Yugoslavia, and from 20:00 to 23:00 with Karajan.'[124] Two years later the principal horn reported playing forty-two hours in a week, though this was half, he added, what the string players regularly clocked up. Even when the orchestra had an exclusive contract with Philips they were still permitted to record on other labels using pseudonyms, the Vienna State Philharmonic, the Vienna Philharmonia Orchestra, the Pro Musica Symphony, or simply the Vienna Orchestra.[125] Before too long there were innumerable contractual difficulties, and, since the members of American orchestras were being done out of work, the US unions managed to prevent some American conductors working with the Viennese. But for a time recording activity flourished and as a result of these conditions the SPA label was able to issue recordings of Mahler's Third and Sixth Symphonies, Bruckner's Ninth and Milhaud's Fourth Symphony, d'Albert's opera *Tiefland* and Charles Ives's Second Symphony; Vanguard released four discs of the songs of Mahler, and

Schubert's E major Symphony orchestrated by Felix Weingartner from the composer's sketches, and Schoenberg's Piano Concerto and a series of Mozart's operas *La Finta Giardiniera, The Impresario, Bastien and Bastienne,* and *Il re pastore.*

Not least in importance were the recordings made by the Haydn Society, whose recording activity epitomized that mixture of energy, enterprise, and artistic and financial recklessness that characterized many of these small labels. As a music-loving high school student in Ashville, North Carolina, in 1939, H. C. Robbins Landon realized that he perhaps wasn't going to be the virtuoso pianist that he would have quite liked to be. But taking a hint from a teacher, he decided to devote his energies to telling the world about a composer called Joseph Haydn, whom the world loved but about whom the world in fact knew very little. He chose to study music at Boston University precisely because the head of the music faculty was Karl Geiringer, a world authority on the composer. Robbins Landon recognized immediately the potential of the long-playing record to revolutionize public knowledge of Haydn's music. How else but by such a medium could there be familiarity with such a body of music – 106 symphonies, 62 piano sonatas, 68 string quartets, 45 piano trios, 34 string trios, 126 baryton trios, 14 masses and two dozen operas – most of which could never find a place in the permanent concert repertoire?[126] And at the beginning of 1950 only twenty-five of the symphonies had ever been recorded.

The plan was that the Haydn Society should issue a collected edition of the music and at the same time release recordings. The project did not have organizational funding and opportunities were simply seized as they arose. The whole enterprise was launched with the help of a legacy from his uncle, Francis Le Baron Robbins, his future wife Christa Fuhrmann acted as his organizational assistant, and his aunt Louise Robbins was the narrator on a ten-inch disc called 'Let's listen to Haydn'. She also came to the rescue at one stage with US $15,000. His friend the keyboard player Virginia Pleasants recorded three ten-inch discs of piano sonatas, and a member of the Society's administrative staff, the baritone Richard Wadleigh, sang in the recording of *Orfeo ed Euridice.* One conductor he used was an American he'd bumped into in a Vienna music shop, Jonathan Sternberg, who had come to Austria hoping to gain further conducting experience after several months in 1945 and 1946 spent directing the Shanghai Symphony Orchestra; he recorded seven Haydn symphonies in ten days with the Vienna Symphony Orchestra.[127]

Some of the tapes Robbins Landon issued were Austrian Radio masters: the Society's very first release was one such, issued in April 1949 – the only release on 78s – a performance of the *Harmoniemesse* by Munich musicians at the 1947 Salzburg Festival; so were recordings made in 1942 and 1943 of *The Seasons* and *The Creation*. But most were original recordings. With the Vienna Symphony Orchestra's hourly rate of 38 schillings per player, a Haydn symphony could be completed for about US $200; the *Coronation* Mass, with four soloists, chorus and orchestra, was recorded for $400. 'Hall rental ranged from 900 schillings a session in the Mozartsaal at the Konzerthaus to 1,800 schillings in the Musikvereinssaal, adding perhaps £50 to the budget. . . . Symphonia, the VSO's recording studio, and the Telefunken studio in the suburbs charged about $9 an hour in 1949. Under such conditions, the Haydn Society managed to record even the more elaborate masses for about $1,000 each. . . .'[128] Before the Society was wound up, in 1954, it made recordings of symphonies 43, 50 and 61 in the concert hall of the Danish State Radio building in Copenhagen using Danish EMI engineers with Mogens Wöldike conducting; of all the Haydn Society's discs these last were considered the highest in quality, both technically and musically.[129]

Soon after the Haydn Society ceased activities in Europe,[130] John Culshaw produced an LP of Wöldike and his orchestra playing Haydn's Symphonies numbers 44 and 48, and the Vanguard company, working in Vienna, took up the torch for Haydn, recording Wöldike there in *The Creation*, the *Missa in tempore belli* and the last six symphonies.[131] Robbins Landon has indicated the limitations of this Haydn recording project, the impossibility of engaging the greatest artists and of distributing the recordings in Germany, where they might have had most impact – some were released under licence in England – and the variable technical standards that were achieved. He himself thought that, in America, 'in the long run the effect of all this activity was negligible . . . a few years later the recordings were forgotten'.[132] It seems likely that this is an exaggeration. It is impossible to speculate on all the reasons that led to later Haydn recording projects but the pioneering work of the Haydn Society and the enthusiasm it generated – the 'Nelson' Mass recording immediately sold 5,000 copies – may certainly have decided a later record company to agree to a proposal, or in fact inspired musicians to take an interest in a composer they were later to record. He himself described the impact on a generation of Americans hearing works on Haydn Society discs like the 'Nelson' Mass and the *Trauersinfonie* and *The Creation* for the first time as 'gigantic'.[133]

It was an American, Max Goberman, who in 1960 formed a plan to record all the Haydn symphonies with the Vienna State Opera for his own record label, the Library of Recorded Masterpieces; the project was abandoned after forty-five symphonies on Goberman's premature death in December 1962. A recording of all the symphonies, though, was completed in 1972 with Goberman's orchestra conducted by Ernst Märzendorfer, but these were for the American subscription club Musical Heritage Society and not so widely known about.[134] The real breakthrough came when the complete series was recorded for Decca by Antal Dorati and the Philharmonica Hungarica, nine boxes each of between four and six discs, with a two-record appendix, which appeared between 1970 and 1974. Haydn had become big business. Box sets of discs of the Salomon Symphonies from Antal Dorati's complete series on the Decca label lay in huge piles in London record shops during the Christmas rush in 1974, Robbins Landon remembered, alongside records of the Rolling Stones and the latest Verdi opera.[135] And so it was to continue. Argo, the little English company which had been taken over by Decca in 1957 – though the label preserved its own separate identity – had had a popular success with their recording by the Choir of King's College, Cambridge, under David Willcocks of Haydn's 'Nelson' Mass, released in 1962, which led to a series, all 'The Six Great Masses', the other five being sung by the Choir of St John's College, Cambridge. The works were almost completely neglected before these recordings and it was these discs, the head of Argo thought, that brought them to the notice of English choral societies.[136] Argo also issued all the string quartets with the Aeolian Quartet, eight boxes and thirty-six records, and then one after another came six complete recordings of the piano sonatas, from Argo, Hungaroton, Musical Heritage Society, Vox, a small Italian firm, and Teldec; the first complete edition of the piano sonatas had only been published by the Wiener Urtext Ausgabe in 1963 and 1964. And then, miraculously it seemed at the time, came the most daring commercially of all these undertakings, the operas, almost completely unknown by everyone, in a series conducted by Dorati with the Lausanne Chamber Orchestra and issued by Philips. Finally came the oratorios under Dorati on Decca.[137] 'Every man his own Prince Esterhazy', one critic had exclaimed with delight in 1971.[138]

In the first decade of the long-playing disc a greater amount of recorded classical music and a greater range of the musical repertory was brought into the home than in the entire history of recording during its first half century. There were first recordings of Monteverdi's *Vespro della Beata Vergine*, of Messiaen's organ works (including performances by the composer), of Bach's St John Passion, of Schoenberg's piano and violin concertos, Wagner's *Tristan und Isolde*, Strauss's *Elektra*, *Rosenkavalier* and *Salome*, Verdi's *I Lombardi* and *Nabucco*, Puccini's *La fanciulla del West* and *Suor Angelica*, Donizetti's *Il campanello* and *La fille du régiment*, Rossini's *Cenerentola*, Mozart's *Apollo et Hyacinthus*, *La finta giardiniera*, and *Der Schauspieldirektor*, Haydn's *Orfeo ed Euridice*, Nicolai's *The Merry Wives of Windsor*, and Pepusch's *The Beggar's Opera*; during this decade there were first recordings of Haydn's Cecilia Mass, and of the *Missa in tempore belli*, and of *The Seasons*, of Mahler's *Des Knaben Wunderhorn*, Bruckner's third and sixth symphonies, Dvořák's Third, and Ives's Third, and Martinů's Third, Mendelssohn's First, and Schubert's First, Mahler's third, sixth, seventh and eighth symphonies, Prokofiev's first and second piano concertos, Goldmark's Violin Concerto, Martinů's Concerto Grosso, and his *Sinfonietta la Jolla*, Schoenberg's four string quartets and Bliss's second, and Mozart's K.173, and Arriaga's quartets 1 to 3. During the 1950s there appeared for the first time the complete piano works of Mozart, the complete harpsichord works of Rameau and Couperin, all the symphonies of Sibelius and Vaughan Williams as well as Beethoven and Brahms, all the works with opus numbers of Webern, every note of Tchaikovsky's ballets and of Beethoven's *Prometheus* and Schumann's *Manfred*. In 1960 the American Schwann catalogue listed complete or nearly complete recordings of 250 operas. On electrical 78 rpm discs there had been one complete version of Rossini's *Il barbiere di Siviglia*; in England in December 1960 there were four different LP versions on sale, in North America six. There were four LP versions available of Richard Strauss's *Der Rosenkavalier* in England in 1960, and three in America; on electrical 78s there had been one abridged version, on twenty-six twelve-inch disc sides. Of Mozart's *Le nozze di Figaro* there had been one complete version on 78s, on thirty-three sides; by the end of 1960 five different versions were on sale in England and six in the United States.

Economics and education

How could such record production be sustained? How had potential audiences been created for this flood of music on long-playing records? By June 1954 *The Gramophone* magazine could announce that its circulation had reached 50,000 copies each month, which event prompted the editor to speculate on the reasons for the increasing popularity of recorded music. Underpinning everything, he thought, was the economic context, 'the redistribution of purchasing power brought about by the Welfare State'; the principle had been adopted that music and art and literature and drama, like education, health and social security, were universal goods which ought to be generally available regardless of the ability to pay. The editor of *The Gramophone* was sure that twenty times as many music-lovers were now able to collect records as when the magazine began publication in 1923.[139] And besides rising real incomes, shorter working hours gave further opportunities for recreation and leisure. An average working week was 54 hours before the First War, 48 hours by 1920 and 40 hours by the mid-1960s.[140]

In 1939 the gramophone was described by a sympathetic commentator – he was convinced of its beneficial effects overall on music and music-making – as 'an expensive and slightly troublesome hobby' that had only 'just begun to give adequate reproduction'.[141] The sound of the gramophone was certainly still regarded as unsatisfactory by many music-lovers; twelve years before, a music critic had referred to the 'desiccated and condensed forms of music',[142] referring to the quality of the sound as well as to the truncated versions of works necessitated by the short length of record sides, and while electrical recording had resulted in considerable improvements, still the highest frequency that could reliably be recorded in the late 1930s was 8,000 Hz. It was certainly expensive: at that time the Gramophone Exchange Ltd in Shaftesbury Avenue was offering gramophones at prices of between 30s. (£1.50) and £50. 30s. would have bought a second-hand inferior portable model, and the same amount would have been necessary for a Rondo Popular cabinette in which could be stored fifty twelve-inch or ten-inch

78 rpm discs. An HMV 'non-electric' model 193 gramophone on a walnut cabinet with an ebonized base and pedestal would have cost twelve guineas (£12.60), the 152 model, though, only ten guineas (£10.50). HMV radiograms cost between twenty and twenty-seven guineas (£21 and £28.35), a Marconi 291 radiogram forty-two guineas (£44.10), and the R.G.D. Superhet Seven Auto-Radiogram fifty-nine guineas (£61.95).

Listening to classical music on the gramophone had always been very expensive. You would have paid 10s. (50p) in 1902 for one of the Gramophone & Typewriter Company's Caruso recordings, and a guinea (£1.05) for the highest-priced records in 1904.[143] In the 1930s, EMI's best-known artists appeared on the company's red label discs, ten-inch double-sided records costing 4s. (20p) in 1934, twelve-inch double-sided discs costing 6s. (30p); plum-label discs were cheaper, 2s. 6d. (12½p) the ten-inch disc, 4s. (20p) the twelve-inch, but the twelve-inch buff label disc, with two 'red-label' artists, cost 10s. (50p), and the twelve-inch white label with four or six top performers cost 16s. (80p). This was at a time when the weekly wage was under £3. Before the Second War £250 was the annual income which was regarded as dividing the working classes from the rest of society and only a quarter of households in England were in receipt of more than £250 a year.[144] For most of the population disposable income was spent on the basic necessities: a radio or an iron would have to be saved for. A household in receipt of between £500 and £700 might typically spend £26 or £27 a year, say, on petrol and on running a car, 10s. (50p) on a radio licence, £20 on an annual holiday.

A recording of Mozart's *Le nozze di Figaro*, not quite complete,[145] was released by EMI in 1935; it extended over seventeen twelve-inch 78 rpm discs and was issued in three sets, each set available separately, a useful arrangement, one reviewer thought, since it enabled the 'less wealthy' to acquire the work in parts and the 'more wealthy' to have 'the entire work without delay'.[146] It cost altogether 99s., nearly £5. In 1937 it was followed by *Così fan tutte* on twenty discs, also issued in three sets and costing 120s. (£6) altogether. *Don Giovanni*, released in 1937 on twenty-three discs in three sets, cost 138s. (£6.90). In 1931 Decca had begun to issue ten-inch discs of classical music at 1s. 6d. (7½p) and twelve-inch discs at 2s. 6d. (12½p), and a number of performers had been added to their catalogue by the mid-1930s, including Sir Henry Wood, Hamilton Harty, Boyd Neel and Clifford Curzon. The fourth edition of

Grove's *Dictionary of Music and Musicians* which appeared in 1940 in five volumes cost 30s. for each volume; Stravinsky's autobiography, *Chronicle of my life*, which appeared in English for the first time in 1936, cost 8s. 6d. (42½p), Alfred Einstein's *A Short History of Music* which was first published in English in 1936 cost 4s. 6d (22½p); a hardback novel might cost 3s. 6d. (17½p) – 7s. 6d. (37½p) in a luxury edition – a bible for school use also 3s. 6d. (17½p). Penguin paperbacks were launched in 1935 and cost 6d. (2½p) each. Stalls at Glyndebourne during that first season in 1934 cost £2 on first nights, and subsequently £1. 10s. 0d. (£1.50), and a box cost twenty guineas (£21).[147] In 1930s advertisements in *The Gramophone* elegant ladies in long evening gowns reach into their record filing cabinets ('capable of holding over 400 10″ or 12″ [records]', price six guineas (£6.30)), upon which a tasteful display of cut flowers has been placed; happy children in their pyjamas holding their teddy-bears listen to ' "Children's Hours" from all parts of the World' on the new 'HMV' Autoradiogram while, through an open doorway, their parents can be seen dining with their guests. Clearly gramophones and gramophone records of classical music were aimed between the wars at the middle and upper-middle classes.

The long-playing record was famously launched by Columbia in 1948 at a reception at the Waldorf-Astoria Hotel in New York with the company's representative, Edward Wallerstein, flanked by two piles of discs, on one side a pile nearly eight feet high of 78 rpm discs and on the other a pile of 101 LPs, just over fifteen inches high, representing identical amounts of music.[148] In 1948 the Ormandy-Philadelphia Orchestra recording of Tchaikovsky's Fourth Symphony sold for $7.25 on five 78 rpm discs, but for $4.85 as one twelve-inch LP.[149] To begin with, the LP in England was under £2 for a twelve-inch disc; in 1953 the typical price was 36s. 5½d. (almost £1.82½); *Winterreise* on two LPs in 1953 cost 72s. 11d. (almost £3.65); two Schubert songs on one 78 rpm disc that month cost 8s. 11½d. (almost 45p).[150]

In 1960 the 'predominant' price for an LP was £1 18s. 3d. (about £1.91), in 1970 £2 5s. 11d. (almost £2.29½),[151] and in 1980 £4.69.[152] But as early as 1950 in America, less than two years after the introduction of the LP, the Remington label began issuing standard classics by little-known artists on twelve-inch discs at $1.99 against the usual price of most labels then of $5.45.[153] Now, in the 1950s, record clubs in England began direct marketing of cheap discs, selling by post recordings in pressings which, to begin with, were of poor quality, made from master-tapes with little or no royalties payable, and with non-existent or unsophisticated or careless notes and documentation. But in spite of such deficiencies such record clubs seemed likely to pose a serious threat to the established record companies in 1958. The public had recently changed their old gramophones for the new long-playing record, and now stereo discs had just been introduced, which required new styluses and loudspeakers. And sales were beginning to falter. What should record buyers do? Was there to be another new development within the next few years? In order to reassure customers and prevent them from being seduced by cheap discs by post, Decca created a bargain label, Ace of Clubs, in order to trump the record clubs. The first two issues were of Beethoven symphonies, reissued from original 78 rpm releases. But then came two original recordings, of Rachmaninoff's Second Piano Concerto in which the soloist was Julius Katchen, and Ernest Ansermet's version of Rossini-Respighi's *La Boutique Fantasque*. These twelve-inch Ace of Clubs discs sold for 21s. (£1.05) and were easily obtainable from any record dealer.

Some of the early issues were probably manufactured at a loss, even if the artists were persuaded to accept reduced royalties, but these bargain discs were a great public success and soon other companies had to follow – Deutsche Grammophon with Heliodor, EMI with its Concert Classics label. Through bargain labels Eastern Europe took the opportunity of re-entering the British market, the Czechs with Supraphon at 17s. 6d. (87½p), the Russians with Russian MK. Gradually the whole pricing structure of the market was altered. The Nonesuch label was launched by Elektra in America in 1964 charging $2.98 instead of the full price for a twelve-inch LP, commonly $5.98. Some of the Nonesuch discs were reissues of selected master-tapes from smaller international catalogues, but much was new, and the repertory chosen was an eclectic mix: there were sonatas and symphonies by C. P. E. Bach as well as the Brandenburg Concertos, a large number of Bach cantatas and Haydn symphonies, orchestral and chamber music by Telemann, madrigals by Schütz and concertos from his *Symphoniae sacrae* and his *Psalmen Davids*, Christmas music and dances from *Terpsichore* by Praetorius, Nocturnes by John Field and Rossini's sonatas for strings, but also works by Charles Ives and music by a large number of contemporary American composers, Elliott Carter, George

Rochberg, Stefan Wolpe, John Harbison, Roger Reynolds and George Crumb.

Decca soon afterwards created the Turnabout label in the image of Nonesuch, drawing on the Vox catalogue for source material and designing sleeves which resembled Nonesuch's in order to catch the eye of an already developed market. Nonesuch sold at 25s. (£1.25); Decca priced Turnabout discs at 17s. 6d. (87½p) and they were an immediate commercial success. The selling line on Turnabout was repertory 'off the beaten track'; there was Gregorian chant and there were anthologies of electronic music and Boyce symphonies and chamber music by the sons of Bach, there was Passion music by Demantius and Lechner, there were concertos by Boieldieu and Dittersdorf, quintets by Boccherini, quartets for mandolin, violin, viola and lute by Hoffmann and Giuliani, and concertos by Hummel, for piano, for piano and violin, and for mandolin.

It was not usually possible for established artists of the front rank to make new recordings for the bargain labels, but outstanding younger artists could sometimes be caught before their reputations and their fees had soared. Janet Baker and John Shirley-Quirk made their solo debut recital records for Saga. Repertory was discovered which, though it might not have sold well if issued at the usual prices, did produce good sales and reasonable profits if marketed at these lower prices, chamber music by Elgar, for example, or John Ireland. So the overall repertory on these bargain discs was very wide indeed. The record industry had created an equivalent of the paperback, and these bargain labels were brought before an ever-growing public, distributed through bookstalls and supermarkets as well through record shops.[154]

Sometimes cheaper recordings were criticized for inferior technical quality, for piano sound, for example, which was 'very shallow toned and pinched in dynamic range',[155] but more often the critics saluted the technical and artistic quality of a high proportion of these bargain releases and in their reviews often concluded that a bargain disc was 'superior to the full-price versions available'. 'This record should not on any account be missed', one said of a disc issued by Pye of Handel's Music for the Royal Fireworks, recorded 'as the composer wrote it' with twenty-four oboes, twelve bassoons and contrabassoons, nine horns, nine trumpets, three pairs of kettledrums. It was made on the night of the 200th anniversary of Handel's death during the early hours when

virtually all London's oboes could be employed; 'something of a revelation', an 'inspired recording', it was described as.[156] Reissues of
Furtwängler attracted a great deal of praise; three discs of all the string
quartets of Bartók on Saga costing less than a full-price LP were warmly
received, as were Peter Frankl's discs of all Debussy's piano music on
Vox, 'quite magnificent', a critic enthused.[157]

In 1970 that recording of the Glyndebourne *Le nozze di Figaro*, which
in 1935 on seventeen discs had cost altogether 99s. (£4.95), was reissued on two Classics for Pleasure LPs and cost 35s. 6d. (£1.77½). And
as more and more recorded music was becoming available at cheaper
prices there was increasing affluence: between 1960 and 1970 prices
in Great Britain rose 49 per cent but average pay doubled, and so real
income rose about 30 per cent.[158] Between 1945 and 1974 in Britain the
number of universities, new polytechnics and technical colleges and
colleges for further education doubled; there was a fivefold increase in
the university population, and an almost tenfold increase in higher education, supported by student grants.[159] The LP gave encouragement to
the musically curious who had had little in the way of formal musical
training or education, that 'cultured class', as R. R. Terry had described
it in 1927, that had a wise understanding of books and pictures, which
could 'converse easily and intelligently with authors and painters', but
'in the presence of a Doctor of Music . . . is dumb', since it had been
brought up to think that 'music is a "gift"', that counterpoint and fugue
are 'profound mysteries'.[160] Books on music, such people believed,
were crammed with technical terms and 'enigmatic snippets from
scores'.[161] But now with the LP they 'got to know the music by playing
the disc and they got the habit of reading about music by scanning the
commentary on the back of the jacket . . . [which] innocent practice
established without argument that one's experience of music could be
enhanced, organized, solidified by the use of words – preferably wise,
accurate, and enlivening words'.[162]

By the 1960s recordings had become 'the central fact of lay culture'
in Western Europe and North America, according to one cultural commentator; the long-playing record, he thought, had revolutionized the
art of leisure: 'The new middle class in the affluent society reads little,
but listens to music with knowing delight. Where the library shelves
once stood, there are proud, esoteric rows of record albums and high-
fidelity components.'[163] It was probably because of the long-playing
record and radio, a distinguished art historian thought in 1961, that

music had become 'the most precious of all shared possessions, of all sources of metaphor in our culture'.[164]

DG and Archiv Produktion

The dilemma facing the major German label, Deutsche Grammophon, after the war was that a great number of excellent and experienced German artists whom the company would have wished to use in normal circumstances could not be engaged because of the taint of Nazi collaboration or involvement of some kind, and no foreign artist would wish to be associated with a German label in the 1940s. An adviser to the company on marketing matters suggested specialization in a repertory in which the company could be competitive, and this led, in the words of the head of the company, to the consideration of 'good old German domestic music, or in fact the periods of musical history before the era of Mozart'.[165] It seems likely that a further recommendation of such a repertory was that it might represent an effort to re-establish the authentic roots of German culture at a time when the German nation was numbed at the tragedies and horrors of recent history, the results, many felt, of the distortion and corruption of its traditions. As plans were developed the scheme was extended and elaborated with Teutonic thoroughness and precision to encompass 'practically the whole of the history of Western music from its beginning up to the dawn of the classical era, almost a full millennium'.[166] The whole operation was divided into twelve different 'research periods', from Gregorian Chant to the time of Haydn and Mozart; two of the periods were devoted to composers, one to Bach and one to Handel, but the others had titles like 'The Central Middle Ages (1100–1350)', or 'The High Renaissance (16th century)', or 'Mannheim and Vienna (1760–1800)', and each was subdivided: so 'Period IV: The High Renaissance' had subdivisions as 'The Netherlanders from Josquin', 'At the court of Maximilian I', 'Evangelical church music', 'Social music in Italy', 'Organ and lute', 'Palestrina and his school', 'Dance music', 'The German Lied', 'The French chanson', 'Lassus', 'The Spanish masters', 'The Elizabethan age', 'The instrumental ensemble'. The recordings were issued on a new label, Archiv Produktion, described as the 'History of Music Division of the Deutsche Grammophon Gesellschaft', and the company emphasized its distinc-

tiveness: 'the musical works are offered . . . in their complete authentic form based on the original versions performed faithfully to the original style using historical instruments in "living" interpretations by
highly qualified specialist performers in recordings of the highest standard using the latest technical developments'.[167]

Reviewers were impressed with the presentation of long-playing
discs on the Archiv label, with the fibre sleeves lined with polythene
and with the meticulous documentation: 'We are given the composer's
name with dates and places of birth and death, *full* title (a rarity in itself
these days), key and opus number, *full* particulars of first edition or
location of the MS., edition or arrangement used, list of movements
(with timings) and, in the case of extended vocal works, the complete
text; detailed list of artists, including notes on the provenance of any
early instruments employed, and actual strength of orchestras and
choirs; and finally, along with the names of the producer and engineer
responsible for each side, the place and date of recording . . . disc
surfaces are unfailingly silent and free from pre-echo; the standards
of performance are high; and it is a matter for pleasurable surprise that so many good artists new to the gramophone have been
discovered.'[168]

Amongst the first releases on 78 rpm discs were some Bach organ
works and a Bach cantata, performed respectively by artists who were
to become leading figures in the catalogues: Helmut Walcha on the
Schnitger organ at St Laurents, Alkmaar, restored by Flentrop, largely
to its original form, between 1940 and 1949, one of the outstanding
organs of Europe, and a young baritone called Dietrich Fischer-
Dieskau. There was August Wenzinger, the Swiss cellist and viola da
gamba player who had founded the Schola Cantorum Basiliensis in
1933; there was Hans-Martin Linde, the Swiss recorder player, flautist
– performing on both modern and Baroque flutes – and composer of
German birth who was twenty in 1950. Karl Richter, the German
organist, harpsichordist and conductor, recorded for Archiv; he was
born in 1926 and had been appointed organist at the Thomaskirche in
Leipzig in 1947. Among his teachers had been Günther Ramin, who
had been appointed organist of the Thomaskirche in 1918 and Kantor
in 1940 and who in this immediate postwar period was rebuilding the
choir, which also made records for Archiv. As did another of his pupils,
the American harpsichordist Ralph Kirkpatrick.

The first releases in England, in 1954, through Heliodor, a subsidiary of Deutsche Grammophon, included performances of *madrigali* and *caccie* from the fifteenth-century Squarcialupi Codex, sacred songs by Dufay, and the thirteenth-century *Jeu de Robin et Marion* of Adam de la Halle, Gregorian chant for Vespers of Christmas Eve, songs by Thomas Campian from Rosseter's Book of Ayres, viol fantasias of Henry Purcell, Monteverdi's *Lamento d'Arianna* and the Sonata a 8 sopra 'Sancta Maria ora pro nobis', Carissimi's *Jephte*, Heinrich Schütz's *Musikalische Exequien*, Alessandro Scarlatti's cantata 'Su le sponde del Tebro', and Corelli's Sonata op. 5 no. 15 in D minor, 'La Follia', and Attilio Ariosti's Lesson V for the viola d'amore, Bach's cantatas *Ich will den Kreuzstab gerne tragen* and *Ich habe genug*, Handel's Water Music, chamber music by Telemann, and Mozart's Piano Concerto in A major K.414.

All these developments in repertory and presentation with Deutsche Grammophon followed on from severely practical business considerations. What began as an exercise in economy ended up by setting standards which could not but have important implications not only for the ways other record companies presented their material and influenced the repertory for which tastes were being created, but also – since the work of specialists was now being more widely exposed – for the evolution of performing standards and styles.

Recording artists and repertoire

The big record companies, the multinational companies with huge capital resources, were proud of their ability to record the world's greatest executants performing the towering masterpieces of the central repertory. The dominant aesthetic of the twentieth century may have been formalist and anti-Romantic but the image of the artist as hero, the re-creative artist as well as the creative artist as prophet, priest and king, of conductors – especially conductors – as men of 'energy, self-confidence, and personal power'[169] as Wagner stipulated they must be, has continued to capture the popular imagination. There were certainly a limited number of works that would sell to a very large global audience. But the big companies could record repertory which smaller companies could not begin to contemplate. The long-playing record and stereo made the recording of Wagner's *Ring* a technological and practical and musical possibility. But while the technical and administrative possibilities were formidable they were to some extent assessable; the commercial prospects of the venture could be less easily predicted. Not only were record company executives doubtful that it would be 'any sort of commercial success', so was the producer whose determined advocacy in the end obtained his company's grudging permission. So for financial reasons Decca would not contemplate the project as a whole; the recording of the next opera would be authorized only when the financial success of the previous one could be clearly attested in the chief accountant's log.

Work began in September 1958 taping *Das Rheingold* as the shortest – it would fit on to three LPs, as against five required for *Walküre* or *Siegfried*, and six for *Götterdämmerung* – and so the cheapest. It had never been recorded at all before, and therefore would have whatever market there was to itself. The trouble was that *Rheingold* is not self-contained; it is only produced in the theatre as a prelude to the *Ring* and it has no real 'star' parts, at least not of the kind that bring the public in, though Kirsten Flagstad was persuaded to sing the role of Fricka – a comparatively modest role that she had never sung in public – in part because of the commercial advantage her name would give the records. What finally decided it was the impossibility of casting Birgit Nilsson as Brünnhilde, at that time the world's great singer in the role, the obvious choice, the only choice as far as those Wagner devotees who alone it was thought could guarantee the financial success of the enterprise. She was under contract to Columbia, and while it was hoped she might become available at some stage, in 1958 there was no question of using her. Even when the recording of *Das Rheingold* turned out a resounding artistic and commercial success Decca would still only consider each opera in turn. And yet John Culshaw was convinced that the project was only successfully accomplished because it was 'subject to strict commercial discipline',[170] that financial constraints by and large aided and abetted the striving for high standards, stimulated technical inventiveness and artistic self-discipline, and created conditions in which musicians and technicians and producers worked with the kind of rapt concentration, intense but controlled, that communicated disciplined excitement in the performances, and also ensured that no overtime had to be paid to the orchestra.

If it was generally true – as John Culshaw reported of Decca – that in 1955 most big record companies lacked coherent policies regarding repertory, partly because the companies disliked committing resources too far in advance,[171] this would soon change as the development of a great performer's artistry and the size of the fees he could command became more closely bound up with his recordings and with record company profits. The reputations of the greatest artists – and the sales figures they could inspire – did make possible explorations of repertory which would otherwise have remained unrecorded and largely unknown; the commercial success of Maria Callas and Joan Sutherland meant that the recording of the infrequently heard operas of Bellini and Donizetti became commercial propositions, with enormous sales for even a work like *Beatrice di Tenda*. And the popularity of particular artists led to the possibility of the recording of *intégrales*. Artur Rubinstein was apparently not enthusiastic when the Gramophone Company suggested in the late 1930s that he record all the mazurkas of Chopin; though he was renowned for his interpretation of some of them, most he had never learnt at all.[172] And the same EMI man, Fred Gaisberg, had to worry Pablo Casals persistently in order to persuade him to complete his famous recordings of the unaccompanied Bach cello suites.[173]

It was the youthful high spirits and ebullience and the musical and emotional partnership with Jacqueline du Pré – as well as the transcendent musical gifts – that made Daniel Barenboim so universally popular in the 1960s and therefore made EMI keen that he should cover repertory so exhaustively with series of recordings of Mozart symphonies and piano concertos and Beethoven sonatas running in parallel at the end of the decade. Some older artists viewed with misgiving the developing fashion for young performers to record composers' complete works, at an age, they thought, when they could not possibly 'encompass the whole life's work of a great genius . . . of a Beethoven, a Schubert or a Mozart'.[174] Now, in the age of the longplaying record, reputations and careers were being made through recordings. The President of the American label Westminster claimed that it was his company that discovered Paul Badura-Skoda in Vienna after the war, when he was in his early twenties, that they nurtured his talent, and produced his first records which enabled him to go on and develop an international career, the first time that this had happened, he was sure. Until that time a solo recording artist had to have made a name with the public before he was allowed into the recording studio.[175]

The early music performer

Walter Legge considered in 1960 that for 'the great recording companies . . . the repertoire in which a sufficiently large public is interested, to justify the artistic and technical costs, is still discouragingly limited'. But in fact Walter Legge's own tastes were not particularly adventurous or wide-ranging. He agreed with Ernest Newman, he once said, that 'you can interchange at will any movements of the last twenty Haydn symphonies, and it will make no difference'.[176] He was not convinced that Schoenberg was a 'major composer'. He was emphatically only interested in those he considered major composers and major artists. It was certainly true that the biggest record companies, like EMI for which Legge worked, have always been chary of extending the repertory; unknown music would never earn so much money. The American conductor Erich Leinsdorf complained that the major companies were always unwilling, whether they were 'in prosperity or in distress', to record a work for the first time.[177] And the failure of twentieth-century composers to write for mass audiences, their unwillingness even to contemplate using the new technology to address large audiences, has meant that for mass audiences, for record-buying audiences, the greatest musicians have been the interpreters of old music rather than the creators of new music, figures like Casals, Callas, Horowitz, Michelangeli, Enescu, Karajan, Ferrier, Sutherland, Schwarzkopf. Toscanini was perhaps the first 'greatest', most famous, musician alive to be purely a re-creative artist, to have no aspirations as a composer. As early as 1934 a New York critic complained of 'prima donna conductors': 'Critical comment . . . is almost entirely directed to "readings" of mighty magicians of the conductor's wand. . . . Can [the public] ever again be trained to love music for its own sake and not because of the marvels wrought upon it by supermen?'[178] Beethoven sold records in large quantities, Tchaikovsky sold records, so did Toscanini. But as the impact of the LP grew, so even early music began to create its own supermen. The anthologies of early music on 78 rpm discs had presented musical specimens of 'scientific' significance; now with increasing familiarity in performances on radio and LP disc the particular beauty of different idioms and styles was becoming so familiar that 'questions of historical significance . . . often seemed to be of purely secondary importance', as a 1963 Archiv catalogue had it.[179] A record critic could still reflect in 1953 that 'the notion that "old" music is primitive and unattractive, or at the best "quaint" . . . that it is merely a series of tentative experiments leading towards future glories, dies hard'.[180] But he perceived that an increasing number of music-lovers were indeed finding interest and delight in the earlier ages of music and wondered whether 'the public at large [would] become more adventurous and seek out pre-Bach music and contemporary music, or will the companies have to go on desperately recording more performances of the "Fifth" and "Unfinished" until they themselves are finished?'[181] Two decades later another commentator concluded that medieval and Renaissance music had won 'the kind of acceptance that made it part of the standard repertoire, to be enjoyed and appreciated in the same halls and by the same audiences as existed for Mozart concertos and Tchaikovsky symphonies'.[182]

That this had happened in England he felt owed a great deal to the brief but spectacular career of one particular early musician. David Munrow, born in 1942, was a gifted wind player, first a bassoonist, then a recorder player – and as such completely self-taught, he never passed an examination in music – who at the age of eighteen spent a year in South America teaching on the British Council Overseas Voluntary Scheme. He discovered the folk traditions of South America and returned to England armed with collections of Bolivian flutes and Peruvian pipes. He was to collect folk instruments wherever he went – a Turkish shawm, a Bohemian bagpipe, a Moroccan rabab, a double flageolet, a pottery flute, a didjeridoo, a shepherd's goat bagpipe of Yugoslavia, an Egyptian *nai*. The styles and idioms of folk music traditions and the timbres of some of the instruments he had collected were later to be suggestive when he struggled to arrive at convincing performance styles for medieval music. He was minutely sensitive to timbre and delighted in sound quality; in 1967 he had gathered round him a group of instrumentalists to perform the repertory he was investigating, but then he heard the countertenor James Bowman and invited him to join the group because 'here was the most fabulous "noise" I'd ever heard'.[183] This was the Early Music Consort of London and he directed them during a career which lasted barely a decade. His recordings include recorder concertos by Sammartini and Handel, Purcell's 1692 and 1694 Birthday Odes for Queen Mary, and Monteverdi's Vespers of 1610, and motets and dances by Praetorius, but his most important contributions were in performances of medieval and Renaissance music, Dufay's Mass 'Se la face ay pale', *Music for Ferdi-*

nand and Isabella of Spain, *Music from the time of the Crusades*, and three box sets each of three LPs, *The Art of Courtly Love*, *The Art of the Netherlands*, and *Music of the Gothic Era*.

Why did Munrow create such an impact? First because of his own instrumental virtuosity and the technical expertise and panache and vitality of the musicians he collected round himself. 'As a performer he was a ruthless perfectionist', according to a colleague, 'yet always prepared to take exciting risks which heightened the emotive quality of his style'.[184] He was never predictable. He was small and looked like a clever, good-natured, impish choirboy, and his music-making, though deeply serious, looked fun; he had the ability to make every member of an audience feel as if he or she belonged to an effervescent circle of friends. He was a supreme communicator and teacher, brimful of charm and exuberant vitality, who presented four weekly radio programmes for children for nearly five years and was listened to avidly by music-lovers of all ages. Of the box set of records, *Music of the Gothic Era*, which was released posthumously, one reviewer wrote that 'the records and the booklet are mutually illuminating to an extraordinary degree. . . . The listener is not so much presented with a complementary textbook as drawn into a process of discovery.'[185] Though he was meticulous and painstaking in acquiring the latest scholarly information about the music he was to perform, he hated academic obfuscation and could himself brilliantly encapsulate an epoch, the age of Guillaume de Machaut, the Notre Dame period, or explain a complicated concept like isorhythm.

He was convinced that performers should do their utmost to discover all they could about timbres and articulation and the performing conditions of early music repertories, but in performance he prized above all spontaneity. He loved jazz. He had no wish to exhibit historical specimens; all music worth performing, he thought, should be made to live in an historical present. 'A Machaut song should communicate as directly, albeit in a different way, as one by Schubert', he once said.[186] He recognized that musical presentation in live performances and in recording studio conditions might require subtly different approaches, but prepared for each with equal seriousness. He belonged to a generation that had grown up with LPs; they had played a central part in his musical experience and education; they were not simply adjuncts to musical experience but legitimate means of musical enjoyment and understanding in their own right. It was he who approached EMI in 1969: 'I have many ideas around which records of early music could be sold: would it be possible to have an opportunity to put some forward, backed by tape recordings?'[187] He reckoned that the long hours in the studio represented perhaps a tenth of the time he spent working on the creation of a recording. There was the planning of the programme, ensuring balance and coherence and an expressive progression through the sides of the discs, satisfying himself, for example, that a bold juxtaposition of timbres or moods in different pieces would stand repeated hearings; there was the writing of explanatory notes, and the selection of photographs and other illustrative material.

He himself thought that the twentieth-century enthusiasm for medieval and Renaissance music derived in part from a kind of nostalgia for a largely imaginary past, for better and brighter epochs, for times when life was more wholehearted and experience less fragmented, from a distaste for the violence and bleakness of the twentieth century. He also considered that it was evidence of a failure on the part of modern composers to address a mass audience. Though performances by the Early Music Consort intrigued music-lovers of all ages, they especially appealed to a younger generation who might have been expected to identify with the styles and accents of postwar composers. But in Europe at least, the eccentricities of many composers, the inwardness, the obsessive concern with creating a new musical language, the aggressiveness with which technical concerns were paraded before a bemused and uncomprehending public, all this repelled young audiences who could proclaim their difference by responding with enthusiasm to the charm and friendliness of David Munrow and to the distinctively new timbres he conjured up. For the sonorous image of his music-making undoubtedly had an enormous appeal, its brightness and clarity and translucent textures, its 'cleanness' as one (middle-aged) devotee of the Early Music Consort described it, whose effect he compared with the way Bach's Third Brandenburg Concerto cleared his head, physically and spiritually, when he was a teenager after the war, discovering classical music for himself through gramophone records.[188] Above all, Munrow wished to communicate with and to move his audiences and he succeeded because he was a brilliant musician and a modest, witty and inspirational human being. He was large-hearted and himself easily moved; he adored Elgar and hoped that perhaps one day he might conduct

Falstaff.[189] But he was a depressive,[190] and he died by his own hand at the age of thirty-three.

He had changed things, though. The prejudice against early music as being the refuge for those musicians whose techniques could not quite meet the demands of the mainstream repertory of music after Bach was severely dented, and now early music too had its stars. David Munrow's performing persona radiated warmth and friendliness but he was nonetheless still a magician, a virtuoso wizard whose technical achievements inspired spontaneous cheers but also awe. 'Early music' was now marketable, profitable, and even the major record companies began to devote resources especially to early music on specialist labels like Decca's Florilegium and EMI's Reflexe.

Twentieth-century music: the major labels

In 1957 Columbia issued a box set of four long-playing records of 'the complete Webern'. This was at a time when Webern was being created a patron saint by the avant-garde, partly because of the clarity of his structures and the ease with which they could be analysed. Inevitably the mystery that surrounded him made him all the more attractive: his isolation, his obscurity, his tenacity of purpose, the curious circumstances of his death, the very difficulty of obtaining his scores. Webern was, as Boulez's metaphor had it, 'THE threshold',[191] over which the avant-garde would boldly step into new expressive worlds. But though of crucial importance to a small number of the leading creative thinkers of a new generation of musicians after the war, his music was hardly known in performance. As Herbert Eimert pointed out: 'In thirty-five years of creative endeavour, from 1908 to 1943, Webern wrote thirty-one works. None of them was a sensation, a landmark, a hit. . . . None of them imprinted itself on the musical consciousness of the times, in either a good or a bad way.'[192] Crucial though he might be to a handful of young composers – themselves little known to the general public – Webern was completely unknown to the musical world at large. And yet in 1957 Columbia issued a set of four long-playing records of 'the complete' works, all the works of Webern, this was, with opus numbers. In fact Columbia only agreed to these discs because the most famous of their recording artists insisted upon it. Stravinsky refused to record unless his associate Robert Craft was allowed to use time at the end of a Stravinsky session, or to go overtime, in order to tape one more of Webern's short pieces. Craft was always given the 'stingiest' amount of studio time; none of the recording sessions at which the Webern set was recorded were given over to Webern completely, and Stravinsky himself contributed to the Columbia studio costs. And it was Stravinsky – not a company man – who sat in the control room and acted as a kind of producer for the Webern recordings.[193] This was not just disinterested philanthropy, not simply altruistic generosity; Stravinsky was eager to discover this music for himself, to feed his own creative needs, to align himself with what he considered the most interesting and progressive creative thinkers of a new generation. When he said 'we' during these years, he explained, he meant 'the generation who are now saying "Webern and me"'.[194]

The players Robert Craft used for these Webern performances were freelance musicians working for Hollywood film companies. When he had obtained the music – most of the scores photostats of Webern's own manuscript – and had had parts written out, Craft rehearsed the musicians individually, and bribed them by allowing them to play in addition other music at the concert series he was running at that time – Monday Evening Concerts, Evenings on the Roof – a Brahms or a Beethoven sonata, for instance. No-one was paid for rehearsing, and for a performance only $28. In the end there was a certain prestige in being involved, as it became recognized that the discs would be a trail-blazing.[195] The release of these discs was hailed as an event of the greatest significance by critics, 'this wonderful box set' Ernst Krenek called it,[196] and Jeremy Noble, reviewing it in *The Gramophone* in 1959, noted that it had attained 'an almost legendary status among people with any interest in contemporary music'.[197] He considered it the twentieth-century equivalent of the sixteenth-century 'musica reservata', essentially music for the connoisseur.[198] No doubt sales would hardly have justified Columbia themselves investing in such a project and covering session costs and artists' fees in the normal way. But undoubtedly the records created an interest in the music far beyond the hermetic cabals of avant-garde musicians themselves.

In the 1960s the classical division of Columbia Records (CBS) issued individual compositions by avant-garde composers such as Cage, Feldman, Boulez and Karlheinz Stockhausen, and the complete works of several still controversial twentieth-century composers such as Schoenberg and Varèse, and a 100th anniversary album of the music of Charles Ives in 1974, and in 1979 the complete works, or almost the complete works, of Carl Ruggles. But in general a very small amount of contemporary music was issued by the major record companies and what was issued of modernist music from the Second Viennese School onwards was done in a haphazard and unmethodical way. When the major record companies did issue contemporary music it was very often subsidized in some way. Before the Second World War the British Council had carried out a survey of all the British music on record and identified 'lamentable gaps' – in old music as well as new, works by Byrd and Purcell, some of which they then proceeded to fill by sponsoring recordings through the Gramophone Company and Decca; in this way were released recordings of Bax's Third Symphony and *The Garden of Fand*, Berkeley's Divertimento, Bliss's Piano Concerto, Bush's Dialectic Quartet, Finzi's *Dies natalis*, Moeran's Symphony in G minor, Vaughan Williams's Symphony no. 5 and *Flos Campi* and Michael Tippett's Second String Quartet.[199]

In 1965 the first discs were released by EMI in a project called 'Music Today', whose aim was to record modern works 'which do not appear very frequently, if at all, in the concert repertoire'.[200] The sponsor was the Calouste Gulbenkian Foundation and the aim of the series was 'to present a broad conspectus of the musical scene over the past 30 years',[201] avoiding musical propaganda and musical party lines, as an adviser on the project explained. There was Schoenberg's Suite for Strings, written in 1934, which is firmly set in the key of G major, and, for that reason, avoided by the doctrinaire champions of atonality and yet also bypassed by those who rejected Schoenberg and all his doings as the 'destroyer of tonality'; on the same disc there was Benjamin Britten's little-known Prelude and Fugue for Strings op. 29 of 1943, and the cantata, *Ô Saisons, Ô Châteaux* (1946), by Elisabeth Lutyens, a composer who took account of Schoenberg's stylistic concerns and who, as a result, made little headway to begin with amongst her compatriots, the insular and conservative English. The series included a disc devoted to the Schoenberg pupil Roberto Gerhard, Spanish by birth but English by adoption, one with Kurt Weill's two symphonies, another of music by the Greek composer who had composition lessons with both Schoenberg and Weill, Nikos Skalkottas; there was a disc of works by Harrison Birtwistle, another of music by Peter Maxwell Davies, one with pieces by Messiaen, Boulez and Koechlin, one with music by Dallapiccola, Busoni and Wolpe.

Glock and the BBC

In England interest in twentieth-century music and in the newest music was fuelled by the appointment in 1959 of William Glock as the BBC's Controller of Music. Glock was an exceptionally open-minded critic, writer, teacher, lecturer on music, pianist – he had been a pupil of Schnabel in Berlin in the 1930s – and persuasive advocate of new music. He was determined to undermine the Corporation's 'middle-of-the-road' policy regarding contemporary music; 'broadcasting on the whole', he thought, 'still gave the impression that contemporary music was led, for example, by Samuel Barber in the United States and by Poulenc in France'.[202] He had an obligation, he thought, to allow musicians and music-lovers to acquaint themselves with what the best creative minds of a younger generation in Europe were achieving, to understand the preoccupations of Boulez and Stockhausen in Europe and John Cage in America. He devised series of broadcast concerts which boldly juxtaposed music of different periods and in different styles, from the fourteenth century to contemporary works. He programmed Schoenberg's *Serenade* with the Beethoven Septet, *Pierrot Lunaire* with the Goldberg Variations, Byrd's *Civitas sancti tui* and *Assumpta est Maria* with Boulez's *Improvisation: Une dentelle s'abolit* (from *Pli selon pli*), Machaut's *Messe de Nostre Dame*, a repeat of the Boulez and, to finish with, two more motets by Byrd, *Ave Regina coelorum* and *Beata viscera*. Glock juxtaposed Tallis and Schoenberg, Byrd and Dallapiccola, Carver and Cornelius Cardew; he sandwiched each part of Tallis's Lamentations between chamber music by Haydn, Webern and Hindemith; he placed Schoenberg's *Verklärte Nacht* between Cornysh's *Salve Regina* and Taverner's Mass 'Gloria tibi Trinitas'.

And for such adventurous programmes there was often an audience at home of 100,000, 'enough to have filled the Wigmore Hall or St John's, Smith Square, 150 times'.[203] Glock also revolutionized the repertory played at the Henry Wood Promenade Concerts, concerts on a different scale altogether. On many of the Prom evenings the audience in the Royal Albert Hall would number four or five thousand and increased television coverage with the opening of BBC2 in 1964 meant that the total of those viewing and listening to the Proms at home in the late 1960s must have reached between fifty and a hundred million each season.[204] From the beginning he was determined to introduce to the large, non-specialist Prom audiences those twentieth-century masterpieces which had hitherto been kept from them; among the works he included in the first Prom season he organized in 1960 which had never before been heard in the series were Debussy's *Jeux*, Schoenberg's Orchestral Variations op. 31, Webern's Six Orchestral Pieces op. 6, Bartók's Sonata for two pianos and percussion, and Stravinsky's Symphony in C, Symphony in Three Movements, and *Oedipus Rex*.[205] These explorations were possible, Glock was sure, since by the late 1950s a new audience had been created, 'more knowledgeable and sophisticated', through the Third Programme itself and through the long-playing record.[206]

In the late 1960s the programmes of the BBC Symphony Orchestra were exceptionally adventurous and wide-ranging, Colin Davis cultivating the eighteenth- and nineteenth-century classics, and others – and in particular Pierre Boulez, who was to serve as Chief Conductor between 1971 and 1975 – exploring twentieth-century music and contemporary music. In a few months of 1967 and 1968, for example, were heard the British première of Penderecki's *Music from the Psalms of David*, Dallapiccola's *Tre Laudi*, Gilbert Amy's *Triade*, Stravinsky's *Le Rossignol*, Gunther Schuller's *Seven Studies on Themes of Paul Klee*, Henze's *Five Neapolitan Songs*, with the performances directed by Boulez including works by Berg and Varèse and Messiaen and Schoenberg and, with Michel Tabachnik and Edward Downes, Stockhausen's *Gruppen*.

Boulez was perceived as an 'educator and stimulator' of public taste,[207] which were essentially the roles William Glock himself wished to fulfil. He wanted to offer the public 'every imaginable kind of good music', but also thought it necessary to emphasize, at any given moment, to give a little more than their 'natural share' of programme time, certain works which might have previously been neglected for whatever reason, or works which might catch public imagination because of particular changing circumstances – because of the passionate advocacy of a rising star performer or a brilliant new ensemble, or because of the particular concerns of a composer or group of composers – which circumstances could only be discerned by hunch, or by sympathetic judgement, or by sensitivity and tact, and only exploited by a willingness to take risks. This kind of emphasis Glock described as 'creative unbalance'. It followed from a determination not simply to reflect but to assist in forming public taste and to anticipate its enthusiasms.[208] When he was once asked what he wanted to offer radio listeners, he answered: 'What they will like tomorrow.'[209]

Subsidies for new music

But still, on commercial recordings new music remained largely the province of specialist labels. It always had been. In America the subscription publication *New Music Quarterly* (later *Edition*) – founded in 1927 – published 'ultra-modern' new scores (the publisher's description in the first issue)[210] by North Americans chiefly, but also some Central and South Americans, some Soviet composers and miscellaneous other works – Schoenberg's *Klavierstück* op. 33b, and Webern's *Geistlicher Volkstext* op. 17 no. 2 among them.[211] Between 1927 and 1942 it was run by the composer Henry Cowell, and Charles Ives kept the enterprise afloat with monthly contributions of $100.[212] Between 1933 and 1948 discs were also issued; the label was first called New Music Quarterly Recordings and then after 1940 named New Music Recordings.[213] In all, sixty-four sides were issued, sixty-two works by thirty-eight composers, and all were first recordings. The artists included the flautist Georges Barrère, Bernstein and Copland as pianists, Quincy Porter playing his own *Suite for viola alone*, the harpist Carlos Salzédo, and the conductor Nicolas Slonimsky – conducting the earliest orchestral music by Ives on record – and Joseph Szigeti in the first recording of Ives's Violin Sonata no. 4.[214] There were recordings of music by Crawford, Riegger, Chávez and Adolph Weiss; in 1934 Nicolas Slonimsky conducted 'Barn Dance', an excerpt from Ives's *Washington's Birthday* and 'In the Night', the third piece from Ives's *Theater Set* for chamber orchestra, and in 1938 Varèse's *Octandre*. Subscribers received four twelve-inch records per year, while non-subscribers could purchase single discs through The Gramophone Shop in New York, an outlet at the time for rare, esoteric items and obscure imports.[215]

Composers' Recordings Inc. was founded in 1954 by two composers, Douglas Moore and Otto Luening, and the record producer Oliver Daniel of CBS. It was originally funded by the American Composers Alliance, an organization collecting royalties on performances for unpublished composers. ACA licensed recording rights to companies like RCA, Columbia and Mercury, and had inserted a retrieval clause by which tapes reverted to ACA should a disc be deleted. So these tapes could be reissued by the new company; there was also start-up money from the Alice M. Ditson Fund of Columbia University and a recording award from the American Academy and Institute of Art and Letters. In 1977 CRI became a not-for-profit corporation, and therefore had tax-exempt status, and from the mid-1980s it has actively sought funds from charities, corporations and private individuals. The main responsibility for covering the costs of producing a master-tape for CRI had always been the composer's, by means of a patron or a grant, and universities gave assistance, and foundations and corporations helped; the American Academy and Institute of Arts and Letters, the Naumberg Foundation, and ACA gave regular recording awards. The emergence of the label occurred at a time, the 1950s, when the curricula of American university music departments were widening to include composition and performance; suddenly there were many more jobs for composers, composers moreover with steady salaries and access to grants and awards, whose professional advancement required evidence of their activities, who wished to keep abreast of their colleagues' creative endeavours over a vast continent. Elliott Carter remarked that he would rather buy a recording of new music for both artistic and financial reasons: the score of one of his twenty-minute pieces cost, in the mid-1980s, $100, a recording of the same piece cost then half of $9.95, being one side of a twelve-inch LP. So new sources of funding were available and a very small but dependable market had been created; the average sale in 1984 of each CRI release was about 1,000 copies, the size of the initial, and often the only pressing. Sales might settle down later to perhaps one hundred copies a year, but the recordings all remained in print and available.

The label seemed to embrace repertory of widely differing styles, music with or without tonal centres, works constructed with tone rows, works in conventional forms and traditional instruments and works for electronics, composers as diverse as Ned Rorem, Milton Babbitt, Sessions, Crumb, Ralph Shapey, Barbara Kolb, George Rochberg, Joan Tower and Ezra Sims, and anthologies, 'Voces Americanas' – of composers drawing on the 'Hispanic heritage' – of electronic music pioneers like Otto Luening, and Ussachevsky and Davidovsky. And yet it did not avoid criticism, of pursuing an 'ideology', of bias towards the new-music academic establishment, and particularly the styles of East Coast university composers, the 'Columbia-Princeton' axis. Minimalist composers – Reich, Riley, Glass, Adams – did not figure among its composers. Philip Glass started his own highly successful record company, which required no subsidy. In the view of some, CRI ghettoized new music, sustained new music as the preserve of a self-serving community of academic composers who were sustained by grants and subsidies. CRI seemed to acknowledge their staid image and the limited stylistic range of the music they issued when they launched in 1992 an 'Emergency Music' series, featuring young composers 'working in non-academic styles, often drawing on minimalism and popular music'. Certainly recordings of the music released by CRI over the decades were not profitable, and recordings of performances of this repertory would never have been made at all without subsidy and sponsorship.[216]

Other countries too created subsidized labels for new music. Musique Française d'Aujourd'hui was an initiative of the Sacem Foundation and Radio France and major French record companies. In England NMC – New Music Cassettes, originally – was founded in 1988 as a charitable company with substantial funding from the Holst Foundation; the company issued singles, mid-length and full-length compact discs of music by living British composers and aimed 'to reflect the seriousness and diversity of contemporary music'.[217] In Sweden there was the label Phono Suecia, founded in 1966 by Sweden's performing rights society, whose function included disseminating information; the society had been making subsidies to record companies and also issuing its own productions since 1948. Phono Suecia discs were devoted to contemporary classical music and jazz and the first recording, issued to mark the International Society for Contemporary Music's 40th World Music Festival held in Stockholm in 1966, contained music by Bo Nilsson, Karl-Erik Welin, Siegfried Naumann and Åke Hermanson. Later came an anthology of Swedish music from all periods, Musica Sveciae, edited by the Royal Swedish Academy of Music and produced in collaboration with leading Swedish record companies; the project was planned in the mid-1980s to comprise about 160 CDs, ten or twelve being issued each year. And then in 1998 came the first issues in a series called Musica Sveciae Modern Classics, twenty CDs of Swedish music written between 1910 and 1945 by such composers as Hilding Rosenberg, Moses Pergament, Erland von Koch, Dag Wirén and Lars-Erik Larsson, the result of collaboration between the Swedish performing rights society, the Swedish

Music Information Centre, the Swedish Broadcasting Corporation, and the Royal Academy of Music in Stockholm. There have been three Anthologies of Australian Music on Disc, a project launched in 1989 by the Canberra School of Music, the Australian Music Centre and the National Film and Sound Archive and funded through the Commonwealth Government, which by 1998 totalled thirty CDs. One of the largest presentations of a country's music, a historical survey also containing new music, was New World Records, established in 1975 to record a comprehensive representation of American music for free distribution to libraries and educational institutions. It was funded initially with a $4 million grant from the Rockefeller Foundation and the aim was to present all aspects of American musical history, building on what CRI, the Louisville Orchestra First Edition Series and the Nonesuch label had achieved through broader and more systematic coverage. The intention was to cover 'everything from concert art to calliope music, marching bands to bebop, film music to field hollers, symphonies to theater songs – music of every genre, spanning well over 200 years of America's history and cultural heritage'.[218]

Composers' attitudes to recordings

A number of composers saw early on in the history of recording possibilities for a new, quite different musical art, with the composer casting his music in finished, final form on the recorded disc. No longer would there be 'deficiencies in the ensemble, no late entries, no "coughing" horn players, no broken strings, no out-of-tune tympani, no mistakes in interpretation', enthused a young German composer in 1925; from now on the musical work of art would be fixed on a disc 'with mathematical precision'. He confidently proclaimed a new era and welcomed it with the greatest relish: 'Sentimental resistance won't be able to hamper the development of music. . . . The role of the interpreter belongs to the past.'[219]

When composers between the wars did write for the gramophone – which was very rare – it was not in an endeavour to create new sounds and new worlds but simply to reproduce old ones more conveniently. In 1934 Roy Harris wrote a piece for flute and string quartet to fit on the single side of a twelve-inch disc called *Four Minutes and Twenty Seconds*,[220] and Stravinsky wrote his *Serenade* for piano in four movements, each of which was designed to fit on a single side of a ten-inch disc, to avoid, as he said, 'all the trouble of cutting and adapting'.[221] And even the enthusiasm felt by many composers for tape in the 1950s soon evaporated when it became clear how time-consuming and inflexible the generation of sounds was still, even with the manipulation of tape and with a mixture of electronic and acoustic sound sources. When it took three or four weeks' work to construct a minute of electronic music,[222] as it did in one of the best-equipped studios of the 1950s, at Cologne Radio, it was not surprising that so few composers were attracted to the new medium. Few were given the chance to experiment, and few had the tenacity and patience to carry experimentation through into finished works of art. Stockhausen was one who would not be deflected from creating with such intractable materials and with his *Gesang der Jünglinge* created a work which has retained its sophisticated power and originality. It mingles transformations of a boy's voice singing the text of the Benedicite with electronic sounds. But though it was soon issued as a disc[223] it was originally conceived for performance in Cologne Cathedral, issuing from five separated loudspeakers, and the space was conceived as an integral part of the work. And a work like Stockhausen's *Sternklang* was written for five groups of instruments spread out in an open-air setting, and the stereo recording can only begin to suggest the envisaged effect.

Even with the comparatively primitive techniques of the 1960s, popular music was evolving different kinds of music and different kinds of musical creation, with the performers working with a producer, using the recording studio and sixteen-track tape recorder to piece together little bits of music, and single lines of sound, in ways not unlike the composer wrestling with a work's constituent parts, with tiny fragments of his music as he struggles to build up structures on manuscript paper. One of the most famous early examples of this is the Beatles' album *Sgt. Pepper*, which was released after the group had announced they would give no more live concerts but exist solely as a studio band. It was only with the arrival of the synthesizer in the mid-1960s and with the development of compositional programmes for computers, and then, in the mid-1980s, the digital equipment for sound synthesis, that composers had the means of creating music more easily, that composers could work alone without the need for very expensive facilities. And yet even then few exploited these possibilities,

and fewer still aimed to create works for publication by means of commercial disc or cassette.

It's true that the American label Nonesuch commissioned a number
of composers in the late 1960s to create works for long-playing disc,
including Charles Dodge's *Earth Magnetic Field*,[224] Donald Erb's *Music
for instruments and electronic sounds*,[225] Eric Salzman's *The Nude Paper
Sermon*,[226] Morton Subotnick's *Silver Apples of the Moon*,[227] *The Wild
Bull*,[228] and Charles Wuorinen's *Time's Encomium* for synthesized and
processed synthesized sound.[229] But these seemed not to be presented
for a wide general audience of music-lovers greedy for new musical
experiences but rather self-consciously for a community of composers,
especially composers in American universities who, in the second half
of the twentieth century, have been as characteristic a feature of the
musical community as composers in the employ of German princes in
the eighteenth. Charles Wuorinen introduced his work on the sleeve
by explaining that 'the basic materials are the twelve tempered pitch
classes and pitch-derived time relations'. The RCA Synthesizer at the
Columbia-Princeton Electronic Music Center in New York would of
course be 'familiar through several works of Milton Babbitt'; and, lest
his potential audience was unsure whether this composer could be led
into the drawing-room, or at least the common-room, eloquent testimony was given as to his suitability, for he had been 'the recipient of
numerous grants and awards, among them the Lili Boulanger Memorial Award, BMI-SCA Awards, Bearns, Alice M. Ditson, and Guggen-
heim Fellowships, and commissions from the Ford Foundation,
Berkshire Music Center, Koussevitsky, and Fromm Music Foundations'. And he had been honoured by the American Academy of Arts
and Letters. Lest anyone still harboured the suspicion that Donald Erb
was not a really serious composer because he had written this piece for
a commercial recording, he assured his audience in the sleeve-note that
Reconnaissance, 'a composition in five movements' – the title 'simply
gives some clue as to the rather exploratory nature of the piece' –
though it had undergone 'extensive revision' for this recorded version,
in fact in earlier versions had been performed in the 1967 Music In
Our Time concert series in New York, at Expo '67, and at the Monday
Evening Concerts in Los Angeles.[230]

Alexander Goehr thought that the character and idiom of much
avant-garde music of the second half of the twentieth century – he was
thinking particularly of the music of György Ligeti, of Elliott Carter, of

Xenakis, and of Birtwistle – seemed ideally suited to the recorded medium.[231] This was partly because of this music's intricacy, partly because much of it was constructed out of tiny figures and motifs endlessly repeated, partly because of the absence of long, 'expressive' lines, partly because of its impersonal character. Goehr recognized that the cause of modern music 'would be significantly furthered if, instead of sponsoring endless concerts of first performances, resources were allocated for recording new works', works which, he thought, could be conceived just for records.[232] These comments, made by a distinguished and well-informed creative musician, are odd only because they were made in 1987. Musicians had been expressing such views for decades, and other kinds of musicians, popular and experimental composers, had been attempting to realize such ideas for many years. Surely, the German composer Herbert Eimert wondered in 1955, isn't it the symphony recorded on tape or disc which is the synthetic article, and electronic music, the music especially created for the disc or the tape which is the real thing?[233] But it was unusual, still, in the 1980s, for most composers who felt they belonged to the central European traditions even to imagine themselves working in this way, mastering the studio techniques required or engaging in collaborative acts of creation. And a fundamental reason for the attitudes of a great many composers towards commercial recordings derived from their suspicion of mass audiences.

When audiences change, the character of music changes, history has repeatedly demonstrated. The twentieth century has witnessed a revolutionary change in music, the development of an enormously enlarged potential audience, and many commentators have pointed out that most composers seem steadfastly to have refused to acknowledge this fact. And some have damned them as a result. After the Second World War, one of them thought, 'composers essentially abrogated their responsibilities as citizens in the name of their art'.[234] Most of the classical musicians in Europe and America in the twentieth century discovered themselves and their love of music through the masterpieces of the great classical tradition, through Bach and Mozart and Beethoven and Brahms and Wagner and Debussy. They contemplated the tradition with awe as well as love, and felt acutely a sense of responsibility to preserve its richness, to create works of comparable technical sophistication and emotional profundity. They lived, as the American composer Aaron Copland put it, 'in constant communion with great works, which in turn seems to make it *de rigueur* for them to attempt to emulate the great works by writing one of their own on an equivalent plane'.[235] In attempting to encourage his fellow musicians to take changed circumstances into account, Copland denied that he was advocating a watering down of musical ideas for mass consumption; he insisted he was simply stating what for him was obvious, that different occasions will require different kinds of music; some times and occasions and audiences will require 'complex' and 'dense' musical arguments, other audiences on different kinds of occasions will require 'simpler', more 'direct', less 'severe' or 'abstruse' styles, and there seemed to him no reason why the same composer should not become fluent in cultivating different styles or manners for different occasions.[236] Some of the modern composer's output at least should surely address the large audiences now available through recordings. Hindemith after all had declared in 1928 that the days were over of composing for the sake of composing; the modern composer wrote for a purpose, and the demand for music was so great that it was essential that the function of a particular musical work should be understood and clearly defined by those who created music and those who used it. But a Romantic, nineteenth-century concept of the creative artist remained enormously influential in shaping the way many composers – as well as many audiences – regarded their activities. As one of the leading avant-garde musicians after the Second World War expressed it, composing music is 'a gesture of communication, but communication with the unknown, with the infinite'; the composer must remember his responsibility not only to the public, but to himself, 'a responsibility that should lead him to turn to . . . the public of the future'.[237] In the circumstances it was hardly surprising that Aaron Copland so seldom found young composers in the 1950s who were willing to contemplate writing 'a good piece for high school band'.[238]

The weight of the tradition and the fear of compromise, of dilution for a mass audience, preyed on the minds of many of those who had been called to become creative musicians. It required a particular combination of visionary and humanitarian to respond enthusiastically to the challenges and opportunities recordings offered towards the end of the century. One such was the eighty-year-old Michael Tippett, who had devoted his life to attempting to fashion 'images of abounding, generous, exuberant beauty in an age of fear, mediocrity and horror comics';[239] he wished he had been younger and able to acquire the techniques which would enable him to address the new kind of fragmented audiences, the solitary listener, the small group listening at home: 'I can't go into the studio and learn how to make records myself using the latest electronics. But I'm fascinated by what is done. You publish your music through a record which then goes round the world. The recording belongs to human beings.'[240] But after a hundred years of recordings it remained true that most composers working in what they might agree to designate the West European traditions did not wish to write for and to find new audiences through recordings.

Duplication of repertory

With each technological development – from acoustic to electrical recording, from shellac 78 rpm disc to vinyl 33⅓ rpm disc, from mono to stereo, from analogue to digital, from LP to CD – a market was created for duplication of the recorded repertory, to hear the most popular repertory recorded afresh with all the benefits of improved technology. But there were many recordings which were so popular or which preserved performances of such distinction and insight that there were constant demands that these be kept in the catalogues or reissued. Many recordings from the early 1900s were still in the catalogues twenty years later, and from the early 1920s to the late 1940s HMV retained in circulation a selection of their early recordings, in the so-called 'Catalogue No.2', containing 'records of unique and historical interest', preserving 'the art of a past generation', giving 'a wonderful impression of the art and personality of many famous figures – now, alas, removed by the hand of death . . . singers, players, composers and conductors whose names are among the greatest that the musical world has ever known', records which 'are imperfect, technically, as compared with those made . . . by improved modern processes' but which should still be preserved because of 'their interest and importance'. Here were found some of Caruso's early records, Saint-Saëns playing three of his piano solos and accompanying Gabrielle Guillaume in his *Elégie* op. 143, Grieg playing his 'Au Printemps', Joachim playing a Brahms Hungarian Dance, Sir Charles Santley singing John Hatton's character song 'Simon the Cellarer' and his 'To Anthea' and 'The Vicar of Bray', and famous performances by

Tamagno and Sarasate and Battistini and Tetrazzini and Melba and McCormack, by Clara Butt and Edward Lloyd and by Chaliapin, Pachmann and Paderewski.

In the early 1950s many critics were fearful that with the appearance of the long-playing disc many recordings from the first half of the century would vanish for ever. In the first few years very little was reissued in England, though there were historical reissues in the United States. But by the mid-1950s there were LP reissues of Caruso, Supervia, McCormack and in 1956 a five-LP set called *Fifty Years of Great Operatic Singing*. In 1961 HMV issued two LPs to mark the death of Sir Thomas Beecham, an anthology of recordings made between 1915 and 1958. The centenary of the birth of Dame Nellie Melba was marked by a selection of recordings made mostly in 1904; in 1962 Pathé issued three-disc volumes of early vocal recordings: *L'Age d'or de la Scala de Milan*, *L'Age d'or de l'Opéra*, and *L'Age d'or de l'Opéra Comique*; in 1963 American Columbia's 1903 'Grand Opera Series' was issued on two LPs. In 1969 Caruso's 1904–6 US recordings were reissued. In 1973 EMI released a set of two discs and a 64-page booklet marking seventy-five years of commercial recording. In 1974 Deutsche Grammophon issued a five-disc set of historical recordings which included Nikisch's 1913 version of Beethoven's Fifth Symphony and in 1976 a two-disc set to mark the centenary of the Bayreuth Festival; in the same year World Records issued a five-disc set of Beecham's interwar recordings of Delius together with a reprint of Beecham's book on Delius, and HMV issued *The Art of Maria Callas* as a four-disc set, and a five-disc set of *Dame Nellie Melba – The London Recordings (1904–26)*. In 1979 Pearl released *The Art of John McCormack, 1904–1928*, a six-disc set. Between 1977 and 1989 HMV issued four box sets of 'The Record of Singing', forty-six LPs in total, containing performances by more than 700 singers from the first half of the century. The first volume contained recordings made up to 1914, the second volume recordings made between 1914 and 1925, the third between 1926 and 1939, and the fourth made between 1939 and 1954. EMI have had a long-running series of LPs and CDs called *Great Recordings of the Century* and there has been an 'HMV Treasury' series on CD as well as on LP: 'Dame Nellie Melba – the London Recordings', and collections of Lipatti, Kreisler, Ferrier, Gigli, Cortot, Harriet Cohen. In the 1970s there were anthologies of 'Great Tenors of the World', and 'Great British mezzo-sopranos and contraltos', and a disc of vocal reissues put out to coincide with the publication of John Steane's book of the same name, *The Grand Tradition.*

The technological advantages of digital recording and the CD increased this activity enormously with labels like Nimbus's Prima Voce and Pavilion's Pearl and Opal labels, and Testament, and Romophone, and Biddulph, and Symposium, and many others, all devoted to reissues of old material. The same recordings have been assembled and reassembled in endless anthologies: of the complete commercial recordings of an artist, of all these but with the addition of pirated radio tapes of live performances, and perhaps some rehearsal material that has recently come to light; of the 'early' recordings made by a performer, or the recordings made in Europe, or all the Beethoven performances, or in anthologies of English singers, or in anthologies of sopranos, or as issued previously but with a different transfer 'philosophy' – employing different transfer techniques, using computer-enhancing equipment, or avoiding any electronic treatment and playing discs on an acoustic gramophone through an enormous horn and using thorn needles which reproduce limited frequency range but sound sweeter to some ears, giving a voice more immediacy and character.[241]

Mechanical copyright resides in a recording for fifty years, after which time the recorded performance enters the public domain. If the musical work recorded is itself in the public domain – if it's a symphony by Beethoven – all that it is necessary for a company to do is to locate a copy, remaster it and market and distribute it. The old and large record companies have huge advantages since they have usually built up archives of original recordings, often metal masters of shellac discs, or if not metal masters then at least mint copy wax masters, and master-tapes of LPs or even first-generation tapes before the final edited tape used for the tape-to-disc transfer. But many small or very small companies devote themselves to this activity. Peter Biddulph sold violins but contemporary violin-playing he did not like; he disliked the absence of finesse, the way players were encouraged to make more and more 'noise', the standardization of tone qualities and styles of playing, the lack of idiosyncrasy. So he created the Biddulph label in 1989 and hoped that young players would absorb 'the gracefulness of Kreisler, the sensuousness of Thibaud' and so enrich their playing. The success of the label has led to piano and orchestral reissues, and a growing number of new recordings.[242]

The ability of the performer's name alone to generate sales meant that record companies would be keen for major artists to re-record repertory. Performing artists obviously develop and change and many have stressed that a recording is just one interpretation of a work; the day after it would have been different. And even if for Alfred Brendel himself an earlier interpretation of a Beethoven sonata does not now accord with his 'view' of the work, if an earlier recording has now been superseded, connoisseurs of his art may disagree, or may wish to preserve all such an eminent artist's interpretations of a piece, however slight the perceivable differences might be, and less experienced music-lovers know only that they have been recommended to buy Beethoven and Alfred Brendel, and most record companies see no point in declaring in bold type that a record was made forty-three years ago. So Brendel has recorded the Beethoven sonatas complete three times, and the Beethoven concertos complete four times, and all of the versions remain marketable.

But the result of accommodating a performer's whim has often been to create duplication which neither the record company nor the world appeared to want. In the 1950s Decca had a contract with the conductor Ernest Ansermet, who was renowned for his interpretation of Ravel and Debussy, Stravinsky and Bartók. His Orchestra of the Suisse Romande in Geneva was not outstanding in Decca's view but it was the cheapest on their books. But with it Ansermet wished to record Mozart, Beethoven and Brahms, which repertory Decca wanted to record with another orchestra on their books, the Vienna Philharmonic, who did not wish to be conducted by Ansermet, who anyway wished to use his Geneva musicians. It was the failure to resolve problems like these that would result in duplication that all but the most devoted fans of a performing artist would regard as unnecessary.[243] 'Unnecessary' recordings might also be made because a surplus of record company money at the end of the financial year would be taxed if it were not used up on making recordings, and a session taping well-known works could be quickly and easily arranged.[244]

So decades of performances of the same repertory which modern technology allowed to be reissued considerably enhanced, and the idiosyncratic interpretations of several decades by powerful recreative artists, and the great variety of performances of repertory from Bach to Elgar which have been fostered by the advocates of historically informed performing styles meant that a music-lover in England in 1998 could have chosen from ten recorded performances of Byrd's five-part Mass then available in the shops; from thirty-one of Bach's Mass in B minor; from thirty-nine sets of the Six Brandenburg Concertos, including the Paris École Normale under Cortot recorded in 1932, the Busch Chamber Players recorded in 1935, Karl Richter in 1958, Benjamin Britten and the English Chamber Orchestra in 1968; from thirty-three CD sets and two video performances of Handel's Messiah, including six versions of Mozart's arrangement of the work, and from five video performances; and from thirty-two CD sets of *Don Giovanni*, including the 1936 Glyndebourne Busch recording and the 1984 Glyndebourne Haitink version, Rosbaud's 1956 recording, Fricsay's 1958 recording, Leinsdorf's 1959 recording, Giulini's 1959 recording, Klemperer's 1966 version, Karl Böhm's 1967 version, and Colin Davis's 1973 recording with the Royal Opera House. There were two videos and 102 CDs available in 1998 of Mozart's Symphony no. 40; there were 108 CDs and four versions on video of Beethoven's Ninth Symphony; there were ninety-seven CDs and one LP of Beethoven's Fifth Piano Concerto; there were thirty-seven CDs of Fauré's Requiem. There were sixteen CD sets of *Tristan und Isolde*, one video recording, and a CD of the 1926/7 recordings of the abridged version conducted by Coates, Blech and Collingwood; there was Robert Heger's 1943 version, Knappertsbusch's 1950 interpretation, there was Furtwängler's 1952 version, Solti's 1960 recording, and Karajan's version recorded in 1970 and 1971. There were nine CD versions of *Der Rosenkavalier* and four video recordings on sale; the sound recordings include an abridged 1933 performance conducted by Robert Heger, a 1942 performance conducted by Clemens Krauss, a 1954 performance conducted by Erich Kleiber, a 1956 version conducted by Karajan, a 1968 performance conducted by Solti, and a 1969 performance conducted by Karl Böhm. There were fifty-four recordings of Stravinsky's *The Rite of Spring* available, including Rex Lawson's on pianola, an arrangement for four pianos, Stravinsky's own performances from 1929, 1940 and 1960, Monteux's in 1951, Eduard Van Beinum's in 1946, Igor Markevitch's in 1951 and 1959, Ernest Ansermet's in 1957, Boulez's in 1963, and in 1969, and in 1991, and Robert Craft's in 1995.

Live and recorded repertories at the end of the century

Towards the end of the century record companies recognized ever more specialized markets and tastes. In 1995 EMI Classics divided their labels into full price, mid-price and bargain price compact discs and each category was divided by repertory. The full-price labels included four categories: *Baroque Special*: 'Music from the time of J. S. Bach, his forerunners, contemporaries, and successors' performed in 'authentic interpretations by young and aspiring ensembles'; *British Composers*: the works of British composers in new recordings; *Composers in Person*: a series of historical recordings of composers performing their own music, Elgar, Falla, Messiaen, Lehár, Roussel, Strauss, Stravinsky; *Reflexe*: devoted to 'authentic' performances 'from Early Music to the Romantics; its aim is to re-create the sound world of the composer'. In the mid-price category there were eight: *British Composers*: the works of British composers in reissued recordings; *Eminence*: 'The mid-price Classical Collection of top quality new recordings and reissues with foremost EMI artists'; *L'Esprit Français*: works by French composers of the nineteenth and twentieth centuries; *Matrix*: 'The Matrix series aims to open up new horizons to the more adventurous music-lover who is just starting to look beyond the standard repertoire for less familiar repertoire'; the series offered 'lesser-known works from the past 150 years'; *Références/Great Recordings of the Century*: 'with an emphasis on the pre-1955 era, this series includes legendary performers such as Caruso, Casals, Furtwängler, and Heifetz'; *Reflexe*: the 'authentic' performance mid-price series with 'many pioneering performances from the Early Music revival'; *Studio*: 'reissues featuring great names in wide-ranging repertoire – artists include du Pré, Richter, Menuhin, Oistrakh'; *Studio + Plus*: this series offered 'essential repertoire . . . performed by artists such as Karajan, Perlman, and Muti'. And at budget price there were three more: *Classics for Pleasure/Lasar*: 'Best-known classics in distinguished performances'; *Profiles*: a series of 2CD sets of 'vintage EMI stereo recordings from the 50s and 60s featuring artists such as Solomon, Giulini, Kletzki, Kurtz and Kogan'; *Rouge et Noir*: 2CD sets 'with an intriguing combination of repertoire and artists'.[245]

Some of the small independent labels were very specialized indeed. Gimell for its first two decades recorded almost exclusively Renaissance unaccompanied polyphony and Collegium only English choral music; and these two labels were formed to record particular performing ensembles, Peter Phillips and the Tallis Scholars, and John Rutter and the Cambridge Singers. Bis was started by the husband of a flautist who was unable to obtain a record contract with an existing label.

Harmonia Mundi was founded as a result of a bet between journalists that one of them couldn't set up a record company, and its earliest recordings, in the 1960s, were of historic organs because production costs were low and there was a growing interest at that time in the sonorities of Baroque instruments.

The German label ECM, Editions of Contemporary Music, was founded in 1969 by a professional musician called Manfred Eicher, trained as a violinist, double-bass player and in composition, who considered creating a distinctive label a form of musical creativity. The repertory of ECM evolved simply 'through instinct', through the particular enthusiasms of the owner. The first releases were of Jan Garbarek and Keith Jarrett, and later ones have included the American minimalists Steve Reich and John Adams and the Estonian Arvo Pärt. Eicher's enthusiasms include painting, theatre and photography, and sleeve and booklet designs are his own;[246] the recorded music and its presentation are considered as an aesthetic whole; critics have remarked on the clarity and the bleakness and simplicity of much of the repertory, and on these same qualities that distinguish the acoustics chosen for recording and the design of record and sleeve. The label's distinctiveness is itself sometimes taken as a cultural badge; in 1994 a music critic reported overhearing two urbane music-lovers outside a concert hall discussing the kind of music they liked best: 'ECM', said one; a 'terse but entirely satisfactory response', in the view of the music critic.[247]

Nearly all independent labels issued a wide miscellaneous repertory; the major labels wished to record, principally, the greatest performing artists in the greatest repertory; when a taste, a market, had been created, the major labels sometimes moved in or even took over the pioneering label, Decca taking over Argo and L'Oiseau-Lyre, or Koch buying Schwann in 1987, or Philips taking over Gimell. The small independent labels could not afford the greatest artists, so they exercised their skill and cunning and identified markets for other repertories, for unknown music. Occasionally a small label did record a star performer: Bis recorded the first lieder recital of Birgit Nilsson; the managing director of Capriccio had been mightily impressed with Sándor Végh conducting Mozart in what seemed to him a completely new way at the Salzburg Festival in 1986 and was astonished to find that this musician, who was a pupil of Bartók and had played with Furtwängler and Casals, had no existing record contract. So he recorded him in Mozart.

Ninety per cent of the repertory that was issued by Capriccio had been neglected – there were works in the Capriccio catalogue by Kraus and Hasse and Schreker's *Der ferne Klang*, but the company had no ideological rule that it should not record mainstream repertory.[248] It was founded in 1982, and created a name for itself and some capital in the beginning by recording the first complete set of Beethoven symphonies on CD and selling almost half a million copies in the first year after release.[249]

The result of all this activity was that at the end of the century there were vast swathes of recorded repertory never or hardly ever given live performances, many of such works forgotten and unplayed since the time they were written when most of them had received but a handful of performances. There were recordings of works by Kozlovsky, Dubiansky, Teplov, Morkov, Ivanova, Siniavina, Bortnyansky, Kurakina, Lykochina, all of them eighteenth-century composers at the court of St Petersburg; songs by the nineteenth-century Danish composers Peter Arnold Heise and Peter Erasmus Lange-Müller; there was the complete orchestral music of Igor Markevitch, all the piano music of the Norwegian composer Geirr Tveitt, and of the Russian dodecaphonist Nikolay Andreyevich Roslavets, and of William Baines, the Yorkshire composer who died in 1922 at the age of twenty-three; there were anthems and devotional songs by the seventeenth-century Englishman George Jeffreys and secular songs by the twentieth-century Englishman John Jeffreys; there was liturgical music by the Cuban composer Esteban Salas y Castro (1725–1803), *maestro de capilla* of Santiago de Cuba Cathedral; there were works for orchestra by the Scottish composers William Wallace (1860–1940) and Sir Alexander Campbell Mackenzie (1847–1935); there were brand-new performances of Stokowski's arrangements of Mussorsgky and Bach; there were the string quartets of the Viennese-born composer Maddalena Lombardini Sirmen (1745–1818), and the quartets of Othmar Schoeck (1886–1957), and of Ernst Krenek (1900–91); there were recordings of Ferdinando Carulli's works for guitar and pianoforte, there were the complete piano works of Muzio Clementi, and the complete organ works of Max Reger, and organ music by Antonio Diana (fl. ca.1862) and Giovanni Morandi played on the organ built by the Serassi brothers from Bergamo in Piscogne in 1856; there were the complete piano trios of Joseph Rheinberger; there was William Boyce's *Peleus and Thetis*, and Rutland Boughton's *Bethlehem* and Bantock's *Cyprian Goddess* and Georg

Benda's *Cephalus and Aurora*; there was the London version with two pianos of Brahms's *Ein Deutsches Requiem*, there were Mozart's arrangements of Handel's *Ode for St Cecilia's Day* and *Acis and Galatea*, there were Bach's six sonatas for unaccompanied violin BWV 1001–6 and Paganini's 24 Caprices for Violin Solo op. 1 with piano accompaniments added by Robert Schumann, and Karg-Elert's arrangements for organ of Handel's 'Harmonious Blacksmith' variations, and the piano duet arrangements by Max Reger of the Brandenburg Concertos, and by Schoenberg of Schubert's Rosamunde D.797, and of Bruckner's Symphony no. 3 by Mahler, and of Mahler's Symphony no. 6 by Alexander von Zemlinsky, and of his Symphony no. 7 by Alfredo Casella.

In his book on Bach published in 1909 Parry expressed the view that because of the 'nature of his "artistic impulses"' the composer in his cantatas 'wrote as for the ideal performers he called up in imagination'. He doubted that these works had ever received anything like adequate performances in Bach's lifetime and there was little likelihood of the conditions being created in the future, he was sure, that would allow the development of the necessary performing skills. 'The melancholy conclusion seems inevitable that the greater part of this vast region of art is inaccessible except to those who can read it in imagination, and divine the wonderful revelations of the personality of the composer without the aid of their ears.'[250] But broadcasting and recording have created the conditions in which this music can be heard again.

The BBC began transmitting the cantatas in May 1928 in a weekly series of live broadcasts before invited audiences; when the Third Programme was founded in 1946 Anthony Lewis suggested that the complete Bach cantatas should be transmitted every seven years.[251] And by the 1970s two complete recordings were begun, though with considerable commercial reservations all round. Teldec began recording its complete cantata series in 1970, with some of them directed by Harnoncourt and some by Leonhardt; the series was completed by 1985 and released on eighty-three CDs, a total playing time of about 3,870 minutes. Helmuth Rilling's series, begun in 1969, was issued on various labels and also completed by 1985; this was released on 100 LPs in 1985 and in 1995 on sixty-nine CDs.

The Harnoncourt/Leonhardt set used contemporary instruments

and boy trebles and there were hardly ever any concert performances by these forces at that time. In fact the only 'performances' that were then possible were recorded ones, that is ones that were stitched together from several attempts, since neither the boys, nor the players of the Baroque trumpet, nor of the oboe d'amore, nor of the oboe da caccia had the virtuosity to meet Bach's technical demands. Holland has no tradition of boy trebles (though even English trebles would find these parts cruelly demanding), and female sopranos – and female altos singing with falsettists – have generally been employed in live performances given in Holland since those days. But the experience gained in making these recordings did enable wind players to acquire the expertise and the facility to give convincing live performances. And the experience of listening to these make-believe performances created audiences for these works. When Ton Koopman began recording another series of the cantatas in the 1990s, organized alongside were concert series given in Amsterdam, Rotterdam, The Hague and Utrecht.[252]

So the twentieth century has seen an almost incredible widening of the repertory of European art music that can be heard in performance. A lot of music is heard in live performances that would never be performed had recordings not created the tastes for it in audiences or given musicians the opportunities to acquire the necessary performing techniques. And there are large parts of the repertory that cannot be sustained by the economics of concert-giving, which exist simply in recorded performances and never, or hardly ever, are heard in concert halls or opera houses or churches, even much of the music of Henry Purcell, say – the great, long, orchestrally accompanied anthems, the viol fantasias, the semi-operas – even the early symphonies of Haydn or Mozart.

Our view of the history of music has been transformed. We can now, at least potentially, listen to the music of several centuries as we can examine centuries of fine art in galleries and museums. No longer is our experience of music in performance limited to a small number of the works actually composed, those great masterpieces which have been pronounced upon by earlier generations. The canon of great works can more easily be revised; recording in effect discovered Charles Ives and Gustav Mahler. And just as our understanding of Matisse, say, may be enriched by a knowledge of the work of Maurice de Vlaminck and Albert Marquet and Henri Manguin and Charles Camoin, so our appreciation and love of Mahler's art may now be enlarged by experiencing the music of Felix Weingartner, Max von Schillings, Hans Pfitzner and Sigmund von Hausegger.[253] The canon of great works as described by Sir Hubert Parry had a force and coherence that undoubtedly have been lost; infinite subtleties could be communicated when composers and listeners shared a deep knowledge of repertory of wide stylistic range encompassing Bach and Brahms and felt that such music lived in some kind of eternal present. Some have regretted too that the distinction they insisted upon between such works and those they considered merely of antiquarian interest has been lost or at least blurred.

The tastes of music-lovers, just like the skills of executants, have become more specialized; there is simply too much music available for anyone to develop a knowledge, let alone a love, of it all. A one-time controller of the BBC's Radio 3 was sure in the 1980s that the audience for serious music was completely fragmented: people liked organ recitals, or chamber music, or symphony concerts, he insisted, or opera, or the music of the nineteenth century, or new music. They were fierce in their exclusivity. And they certainly didn't like each other.[254] This was a deliberate simplification, but it was undoubtedly true that at the end of the twentieth century it was likely that any musician or music-lover would have developed a taste for an extremely individual and idiosyncratic mixture of musical works. No doubt not all twentieth-century composers or listeners were as energetically eclectic in their tastes as Peter Maxwell Davies was, who could enthuse over Mahler and medieval carols and Giovanni Gabrieli and Sibelius and Dunstable and foxtrots and Schoenberg and Victorian hymn tunes and Beethoven. But certainly there were indeed many who were just as passionately eclectic.

And as more and more older material was released it was not only the variety of repertory available on recordings that delighted some and bewildered others, but the startling differences in performing styles of the same repertory over the decades that made listeners begin to wonder just what performers thought they were doing. Performances of Bach and Mozart and Beethoven by the most admired re-creative artists a hundred years ago, which so moved our grandparents, left most listeners cold, or incredulous, or amused. This would surely be the fate of the most admired performances of our own time, the inescapable conclusion seemed to be. Leonard Bernstein required first of all humility in the executant, 'that he never interpose himself between the music and the audience', that all his efforts 'be made in the service of all the composer's meaning – the music itself'.[255] But what exactly was 'the music itself'?

III
Changes in Performing Styles Recorded

Early and late twentieth-century performing styles contrasted

The Italian soprano Adelina Patti made her adult debut at the age of sixteen in New York at the old Academy of Music. This was in 1859 and for the next half-century she was the most famous operatic diva in the world, her voice a lightweight soprano, lyrical and brilliant in tone. She made her first recordings in December 1905 when she was sixty-two. When she first heard her recorded voice – she was singing 'Voi che sapete' from Mozart's *Le nozze di Figaro* – she did not faint like Hans von Bülow, or lament on her shortcomings like Max Pauer; on the contrary she was mightily impressed: 'She threw kisses into the [recording] trumpet and kept on saying: "Ah! mon Dieu! maintenant je comprends pourquoi je suis Patti! Oh oui! Quelle voix! Quelle artiste! Je comprends tout!"' But it was said with such childlike wonder and excitement that her accompanist was moved rather than appalled.[1] When today we listen to her singing the simplest songs like 'The last rose of summer', or Stephen Foster's 'Old Folks at Home', the frequent portamentos make her singing style sound immediately very old-fashioned, but the actual tone quality is exceptionally pure, steady and transparent, especially so for a soprano in her sixties. There is generous rubato by the standards of the late twentieth century, and it is constantly employed. Her account of Bellini's 'Casta diva' will surprise those used to performances by Maria Callas or Leontyne Price not only because of the rubato and portamenti but especially because of the ornamentation added to the repeated verse, of which there is no hint in the score, and the greatly extended cadenza at the final cadence; the trill by Patti at this cadence (added by most singers throughout the century) is rapid and narrow – it could almost be mistaken for the kind of continuous vibrato employed by most modern opera singers – beautifully controlled, subtle and unforced, and gives a hint of a smaller-scale operatic style than any cultivated in the opera houses at the end of the twentieth century.

Similar characteristics are demonstrated in the recordings of an Italian contemporary of Patti, the brilliant high baritone Mattia Battistini, who made his debut at the Teatro Argentina in Rome in *La favorita* in 1878. Some contemporaries maintained that the colour and tone quality of his voice were never adequately captured on records – that they didn't 'give you a *shadow* of his real quality . . . his voice was so beautiful, you cannot imagine', was Alexander Kipnis's opinion in 1973[2] – but the rubato, the portamenti, the narrow, quick, flickering vibrato with some long notes characterized by an apparent absence of any at all, these are all easily discernible. And most startling of all, as with Patti, the actual notes – a great many of them – that aren't in the score at all, the ornamentation of melodic repeats and of internal cadences and the insertion of extended cadenzas at the ends of cabalettas and cavatinas. The pulse is constantly varied, held steady for barely two bars together; sudden fermatas are introduced just before cadences, and regularly before intermediate ones, not just for emphasis at the very end of an aria. Battistini continually adds ornamentation to the line as written, and where the composer has inserted *fioriture* in small notes he rarely keeps to these but embellishes in his own way. He will shorten long notes at the ends of phrases, he will sing through rests to create a long phrase out of two shorter ones. It is unimaginable that even the same performers could ever repeat these inflections exactly, since there is obviously a desire to avoid precise synchronization all the time. If the recordings he made of arias from *Ernani* in 1906 and 1907 are compared with the performing style exemplified by Renato Bruson on discs first released in 1983[3] it is the steadiness in tempo and the meticulous coordination between singer and accompaniment in these modern performances – and these are live performances – that strike the listener first of all. The music performed at the end of the century is a much more literal realization of the notes on the page. Where Bruson does add to the score, by inserting an expected cadential cadenza on the pause of a final cadence, for example, as at the close of the cavatina 'Oh, de' verd'anni miei' in Act III, his interpolation will be much shorter and simpler and less exuberant than Battistini's.

The modern listener is frequently surprised by the lack of coordination between singer and accompaniment, by the way in which voice and accompaniment are permitted to go out of phase. Just as there is a freedom – or as we might consider now, a lack of coordination – between singer and accompaniment in the recordings of Patti or Battistini, so are there similar dislocations in the performance of Chopin's Nocturne in D flat op. 27 no. 2 recorded by Vladimir de Pachmann in 1925, or in Paderewski's performance recorded in 1924 of Schubert's Impromptu in B flat, D.935 no. 3, where time after time the bass anticipates the note in the melody. And in both there are slight accelerations through unimportant or ornamental melody notes and stresses, tenutos, on strong beats or on important melody notes. And such characteristic features of articulation and emphasis are not limited to the nineteenth-century repertory; they are just as apparent in the performance of Bach's *Italian Concerto* recorded on the harpsichord by Violet Gordon-Woodhouse in April 1927[4] as they are in early recordings of piano works by Chopin or Beethoven or Schubert or Mendelssohn or Brahms.

A recording made about 1930 of Bach's Concerto in D minor for two violins BWV 1043 recalls in some of the most characteristic features, of the player of the first violin part especially, Arnold Rosé, the performing style of Adelina Patti, with frequent portamenti and sparing use of vibrato.[5] His fellow soloist, his daughter Alma Rosé, does not follow him quite stylistically – she fails to observe all the portamenti he inserts, and usually slides much more quietly than her partner – and he himself is not absolutely consistent in the way he places slides in repeated or transposed passages.[6] Leaving aside differences in bowing technique, in the application of slides and vibrato and rubato, between such a performance and versions from the 1960s, and 70s and 80s, it may be the improvisatory nature, the slight air of disorderliness, of spontaneity, which disconcerts a modern listener most of all. Precise consistency in phrasing and articulation which is carefully planned by players and singers at the end of the century is not a feature of those in the earlier decades.

Rachmaninoff and Kreisler interpret Grieg's Sonata for violin and piano in C minor op. 45 in September 1928 as two distinct musical personalities;[7] Rachmaninoff announces the long theme of the slow movement with a great deal of tempo fluctuation and all kinds of unnotated emphases and rhythmic distortions which are not imitated by Kreisler when he repeats the material in his own highly distinctive manner. The famous recordings of Beethoven quartets by the Busch Quartet are performances of four distinct musical personalities interacting, as they might express it, rather than the smooth, effortless, meticulous and precisely coordinated and integrated ensemble speaking with one voice characteristic of the 1990s. Menahem Pressler, the pianist of the Beaux Arts Trio, revered musicians like Cortot, Thibaud and Casals who played as a trio, or Rubinstein, Piatigorsky and Heifetz, but to him their performances weren't chamber music: 'Everyone follows his own flight of fancy.'[8] Pressler hears three inimitable musicians, each with a highly distinctive musical character and personality, but for him in such interpretations Schubert's 'own personality' is obscured. In his opinion the Beaux Arts 'established the piano trio . . . we achieved a sense of balance that is to this day unequalled'.[9] Needless to say, this is a late twentieth-century view and would not necessarily have been shared by the music-lovers of earlier decades in the century.

One of the most startling aspects of Nikisch's famous performance of Beethoven's Fifth Symphony recorded in November 1913 is the flexibility of tempo, the fluctuations in time, the way the tempo ebbs and flows;[10] the overall speed of the movement is not particularly remarkable to late twentieth-century ears, but a characteristically modern performance, like John Eliot Gardiner's with the Orchestre Révolutionnaire et Romantique, rarely deviates much during the course of the movement from the speed established at the beginning.[11] Towards the end of the first movement's exposition Nikisch is conducting at about minim (half-note) = 93, but he slows down with great emphasis, more than twenty metronome marks, to introduce the second subject. The same flexibility over tempo is observable when he accompanies Elena Gerhardt on the piano in 'Ich grolle nicht' from Schumann's *Dichterliebe*; this strikes a modern critic as, at best, 'interesting': 'The singer caresses and lingers when she wants to – and she wants to often. The pianist rarely makes two consecutive quavers [eighth-notes] sound the same length.'[12] But the way in which Nikisch does not detach the last three chords is too much for this modern critic; 'demonstrably wrong', he judges it,[13] because it deviates from what is clear and unambiguous in the printed score, the playing appears simply to ignore Schumann's instructions. But then recordings show clearly that composers themselves appear cheerfully to ignore what they have painstakingly notated in the score.[14]

Some of the strangeness and quaintness of Nikisch's 1913 performance of Beethoven's Fifth Symphony derive from it being an acoustic recording and from the abbreviated scoring that this necessitated; but Elgar's performance of his own 'Enigma' Variations made in 1926 electrically – and so enabling a regularly constituted orchestra to play under more or less normal conditions – demonstrates many of the same peculiarities in instrumental sonority and style and some of the same idiosyncrasies in inflection and articulation. Variations II and VII Elgar takes considerably faster than his own metronome markings; 'Nimrod' he begins exceptionally slowly (at crotchet (quarter-note) = 40 against a marking of 52) but accelerates to 56 just before the movement's climax. In variation III the triplet semiquavers (sixteenth-notes) in the third bar are played as if they were demisemiquavers (thirty-second-notes) and throughout the performance there is an absence of that meticulous attention to ensemble and to rhythmic accuracy that is so characteristic – we realize when listening to recordings from the past – of performances at the end of the century. The opening performance of the theme is distinguished by slides, many of them undisguised, just as loud that is as the notes before and after them, and in 'Nimrod' too there are prominent portamenti. The string sound throughout is full-bodied and straight, uninflected by continuous vibrato, as is clear from the solo viola passages in variations VI and X. And there is good evidence that Elgar considered this performance entirely satisfactory, characteristic and fully realizing his intentions. It is certainly not odd or eccentric when compared with performances of Elgar's music at that time by other conductors; and although he had a reputation for fast speeds, others often took his music just as fast and some of them at times even faster.[15]

The performance of the first movement of his Organ Sonata op. 28 recorded by G. D. Cunningham in 1930[16] belongs to the same world. Cunningham, much admired at the time as a stylish and idiomatic performer, takes 7′08″ over the complete movement whereas Herbert Sumsion on a 1965 disc takes 8′38″,[17] Christopher Robinson on a disc released in 1976 takes 9′17″,[18] and Stephen Cleobury recorded in 1991 takes 9′13″.[19] Admittedly these later performances are in large resonant buildings, in Gloucester Cathedral, Worcester Cathedral and the chapel of King's College, Cambridge, whereas Cunningham plays the instrument in the much drier acoustic of Alexandra Palace, and the players may have modified speeds to suit the acoustical environment. But then Simon Preston's performance issued in 1967 lasts 8′55″[20] and this, like Cunningham's, was recorded in a concert hall, in the Colston Hall in Bristol. The piece bears the tempo indication 'Allegro maestoso' and carries no metronome marking; Cunningham's performance begins at crotchet (quarter-note) = 90, quite close to the initial tempo adopted in most modern recorded performances. But his performance is much more improvisatory in tone, with much more flexibility in the speeds adopted. Just before the final big rallentando – not marked in the score – Cunningham whips up excitement with a sudden accelerando where he touches crotchet (quarter-note) = 140. There are a number of other departures from the score not followed by later performers: he rolls the D major chord at the opening of the movement's second subject, and whereas in most modern performances players simply stop the oscillations at the end of the succession of trills just before the recapitulation, Cunningham inserts a very elegant turn, which perfectly fits the sweep and improvisatory élan of the movement's progress in his hands. He is not averse to the slight jolt caused by adding ranks in mid-phrase, whereas most players today would make it a point of honour to draw stops deftly and unobtrusively in the split seconds between phrases. In other words this performance by G. D. Cunningham, like Elgar's own performances of his orchestral music recorded at this time, is much more fluid, much more impulsive, vigorous, volatile, informal, vibrant, with a sense of direction that sweeps all before, at moments infinitely tender, much more improvisatory than we hear today and with much less attention to clarity of detail and precision.

The earliest styles documented

Recordings can give hints at least about much earlier performing styles than is often supposed. There are two cylinders made by the Danish baritone born in 1819, Peter Schram, who appeared with Jenny Lind, singing extracts from Leporello in *Don Giovanni*, his most famous role;[21] there are recordings of seven singers born in the 1830s and twenty-four born in in the 1840s, four hundred sides or cylinders in total, all of them artists formed before the stylistic transformations wrought by Wagner and the Italian *verismo* school, and some of them collaborators of Brahms and Verdi and Wagner and Grieg and Sullivan.[22] There are recordings by singers who worked with Verdi on roles they sang in premières, like Tamagno and Maurel and Pini-Corsi and De Reszke, and singers for whom he expressed particular admiration like Battistini and Bellincioni and Nordica, and for the singer he praised for her 'marvellous execution' and as demonstrating 'the purest style of singing', Adelina Patti, though none of her recordings are of his music.[23] There are recordings by Joachim, who played Mendelssohn's Concerto under the composer's direction in the 1840s and for whom Brahms wrote his Violin Concerto, whose style was completely free from the continuous vibrato that Kreisler introduced, who in fact 'disdained' it, Kreisler remembered. There are recordings of works by Chopin played by Raoul Pugno, who was a pupil of Chopin's pupil Georges Mathias, and recordings by other 'grand-pupils' of the composer like Moriz Rosenthal and Aleksander Michalowski and Raoul Koczalski – all pupils of Karol Mikuli – and Alfred Cortot and Edouard Risler, both pupils of Émile Decombes.[24] There are recordings of seventy-eight compositions by Liszt played by pupils of the composer including Frederic Lamond, Conrad Ansorge and Arthur Friedheim.[25]

Aspects of stylistic change can be glimpsed by means of the advice given in famous treatises and instruction manuals like M. Garcia's *Traité complet de l'art du chant* or Joachim and Moser's *Violinschule* of 1905, or Leopold Auer's *Violin Playing as I Teach it* of 1921, or Carl Flesch's *Die Kunst des Violinspiels* of 1923 and 1928, or in dictionary definitions, like the entries for 'vibrato' or 'tremolo' in successive editions of *Grove*. In the first edition readers are warned that vibrato could easily degenerate into a mannerism when the effect becomes 'either painful, ridiculous, or nauseous, entirely opposed to good taste or common sense, and to be severely reprehended in all students whether of vocal or instrumental music';[26] in the third edition of 1928 the writer accepts that as an 'emotional effect produced by physical means it has obvious dangers, but no string-player's technique is complete without its acquirement'.[27] Some styles, though, and some aspects of performing style it would be extremely difficult to reconstruct in imagination without recordings; orchestral styles have never been prescribed in manuals and it would not be possible to gauge the effect of instructions regarding portamento, say, written for a solo string player, when these were applied by an entire string section. And ultimately performing styles and techniques cannot be described by analysis of their component parts but by the effect of the fusion of characteristics, by the complex interaction of timbre and articulation and movement and flow. Hence the particular value of sound recordings, demonstrating stylistic traits in context, as part of an artist's voice or personality.

A summary of the changes that have been perceived

Through recorded performances it is now possible to scrutinize several decades in the lives of some of the greatest and most famous works in the standard repertory. Researchers are beginning to collect a horde of information about recorded performances, armed with stop-watches and metronomes and tuning forks, and also now with computer programmes which can analyse and give data on aspects like flexibility of speeds which are all but impossible to collect with conventional methods. What are their investigations revealing? Are any generalizations possible?

The discographic evidence suggests that Chopin's music is in general played slower today than it was at the end of the nineteenth century, contradicting what even many experts have assumed. The illusion of greater velocity seems to arise from much neater articulation and greater clarity and attention to detail.[28] There is clear evidence that conductors today generally take Brahms's orchestral music rather slower than he did or his contemporaries did, as they do with Elgar, but recordings demonstrate that initial tempos have not altered drastically; it is through tempo fluctuations, through accelerations, that overall timings are reduced.[29] There is evidence that the first movement of Bach's Fifth Brandenburg Concerto has been played faster and faster during the century,[30] and it is certainly true that in those repertories that have been played by musicians using historic instruments or modern copies and perhaps more alert to some of the niceties of historical style, performances have been characterized by fleetness and lightness and transparency. This is now true even in Brahms as it is conducted by Roger Norrington.[31]

Performing styles of the early twentieth century were characterized by sparing use of vibrato by string players, its discreet use by singers, and the general avoidance of vibrato on woodwind instruments by most players except those of the French school; the frequent use of prominent, often slow, portamento by string-players and singers; the use of substantial tempo changes to signal changes of mood or tension, and the adoption of fast maximum tempos; varieties of tempo rubato which included not only detailed flexibility of tempo, but also accentuation by lengthening and shortening individual notes, and the dislocation of melody and accompaniment; and a tendency, in patterns of long and short notes, to shorten the short notes, and to overdot dotted rhythms. The introduction of vibrato and a more discreet use of portamento is a twentieth-century phenomenon observable in both vocal and instrumental performing styles. The practically universal application of vibrato by the 1950s and 60s and 70s makes its absence in recordings of the early decades of the century immediately noticeable. (Its suppression by those attempting to imitate Baroque performing styles, especially on string instruments, has led at the end of the century to a general conscious or unconscious re-evaluation of its expressive possibilities.) It is the absence of vibrato and of dynamic nuances which makes much flute and oboe playing in the earlier part of the century sound flat, unpolished, unsophisticated, 'unmusical' we are tempted to say.[32] The interpretation of rhythm has become ever more literal, and distortions such as overdotting are now, at the end of the century, rarely heard in Beethoven or Brahms or Elgar in passages where a century ago they were commonplace; and there is much less flexibility in tempo. Certainly through the middle decades of the century it was drummed into the heads of music students that they should guard against any tendency to accelerate with a crescendo; this was a mortal sin. It hasn't been for very long, apparently; Strauss would do it, and Rachmaninoff, and Elgar.

Most of these features can be very clearly demonstrated. Recordings of the slow movement of Bach's Double Concerto, for example, exemplify the growth of vibrato and the decay of portamenti very clearly. That recording of about 1930 shows the distinctive portamento styles and absence of vibrato of Arnold Rosé, a player who had led the Vienna Philharmonic Orchestra from 1881, whose style was described by Carl Flesch as 'that of the [eighteen] 'seventies, with no concession to modern tendencies in our art'.[33] A recording made in January 1915 with a string quartet instead of a body of strings has as soloists Efrem

Zimbalist, the Russian-born violinist who studied with Leopold Auer at the St Petersburg Conservatory in the early years of the century, and in stylistic contrast to him – which contrast would have delighted contemporary audiences just as it has puzzled and perhaps irritated later violinists – the man who almost single-handedly created the style and the taste of modern continuous vibrato, Fritz Kreisler. The kind of international classical style of violin playing of much of the twentieth century, continuous vibrato, intense projection, absence of portamenti, and the consistency in articulation and phrasing characteristic of musicians in ensemble generally, is well exemplified in a performance by Itzhak Perlman and Pinchas Zukerman with the English Chamber Orchestra under Daniel Barenboim released in 1972.[34] A 1990 recording with Elizabeth Wallfisch and Alison Bury and the Orchestra of the Age of Enlightenment is at Baroque pitch, with very little vibrato – certainly not continuous at all – and a gentle lilt which probably derives from the style which was forged in London in the 1970s, itself a conscious reaction against the mannered style, as the English players considered it, of the Dutch and Austrian players which became well known in the 1960s.[35] A parallel progression could be traced with 'Voi che sapete', that Mozart aria recorded by Adelina Patti in December 1905, and by Luise Helletsgruber with the Orchestra of the Glyndebourne Festival Opera in June 1935,[36] by Tatiana Troyanos with the Orchestra of the Deutsche Oper in Berlin in March 1968,[37] and by Alicia Nafé in August 1987, with the Drottningholm Court Theatre Orchestra,[38] such recordings as these demonstrating similar changes in vibrato and portamento and articulation and ensemble.

To study musical performances is to study gestures, whatever else it may be. How do particular sounds and particular timbres and ways of articulating musical notes come to have special significances? How and why do such gestures change? How can we account for the restraint and emotional coolness increasingly characteristic of twentieth-century performing styles, for this decrease in volatility and for the gestures that convey this coolness to audiences and to the listeners of recordings? Musical performances a century ago, like all forms of public speech and declamation, were more rhetorical, almost as if the performer were enunciating a narrative for the first time and it was important for the storyteller to ensure that the essential elements were grasped, to give particular emphasis to certain passages but to throw these into relief by lightening others. And while the broad outline of an overture, or a symphony or a concerto would be known to most of the audience at a concert at the end of the nineteenth century, it would have been true that few listening would ever have heard a particular work many times, and many would have never heard it at all before, whether it be by Beethoven or Mendelssohn or Stanford or Brahms or Coleridge-Taylor. And the curl of the lip and the flashing of the eye were important components of much of the repertoire then being presented to the public. In the 1950s a historian examined political and dramatic rhetoric in the 1830s and 40s and concluded that the eloquence heard in speeches on the radio in England in the middle of the twentieth century would not have been considered eloquence at all a century earlier.[39] In the third edition of *Grove's Dictionary* published in 1928, at a time when performing styles, just like compositional styles, were all clearly avoiding the grand gesture, Fox Strangways cautioned against the use of too much rubato lest the music become like correspondence 'which is too much underlined'.[40] The lessening of rhetorical emphasis in musical performance seems to have its counterpart in all kinds of public speaking, and in the smaller-scale gestures of film and television acting. It's possible to observe a greater rhythmic literalness emerging even in Elgar's own recorded performances, between, say, his 1926 and 1933 recordings of *Cockaigne*, with groups of semiquavers (sixteenth-notes) less hurried, played with less abandon and more care in the later performance, but, as the expert on Elgar's own recordings points out, there is no reason to suppose that Elgar preferred the newer style.[41] Elgar's response to the Gramophone Company's suggestion that he re-record *Cockaigne* on three sides was: 'By all means do "Cockaigne" again: is there anything wrong with the old four side records?'[42]

How can changes in performing styles be accounted for?

How do these changes come about? And first of all, what were the forces that shaped the Romantic styles that the earliest gramophone records document? For Wagner, music to be truly expressive had to be quiveringly alive, it had to reflect the minute emotional changes of each suceeding phrase of the music's unfolding, which Wagner recognized in Beethoven, in his 'emotional, sentimental music', in which 'the manifold changes of a series of variations are not merely strung together, but are now brought into immediate contact, and made to merge one into the other'.[43] Hence the importance of the piano and piano music for the Romantic musician in which one controlling intelligence could articulate the ever-changing emotional or spiritual import of the sounds. When in 1845 Moscheles tried to explain the style of performance he was aiming at to the players of the Philharmonic Society, he compared their performance 'with the fingers of an admirably trained pianoforte-player's hand. Now, will you allow me to be the hand that sets these fingers in motion, and imparts life to them?'[44]

Certainly Wagner wished the conductor to be the nerve- and brain-centre of the orchestra; he did not want conductors to be classicist time-beaters. Beethoven's symphonies demanded conductors of 'energy, self-confidence and personal power' who must inspire in their players fluidity and flexibility in tempo and a subtlety in dynamic, tone quality, articulation and phrasing which will hardly be encapsulated in any system of notation. There is some evidence that Beethoven did introduce modifications in tempo to make clear a passage's structural significance.[45] But it is also true that Wagner wanted interpretation of Beethoven essentially in a style he thought appropriate to his own music dramas. At any rate the style he attempted to cultivate with the orchestras he conducted in the 1850s, whether in Beethoven or in his own pieces, was still – regardless of whatever success men like Moscheles may have already had – to all intents and purposes a new one, and evidently foxed orchestral players, at least on first experiencing it: 'the strange and significant movements of his long baton bewildered the players, and put them out until they began to understand that it was not the time-beat that ruled, but the phrase, or the melody or the expression'.[46] A London violinist complained of the way that Wagner 'prefaces the entry of an important point or the return of a theme – especially in a slow movement – by an exaggerated ritardando; and . . . reduces the speed of an allegro – say in an overture or the first part of a symphony – fully one-third immediately on the entry of a cantabile phrase'.[47]

From a number of vivid accounts we can glimpse something of the character of pre-Romantic styles of performance. In 1880 Ernest Walker was taken to one of the Saturday afternoon popular concerts at the Crystal Palace where since 1855 the conductor had been a German, August Manns, 'a gallant, picturesque figure with a symmetrical mane of snow-white hair and his velvet coat'.[48] Walker admired his performances, they constituted his musical education, he was musically formed by them, he said looking back in 1931. Never did August Manns 'show off', his tempi were always 'normal'; quick movements were often taken 'somewhat slower than is now customary'.[49] He remembered the finale of Beethoven's Fifth Symphony as being 'a very dignified and steady *Allegro maestoso* all through'. He granted that in some modern music 'of the dramatic and emotional type . . . his conception lacked colour and undulation', as he put it, and could 'not disadvantageously have been subtler'.[50] He remembered the striking difference between the interpretations of Manns and Hans Richter with the same body of men. But he was profoundly grateful to Manns for having shown him that great music 'must be seen spaciously and whole. He would have scorned to use a drop of that red ink of which so many a conductor of the present day seems to possess an inexhaustible bottle at the end of his baton; not for him those dreadful pullings-up of the second subject and all the rest of it, those contagious habits of tearing an organism into snippets in order to make "points" intelligible to the unmusical.'[51] When this rather serious and intellectual musician speaks of 'modern' music 'of the dramatic and emotional type', he means Wagner and Liszt.

So the Romantic styles of performance, in the formation of which Liszt and Wagner were the pre-eminent exemplars, emphasized the originality and individuality of the performer and the spontaneity of musical re-creation and the importance of conveying an air of improvisation, however complicated and involved the compositional processes, however demanding the work of instrumental or vocal virtuosity. This was accepted by everyone; even for as sober and conservative a commentator as Ernest Walker, who loved Brahms more than Wagner, and Schumann more than Liszt; 'no performance worth anything, of any music, remains mathematically level, either in time or tone, for more than a very limited period. This we all take for granted. . . .'[52]

Composers and performers explained the need for the characteristic features of Romantic performing styles in different terms. Chaliapin wondered why an agent should pay £400 for him when he could obtain a perfectly adequate performance for £40 if all that was wanted was a singer who would obediently follow the beat; music must never be taken in 'a fixed and flexible tempo', or at least wasn't by a true artist.[53]

To play Chopin's Nocturne in G minor with pious respect for a metronome marking would be, in Paderewski's opinion, 'as intolerably monotonous, as absurdly pedantic, as to recite Gray's famous *Elegy* to the beating of a metronome'.[54] And he was equally sure that to play Mozart and Haydn and Bach, and even Frescobaldi, these 'Olympian predecessors' who may have lived 'on a plane above that of our present-day nervousness and excitement', it was necessary to infuse life into their works through 'some *discretional power*', some '*Tempo Rubato.* . . . A great artist's performance of a noble work ought to sound like spontaneous improvisation. . . . '[55] The religious and mystical Charles Tournemire, who had studied with César Franck at the end of his life and succeeded him as organist at St Clothilde in Paris in 1898, stressed the importance of improvisation for his teacher and those improvisatory qualities in performance which must be recaptured if the Master's music is to live again, when 'an ardent, creative spontaneous imagination' will synthesize sovereign musical intelligence with 'vibrations intérieurs', profound musical thought with 'psychic phenomena' and the 'rhythms of the heart',[56] and so create a kind of spiritual intoxication necessary if those sublime moments of revelation are to be attained when it seems the organist himself is no longer in conscious control but guided by some inspiring angel.[57]

It is these determining features of late nineteenth- and early twentieth-century style which are heard clearly in the earliest recorded performances. They are heard when Rachmaninoff plays his *Rhapsody on a Theme of Paganini*, when Elgar conducts his Violin Concerto, when Grieg plays his *An die Frühling* – like a sentimental schoolgirl, as one commentator perhaps anachronistically described it in 1974.[58] But it is also clearly heard in composers and works whose aesthetic world we do not immediately associate with these features, with expressive rubato and imprecise ensemble, in the recorded performances of his own works by Bartók, for example, described by a distinguished interpreter of them in 1997 as 'unbelievably lyrical and romantic, tender and rhythmically subtle'.[59] But, as he points out: 'The style is rooted in nineteenth-century *rubato* with chords that are notated together. The way he arpeggiates them is very distinctive; he very seldom plays chords together.'[60] In his own *Gavotta* op. 32 no. 3, which he recorded in 1932, Prokofiev is not at all rhythmically strict, playing groups of short notes lightly and hastily, throwing them away, almost like grace notes, but giving particular emphasis to the main beats,[61] just like Poulenc does in his *Caprice* in C ('d'après le Final du Bal Masqué') and Bartók in the first movement of his Suite op. 14.[62] The emphatic tempo modifications in a 1927 performance of Orlando Gibbons's *Hosanna to the Son of David* by the choir of St George's Chapel, Windsor, strike us today as melodramatic and absurdly exaggerated, and particularly curious when as we know these English church musicians were striving for an 'untheatrical' and 'unemotional' effect.[63] The impact of such details, though, can only be assessed and imagined in the context of the performing traditions existing at the time.

The influence of recording on performing styles

Recordings have not only documented the changes, the technology itself has been a hugely influential agent in bringing these changes about. Editing and splicing techniques have made it possible for recorded performances to be manufactured from which any kind of inaccuracy or blemish has been removed. One result of this has been that a listener's expectations in the concert hall, in live performances, are based on the standards achieved or seemingly achieved in performances on discs, the kind of performances that most music-lovers listen to most frequently.

Everyone is sure that broadcasting and recordings, recordings especially, have driven up standards. In 1938 an English novelist noted with satisfaction and relief that the amateur pianist and amateur singer had been driven from drawing-rooms by the radio and the gramophone.[64] In 1932 an English choirmaster had welcomed broadcasting and the challenges it posed for English choirs: 'The microphone is a relentless truth-teller. But it is good to have to stand up to it, because a choir can only do so after untiring team-practice and the most devoted self-effacement for the sake of the music and its purpose.'[65] He was equally enthusiastic about recording for the gramophone and equally sure of the beneficial effects it would have in the long run: 'Is there any church music recording that has reached, or (as one may someday hope) begun to reach, or to surpass, Toscanini's orchestral recording? Does that mean that we cannot reach such a standard? Of course it does not.'[66]

Magnetic tape and the long-playing record had an even greater effect on standards in the second half of the century; 'profound and wide-

spread' was their influence, in the opinion of the most famous recording producer of his time. He considered that the effects of editing and
splicing of tape, which enabled recorded performances to be 'more polished and accurate than those normally heard in concert halls and
opera-houses', to be 'most salutary'.[67] Since performers' reputations by
the 1960s were made principally by their recorded performances on
which all care was lavished by the artist himself and the team of engineers and producers, the performer felt obliged, this producer thought,
to equal this standard in his public performances.[68] Not all performers
or even record producers have considered imitating recorded performances desirable,[69] but nonetheless it has been agreed that audiences'
expectations have been changed through the characteristics of those
performances most of them hear most frequently, performances on
record.

But raised standards of performance alone cannot possibly be held
to explain the changes in fundamental characteristics of performing
styles in the twentieth century. In Chopin's Waltz in A flat op. 42
Vladimir Ashkenazy in his recording released in 1983,[70] and Jean-
Bernard Pommier on his 1994 disc[71] and Peter Katin on his 1994 disc,[72]
and countless other pianists on discs from the last few decades of the
twentieth century, distinguish carefully between every quaver and
semiquaver – eighth-note and sixteenth-note – throughout the piece;
Rachmaninoff in a long passage in his 1919 recording plays quavers
and semiquavers both as semiquavers.[73] But it would be absurd to
suggest that Rachmaninoff would have been unable to make the distinction clear if he had wished to. Musicians came to denounce the
characteristic portamenti employed by such players as the members of
the Flonzaley Quartet, one of the first string quartets to record, as 'taste-
less and nauseating', in the words of one distinguished conductor, the
style, he said, of those musicians who provided entertainment in the
kind of cafés and tea rooms where the food possessed similar qualities.[74] But the care and subtlety with which the Flonzaley Quartet
employed this expressive device, as they would have regarded it, can be
heard in their performance with Harold Bauer of Brahms's F minor
Quintet op. 34 recorded in December 1925[75] where they avoid any slides
completely at the opening of the work to achieve a real unison with the
piano. The Royal Albert Hall Orchestra with whom Elgar recorded his
'Enigma' Variations in 1926[76] certainly could have distinguished
between the demisemiquavers (thirty-second-notes) and triplet

semiquavers (sixteenth-notes) in the third of the 'Enigma' Variations, as modern conductors do, as Barbirolli does, for example, in his 1962 recording with the Philharmonia.[77] The point is, the players did not wish to in 1926, and perhaps even more to the point, it seems clear Elgar did not wish them to either.

At the same time it was early recognized that recording requires the musician to cultivate a more intimate tone of voice, that when he stands before the microphone he is in effect singing or playing to an audience of one or maybe at most two or three in a small domestic setting. Lorin Maazel found that he was adjusting the spacing between the chords at the close of the Fifth Symphony of Sibelius in his interpretation, shortening silences whose effect in the large spaces of the concert hall was powerful but which, on playback in the control room, simply sounded mannered.[78]

Some musicians found the highly individual and characteristic interpretations of Furtwängler 'intense and revelatory' in live performances, but considered it was those very idiosyncrasies which made them great in the concert hall that caused them to 'wear out' on record.[79] It was the 'spontaneity', the 'unrepeatability' of Furtwängler's art that would prevent it living on in recordings; it was the 'infantile fears of emotion' of the late twentieth century that would have to be overcome, one commentator thought, if such music-making was to be appreciated again. 'He was the very opposite of a gramophone record.'[80] Alfred Brendel consciously aimed to avoid any 'exaggeration' in the recording studio, for the kind of interpretation 'that will bear frequent hearing'.[81] Christopher Hogwood sometimes attempted to restrain his musicians because he has felt that risk-taking, 'wild risks' and 'fantastic cadenzas', improvisatory élan, spontaneity and dangerous living which would certainly elicit cheers in a live performance 'nearly always pall on repeated hearings'.[82]

Towards the end of the century some musicians who had lived through the recording revolution were uneasy. They considered that styles had been moulded too much by the microphone, that after a decade or two of tape recording, studio sessions were having a deadening effect on music-making, that the price of technical perfection and blameless accuracy and neatness and control was too high and that much had been lost in élan and spontaneity, and that music-making had become dull and homogenized and standardized. Claudio Arrau referred to 'this silly perfectionism that people appreciate too much', and to a lack of 'poetry' and 'nobility'.[83] A critic compared the singing of songs by Hugo Wolf in the 1960s and 70s with recordings from the 1930s and found the earlier styles 'more direct and whole-hearted, less-self-regarding and concerned with minutiae'.[84] Everywhere in the 1980s could be heard lovely sounds, an orchestral player was sure, beautiful intonation, perfect articulation, 'but no music in between it all'.[85] The effect of studio recording on performing artists had not only been 'purifying but also sterilising, not only concentrating and distilling but also petrifying', in Alfred Brendel's words in 1983: 'The interpreter who aims at accuracy risks less panache, lesser tempos, less self-oblivion', he thought. The time had come, so much having been learnt from studio recordings, for the performer to 'learn from concerts once again'. Under special circumstances, he thought, recordings of live performances should be made in order to restore those vital elements of spontaneity and tension which characterize vital interpretations. The first live performance Brendel allowed to be issued on disc was of Beethoven's 'Hammerklavier' Sonata op. 106, one of the 'biggest and most dangerous works' in the repertory, and this deliberately, for while it is undeniable that the player cannot function at the same high level for an hour or so, nonetheless a piece of this size and scope, he thought, stands most to gain in an actual performance in 'boldness, absorption and vision'.[86]

Brendel had given performances of the complete cycle of Beethoven's piano concertos with James Levine and the Chicago Symphony Orchestra in 1977 and 1979, and in 1983 he recorded two series of live concerts of all the works in Orchestra Hall in Chicago. It would have been unwise, even foolhardy, the pianist thought, to have relied on a single performance of each work, for both technical and musical reasons, and the availability of two recordings gave the opportunity of combining 'the benefits of concert and studio'.[87]

By the end of the century there was clear evidence that some performers wished to cultivate a freer, more flexible, more improvisatory approach, to seek to suggest a greater degree of spontaneity, which seemed partly at least a reaction against the studied perfection of recorded performances. When Anne-Sophie Mutter played Beethoven's violin sonatas in London in October 1998 a London critic marvelled at these 'far from traditional accounts: pregnant pauses, exaggerated rubati and highlighting of mysterious modulations all resulted in intensely personal interpretations'.[88]

Anti-Romantic and formalist trends:
neo-classical performing styles between the wars

But recording and broadcasting themselves cannot be held solely responsible for effecting the changes so clearly documented on discs and tapes. Changing repertories and changing physical contexts – different kinds of performing spaces – have also modified styles; bigger voices in opera may have developed not only from composers writing for bigger orchestral forces, but also because of bigger opera houses, because of the economic need to play before bigger audiences.

Gestures of any kind become meaningful through their total contexts, certainly the physical surroundings in which they are made, but also the aesthetic, intellectual and social settings in which they are made. Recordings have clearly documented the taming, as some might see it, the moderating, the cooling, the classicizing of performing styles. Certainly the 1920s were characterized by disillusion, by a distrust of dramatic gestures after the high-sounding rhetoric and propaganda of the Great War. In 1928 an English critic published a book on the art of writing English prose in which he condemned the literary style of a passage of Churchillian prose for its artificiality, its stale images, its redundant epithets, whose aim he suggested was 'not so much an aggrandization of the theme as an aggrandization of the self'.[89] The note of heroism sounded hollow in these postwar years, when grand and confident poses seemed dishonest, or fraudulent, or merely ridiculous. 'Eloquence' seemed artificial; men and women were described as 'waxing eloquent' when they couldn't quite be believed. A High Victorian might yet be convinced that he could be master of his fate and captain of his soul, but as the implications of Darwin and Freud permeated artistic and intellectual consciousness the twentieth century became not so sure. And a music historian who viewed these developments with alarm and anguish noted that the new music despised 'not merely sentimentality but every serious expression of feeling', and that it 'insulted' the 'romantic adoration of beauty, regarding it simply as hypocrisy'.[90]

So between the wars Claudio Arrau detected the emergence of a new kind of performing musician whose concern was for 'a just mode of interpretation', for a closer observance of the composer's text, in contrast to the 'arbitrary' and 'false' accounts given by an earlier, pre-Great War generation. Now, he thought, musicians' concern was to 'render intact' the thinking of the composer and not to use the work of art as a pretext for self-expression or for 'sensationalism'.[91] Edwin Fischer numbered Stravinsky, Hindemith and Bartók and Arturo Toscanini among what he calls the 'purifiers' of music; the kind of performance that the new men of the 1920s and 1930s aspired to, he says, was one that 'accords exactly with the composer's intentions, respects the note-values and all the composer's directions, is stripped of all unnecessary trimmings'.[92] Artur Schnabel, one of these 'new artists' known for his sobriety and austerity and lack of self-indulgence, required that every trill, every pause in a Beethoven sonata, even a rest between two movements should be counted out.[93] This was a time, Alfred Brendel remembered, when piano students played Beethoven as if he had learnt composition with Hindemith.[94] And Hindemith was indeed a composer who expressed this new anti-Romantic spirit of coolness and neutrality and functionalism and an absence of frills and profundity: '. . . my things', he said – not 'my works' – 'my things are perfectly easy to understand'.[95]

Neo-classicism itself was in part a reaction to late Romanticism, against hypersensitivity, against emotional extremes, and it emphasized the virtues of detachment and an absence of personal involvement. Such characteristics could be detected as much in the performing style of Toscanini as they could in the compositional styles of Hindemith or Milhaud or Poulenc. The terraced dynamics and the motor rhythms exemplified in countless recordings of Baroque music in the middle decades of the century derived not so much from the unequivocal testimony of eighteenth-century manuals on performance practice but more from prevailing twentieth-century aesthetic concerns of which Stravinsky was the pre-eminent exemplar and articulator. The German conductor Hermann Scherchen writing in 1929 explained that in Stravinsky's recent works 'there is neither a *crescendo* nor a *diminuendo*. . . . All romantic expressive adjuncts . . . *accelerando, ritardando,* or *rubato* [are] ignored . . .'; and changes of tempo bear strict proportional relationships to one another.[96] Scherchen is distinguishing between the styles necessary for idiomatic performances of Stravinsky and those for classical composers and for the romantic repertory. But it was never possible to compartmentalize strictly. Taste after all was being formed by audiences listening to Bach and Beethoven and Stravinsky. And specialization among performers hardly existed between the wars, as Wanda Landowska acknowledged; musicians at that time were like 'country doctors', she said, 'who treat all ailments' and play 'Scarlatti, Brahms, Cabezón, Bach, Beethoven, Schumann, Handel or Chopin, as well as the most recent composers'.[97] Elisabeth Schwarzkopf sang in the first performance of *The Rake's Progress* in September 1951 and a few months later she was recording Purcell's *Dido and Aeneas* with Kirsten Flagstad. Even when times changed, as Landowska was sure they would, and specialists did emerge, the different worlds were never hermetically sealed; the extent to which a large symphony orchestra using modern instruments could consciously adopt – and wished to adopt – the lightness and fleetness of orchestras using contemporary instruments can be heard in 1982 in the Amsterdam Concertgebouw Orchestra's performance of Mozart's Fortieth Symphony under Nikolaus Harnoncourt.[98]

And so the anti-Romantic aesthetic laws formulated by many of the best-known composers between the wars and encapsulated most powerfully in the music of Stravinsky, and articulated by him in a number of pungent diktats, became enormously influential, and commentators and scholars and explicators, almost without thinking – since clear contemporary evidence for them was almost non-existent – attached without difficulty these defining characteristics to the music of Bach and Handel and Vivaldi. As a scholar of performance practice put it: 'Certainly the style of . . . the age of Bach and Handel is most memorably characterized by an important rhythmic feature: the uniformity of its metrical pulse. This is in turn but one facet of a regularity that pervades the texture of the music. As a result the typical movement of this period is indeed a *movement*, i.e. a piece composed in a single unvarying tempo.'[99] Arnold Dolmetsch, though, had examined the same sources and come to quite different conclusions. Rubato, he thought, was 'as old as music itself'. It was as common in the seventeenth and eighteenth centuries as in the early twentieth, he was sure.[100] And he urged players to 'follow their own instinct' in order that 'the music . . . come to life'.[101]

Non-developmental forms and the technical and expressive demands of new music

The cultivation by important twentieth-century composers of static non-developmental forms, various kinds of so-called block-forms, stark juxtapositions of highly contrasted sections – of which an early *locus classicus* was Stravinsky's *Symphonies of Wind Instruments* – and forms which have avoided the dynamism of tonality, of onward development and forward propulsion to a climax or series of climaxes – in Debussy, in Messiaen, for example – these too perhaps have also militated against the cultivation of narrative styles of performance with sweep and flexibility of articulation and dynamic and tempo.

Certainly the technical demands of the new music were important in influencing performing styles; the rhythmic demands in *The Rite of Spring*, in *The Soldier's Tale*, or in Stravinsky's Octet, or in such works as Manuel de Falla's Harpsichord Concerto written between 1923 and 1926, or Milhaud's jazz-inspired *La création du monde* of 1923, or Bartók's Second Piano Concerto of 1931, or those adoptions and adaptions of dance rhythms like rumba and tango which had to be painstakingly learnt by classically-trained concert musicians and required demisemiquaver (thirty-second-note) by demisemiquaver attention to detail in order to ensure adequate co-ordination and a convincing interpretation – such music precluded the application of a great deal of *tempo rubato*.

Schoenberg was sure that the manner of performing nineteenth-century music that emerged after the First War, with all 'emotional qualities and all unnotated changes of tempo and expression' suppressed, with 'a certain frigidity of feeling', was of American origin and derived from 'the style of playing primitive dance music . . . in a stiff, inflexible metre'. European conductors and instrumentalists, suddenly fearful lest they be called 'romantic' or 'sentimental', immediately capitulated, much to Schoenberg's astonishment and irritation.[102] Jazz styles were felt by many to have been an important contributing factor to the flattening out of tempi, to the emergence in art music performance of a metronomic steadiness of pulse as a distinguishing feature of twentieth-century performing styles, an avoidance of the kind of rubato that Wagner and Liszt considered the very lifeblood of music-making. Milhaud recalled the arrival of a jazz band at the Casino de Paris in 1918 and the delightful shock of its rhythmic novelties, the incisive syncopations against 'a foundation of steady regularity like that of the circulation of the blood, the beating of the heart or the throbbing of the pulse'.[103]

'I write chorales like Bach', Erik Satie explained in 1914, 'except not so many as him, and mine aren't so pretentious.'[104] The ghost of Beethoven, the quintessential Romantic musician, had to be scared off, repudiated: 'le vieux sourd',[105] Debussy dismissed him as. 'The late quartets?' said Stravinsky. 'Worse than the other ones.'[106] Such remarks were of course intended in part to shock, to provoke, and to debunk the pretentiousness of worshipping intellectuals who did not know Beethoven but knew what attitude they were supposed to adopt. And of course Satie and Debussy and Stravinsky recognized Beethoven as a genius of the first rank. But also such uncompromising remarks were to make plain – to themselves as well as to others – that their own aesthetic stance was very different.

A classic romantic description of what the musician does was Schopenhauer's famous characterization of him as 'the interpreter of the profoundest wisdom speaking a language which reason cannot understand'.[107] More characteristic of the twentieth century than such transcendental or metaphysical notions was Stravinsky's formulation that 'All music is nothing more than a succession of impulses that converge towards a definite point of repose',[108] or Honegger's that music is 'geometry in time'.[109] The desire of many younger performers between the wars for sobriety and straightforwardness inevitably had affinities with the dominant intellectual trends of the time, with a desire to bring everything down to brass tacks, with the simple geometric forms of Bauhaus-inspired architecture and design, with a practical 'scientific' spirit of enquiry that focussed attention on the words of a literary text, or the notes of a musical score, that concentrated on the material reality of works of art.

For many years Stravinsky recoiled from the music of Beethoven, he tells us in his autobiography, alienated by the popular images and connotations of the tousle-headed genius in his garret, turning his back on emperors and princes and taking destiny by the throat. During the composition of his Piano Sonata he began to examine Beethoven's scores again and what provoked his admiration was the 'tremendous constructive force' he found in them.[110] To make his own attitude clear he quoted Mallarmé: 'It is not with ideas that one makes sonnets, but with words.'[111] Music was made out of notes, the new men maintained, not out of ideas or feelings, nor was a musical work the expression of a composer's mind or the reflection of some social reality or the incarnation of some transcendental truth. To understand a piece of music was to see how it worked, to take it to bits like a machine and analyse how the composer had assembled the component parts into the overall structure, rather like a piece of engineering. Such formalist convictions were to remain a dominant strand in aesthetics and in writing and thinking about music, as well as in composing and performing it, for the rest of the century.

There was no need for commentators to spin out a string of elegant epithets on the 'beauty' of the great works of the past; what was required of scholars and historians was 'factual stylistic analysis' which should take the music to pieces 'as a mechanic does a motor' in order to demonstrate the 'specific effect' of the notes, as Manfred Bukofzer explained in 1947.[112] And this applied whether the work was by Guillaume de Machaut or Karlheinz Stockhausen. Those composers at the Darmstadt Summer School after the Second War despised performers and their 'charming mannerisms – the sudden diminuendos, the unnotated lengthening and shortening of notes, the irrelevant pauses, the squeezing of phrases for maximum expressivity'; they assumed 'quasi-scientific identities' and did not imagine their music out of gestures, phrases, motifs, melodies, but simply formulated 'matrixes' and performed operations on these in order to generate complete works,[113] many of them cherishing 'a post-Webernian ideal of a purified, crystalline musical structure'.[114] The initial aim of at least some of the young Darmstadt composers in the 1950s was first of all the formulation and the construction of the components of a new language purged of elements of conventional expressivity.

When Pierre Boulez's *Structures*, Book I, was given its first broadcast on the BBC in 1957 the announcer provided a lengthy introduction to clarify certain points, an explication being listened to not by specialists but by a broad, miscellaneous audience of music-lovers at peak listening time on the Third Programme. The style and content give some indication of the asceticism and purity of motives and otherworldliness of this generation of composers, but hint also perhaps at its vehemence and self-righteousness: the 'discoveries' of Stravinsky, Bartók, Schoenberg and Webern, the announcer explains, are for Boulez 'a stepping-stone to further experiments. . . . The durations of the notes themselves are derived from two tables of permutations of transpositions of the row and its inversion with reference to the order number of the row. . . . "Serial structure of notes tends to destroy the horizontal-vertical dualism, for composing amounts to arranging sound phenomena along two co-ordinates, duration and pitch." '[115]

In 1969 the composer and pianist Roger Smalley considered that phrasing, articulation and tempo were no longer 'adjuncts' to the notes, no longer expressive ornaments of the musical 'argument' which was articulated traditionally through themes, motifs and harmonic progressions, but essential components of the argument itself and so they 'must be realized with an equivalent degree of accuracy'.[116] Such preoccupations of composers and performers of new music in the second half of the century might be anachronistically projected back on to earlier music, especially if the composer concerned was one in whom the later musicians recognized features of a sound world or tone of voice they thought they shared or from whom they claimed to derive certain technical procedures. In 1965 the pianist Stephen Pruslin explained that in Debussy 'the succession of sounds no longer *represents* the meaning, but *is* the meaning . . .'. A proper interpretation of a piece by Debussy, he maintained, required the performer simply 'to produce the sounds as perfectly as possible'.[117]

Bucking a trend: the clarinettist

It is against such norms or trends that individual performances acquire their distinctiveness and particular expressivity. Against that background the surface is of the greatest subtlety and complexity; there are national styles, not formed by abstract canons of 'national taste' but moulded by outstanding players and teachers, or by developments in instrument making, for example; there are styles and timbres created to meet the demands of particular composers and repertories, Wagnerian tenors, for example, or voices nurtured for Verdi, or sopranos for Mozart, or mezzo-sopranos for Rossini. Performing skills have always thrived on competition, on the existence of different traditions, on the differences between, say, the tone colour and kinds of articulation possible on the metal flute that was introduced towards the end of the nineteenth century in France and Belgium and Italy, and the styles cultivated in those countries that retained the wooden flute much longer like Germany and Eastern Europe and Britain, where a number of leading players used the wooden flute even after World War II. All such differences in the twentieth century can be examined by means of recordings.[118] Some stylistic particularities actually seemed to buck the main trends. At least at first sight, clarinettists appear to have remained immune from the general tendency to cultivate and develop vibrato, or at least have been much more reluctant to. Why should this have been so? Why should certain performers seemingly have refused to accept changes in stylistic norms? There is no general rule. The pure vibrato-less sound of the clarinet can certainly evoke, in the words of one of the century's most famous players, the 'cool, flawless beauty of a marble statue or a piece of perfectly polished wood',[119] which remarkable tone quality players clearly might have wished to continue to cultivate. But it seems equally likely that players wished to distance themselves from jazz styles. Between the wars many musicians in both Europe and America considered jazz poverty-stricken in its melodic, rhythmic and harmonic resources and at the same time in its overall style and effect a cultural threat, essentially an aphrodisiac, a challenge to the civilized values of Western Europe, an incitement to lewdness. The sounds and styles of jazz belonged to *La Revue nègre* showing at the Théâtre des Champs-Élysées in 1925 and starring Josephine Baker, the animality and sensual fury of whose contortions on stage conveyed even to smart Parisians a disturbing primeval barbarism, 'a return to the manners of the childhood of man' it was described as.[120] So it's perhaps not so surprising that clarinettists playing Mozart's Quintet should have wished to eschew any suggestion of the reedy, edgy tone and the leering, physical jaw-vibrato cultivated by jazz-players. It's true that Reginald Kell introduced a degree of vibrato into his playing when he was a member of the London Philharmonic Orchestra where he was much influenced by the principal oboe Leon Goossens, who himself had pioneered vibrato on his instrument. And he caused as much outrage among all right-thinking clarinettists as Josephine Baker did among all right-thinking citizens.[121] But even at the end of the century, Jack Brymer was still only very gently suggesting that clarinettists should perhaps just consider developing subtle kinds of vibrato that at times their instinct might allow them to bring into play.[122]

Trail-blazers

So performing characteristics or norms of style shifted through general artistic and aesthetic and intellectual movements. But also the particular achievements of individual artists or performing groups might be of crucial significance: musicians like Kreisler and Heifetz, like Toscanini and Horowitz, and the countertenor Alfred Deller, and the oboist Leon Goossens, and the horn-player Dennis Brain, and David

Willcocks and the choir of King's College, Cambridge. And in the twentieth century the mastery and idiosyncratic brilliance of outstanding executants of this kind have had the kind of far-reaching effect on performing styles that would have been inconceivable except for recorded performances. The cultivation of continuous vibrato on string instruments in the twentieth century probably owed most to the example of Fritz Kreisler, though the precise origins of his own style remain, even to an expert, 'obscure'.[123] The pedagogue Carl Flesch described Kreisler as 'driven by an irresistible inner urge'.[124] Some kind of continuous vibrato had certainly been applied by the Polish virtuoso Henryk Wieniawski, a pupil of J. L. Massart with whom Kreisler had studied at the Paris Conservatoire. The assumption must be that Kreisler had heard about this stylistic trait, or had had its elements demonstrated to him by Massart – he himself never heard Wieniawski – and then he developed it in his own way encouraged by his teacher.

Clearly the appreciation of other discerning musicians will embolden a performer to push beyond currently accepted limits an idiosyncratic and personal expressive style. It can only have encouraged Reginald Kell in 1935, at a time when his colleagues in the Covent Garden Orchestra were muttering about his experiments with vibrato, that one day during the rehearsals for *Tristan* Furtwängler stopped the orchestra, pointed at the first clarinettist and asked him his name: 'You are the first clarinettist I have heard who plays from the heart.'[125] No doubt Leon Goossens's conviction as to the rightness and beauty of his application of vibrato to oboe tone, as refining and sweetening its quality, was reinforced by the favourable comments he received from conductors and critics at a time when he had to suffer 'a great deal of abuse and jibing' from other players.[126] Perhaps it was the early age at which he was exposed to the Belgian player Henri de Buscher, the delicacy and flexibility of whose tone provided the starting-point for his own experiments, the contact with de Buscher at an age when his own ideas were still forming, that bred in him a sureness about his own taste later. And doubtless without the transcendent technical expertise and expressive power he possessed in all other aspects of the oboist's art his innovations in tone quality would never have been so widely imitated. He won over even those whose tastes had been formed decades ago like Elgar, who at the age of seventy-five listened to the test pressings of his recording of *Froissart* and exclaimed: 'Leon G's oboe passages . . . are divine – what an artist!'[127]

And Alfred Deller, the countertenor, who developed his voice empirically, who saw the virtuoso parts written for the voice by Purcell and pushed the technical and expressive techniques he had acquired singing a much less demanding repertory in church and cathedral choirs, convinced Michael Tippett that 'this was the voice that Purcell wrote for'.[128] 'Suddenly', in Walter Bergmann's words, 'there was Purcell again.'[129] It may be doubted that Deller's voice in fact resembled in tone quality any that Purcell may have used, but it was new, and it was used with commanding virtuosity. Soon, through Deller's broadcasts and numerous records, there were, as Tippett put it, 'countertenors everywhere'.[130] Tippett really meant that it seemed there were countertenors cropping up all over London. But by the end of the century, principally by means of recordings, the countertenor had indeed established itself as a voice on an international platform. After Deller there came James Bowman and Charles Brett and Paul Esswood, and after them Michael Chance and Christopher Robson, and then the Belgian René Jacobs, and the German Jochen Kowalski and the American Derek Lee Ragin, and then Artur Stefanowicz in Poland, and Andreas Scholl in Germany and Dominique Visse in France, the Americans Brian Asawa and David Daniels, and the Austrian Arno Raunig and the Canadian Daniel Taylor. These voices were not in any sense copies of each other, but each intensely individual and idiosyncratic like Deller himself, and the defining characteristics of each singer or of discernible trends were formulated and debated and fought over. Bowman could declare in 1999, with the genuine unappreciativeness of the performer, that the 'Americans like a brash, wobbly sound and despise the clean English style. The Germans tend to be over-dramatic, though not as hysterical as the Americans. The French style is insufferably affected, a stabbing at the notes.'[131]

Conscious and unconscious changes in the singing of English cathedral choirs

Throughout the century important though barely perceptible changes have certainly occurred continually in performing styles through the instinct of performers in new situations, some of them created by recording. The choir of King's College, Cambridge, taken by many in the 1960s to epitomize the sound of the English cathedral or collegiate choir, became hugely influential through the great number of LPs the choir made at the time under David Willcocks. During that decade, however, the sound the choir made altered significantly. This change in sound and style was not intentional; only when it had happened did the choirmaster notice and attempt to account for it. He chanced to listen to two recordings, one from the late 1950s and one from the late 60s, one after the other, and realized that the choir had instinctively developed a bigger, brighter and more penetrating sound and a rhythmically more pungent style over the decade. These changes were the result in part, he concluded, of making recordings with orchestras in repertory new to the choir, Bach's St John Passion, Vivaldi's Gloria, Handel's Chandos anthems, and masses by Haydn.[132] Five minutes away from King's College in Cambridge is St John's, with another famous chapel choir; the starting-point for its stylistic evolution in the 1950s was the choirmaster's wish to 'do something different' from their rivals down the road.[133] And it was recordings that provided inspirations and models: George Guest was impressed by the sounds of the choir at Montserrat Abbey, near Barcelona, which he had heard singing Victoria on a recording made in 1953,[134] and also by the Copenhagen Boys' Choir who had come to the Aldeburgh Festival in 1952 and had then made a recording of Britten's *Ceremony of Carols* with the composer conducting released in 1954.[135] Guest aimed to cultivate in his boys not the ethereal beauty of the King's boys but 'much bigger, more dramatic voices', developing in each boy 'a range extending over three octaves, from E flat or D below middle C to the G above top C' and encouraging them when singing top notes not to maintain a relaxed physique but 'to adopt something of the poise of an all-in wrestler'.[136]

Scholarship and performing styles

In the 1980s and 90s the sound of English choirs like the Tallis Scholars and The Sixteen singing fifteenth- and sixteenth-century polyphony particularly became well known to music-lovers all over the world through recordings; in Japan it was especially admired. It was characterized again and again by the same epithets, 'ethereal', 'otherworldly', 'pure', 'impersonal'. The distinctiveness of the style was clear, and evidenced as much from the vigorous dislike of some as from the enthusiasm of others; critics referred to the 'coldness' of the style, to its lack of 'personality', to its barren meticulousness, to 'under-interpretation'. The wider audience for these recordings would recognize the generalized sound and style of the English cathedral choir, the style of King's College, rather than St John's College, Cambridge. But the forces that moulded it were quite specific.

In the 1960s a young scholar was carrying out scholarly research at Oxford on the music of John Sheppard, who had been in charge of the music at his college, Magdalen, in the 1540s, and in 1961 he had formed a male voice ensemble of choral scholars to perform the music he was studying. David Wulstan gradually became convinced that most performances of a great deal of sixteenth-century sacred music were flawed stylistically since the music was being sung at the wrong pitch. It had long been recognized that much Jacobean sacred music was probably performed about a minor third above present-day pitch. But Wulstan considered that there was sufficient evidence to indicate that such upward transposition should be applied to the repertory going back to the music in the Eton Choirbook, assembled in the 1490s. Such conclusions immediately created obvious practical problems; boys certainly sang this repertory in the sixteenth century but the high tessitura could not have been sustained by the choirboys that Wulstan had sung with as an academical clerk at Magdalen College. He set out to demonstrate that such voice parts would have been within the capabilities of some boys in the sixteenth century, however; in the early Tudor period, he maintained, boys' voices did not break until they were eighteen or thereabouts and the increased size, strength and intelligence of the possessors of unbroken voices meant that they could negotiate a line which for their twentieth-century successors would be cruelly high. The use of present-day boys' voices being 'problematic', Wulstan related, 'women's voices were . . . substituted and incorporated into the ensemble. The change introduced a painful transition from what was by now the well-established excellence of the men, through an uncertain period when the women's voices threatened the homogeneity of the group, and in which their lack of apparent success met with insistent demands for a return to the earlier make-up of the ensemble. These tribulations came to an end, however, when persistence was finally vindicated and the high treble voice triumphantly reconstructed. It was not without irony that the agility and boyish clarity of the women's voices were by now perceived as typifying the tone quality of the Clerkes.'[137]

How did these young women learn to sing like boys in sixteenth-century English choirs? What texts or tracts or iconography did they consult in order to assimilate the style and perfect the techniques required? Of course there was nothing, or practically nothing. All they could do was imitate a model, and fail to reproduce it exactly because of their own particular vocal qualities and distinguishing features, or develop or extend it into something slightly different. The women who began singing in the Clerkes were all young, undergraduates or recent graduates, and were capable of producing a clear, bright tone characterized by a virtual absence of vibrato, yet each of them able to sustain a stronger and fuller sound than most choirboys can. A model was near at hand, in the chapel of Magdalen College itself, which possessed a fine choir of boys and academical clerks. And many of the lower voices the women were to sing with, the altos, tenors and basses, had been academical clerks in this college choir. It was the inspiration for the Clerkes' vocal colour and general style, a manner of singing highly characteristic of the English cathedral tradition as it had evolved in the twentieth century. Bernard Rose, who directed the choir between 1957 and 1981, had been a choirboy himself at Salisbury Cathedral in the 1920s. The general style of the choir under his direction was described in a review of a recording of their singing Tomkins released in 1979, a style characterized by 'gentle but clear articulation and ... fine balance' in which no attempt was ever made 'to cheapen the music by exaggerated phrasing or tempi', and in which everything was always 'in its place and well controlled'; 'a gentle serenity' informed all the performances.[138] But this was a style which owed most to Victorian ideals; the impersonality and the avoidance of flamboyance, the poise and the absence of rhetoric seem to have stemmed from a concern to create a sense of wonder and awe and reverence, seem to have emerged from particular concerns at the end of the nineteenth century owing much to characteristic emphases in the spiritual and devotional life of the Tractarians and to English society's conceptions of fitting behaviour and decorum. Similarly constituted choirs of men and boys have been singing in English cathedrals almost continuously since the sixteenth century, but what has survived of sixteenth-century singing styles and timbres it is impossible even to begin to speculate. And the minute particulars of the style were forged expressly for Magdalen Chapel, which was where most of the Clerkes' concerts were given for many years, and it was a style that many of the women who sang in the choir had experienced through attending services there. The standards attained by the all-male choir during the first five years of its existence were formidable and certainly challenged and inspired the first generation of women singing the treble and mean parts. Individual oustanding voices too set standards and suggested the cultivation of distinctive styles and timbres; among the first generation of Clerkes' countertenors was James Bowman, a one-time choral scholar at New College, the strength and colour of whose voice and whose sense of style influenced a whole generation of singers at Oxford.[139]

A musicological hunch or theory has had little or no effect unless it has been taken up in performances which have been widely disseminated through broadcasts and recordings, and the fruits of Wulstan's researches were so disseminated.[140] The starting-point for the singing style of the Clerkes had been a matter of historical scholarship. But Wulstan's theories,[141] it must be said, were never universally accepted. Wulstan insisted that the high treble voice fell into disuse during the course of the sixteenth century, the Cambridge scholar Roger Bowers that 'its first appearance can apparently be dated with some confidence to the 1570s'.[142] Wulstan saw his own researches as bringing the work of earlier researchers who demonstrated the importance of the minor third upwards transposition to its logical conclusion; Bowers described Wulstan's theories as they related to pre-Reformation choirs as 'unsustainable and invalid'[143] and as they related to notation 'entirely imaginary'.[144] Bowers conceded that 'changing patterns of nutrition have made twentieth-century men and boys taller and heavier than their sixteenth-century ancestors', but denies that these factors 'have affected the prevailing pitches of their respective voices'.[145] 'Neither physically nor vocally . . . can the early Tudor chorister have differed very much from his present-day successor.'[146] And yet Bowers's theories, meticulously researched, plausible, cogently presented, were not applied in actual performances. Meanwhile through their concerts and broadcasts and recordings the Clerkes of Oxenford developed tastes and cultivated audiences; there arose other choirs of similar constitution and with similar ideals regarding sonority and style, two of which became particularly well-known through concert performances in this country and abroad and through recordings and broadcasts, The Sixteen and The

Tallis Scholars. These choirs did not deny their paternity but inevitably stressed the differences between themselves and between other choirs like the Taverner Choir and the cathedral and college choirs who also sang this repertory.[147]

Scholarship has certainly had an influence on the way performing styles have developed and evolved, but not surprisingly performers have learnt from, and reacted to, the styles of contemporary performers much more than from the researches of musicologists. Even a performer as respected for his awareness of historical performing conditions and sensitivity to historical styles as Gustav Leonhardt explained that instinct and hunch and experiment and imitation of others' efforts came first with those Netherlands early musicians like himself and Frans Brüggen, and Anner Bylsma, and Sigiswald and Wieland and Barthold Kuijken: 'We never talked about any issues. . . . We played, and each one studied the pieces. We played – we had no theories. . . . I was investigating all the time, but from a tradition to a wealth of general concepts. And maybe . . . [our style] is all wrong; I don't know, it could be.'[148]

Changes in the performing styles of fourteenth-century chansons

The changes in the performing styles of pre-Bach repertory as documented by recordings have often been especially striking but the dynamics driving the changes are of a similar kind to those that bring about modifications in performances of Mozart or Beethoven or Brahms. Why did the New York Pro Musica perform Guillaume de Machaut's virelai *Douce dame jolie* on a recording issued in 1967 with two solo sopranos and a solo bass and an instrumental ensemble of gamba, recorders, bells and tabor, and David Munrow perform the same work on a recording issued in 1973 with a solo tenor, two countertenors, and a baritone, a sopranino recorder, cornetts, rebecs, citole and tabor,[149] whereas Christopher Page in his 1983 recording of Machaut's chansons with Gothic Voices gives this work to an unaccompanied contralto?[150] Clearly there is no agreement regarding many matters of performance practice and performing style of this fourteenth-century repertory, and in fact there will never be confident resolution of questions pertaining to speed, dynamics and dynamic shading, pitch and vocal quality and articulation and the even more fundamental aspect of the performance, which voices or instruments actually took part in particular works. How then did different musicians come to decisions about style?[151] The text of this particular chanson gives a twentieth-century performer no definitive clues: 'Fair sweet lady, / For God's sake do not think / that any woman has mastery / over me, save you alone.' David Munrow says in his liner notes that '[i]t is difficult to believe that the melody of . . . *Douce dame jolie* is anything but joyful, exuberant and extrovert, yet the texture fluctuates between a confident assertion of love and the conventional despair of a tormented heart.'[152] Munrow says elsewhere: 'The people of the Middle Ages and Renaissance liked gorgeous colours in their clothes, sharp contrasts in their paintings, and highly spiced dishes at their table. The characteristics of their musical instruments were equally individual and uncompromising.'[153] And his manner of performing *Douce dame jolie* seems to be informed by such an encapsulation of the age. In fact these are views which clearly derived from the picture powerfully presented in a highly influential history book first published, in Dutch, in 1919, and then in English five years later, Johan Huizinga's *The Waning of the Middle Ages*. This famous book worked its way into general perceptions of every aspect of medieval life and culture; it suggested that the fourteenth and the fifteenth centuries were not so much preparations for the Renaissance – an old and familiar idea – but a period of dying, of 'waning', of the 'autumnalness' of the original Dutch title, and that during these years men escaped from the violence and brutality of their lives into beautiful fictions like chivalry and courtly love.

In 1929 the musicologist Rudolf von Ficker, who was certainly influenced by the atmosphere conjured up in Huizinga's book, associated Machaut's music with a kind of naive, desperate thirsting for colour and brilliant sonorities and lively movement which Huizinga found to be so characteristic of the waning Middle Ages: 'Now let your mind conceive how the metallic boy voices were mingled with the gentle tintinnabulations of the glockenspiels, cymbals, triangles and so on then in use, together with the dulcet tones of the viols, while the long sustained notes of the lower parts were sung by smooth tenor voices, supported by the manifold wind instruments. Thus you have some idea of the dazzling tone magic of such motets.'[154] Huizinga and von Ficker didn't influence performers at first. Of course very little of this music was performed between the wars. In order to re-create the timbres that Rudolf von Ficker described, the early music movement revival had to stimulate enough interest in old instruments to create a demand for their commercial manufacture by such firms as Hermann Moeck in Celle, and to create a large enough audience through radio and records to sustain the livelihoods of musicians devoted to the exploration of these new repertories. By the 1950s there was the LP and there were a number of musicians who were convinced of the music's interest and power and subtlety, and energetic enough to develop the necessary technical expertise. They were also keen to explode any of those notions of quaintness and eccentricity that undoubtedly were still associated with this repertory; 'For most people', a critic commented in 1955, 'music before Bach is a fairly precious cult of museum pieces.'[155] And some of the performances then heard did not encourage the sceptical; a radio critic described a programme on the Third Programme of late fourteenth- and early fifteenth-century English music from the Old Hall manuscript as 'little more than a form of monotonous highbrow yodelling'.[156]

The American Noah Greenberg formed one of the most influential early music groups of all in 1952, the New York Pro Musica and in addition the Pro Musica Chorus and the Primavera Singers. Not himself a scholar – though he eagerly consulted such experts as Gustave Reese and Edward Lowinsky – nor indeed a virtuoso executant, Greenberg was an extrovert, ebullient, passionate lover of early music with an energetic, robust, rather jerky conducting style which elicited in his performers forceful, animated responses; early music, he thought, must never sound 'quaint'.[157] In their performances of Machaut the New York Pro Musica drew on the evidence of the representations of musicians in medieval art, on literary descriptions of music-making, and on Machaut's own lists of instruments and his own remarks on the performance of a few of his own works. Scholars seemed fairly sure that the written composition could at least on occasion represent 'only the skeleton of the performed one', as Reese explained; there are no parts suitable for chime-bells in the musical manuscripts that have survived and yet chime-bells 'are depicted in many miniatures of the period and are mentioned in literary sources'; and it's known that drones were widely used but none are notated.[158] So in the simpler monophonic pieces like *Douce dame jolie* Noah Greenberg would add instrumental parts, for recorders, sackbuts, crumhorns, gambas, vielles and percussion instruments, and introduce elements of improvisation. It also made good sense as this repertory was written for a society in which instrumental music had high cultural status.

Such songs by Machaut would be built up into recital programmes performed by the New York Pro Musica, which became a highly successful touring band; in the 1966–7 season it gave more than a hundred concerts.[159] And undoubtedly the style and instrumentation of particular chansons would be influenced by the requirements of satisfactory programme planning, of a song's position in the overall scheme of things: it would probably be desirable that the opening items of each half of a concert grab the listener's attention and the closing item present a rousing conclusion, for example, and so the same piece might be given a more forceful or livelier interpretation in these positions than it would have received had it been programmed elsewhere. And the same would apply in broadcast or recorded recitals. This was an ensemble which revelled in the virtuosity of its members in repertory which had often previously been cultivated by those of modest instrumental and vocal attainments, and these musicians were constantly on the lookout for opportunities to display their prowess. They all wanted to be used; in a touring band they all had to earn their fees, after all. And so these performances of the 1950s and 60s reflected that view of the late Middle Ages painted by Huizinga in 1919, as an epoch when aesthetic enjoyment most often seems to spring from 'sensations of luminous brightness or of lively movement'.[160] But they also reflected, among other factors, the economic state of musical instrument manufacture, and the tastes of an emerging audience of discerning connoisseurs which still had to be wooed with ear-catching timbres.

Inevitably the view of the Middle Ages built up by Huizinga was subsequently developed and revised and modified and complicated by later historians, and musicians have taken hints from these revisions. They have come to see Noah Greenberg's and David Munrow's interpretations for what they obviously are, what anyone's realizations of this music must be, a personal vision, and later players and singers have wanted to create their own views and their own performing styles. Christopher Page's later historical researches suggested that this music by Machaut was sung not by minstrels but by chapel singers and that at least in some households in late-Medieval France, exclusively vocal performance was common. And he put the theory into practice in performances by his group Gothic Voices. It was a particularly attractive theory in England where the college choirs of Oxford and Cambridge produced a steady stream of singers with the straight clear timbres thought particularly apt for this music.[161] But even if these performances were historically more accurate than before in using voices alone, it's unlikely that the timbres and qualities of the voices used by Machaut were much like those of Gothic Voices. The performances convinced because of their expertise and their stylishness, and they attracted attention because they were new.

Even in the years when it was usual for thirteenth- and fourteenth-century chansons to be performed with instruments, there were very different performing styles that jostled for attention. Thomas Binkley and the Studio der Frühen Musik examined the techniques of folk music and non-European musics that had very ancient traditions of performance in an attempt to discover clues and hints about the performing styles of Medieval European music.[162] When they performed the simple tunes of the trouvères, French songs of the thirteenth century, for example, they applied to them techniques derived from Spanish and North African folk music, adding instrumental accompaniments but also improvisatory or quasi-improvisatory *ritornelli*.[163]

Changing styles in Webern performance

Performances of the orchestral music of Anton Webern in the 1950s, and especially of the works from the Symphony op. 21 onwards, emphasized the fragmentary nature of the music – the way it was constructed, the pointilliste nature of the instrumentation, with only a note or two or just a handful being allocated to a single instrument or part at a time – emphasized the exiguous textures and the wide range of pitches and the sudden dynamic contrasts, and presented a rather jagged, hard-edged profile. But gradually through the 1960s and 70s performances of late Webern began to emphasize continuities, to discover the lines that might be constructed from the flecks and flashes of different colours and timbres, and these later performances created softer, subtler, more flexible contours. Why did this happen? Which performing style is the correct one?

Webern's music was so unlike the other music of its time and of the late nineteenth century that the performers at the time it was composed, those few who knew anything about it at all, found it very difficult to grasp its essential character. Otto Klemperer, who conducted the Symphony op. 21, once in 1931 and again in 1936, confessed that he simply didn't understand it.[164] And the difficulties were compounded by the notational complexities, by the continuities – if indeed they were intended to be projected and experienced as continuities – being invisible to the individual orchestral player. Only with experience and long familiarity with particular works could players hope to master the idiom. In the 1950s most orchestral musicians possessed no knowledge at all of any appropriate style for this music. The orchestral works in the series of recordings made by Robert Craft in the 1950s were not based on live concerts and for a number of the works each player had to be coached individually 'until he had learned his part like a cipher'.[165] The music appeared to these musicians as enigmatic and secretive as its creator. Even Stravinsky, who hailed Webern as 'a perpetual Pentecost' and described his works as 'dazzling diamonds',[166] said that he wondered 'if even Webern himself knew who Webern was'.[167]

But a small number of avant-garde composers in the 1950s, Stockhausen, Nono, Pousseur, Ligeti, Boulez and their followers and disciples, did know who Webern was: in his own music Ligeti wanted to avoid, at all costs, 'great, whirling passions, all grand expressive gestures'[168] and in Webern Ligeti saw 'expressionism . . . so overstrained that it can no longer be seen as expression', it has turned 'into a statue of itself'.[169] The super- or hyper-expressionism which the notation might seem to imply was misleading; in Webern's late works at any rate, the expressionism had transformed itself into an effect at once 'crystalline and deep-frozen', as Ligeti describes it.[170] A passage from a German encyclopaedia published in 1954 in an article on their new generation of composers explained that these musicians acknowledge Webern as their master: 'What we hear is only single notes, high and low, first faster, then at a slower rate, and from time to time a glissando or a harmonic tone. These do not constitute the work's meaning, but are merely symbols that we have to put together to make the whole. This kind of music requires a much more active participation from us as listeners. We experience to a certain extent only the material: the form has to be worked out.'[171]

The recordings of Webern supervised by Craft were the first that became widely known;[172] they were recognized as a landmark and saluted by the critics who noted, however, 'a certain dryness and lack of sensuousness'[173] in the interpretations, that some of them strove more for an absolute clarity and precision than towards a projection of emotional intensity. These qualities certainly were in part the result of the difficulties being experienced by the players; but the performances also reflected the prevailing notions of the composers particularly interested in these works, those composers of the avant-garde who were analysing them and describing them and assessing their importance from their own creative points of view, with the result that the performances are characterized by broken-up lines and textures, by strict tempos and an absence of rubato, and by impersonal, terraced dynamic levels.

Pierre Boulez has been an advocate for this music over five decades and his performances have chronicled the evolution of the performing style, or, it may be truer to say, he has discovered in this music a different kind of expressiveness in performances of such power and authority that they have been taken as the starting-point for others' explorations. The earliest recorded Webern performances of Boulez – of the Symphony op. 21 at the 1956 season of his Domaine Musical concerts,[174] and of the Cantata no. 1 op. 29 and the Cantata no. 2 op. 30 at the 1957 season[175] – demonstrate clearly the same salient features as the Craft recordings. But in his recordings of Webern's scores issued in 1979 – though most of them were made ten years earlier – Boulez achieved a flexibility and subtlety in his interpretations that were, in the words of Wilfrid Mellers, 'strictly speaking, a revelation; what it reveals is the continuity of lyrical line beneath the apparent fragmentation. The song sings in a metaphysical heaven, infinitely far off; yet, supported by a structure of fine steel, sing it does, infinitely tender.'[176] The performances of Webern Boulez heard in the 1950s repelled him, he said later:

> there was a complete lack of continuity between the instruments, no flexibility in the structures, and no feeling of transition from one part of the work to another. . . . You have to discover how an instrumentalist can play an isolated sound in a way that links it *intelligently* with what has gone before and what follows. You must make him understand a pointillistic phrasing, not just with his intellect but with his physical senses. So long as a player does not realize that when he

has a note to play it comes to him from another instrument and passes from him to yet another, or that if he has an isolated note it has a precise role within the polyphonic texture, then he will be incapable of the concentration necessary to make his note interesting. He will then produce a note that is 'stupid', divorced from the context. This is why those earlier performances of Webern had seemed idiotic to me: the musicians did not seem to understand their roles. They played stupidly, and this was reflected in the resulting sonority, which also became stupid.[177]

Certainly the differences were the result of his own developing mastery as a conductor during the 1950s and 60s and later, as well as players' growing confidence and familiarity with the idiom. But they were just as clearly the result too of his own creative concerns. He was attracted at first 'by the organisation and structure of [Webern's] language', when he himself was concerned with exploring the possibilities of total serialism and creating such works as *Polyphonie X* and Book I of *Structures*; only later did he become aware of 'the expressivity, of the phrasing you had to give – a phrasing which goes with the dynamic and the rhythm'. Boulez described this as 'a radical revolution in my thinking about Webern'.[178] It was as much a radical revolution in his own creative thinking as in his re-creative ideas, and clearly the two are inseparable. His experience as an orchestral conductor, and perhaps particularly as a conductor of Webern, the acquisition of a mastery which allowed him to direct musicians more freely and more flexibly, showed him practical and expressive possibilities that stimulated his interpretative ideas and also fructified the creative imagination that was to express itself in such works as *Pli selon Pli*, *Éclat/Multiples* and *Rituel*, the strength of whose steel-like structures is as apparent as the sensuous, infinitely subtle, elusive, kaleidoscopic surfaces.

Which performing style then is correct? No performing tradition at all was established in the composer's own lifetime. Even in Austria, even in Vienna – where he was highly esteemed as an excellent musician – his own works were hardly ever performed, and when they were, were greeted with astonishment, incomprehension, and mild ridicule by performers as well as audiences.[179] And then forgotten. The only recording issued during Webern's lifetime was of his String Trio op. 20, a performance by the Kathleen Washbourne Trio released in

1939.[180] The composer was sent a copy of the record and he set down his impressions in a letter to his pupil Willi Reich: 'The recording of my Trio is, as a recording, very good. But the performance! I recognize the presence of diligence and the best of intentions, but not really my music. I am convinced, however, that it would have turned out much better if only one had given the players a few pointers. Nonetheless I certainly respect the accomplishment.'[181]

The few pointers or hints that Webern gave in other contexts suggest that the qualities emphasized in the performances of the 1950s resulted in what Webern might have regarded as distortions. The most striking is his remark muttered to the pianist Peter Stadlen after a performance of his Symphony conducted by Otto Klemperer: 'A high note, a low note, a note in the middle – like the music of a madman!'[182] Which some might accept as a description of the postwar interpretations that so repelled Boulez. And Peter Stadlen, who worked with the composer on the Piano Variations for their first performance in 1937, did suggest quite another style of performance from the jagged, pointillistic style favoured in the 1950s. Webern treated 'those few scrappy notes', Stadlen recalled, 'as if they were cascades of sound. He kept on referring to the melody which, he said, must be as telling as a spoken sentence. This melody would sometimes reside in the top notes of the right hand and then for some bars be divided between both left and right. It was shaped by an enormous amount of constant rubato and by a most unpredictable distribution of accents. But there were also definite changes of tempo every few bars to mark the beginning of a "new sentence".'[183] Stadlen also remarked on the great importance Webern attached to 'a conscious use of the sustaining pedal (although there are no pedal marks) not only as a means of varying the tone colour but also to make up for the angular thinness of the texture and to increase the sheer volume of sound in climaxes'.[184] Hermann Scherchen Webern considered 'the best conductor for his works', according to his pupil Karl Amadeus Hartmann;[185] Scherchen it was who conducted the first performance of Webern's Variations for Orchestra op. 30, and the first performance of *Das Augenlicht* in June 1938 at the International Society for Contemporary Music Festival in London. In his *Handbook of Conducting* published in 1929 Scherchen constantly emphasizes the singing line: 'Often', he says, 'we conductors encounter orchestral playing in which . . . accuracy, elasticity, even-

1. The first gramophone on sale in England. It was made in Germany about 1894 by Kämmerer and Rheinhart of Waltershausen and imported to England by Parkins and Gotto, toy manufacturers of Oxford Street. The machine played five-inch records, about the size of a modern CD. The horn is not original. (British Library)

2. An 1914 advertisement for a 'Vocalion' gramophone in *The Strand* magazine. (British Library)

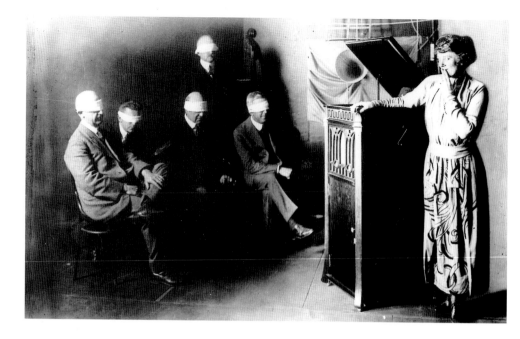

3 (*above*). A publicity photograph of Frieda Hempel, an Edison recording artist, with Edison employees posing as listeners to a 'tone test', a recital of music and musical 're-creations' on the phonograph. The public had to guess whether the artist was singing, whether the phonograph was playing alone, or whether singer and machine were sounding together. Thousands of such public recitals were given before millions of Americans by the Edison Company between 1916 and 1925. (United States Department of the Interior, National Park Service, Edison Historic Site)

4. 'The Byrd Tercentenary', an advertisement from *The Gramophone* vol.1, no.3, August 1923. (British Library)

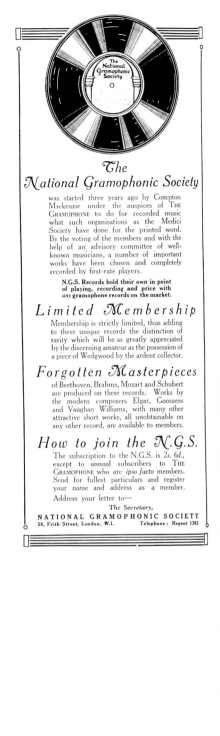
5 (*left*). Advertisement for The National Gramophonic Society, from *The Gramophone* vol.4, no.10, March 1927 p.405. (British Library)

6. Imprimatur of Maurice Ravel: 'Je viens d'entendre les disques de mon quatuor enregistré par le "International String Quartet". J'en suis tout à fait satisfait tant au point de vue de la sonorité qu'à celui des mouvements et des nuances.' The recording was released as National Gramophonic Society discs 78, 79, 80, 81 (4 double-sided 12" discs). From *The Gramophone* vol.5, no.4, September 1927, p.139. (British Library)

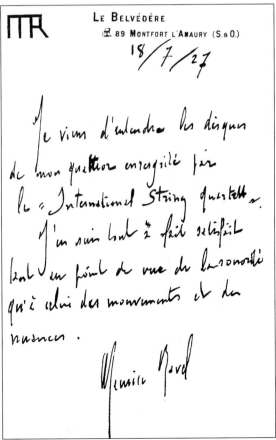

7 (*left*). Elgar in a recording studio on 20 January 1914 when he recorded his *Carissima* (Gramophone 0967, a single-sided 12" disc). The tape wound round the horn is to soften the tinniness of the sound. (British Library)

8. Sir Henry Wood conducting the New Queen's Hall Orchestra on 2 July 1919 when he recorded Liszt's Hungarian Rhapsody no.14 in F minor S.244/14 at Columbia's London recording studio. Recording: Columbia L1412, a double-sided 12" disc. (EMI)

9. Recording Verdi's *Don Carlos* in Walthamstow Town Hall in August 1970. Recording: EMI set SLS 956, a four-LP set. (EMI)

10. Tape-editing: the editor prepares to splice two pieces of tape; locations on the brown tape will be marked with a yellow pencil and cut with a razor blade; adhesive splicing-tape is applied to the back so the oxide surface remains uninterrupted. (British Library)

11. David Munrow (centre) playing an alto curtal with Roger Brenner on the right and Alan Lumsden on the left, both playing tenor sackbuts in Studio 1, Abbey Road. (EMI)

12. The head of the International Artists Department of *His Master's Voice*, Fred Gaisberg, pours coffee for Artur Schnabel; the record man encourages the musician. (EMI)

13. The record producer Walter Legge, on left, in the playback room with, from left to right, the pianist Lev Oborin, the violinist David Oistrakh, and the cellist Svyatoslav Knushevitsky; the record man produces the musicians. (Hulton Getty)

14. John Culshaw and Benjamin Britten interpreting the musical score for the disc. (Decca)

Third Programme

464 m. (647 kc/s)

6.0 p.m. CHAMBER MUSIC

Quartet No. 3 in A, Op. 30
William Wordsworth
Quartet No. 3......*Elizabeth Maconchy*
played by the
Macgibbon String Quartet:
Margot Macgibbon (violin)
Lorraine du Val (violin)
Jean Stewart (viola)
Lilly Phillips (cello)
(BBC recording)

6.40 Recorded in New York
THE REVOLT
OF THE AUTHORS

Talk by Mary McCarthy about
the Muse and the Academy

A picture of American writing in its
current uneasy relation with the
university: 'the short story seminar;
the writers' conference; the critical
exegesis; the courses in how to
understand fiction and poetry; and
the modernised classroom as host to
a new blight of conformity'
(Yesterday's recorded broadcast)

6.55
BBC
NORTHERN ORCHESTRA
(Leader, Reginald Stead)
Conducted by Vilem Tausky

Overture: Julius Caesar....*Schumann*
El Salon Mexico.............*Copland*
Symphony No. 5.................*Jirak*

The Czech composer, Karel Boleslav Jirak,
who was born in Prague in 1891, studied

with Novak and J. B. Foerster. During
the First World War and the nineteen-
twenties he held several conductor's posts
in Czechoslovakia and Germany, and from
1930 to 1934 was professor at the Prague
Conservatoire. Shortly after the last war
he settled in the United States, and is at
present living in Chicago, where he is a
professor at the Roosevelt College of Music.

His Fifth Symphony was written between
October 1948 and March 1949, and was
awarded a prize in the Edinburgh International Festival Competition (the other
prizewinner being William Wordsworth,
with his Second Symphony). Jirak's symphony, like Wordsworth's, was first performed at the 1951 Festival by the Scottish
National Orchestra under Walter Susskind.
Less uncompromising in style than many
of his works, it is scored for a large
orchestra and is in four movements. The
first, in orthodox sonata-form, has a slow
introduction; the second, an Andante, is a
strict passacaglia; the third is a Scherzo;
the last opens with a slow introduction and
based on that of the first movement, and
makes use of themes heard earlier in the
work.
Deryck Cooke

8.0 THE PROBLEM
OF RELIGIOUS BELIEFS

Discussion by the
Epiphany Philosophers

(BBC recording)

To be repeated on Saturday at 10.0

---

194 m. (1,546 kc/s)

8.45 DOMENICO SCARLATTI

Sonatas:
L. 418 in D; L. 103 in G
L. 205 in C; L. 381 in F
played by
Fernando Valenti (harpsichord)
on gramophone records

followed by an interlude at 9.5

9.10   'LOVE
AND FREINDSHIP'
by Jane Austen
Adapted for radio and produced
by Terence Tiller
Music composed and conducted
by Anthony Smith-Masters

Isabel....................Thea Wells
Laura...................Brenda Dunrich
The young Isabel........Sarah Caisley
The young Laura......Prunella Scales
Laura's father............Neil Tuson
Edward.................Frank Duncan
Augusta..................Patricia Brent
Sophia................Susan Kennaway
Augustus................David Spenser
Gustavus..........Alexander Davion
Lord St. Clair.......Reginald Thorne

To be repeated tomorrow at 7.30
Frank Swinnerton writes on page 6

10.10   SCHUBERT

Julius Patzak (tenor)
Frederick Stone (accompanist)

Alinde (Rochlitz); Sprache der Liebe
(Schuber); Ganymed (Goethe);
Litanei; auf das Fest Aller Seelen
(Jacobi); Sei mir gegrüsst (Rückert);
Du liebst mich nicht (Platen); Die
Liebe hat gelogen (Platen); An den
Mond (Hölty); Rastlose Liebe
(Goethe)
(BBC recording)

The eighth of a series of twelve Schubert
Lieder recitals, devised by Richard Capell.
Next programme: November 10

10.45 PROSPECT OF BRITAIN

An observer's impressions
of current life and opinion
A series of eight talks
by Christopher Salmon

1—Beginning the Journey

In this opening talk Mr. Salmon suggests
that national life should be described not
in political or economic terms but as a
fabric made up of personal relations.
(Recording of Sunday's broadcast)

11.5 CHORAL CONCERT

Choir of Salisbury Cathedral
Conductor, Douglas Guest

O Maria et Elizabeth.*Gilbert Banester*
O Lord make thy servant Elizabeth
our Queen to rejoice in thy strength
William Byrd
(Recorded broadcast of June 6)

11.30   Close Down

---

15. The billing in *Radio Times* for the BBC Third Programme evening selection for Wednesday 4 November 1953; the Third Programme began in September 1946 and transmitted old and new musical repertory that had up till then rarely been heard even by specialists and scholars; the talks, drama and documentary programmes which were interwoven with music were not intended as light relief. From *Radio Times*. (British Library)

Instrumental Records

Issued in Album Series No. 78

CORTOT (*Pianoforte*), THIBAUD (*Violin*), AND CASALS ('*Cello*)

12-Inch Double-sided Red Label Records ....8/6 each

DB 1223 { *TRIO No. 7 IN B FLAT MAJOR,*
Op. 97—(The Arch-Duke).....................BEETHOVEN
1st Movement—Allegro moderato—Parts 1 and 2

DB 1224 2nd Movement—Scherzo—Allegro—Parts 1 and 2

DB 1225 3rd Movement—Andante cantabile, ma pero con moto—
Parts 1 and 2

DB 1226 3rd Movement—Andante cantabile, ma pero con moto—
Parts 3 and 4

DB 1227 4th Movement—Allegro moderato—Parts 1 and 2

The Thibaud–Casals–Cortot trio is a combination almost unique in musical history. Not since the days of Joachim and Piatti have such illustrious artists forsaken the attractions of solo playing for the supremely beautiful, but less glamorous Chamber Music. Listening to Cortot, Thibaud or Casals as soloists we are at once aware of individual and compelling personalities, yet so great are they as artists and so sincere their devotion to their art, that as a chamber music trio they play as with one mind. That unanimity is, of course, the secret of the greatness of the trio.

Beethoven's Trio in B Flat, Opus 97 (called the " Archduke " because it was dedicated to his friend and pupil the Archduke Rudolf), is generally admitted to be the greatest of all Pianoforte Trios. It was composed during the winter of 1810, but not performed in public until April, 1814. It is worthy of note that Beethoven made his last public appearance as a pianist in this work.

If we take the customary division of Beethoven's lifework into three periods we find this trio at the end of the second phase. It is a work of great emotional depth and yet instant appeal, and you will find, particularly with the third movement, that each repetition reveals a host of new beauties. The slow movement is indeed one of Beethoven's noblest inspirations.

Cortot, Thibaud and Casals have achieved a great performance, which has been recorded with absolute fidelity.

16. The Cortot-Thibaud-Casals Trio; HMV 'New Records' Catalogue, mid-April 1929 (British Library)

The LP sleeve presented a new format for designers and artists, and designers subtly or not so subtly emphasized composer and work, or performer, or style of performance, depending on the supposed most likely audience. The same performances of the same repertory might be repackaged for markets with presumed different levels of sophistication.

• • •

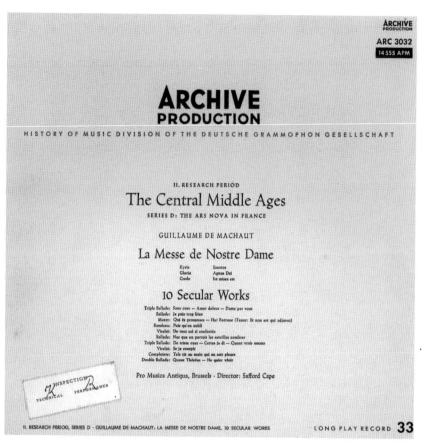

Archive Production emphasized unfamiliar repertory in historically aware performing styles and sonorities; Archive covers proclaimed their serious intent and insert cards with each disc gave details not only of performers on a recording but also of instruments being played, editions used, location of the recording, and the name of the producer and engineer.

17a. (*above*) Guillaume de Machaut: *La Messe de Nostre Dame* Archive Production ARC 3032, a mono LP recorded in 1956

facing page

17 b (*above*) and c. Sleeve and insert cards for the same LP(British Library)

Com-poser	Name: **MACHAUT, Guillaume de**			born: on: ca. 1300 at: Machaut (Ardennen)	died: on: 1377 at: Rheims		ARCHIVE PRODUCTION
	Title: **La Messe de Nostre Dame**			No:	Key:	Opus:	INDEX CARD · HISTORY OF MUSIC DIVISION OF THE DEUTSCHE GRAMMOPHON GESELLSCHAFT
Work	Type of Composition:	Complete work:	No:	Movements/Tempi:		Duration	
	Instrumentation: **4 voices**	Place of composition: **Rheims (?)**	Year: **1364(?)**	Kyrie I / Christe / Kyrie II/III Gloria Credo Sanctus Agnus Dei Ite, missa est Total timing with pauses		5'14 5'04 7'36 4'43 4'16 1'18 28'44	
	Text:	Place of first performance:	Year:				
	Origin/Source: **Paris, Bibl. nat. franç. 22546 Paris, Bibl. nat. franç. 9221**	Place of first publication:	Year:				
Edition	Version:	Critically revised material: **Charles van den Borren Safford Cape**		Place of publication:		Year:	
	Publishers:	Edition No: **(see reverse side)**		Volume:		No:	
Per-formance	Soloists: **Pro Musica Antiqua (see reverse side)**	Conductor: **Safford Cape**		Orchestra:		Size:	
		Instruments: **(see reverse side)**		Choir:		Size:	
Recording	Place: **Brussels**	Producer: **Dr. Fred Hamel**		Research period No: **II The Central Middle Ages (1100—1350)**			
	Hall or studio: **Palais du Comte d'Egmont**	Technical supervisor: **Werner Grimme**		Series No: **D The Ars Nova in France**			
	Date: **1/31 & 2/1/1956**	**1** 12" Sides		Archive No: **ARC 3 032 a 14555 a**			

Performers

Elisabeth Verlooy, Soprano
Jeanne Deroubaix, Alto
René Letroye, Tenor
Franz Mertens, Tenor
Willy Pourtois, Bass
Silva Devos, Recorders
Janine Rubinlicht, Treble-fiddle
Gaston Dôme, Tenor-fiddle
André Douvere, Tenor-fiddle
Michel Podolski, Lute

Instruments:

Recorders: Descant, by Hermann Moeck, 1952
Alto, by Franz Küng, Schaffhausen/Switzerland 1953
Tenor, by Gobel, Oxford 1950

Treble-fiddle: by Pietro Aaron: "Thoscanello de la musica", 1531, reconstructed by Otwin, Hannover 1932

Tenor-fiddles: by Francesco Francia: "Madonne tronante", reconstructed by Otwin, Hannover 1932

Lute: Double-choired Tenorlute by Peter Harlan, Markneukirchen 1930

New Editions:

Jacques Chailley, Messe Notre-Dame dite du Sacre de Charles V, Paris 1948, Rouart & Lerolle

Armand Machabey, La messe à quatre voix de Guillaume de Machaut, Liège 1948, Aelberts

Guillaume de Van, Guillaume de Machaut, La messe de Notre Dame, Rome 1949, American Institute of Musicology

Hanns Hübsch, La Messe de Notre Dame, Heidelberg 1953, Süddeutscher Musikverlag Willy Müller

Heinrich Besseler, Guillaume de Machaut, Musikalische Werke Volume IV, Messe und Lais, Leipzig 1943 and 1954, VEB Breitkopf & Härtel

OL 50062

FRANÇOIS COUPERIN - LE - GRAND

COMPLETE WORKS FOR HARPSICHORD

RUGGERO GERLIN

(Pleyel Harpsichord)

LONDON

·

EDITIONS DE

L'OISEAU-LYRE

·

Long playing 33⅓ r.p.m. microgroove record

18. Sleeve for L'Oiseau-Lyre's recording of Couperin's harpsichord works issued in 1955. Recording: L'Oiseau-Lyre OL 50062 a mono LP. (British Library)

facing page

19 (*above*). 'The Symphonies of Joseph Haydn', Symphonies numbers 12 and 56 in the projected series of all the Haydn symphonies conducted by Max Goberman. Recording: Library of Recorded Masterpieces HS5, a stereo LP released in 1962 (British Library)

20. Bach: *St John Passion* 'Erste Schallplattenproduktion in Originalbesetzung mit Originalinstrumenten', released in 1966 with no details about the performance on the front cover; the conductor was Hans Gillesberger. Recording: Telefunken Das Alte Werk SKL19 (three stereo LPs)

THE SYMPHONIES OF JOSEPH HAYDN

HS 5   Symphony No. 56 in C Major □ Symphony No. 12 in E Major

LIBRARY OF RECORDED MASTERPIECES

In Nomine Domini

Joseph Haydn mia

STEREOPHONIC

Laus Deo.

DAS ALTE WERK

KOSTBARKEITEN AUS DEM MUSIKALISCHEN VERMÄCHTNIS ALTER MEISTER

J.S.BACH
JOHANNES PASSION

Erste Schallplattenproduktion in Originalbesetzung
- mit Originalinstrumenten

GRAND
PRIX DU
DISQUE

21. Chopin Waltzes played by Tamàs Vàsàry on DG SLPEM 136 485, a stereo LP released in 1966. (British Library)

22. Reissued in 1972 in the Netherlands as Polyphon 2542 008, a stereo LP. (Jaco van Witteloostuyn)

23. Stockhausen: Gruppen, Carré, DG 137002, a stereo LP released in 1968. (British Library)

24. *Greatest Hits Karlheinz Stockhausen*, Polydor set 2612023, two stereo LPs released in 1973. (British Library)

25. Florence Austral. Recording: Rubini RDA 005, a mono LP released in 1983. (British Library)

ness, power . . . are united, but in which we miss one thing: the soul of the music, the song that gives life to musical sounds. . . . All music, both in conception and in actualisation is singing.'[186] And again: 'Melodies that are not given out by one soloist throughout, but pass, in subdivision, from one instrument to another, cannot be correctly performed unless each player sings the whole of them as they are played, and contributes his share in accordance with the conception of the whole thus formed.'[187] The conclusion then would be that Webern did indeed wish for great flexibility in time and the moulding of lines through the changes in instrumentation and colour.

Klemperer requested the composer play through the Symphony to him on the piano before he was to conduct it: 'He came and played with enormous intensity and fanaticism . . . passionately.' The conductor had to explain that he simply was not able to bring such intensity and flexibility to an orchestral performance.[188] And the pianist Edward Steuermann, who took part in the first performance of the Concerto op. 24, remembered the composer playing passages from its first movement on the piano for him: 'He played so freely that I could hardly follow the music. . . . When he conducted, however, he was not so free; I suppose one cannot be, or at least he could not.'[189] So performances that would have won the composer's wholehearted approval may not have been realizable; at any rate they were unrealized.

Peter Stadlen detected a dual attitude of Webern towards his own music, the components of which in his opinion were never reconciled: a fanatical concern with 'autonomous structural sense' which the composers of the late nineteenth century he considered had sacrificed, and at the same time a passionate 'urge to express extra-musical contents'.[190] Boulez was himself fanatically concerned and preoccupied with establishing a new musical grammar in the 1940s and 50s; he wanted, he said, to construct a musical language from scratch. He had 'a horror of discussing verbally what is so smugly called the problem of aesthetics', he said in 1948 at the age of twenty-two: 'I shall prolong this article no further; I prefer to return to my lined paper.'[191] It might be claimed that in the 1940s and 50s young composers like Boulez and Stockhausen were interested not in the music of Webern but simply in the music's grammar, in its technical processes. Later, when Boulez had taken from it what he needed, he could investigate the music's style as well as its grammar and logic. But it may be that the style he eventually cultivated in performances of Webern derived from his own concerns about style in his own music rather more than Webern's.

Such conundrums have not caused difficulties for Boulez; the 'correctness' of a performing style is for him a meaningless concept. The 1950s and the 1980s were inevitably different worlds; the total context had changed. The performances of the 1950s were for an epoch and for a generation which was concerned to do away with all conventional musical expressive gestures and rhetoric. The assertiveness and roughness and rawness of some of the playing was part of its expressiveness, its defiance, maybe, its determination to strike out along new paths. By the 1980s there were different imperatives. No solutions to the problems which preoccupied the avant-garde of the 1950s had been found, but by the 1980s no solutions were necessary; there were other problems and other aesthetic challenges. There was much more old music in the air, there were the musics of different classical traditions and the folk traditions of the world; recordings most of all had changed the contexts. Such performances of Webern as Boulez's of the 1960s and 70s revealed music to a younger generation of people like the Englishman Jonathan Harvey which, though created in an Expressionist crucible, yet fused into a compound 'closer to Palestrina, with its own de-emphasized floating curves, and modal oriental music, rather than its own recent past'.[192] In England in the 1980s Harvey sought, like Boulez, he said, 'balanced universes of sound, poised without any rootedness, and this to my ear tends to come closer to the objective musics of our own distant past and of the east – objective in that they're more concerned with collective and spiritual existence'.[193] Liberation from tonal gravity in a consistent style was first achieved this century in the works of Webern, starting with the Symphony of 1928, according to Harvey. 'Significantly, at that point Webern ceased to be an expressionist, striving after extreme expression. He suddenly relaxed, basking in the radiance of the new feelings, the new consciousness. The music is not disruptive any more, but poised in a clear space.'[194] In late Webern, in the Stravinsky of the *Symphony of Psalms* and in the serial works, as in the polyphony of Thomas Tallis, as in many eastern musics, 'time is shot through with timelessness'. For Boulez the search for authenticity of musical expression is not a search for historical verisimilitude; for him 'memory' and 'tradition' are not the key elements of musical interpretation; for him the 'truth of any interpretation is essentially transitory'.[195] It is a sign of weakness, he has reiterated, not to have the confidence to remake the masterpieces of the past for contemporary needs. Boulez himself has betrayed no such weakness.

Twentieth-century concepts of the musical work

After listening to a concert conducted by Elgar in 1929 the music critic of *The Times* urged recording companies to make discs of the composer conducting his own works so that posterity would know how he meant his music to sound; Elgar's music, 'in spite of the meticulous markings' in the scores, 'is written in his head, and only there. Such things as the pauses and accents, directions for *rubato . . .* and such indeterminate suggestions of mood as his favourite *Nobilmente*, acquire their authoritative interpretation only from him. He knows where to throw the emphasis in each phrase, so as to give it eloquence. . . . His mind, especially in the oratorios, moves in a region for which notation offers no precise record.'[196]

But although performers can hear what Elgar and Strauss and Prokofiev and Stravinsky actually did – or at least can scrutinize and as it were 'interpret' the recordings and come to some confident conclusions about their performances – and could aim to reproduce these interpretations, they don't attempt this. What then are they doing? What is interpretation? What in the first place is the musical work and what exactly is it that composers do?

The composer writes down as if from dictation a perfectly finished musical work from a performance in his head of magisterial authority. That is the picture. Of course nobody ever believed that such a process happened literally, except a few Hollywood producers. But such a metaphorical account emphasized that the power and coherence of a musical masterpiece derived from forces not wholly within the composer's conscious control, that the work of genius was in some sense a force of nature, that the harmonic and motivic symmetries to be discovered in the work of a master, the balances, and echoes, and pre-echoes, and internal references of every kind, conveying a sense both of inevitability and spontaneity, were not wholly the result of deliberate calculation and manipulation but also of unconscious forces. This picture of the composer as visionary, articulating truths from another world, was encapsulated in accounts of Mozart and Beethoven at work. In a letter Mozart explained how musical ideas would come to him unbidden and how he could survey, as it were, the whole completed composition, even one of the largest scale, 'like a fine picture or a beautiful statue, at a glance. . . . [T]he committing to paper is done quickly enough, for every thing is . . . already finished; and it rarely differs on paper, from what it was in my imagination.'[197] An old German musician remembered Beethoven, sixty years before, describing how he carried musical ideas in his head, often for a very long time, with the fundamental concept never leaving him, until the work stood before him, 'like a cast', and he could quickly write it down.[198] This moment of revelation, this moment of truth, is what performers try to recapture, and not only executant artists but also analysts and historical musicologists and editors and critics.

In fact these moments of revelation never existed. We know now that the accounts were inventions. Notation is not, as Busoni described it, 'an ingenious expedient for catching an inspiration',[199] not a means of 'transcribing the composer's thoughts on paper',[200] as Copland suggested. Composers scribble down fragments on manuscript paper; ideas, or scraps of ideas, a phrase, a motive, a rhythm, a chord, a chord progression, an outline in words of a movement or of a whole work, or as a pattern, a diagrammatic representation. And then they build up structures little bit by little bit, employing techniques they have learnt or developed themselves, pushing notes around, begetting new ideas in the process of working on the manuscript paper.[201]

But the Romantic, nineteenth-century metaphor of the composer as an agent who simply materializes a perfectly imagined, finished form born in a visionary moment has remained enormously influential throughout the twentieth century. It has remained a fundamental component of the way a great many people think about music; it has shaped the way in which listeners form their ideas about a work of art, and composers too when they listen and when they try to explain what they do to the world. Stravinsky, the paradigmatic anti-Romantic, described himself as the 'vessel' through which *The Rite of Spring* passed; John Ireland was 'the amanuensis' of an 'urgent message' in his orchestral work, *These things shall be.*[202] Boulez explains that for the composer more important than being understood immediately is 'the integrity of the message'.[203]

The role of the interpreter variously defined

And what part does the performer play in this metaphor of musical experience? Some composers have suggested that the performer's must be a self-effacing role. The Austrian pianist Paul Wittgenstein, who lost his right arm in the First World War, was the dedicatee of Ravel's *Concerto for the Left Hand,* and made certain arrangements and adaptations of his own to the score which he then played to the composer. Wittgenstein wrote to Ravel: 'Performers must not be slaves.' And Ravel replied: 'Performers *are* slaves.'[204] Stravinsky once said that the conductor he envied was the military band leader, 'who keeps a revolver strapped in a holster by his side, and a notebook in which he mark's a player's mistakes and, for each one, sends him to jail for a day'.[205]

But such attitudes have been uncommon among composers in the last two centuries; most have acknowledged that the function of the performer includes a personal, interpretative element. Berlioz wrote that the primary responsibilities of conductors are 'fidelity to the directions of the composer' together with 'communication of personal conviction, intensity and spontaneity'.[206] If John Ireland saw the composer as the 'amanuensis', he saw the performer as the 'orator' chosen to deliver the 'message'.[207] The two essentials of great conducting that Vaughan Williams described in a letter to Adrian Boult in 1936 were '[f]aithfulness to the composer' and '[t]he power of the conductor to express *himself* to the full *at the moment* – to feel himself in the music & the music in himself'.[208] By 'faithfulness to the composer' Vaughan Williams did not mean merely that the performer must take infinite pains to observe scrupulously the notated symbols; rather he looked in a performer for 'that twin mind which will transmute [the composer's] imaginings into sound, and consummate that marriage of true minds which alone can give his music life'.[209]

And in fact composers themselves are rarely dogmatic. Wilhelm Backhaus used to tell a story of Brahms listening to two very different performances of his B minor Clarinet Quintet, both of which appeared to delight him equally. He explained that 'both performances had been by first-class players, and that in both cases the artists had put their heart and soul into penetrating and communicating his ideas. Although the two readings were totally unalike, both had conveyed his intentions with equal fidelity.'[210] The English pianist Fanny Davies remembered Brahms once telling a performer who had asked about the interpretation of a piece, 'Do it how you like, but make it beautiful'.[211] For 'normal people', Brahms thought, metronome markings 'cannot remain valid for more than a week'.[212] When Nikisch was once rehearsing a Brahms Symphony in Leipzig in the composer's presence, Brahms was very surprised and 'became quite nervous, repeating over and over again: "Is it possible? Did I really write that?" But afterwards the Master came to me, his face beaming with pleasure, and said: "You have changed everything. But you are right – it *must* be like that." '[213]

'You don't play the folksongs according to *my* intentions!' Grieg told Percy Grainger. 'But don't alter a thing. I love individuality.'[214] And when Debussy heard Paderewski playing 'Reflets dans l'eau' 'daintily, with charm, with refinement', in the words of the pianist Maurice Dumesnil, 'and with a pearly technique that would have better befitted a set of variations by Haydn or Mozart', the composer told the pianist that it 'was delightful. Not at all what I had in mind. But please do not alter your interpretation one iota!'[215] The French organist André Marchal, himself renowned as an authoritative player of the music of César Franck, heard this music when he was very young played by two pupils of the composer. Albert Mahout played 'with great flexibility', his interpretations were 'highly nuanced' and with lots of rubato; Adolf Marty on the other hand played quite differently; his interpretations were 'straighter . . . and faster'.[216] And Madame Tournemire remembered listening with her husband to performances of his music which were not at all like his own interpretations. The composer was unruffled: '. . . he understands it that way; let him play it that way.'[217] Messiaen wondered whether there was much point in a student studying his own recordings since – and he conceded it quite cheerfully – 'no one plays Messiaen like that'.[218]

Aaron Copland thought that from the finest interpreters a composer could learn much about his own music, 'aspects of it that he did not realize were there, tempi that are slower or faster than he had himself imagined were the correct ones, phrasings that better express the natural curve of a melody'.[219] And although Stravinsky was adamant that his own recording demonstrated exactly how a particular work should be played, when he recorded it again it was always quite different.[220] It was Bartók who pointed out that the composer, just like everybody else, will never perform the same piece in the same way. 'Because he lives', he said; 'because variability is a trait of a living creature's character.'[221]

Through all the stylistic and aesthetic changes in composition and performance that have taken place in the past century and a half, the role and the function of the executant has been described and defined in similar terms by all kinds of musicians. The image of the re-creative artist most listeners have etched on their consciousness is a nineteenth-century, Romantic one. Wagner declared that in Liszt's interpretation of Beethoven (as revealed to him from about 1853) he found not a mere *reproduction* of the composer's thought but a *re-creation*, actually taking place in the listener's presence.[222] Bruno Walter wrote that 'only he who understands that, under Wagner's baton, the *Ninth* sounded entirely in the spirit of Beethoven and that yet Wagner's own personality fully lived in it . . . comprehends the essence of musical interpretation'.[223] Alfred Brendel was sure in 1961 that all performers 'are of Liszt's time. . . . He created the type we aspire to: that of the universal performer of great stature.'[224] So Sviatoslav Richter, the public was assured in 1961, possessed a technical mastery which knew no difficulties, a mercurial touch and sublime powers of interpretation.[225] 'His unassuming nature and modesty are astonishing. He talks of his successes to no one. . . . He is a man of honour and principle in his relations with people, true in friendship, and deeply devoted to his art.'[226]

The challenge to performers has been encapsulated by Alfred Brendel in this way: 'It is our moral duty to make music in as visionary, moving, mysterious, thoughtful, amusing, graceful a manner as we are able to; but this raises the question "What is it that will move, shatter, edify, or amuse our contemporaries?" '[227] And this is surely a formulation with which a great many performers could agree. Of course performers in the nature of things, psychologically, need to be dogmatic. To give an assured authoritative performance they need to assert, to believe in themselves. Which is one reason why they so frequently claim the authority of the composer for what they do. Rostropovich said about the Sonata Benjamin Britten wrote for him: 'The music of the Sonata is so clear that it is impossible to play it in any other way but the way the composer intends it to be.'[228] Claudio Arrau once told an interviewer that the last thing he wanted to be was dogmatic about matters of interpretation. But when you discuss a particular work, the interviewer replied, you make it clear that in fact there is only one possible way for it to be played. 'Or maybe one of two possible ways.' 'But that's not what you say.' 'I know. But it would make it less disgusting.'[229]

The most admired executants do not seek to reproduce a performance style or manner, however much they might admire another artist or a school or a tradition of performance. The performer strives for some kind of originality, to be fresh, to be different and to startle in the most subtle ways, not for the sake of it – for the performer of Bach or Mozart or Beethoven or Brahms, 'make it new' is not a slogan, modernist or otherwise – but in an attempt to avoid mannerisms and clichés and all kinds of stock responses. In August 1998 Simon Rattle conducted a performance of Beethoven's Ninth Symphony by the City of Birmingham Symphony Orchestra and Chorus which a London critic described as the 'most exciting' interpretation for years, offering 'nothing less than revelatory thinking . . . this was the *Choral Symphony* approached as if it were a new found land'.[230] 'The point about playing Beethoven on old instruments, of course, is to make him sound new', Roger Norrington wrote in the 'Performance Note' accompanying his recordings of the symphonies with The London Classical Players who use period instruments: 'Our aim is to rediscover these great masterpieces, not by ignoring all this evidence, but by placing as much reliance on it as on our own musicianship and interpretative powers.'[231] What performers, re-creative artists actually do is respond to their worlds just like creative artists with their own highly sensitive antennae, guided by instinct towards 'getting it right' according to their own lights. 'The only true criterion is to see what is possible and proper to do', Pierre Boulez has said. 'There are no rigid criteria, ever. You have to consider the contingencies of the period in question and those of today, and then see what works, that's all.'[232]

The nature of musical notation

That performers can re-create as they do is precisely because of those ambiguities in notation about which composers and performers have so often expressed their frustration. Aaron Copland talked of the 'insufficiencies' of notation,[233] and other composers have dwelt on the 'inadequacies' of notation, its 'failures', its 'imprecision', its 'imperfections', of this 'hideously inaccurate', 'notoriously inexact' system. And yet this very peculiar system of notation – the most detailed of any musical tradition in the world – and the developments in it that have taken place over the past five hundred years have been a constant spur to the imagination, and in the nineteenth and twentieth centuries the vitality of the performing traditions of art music in Western Europe has depended in no small degree on these very ambiguities and on the ways they have been explored and exploited by musicians. Wanda Landowska put it very simply: 'There are a thousand different ways of interpreting a piece without ever getting away from its character.'[234]

The precise particular meanings and significances of inflections and emphases and gestures are generated against the norms, against the shifting trends in performing style. All gestures in performing arts, at least in the performing arts in the European traditions, are evanescent because of the emphasis and importance we have put on originality in the last two hundred years. About musical eloquence there can never be agreement. Somebody is always ready to criticize, that is to perform the work in a different way. Schoenberg found the new literalness of younger performers in the 1920s dull and inexpressive, whereas Adrian Boult listened to Casals conducting with 'a mathematical exactness of rhythm' and was thrilled at the way simple rhythmic figures in Schubert's C major Symphony when played 'in *absolutely* strict time, gained in character and point', how such treatment 'put glowing life into the classics'.[235] Just as the Italian pianist Rita Bötticker was puzzled and disappointed when she attended a Bach recital given in Berlin in 1935 by her former pupil Claudio Arrau, one of the new men bearing the standard proclaiming 'Neue Sachlichkeit', the 'new objectivity': 'It's academic!' she told him; 'Why don't you use your imagination? Why don't you use the pedal?'[236] In fact the term 'Neue Sachlichkeit', which became a slogan that commentators strove to apply to a particular aesthetic approach in the arts generally, was coined in 1925 by the director of the Mannheim art gallery as the title of an exhibition of contemporary paintings and drawings and it was applied without wholehearted approval. The curator of the exhibition felt he detected a note of cynicism; the artists, he thought, did not believe 'wholeheartedly any more in *art*'.[237] Stravinsky mocked the old ways, the nineteenth-century styles: '. . . a *crescendo*, as we all know, is always accompanied by a speeding up of movement, while a slowing down never fails to accompany a *diminuendo*. The superfluous is refined upon; a *piano, piano pianissimo* is delicately sought after; great pride is taken in perfecting useless nuances – a concern that usually goes hand in hand with inaccurate rhythm.'[238] But of course such 'useless nuances' and 'inaccurate rhythms' were rhetorical devices deliberately cultivated by musicians like Elgar, who in 1931 implored his orchestra at a Gerontius performance to give him 'all the fire and energy and poetry that was in them', but looked about him and listened and heard 'no soul & no romance & no imagination'.[239] The devout French mystic, the organist Charles Tournemire, was similarly aghast at the unfeeling performing styles of this post-First War epoch, the result he was sure of the spirit of the eighteenth century which obstinately prowled around still, the cold and arid rationalism of the Enlightenment, the poison of religious doubt, which he was sure must be responsible, in the aftermath of the most destructive war in man's history, for this corrupt instinct even on the part of creative and re-creative musical artists of today, of the 1930s, for what was vain, futile, dry, egotistical and purely exterior.[240]

A particular performing style has its effect against shifting trends but also against the particular characteristics of outstanding contemporary individual executants. The performing style of many musicians with long careers can be heard to evolve in subtle ways, taking into account the changing emphases in performing styles. Otto Klemperer was held by one commentator to be the 'most radical and most objective' of Weimar-period conductors.[241] Between the wars Klemperer was perceived as being a comrade-in-arms with Schnabel, as an apostle of austerity, reacting against what they and others saw as the interpretative liberties of an earlier generation of 'romantic' interpreters. As a young man, though, Klemperer had in fact been one of these himself, had modelled himself on Mahler, for whom he had directed the off-stage orchestra in a performance of Mahler's Second Symphony directed by the composer, and was noted for his cultivation of a Mahlerian intensity of expression. Around 1910 he was certainly known as a conductor whose main concern was with the expression of emotion rather than the articulation of form, the director of sometimes rather noisy performances, whose manner on the podium was characterized by vehement and often exaggerated bodily movements. But in 1915 Klemperer discovered Bach and the eighteenth century and he began to be more sympathetic to new developments, and around 1917 and 1918 older critics who had long recognized his mastery began to comment frequently on an 'uncharacteristic lack of commitment'[242] in his performances. When he conducted *The Ring* in Cologne in June 1918 even one of his admirers thought the performance 'too sharply analytical to be entirely authoritative'.[243]

Toscanini has often been considered as the quintessential conductor of the first half of the century, widely regarded as a modernist, a supreme anti-Romantic. A Russian-American composer called Lazare Saminsky writing in 1932 contrasted Toscanini with what he called 'the Romantic and coloristic school' of Nikisch, Furtwängler and Willem Mengelberg; he wrote: 'For purely tonal taste [Toscanini] is entirely a musician of our day, just as much so as a Hindemith, Milhaud or a Poulenc. His very aversion to adorning music, for inflecting it with meaning, with extra-musical content, for emotionalizing what is but pure line and form, is the aversion of today's musician. He is bewitched by the very flesh of music, by its sonority and rhythmic flux; their plan and balance entrance him. In this he is a true neo-classic musician, both Hellenic and modern.'[244] But as many commentators have pointed out, it's much more complicated: Toscanini's performing style seems to have derived not so much from an aesthetic stance but more from psychological factors and his own formative years, from an overpowering will to dominate his players and from his early experience of low standards in provincial Italian centres.

Performing styles change; the corollary of this, that the same musical interpretations, the same musical gestures, the same kinds of emphases, will convey different meanings, will have a different effect, will be judged more or less convincing or successful, at different times, is easily demonstrated by means of recorded performances. In 1928 the Columbia Graphophone Company brought out a set of discs of the first nine preludes and fugues from the Forty-Eight; they were played on the piano by Harriet Cohen. And in 1930 the Company issued the next eight played by Evlyn Howard-Jones. The reviewers noticed differences between their approaches: Howard-Jones was found to be altogether admirable, straight, precise, clear, though one reviewer found him 'a little monotonous and dry at times';[245] Harriet Cohen, who was generally acknowledged as one of the leading Bach players of the time, was on the other hand found to create a 'rare and happy' combination of 'the spirit of Bach and of her own vivid personality', to make Bach live;[246] there was nothing of the museum about her playing, nothing of an antiquarian spirit. One reviewer noted the way she emphasized fugue subjects and though he did not like it much he acknowledged it was one way of doing things.[247] In 1995 those performances by Cohen and Howard-Jones were reissued on CD. An experienced commentator, himself a keyboard player and editor, wrote: 'Of the present two artists, there is little doubt who was the better Bach stylist and the more mature musician – Eugen d'Albert's pupil Evlyn Howard Jones . . . was never as well known as Harriet Cohen but shows himself here to be a pianist of outstanding quality and intelligence, with a refined tonal subtlety and a developed sense of structure. His interpretations, well judged in matters of tempo, are free from the exaggerations and posturings of Cohen . . . [she] adopts the "hunt-the-slipper" interpretations of the fugues (heavy-handedly "bringing out the subject"), becomes swoonily sentimental in the C sharp minor (the end of its fugue pulled about unmercifully), and behaves in the E flat minor Prelude like a tragedy queen.'[248]

What the interpreter actually does

So the performer certainly studies the composer's manuscripts, he refers to Urtext editions, he reads contemporary instrumental instruction manuals, he investigates disquisitions on contemporary aesthetics. He finds out in other words as much as he can about contemporary performance practices. But this is obviously not enough. Then must enter the picture, if a performance is to live, spontaneity, intuition, aesthetic sensibility, a developed instinct. As Mozart played one of his piano concertos he was living a tradition not reviving one, not following rules but creating them. And so in this century was Edwin Fischer when he played a Mozart concerto, and so too were Daniel Barenboim and Murray Perahia and Malcolm Bilson and András Schiff. 'I study, I scrutinize, I love, I recreate,' said Wanda Landowska.[249] It's not that performances by Nikisch or G. D. Cunningham or Elgar or Charles Tournemire are inexpressive; they're simply expressive in their own terms. What today's terms or tomorrow's will be, it's impossible to say. We simply recognize them when a master performer shows us them.

How does the performer develop such an instinct? The performer takes what he needs wherever he finds it, not being inhibited by current, or even yesterday's, notions of musicological correctness, from his teachers, first of all, and from listening to the best players in concerts and recitals, and also by listening to records. The best of contemporary performers, of course, but not despising the old ones. If the performer neglects to listen to these old recordings he may miss opportunities of catching what seems to him the spirit of the music and also of discovering clues about those features of the music which are not notated. But in recordings he may also see opportunities of reviving features of bygone styles by integrating them into new contexts. If recent stylistic norms have emphasized a steady tempo and a literal approach to the text it may be that hearing a contemporary performance of obvious authority will suggest the reintroduction of certain elements to instil an improvisatory élan. In 1985 when he was preparing performances of the Grieg Piano Concerto Christopher Hogwood used recordings by Percy Grainger as 'reference sources'. Grieg loved Percy Grainger's piano playing – 'magnificent',[250] he called it, 'like the sun breaking through the clouds'[251] – and he worked for many hours with Grainger on the Concerto, in preparation for a performance they were to have given together at the Leeds Festival in 1907; in the event the composer died a month before the Festival. Hogwood used the model edition Grainger made of the Concerto for Schirmer's, the recording of the first movement cadenza Grainger made in 1908,[252] and two recordings of the complete work, one with Stokowski in 1945[253] and another in Denmark in 1957.[254] Through the consultation of such sources Hogwood was attempting, he said, 'to institute a sense of historical propriety' in his performances, but at that time, in the mid-1980s, he thought that such a detailed analytical approach towards a twentieth-century war-horse was 'unheard-of'.[255] Such an approach was intended to aid and abet instinctive responses, not to overrule them. The Japanese pianist Mitsuko Uchida has said that she had only one teacher, Kurt Hauser, in Vienna; otherwise she learned from recordings, of performances by the cellist Pablo Casals, the violinist Josef Szigeti, and the conductor Wilhelm Furtwängler. Often, she said, she didn't at first realize how deeply influenced she had been by Szigeti, because she was playing different works on a different instrument.[256] Rostropovich, having played the Bach cello suites all his life, decided in the 1990s that he was ready to record them. He prepared for the sessions by studying, in the absence of an autograph, the copies made in Leipzig by Anna Magdalena and one of Bach's pupils, and then he retired to a hotel room with a bottle of vodka and a stock of discs – Heifetz in the violin partitas, Glenn Gould in the keyboard works – cleansing his mind of lifelong preconceptions. 'Forty-five years I play it one way,' he said, 'now I play another way.'[257]

Many performers have insisted that the search for expressiveness must be unselfconscious and usually unconscious. An experienced and mature re-creative artist did not listen to his own earlier recordings of repertory he was to perform and record again because 'they might give me a deliberate intention to be different. I prefer that the organic process of change, which is normal in human nature, should run its course, rather than to be confronted.'[258] Whatever the approach, whether recordings are sought out or avoided, the aim is the same, to assist the player to achieve the kind of authenticity which equates naturally with the most musical effect. Certainly a new generation of performers has reacted against the studied perfection and accuracy that commercial recordings have habituated music-lovers to, and are eager to immerse themselves, at least temporarily, in Furtwängler or even Paderewski.

An examination of changes in performing styles is in effect an analysis of the 'situational logic' behind them.[259] The performer strives to make his performances alive, distinctive, different in some way. There will always be the personal element: the 'interpretation' of the performer, Josef Hofmann thought, 'however punctiliously he adhere to the text . . . will and must be a reflection of . . . all the faculties and qualities that go to make up his personality'.[260] But differences may also be cultivated consciously and quite deliberately. Just as Mozart writing to his father from Paris in 1778 explained: 'Every symphony here starts with a fast movement, so I start with a slow introduction', so the keyboard player in the twentieth century has performed Bach on the harpsichord or the clavichord instead of the piano, the conductor has directed the Mass in B minor with a choir of thirty voices instead of one of a hundred and sixty – or even with the choruses sung by solo voices – the violinist has introduced different styles of articulation and has cultivated a continuous vibrato. And if such performers convince audiences and other executants, the new performing style, or important features of it, are adopted by more and more players and the old style comes to appear old-fashioned and itself eccentric; the meanings of musical sonorities and gestures are subtly transformed, like fashions in clothes or like the meanings of words, as 'wireless' and 'gramophone' carried different resonances in the 1970s from the 1920s. A performer cannot continue to cultivate the same style in all its details – even if this were humanly possible – and expect the effect of his interpretations to remain the same, to expect that the same musical gestures will convey the same significances to new audiences. Some of the concerns creating the dynamics of change may be like ripples on the surface of the pool, important to performers but not discerned, at least not in their full complexity, by most listeners, such as the different traditions of interpreting the music of César Franck among organists at different Parisian churches. Others may be polarizing issues of interest to all performers and all listeners: to what extent, for example, should performers aim to create the original sonorities of a particular repertory? The rise of violin vibrato during the century provides a simple illustration of situational logic: by the 1990s a critic is complaining that most modern string performances 'have a certain oppressive monotony. . . . Almost every phrase, regardless of content or context, is delivered in the same big, luscious, vibrato-ridden tone . . . a thick wall of throbbing sound come[s] between us and the music.'[261] Alfred Brendel recalled the reaction against 'the excesses of "romantic" performance' which resulted in 'unemotional and drily mechanical abstraction' of Baroque keyboard music. But in the 1970s he was listening to performances of Couperin which resembled 'amazingly' the ' "romanticism" ' of Paderewski's records: no chord without an arpeggio and the left hand constantly anticipating the right.[262]

Styles of performance – just like new compositions – do not emerge in isolation but are linked with others and with their time by many elusive threads. Different performance styles and changes in performance styles traceable only in recordings can tell us something of great importance about which we would otherwise lack any information. To the late twentieth century it seems more suggestive to consider the great masterpieces of the musical repertory less as finished works of art standing outside time than as phenomena shaped by re-creative musicians, by audiences, by those who mould taste, critics, journalists, commentators of different kinds, and by those who present musical performances, entrepreneurs, concert agents, arts administrators, broadcasters, record company men. But this is not at all how scholars have contemplated music history; musicologists have looked at music, at scores and manuscripts and sketches, and analysed music's form and style and meanings from the evidence of the notes themselves. The history of music they can now listen to.

IV
Listening to Recordings

A billion dollar multi-national industry

'Where do you put all those hundreds of CDs you've acquired?' the *Gramophone* magazine asked in 1998,[1] introducing an article giving advice on storage systems. That the ordinary music-lover should own hundreds of CDs, that is, hundreds of hours of recorded music – most of them by and large presumably of classical music – is taken as entirely unexceptional. Even those music-lovers who frequently attended concerts and opera productions in 1998 usually listened to much more music through recordings than they experienced in live performances. Some young composers at the end of the century began to value musical sounds straight from an acoustic source as 'an increasingly scarce, precious commodity', valuable especially, one of them thought, for its fragility and unpredictability.[2] At the end of the twentieth century it was almost impossible not to listen to, or at least to hear, recorded music, to avoid the aural bombardment from recorded music. In the 1970s a young cellist was exhilarated and bewildered by recordings, was trying to make sense of the music that he heard, was trying, he said, to 'define what a musician was', as he listened to records of 'late-60s pop, Classical, jazz, minimalism, serialism, all claiming that "they had the way to the truth"'.[3]

By the end of the twentieth century the recording of music was a huge billion dollar multi-national industry. A report by Schweizerische Radio- und Fernsehgesellschaft in 1979 found that only two per cent of the people it surveyed never listened to music at home, and that more than two-thirds of those aged between fifteen and seventy agreed with the statement 'I can't imagine a life without music'.[4] World-wide sales of phonograms of all kinds of recorded sound in 1994 totalled more than 3,162,000,000, representing a retail value of US\$35,533,000,000.[5] In was true that in the UK in 1994 classical sales of recordings represented less than a tenth of all recordings sold, in Germany the classical sales were nine per cent of the total, in America they amounted to less than four per cent of the total. And the proportion has steadily declined in the past two decades; in 1975 classical records accounted for twenty per cent of all record sales in the UK.[6] In the United Kingdom in 1994 were sold fifteen and a half million classical music phonograms – CDs, LPs, cassettes – in Germany in 1994 nearly twenty million classical phonograms, in North America more than thirty-seven million.[7] These were the three biggest national markets. However the audience for classical music is defined, it is still a mass audience. In 1994 more than 65,000 copies were sold of each monthly issue of *Gramophone*, the leading classical music record review magazine in Great Britain, nearly 45,000 of *Classic CD*, another review magazine first published in 1990, and more than 65,000 copies of *BBC Music Magazine*. So there were, at the end of the century, huge audiences for recorded classical music. And yet, for much of the century, many musicians and music-lovers and musical scholars have been suspicious of recordings, have regarded them as a substitute for 'the real thing', the live performance.

Antagonism towards listening to records

' "Be ye doers of the word, and not hearers only" ' was what Vaughan Williams preached. The best way of getting inside music's meaning was by active participation; the real musical life of a country, Vaughan Williams thought, was revealed not in its great cities and their orchestras and their opera houses and their celebrity concerts but in the quartet parties and madrigal clubs in the towns and villages, in the church choirs and choral societies. Such music-making was threatened by recordings and he regarded the gramophone record, unless used with great care, as a 'superficial' and 'lazy' way of acquiring close knowledge of music.[8] This English love of music-making by amateurs, and most commonly through singing in choral societies, went with a particular view of community and society; it was a demonstration of solidarity, evidence that music could transcend barriers of class and social background and professional attainment; it was a means whereby human relationships could be cemented by an activity requiring the closest cooperation and dedication and involving the contemplation of serious human concerns and great human truths as revealed in the masterpieces of music. And in Germany too: the characteristic emphasis of *Gebrauchsmusik* in the late 1920s and 30s was on the participation of amateurs. Many musicians held that modern music led a phantom existence without a real audience, with no community, and Hindemith was sure that 'the over-cultivation of "music for music festivals"' – 'advanced' music completely beyond the technical capabilities of amateur musicians, however gifted – was leading composers 'up a blind alley'.[9] The motto of the 1929 festival of contemporary chamber music in Baden-Baden was 'making music is better than listening to it'.[10]

Those were reasons for regarding recorded music with suspicion. And if you were going to listen to music, this activity too had to be cultivated with the utmost seriousness and dedication. True musical appreciation required innate musical gifts and sensibilities, some maintained, deep knowledge of the repertories and of the history and conventions of European music, and it was mere sentimentality to imagine that everyone could ever develop a taste for serious music; as the music correspondent of the *Belfast Telegraph* starkly put it: 'music for the million is a blatant hypocrisy'.[11]

Nineteenth-century concepts of great music, the creator's role and the listener's role

The nineteenth century had changed not only the substance of music in Western Europe, but also the ways in which music was listened to, and the ways in which music was regarded. If for the eighteenth century, for Burney, music had been 'an innocent luxury, unnecessary to our being, but a great gratification and improvement of the sense of hearing',[12] or for Johann Georg Sulzer, who classified concert music as an entertainment, 'a lively and not unpleasant noise, or a civil and entertaining chatter, but not one that engages the heart',[13] for the nineteenth, for Schopenhauer, music engaged the heart most deeply of all the arts, it penetrated to the very core of humanity, revealed 'the innermost essence of the world', imparted 'the deepest wisdom'. For many writers and thinkers during the last century music became the quintessential art form and not merely the 'accompaniment to sociability' it had been in the eighteenth century.[14]

There has been very little doubt in the minds of many musical men and women during the twentieth century how 'serious' music should be listened to. One of the reasons why broadcasting and recording would never eliminate live concerts, a contributor to *The Musical Times* in 1939 was sure, was that many people – who he granted may be misguided or uncultured, certainly not connoisseurs, and whose listening was doubtless superficial – liked to *see* musical performers as well as hear them. For him it is clear the ability to concentrate intensely on the sounds of the music's 'argument' was a mark of the highest kind of musical appreciation.[15] The four-minute segments into which recordings still chopped music in 1939 precluded the development of the kind of rapt attention that was necessary for concentrated listening. Men like Theodor Wiesengrund Adorno and Heinrich Schenker described aspects of this widely shared attitude with characteristic rigour and uncompromising severity. Adorno required that full and undivided attention be paid to the music's unfolding, towards assimilating the development of the structure of great music, not to the mere recognition of themes or the enjoyment of instrumental colours or textures: in 'serious music, the instrumental sound is a mere function of the structure with no intrinsic value as an individual sound'.[16] The mastery of great composers was evidenced, according to Heinrich Schenker, in their control of 'fundamental structure'. Ultimately it made no sense to isolate musical ideas, to speak of sections of primary importance and others of secondary importance, to designate 'bridge passages' and 'principal themes'. What was important was the organic nature of the whole, the fundamental structure behind the foreground details, behind those surface features which preoccupy the composer of talent merely and the superficial and dilettante listener, the sort of listener who cries out for a tune, for a 'tasty aural bonbon'.[17] The performer can assist or militate against the revelation of serious music's true import: 'Every musician is familiar with the phenomenon of the "too beautiful" tone which carries with it wrong associations, being comparable to paintings in which a sunset or a girl as "natural objects" can be too beautiful, in naturalistic terms, actually to fulfil the artistic intention of being structurally beautiful.'[18] What the gifted listener seeks to discover is that inner coherence in the structure of the musical material, 'the kind of coherence which is found only in God and in the geniuses . . . through whom he works',[19] in those great and complex structures which can be shown (by Schenker at least) to obey laws of nature. For Adorno Schoenberg was demonstrably a master because his music required 'not mere contemplation but praxis . . . active and concentrated participation'.[20]

How did the music-lover develop these listening skills? The nature of the relationship between incidental surface detail and the underlying structure could be experienced and understood, according to Schenker, 'only by those blessed with special perception'; such 'secrets . . . are neither teachable nor learnable'.[21] No doubt, though, it helped if a listener had been able to hear operas by Wagner between twenty and thirty times each, as Schoenberg had in Vienna by the age of twenty-five, or as the 'average non-professional music lover in Germany or Austria' about whom Schoenberg speaks who before the First War had been to performances of '*Butterfly* twenty times, *Tosca*, *Bohème*, and *Cavalleria* eighteen times each, *Aida*, *Carmen* and *Il Trovatore* fifteen times, *Tannhäuser*, *Meistersinger*, and *The Barber of Seville* twenty times, *Lohengrin*, *The Flying Dutchman*, and *Tales of Hoffmann* nine times, *Faust*, *Figaro*, and *Tristan* about eight times each, *Manon*, *Fra Diavolo*, *Magic Flute*, and *Salome* about seven times, *The Prophet*, *Don Juan*, and *Freischütz* six times, *Fidelio* four times, besides lesser known operas once or twice'. A member of the audience at a performance of his of Beethoven's Fifth Symphony in Vienna had heard previously fifty performances, 'only' fifty performances, as Schoenberg puts it.[22]

Even in those homes away from Vienna or far from those many provincial centres which presented opera in Austria and Germany there would be the kind of deep engagement with musical masterpieces that can come, or could come, from the regular performance of domestic chamber music. Even in benighted England where there would not have been much opportunity for developing close acquaintance with opera if you lived in Ashby de la Zouch, or Hull, or Swindon or Newcastle-under-Lyme, yet there might be performances at home, and if not of string quartets, then at least on the piano, in arrangements of orchestral and chamber music played 'with an aunt or a sister', though by the 1930s this was almost a thing of the past, at least in England.[23] No doubt many such domestic performances didn't reach superlatively high standards – Schoenberg's inability to count irritated his fellow chamber music players.[24] Nevertheless, such contact with the music certainly fostered intimate knowledge of musical masterpieces that assisted the kind of concentrated listening insisted upon by Adorno.

Listening to music as a religious exercise

So this way of listening to music was intimately bound up with the musical experiences of a very small section of society, the highly edu-cated middle class and upper-middle class of Europe. It was of very recent origin. 'In the middle of the first Allegro was a passage I was certain must please them, all the audience were carried away by it – and there was a great applaudissement – but as I knew while I was writing it how strong an effect it would make, I had brought it in again at the end – and now there were cries of "da capo!" The Andante also pleased, but especially the last Allegro; for as I had heard that here all last as well as first Allegros begin with all the instru-ments playing together and generally unisono, I began with 2 violins alone, *piano* for 8 bars – then at once a *forte* – the audience (as I had expected) went *sshh* . . . at the *piano* – then came the *forte* at once – and no sooner did they hear the *forte* than they began to clap.'[25] Mozart is telling his father about the success of a concert in Paris in 1778, of a performance of the Symphony no. 31 K.300a/297. He was clearly very pleased with the reception accorded the work, indeed he would have been disappointed if the response had not been so voluble, since this is precisely what he had planned. He was more used to being com-pletely ignored in Paris when he performed, with the members of the audience chatting as they consumed food or busily made sketches of each other.[26]

But such a noisy audience would not have pleased the American critic who complained that in the 1890s London contained not a single concert hall worthy of the 'most social, the most affecting, the purest of the arts . . . the one most deeply connected with the moral side of civilization'. Music could not be performed before the mob, in cramped conditions; there must be ample room to circulate, seating for no more than 500, 300 would be better, and the hall 'should have pure air, cool temperature', and there should be no suggestion that light entertain-

ment or public banquets might ever be permitted within these hal-
lowed precincts, no hint of 'Mohawk minstrels or fried fish'. It should
be a beautiful building finely decorated and worthily furnished.[27]
Perhaps the critic had been present at the opening concert of the
Carnegie Hall in May 1891, when 'all was quiet, dignified, soft, slow
and noiseless, as became the dedication of a great temple'.[28] The
eleventh edition of the *Encyclopaedia Britannica* published in 1910 and
1911 noted that the 'reverential spirit which abolished applause in
church, has tended to spread to the theatre and the concert room,
largely under the influence of the quasi-religious atmosphere of
the Wagner performances at Baireuth'. At the turn of the century many
music-lovers would have wished the abolition of applause even in
secular halls. If, Hugo Wolf complained, after experiencing the tragedy
of Coriolan's 'annihilated ego', you can babble and criticize and clap,
'you have seen nothing, felt nothing, heard nothing, understood
nothing'.[29]

Listening to music became increasingly through the last century
akin to a religious exercise, the opportunity for a mystical experience,
a matter of intense concentration and attention both to the structure,
to the unfolding of the music's argument, and to the inner meanings
of the sounds themselves. Listening required a mental attitude and a
physical posture of reverence in order to make possible glimpses of
other worlds. To appreciate music – to appreciate art of any kind –
required a detachment from personal needs and preoccupations,
required what Schopenhauer called the 'aesthetic way of knowing'; art
could take people 'out of themselves' as it is still sometimes put.
Kierkegaard wished to close his eyes when he listened to music; visual
impressions merely confused the mind and blunted the impact, he
thought; at performances of *Don Giovanni* he retreated further and
further back from the stage until he decided it was best to stand outside
the auditorium, leaning up against a thin partition, to experience the
full impact of the music.[30]

Pictures provide evidence of this change in sensibility; more and
more during the nineteenth century painters of pictures with a musical
subject focus on the effect of the music, on the listeners rather than
the performers. Lionello Balestrieri's *A Beethoven Sonata* won a gold
medal at the Paris World Fair in 1900 and engravings of it were put
up on domestic walls all over Europe. One listener sits, his hands in
his pockets, another bends forward, his head in his hands.[31] In the

picture painted in 1883 by the Belgian artist Fernand Khnopff called *En écoutant du Schumann*, a lady sits in a domestic interior, her head resting on her hand which covers her face; only at the very edge of the picture is the right hand of the pianist glimpsed.[32]

The music-lover listens in this way because of his conception of what a masterpiece is. That when he writes – at least when he creates a masterpiece – the composer is able to capture something of which he is perhaps not wholly aware, that his music is not the result merely of deliberate calculation and manipulation, that he is guided by some mysterious force, by 'Truth', or by 'Nature', that he moves like a sleep-walker,[33] that the resulting creation is not merely agreeable, pleasing and melodious but in some sense a force of nature with the same vital-izing effect upon a listener as certain phenomena of nature, these thor-oughly Romantic concepts have been held by many kinds of musicians throughout this century. Schoenberg considered that great music 'conveys a prophetic message revealing a higher form of life towards which mankind evolves'.[34] And those remarks of such self-prodaimed anti-Romantics as Stravinsky, describing himself as the 'vessel' through which *The Rite of Spring* passed,[35] and Pierre Boulez, sure that the 'integrity of the message' was 'much more important than to be understood immediately',[36] reveal underlying nineteenth-century con-cepts and categories. The metaphorical truths enshrined in such remarks and in the fanciful accounts of composers penning their works as though by dictation have been essential elements in the aesthetic response of countless music-lovers and in the way musicologists have thought about music and have explained the way we experience music.

Classical music for mass markets

The production of recordings required mass markets. Some thought it possible to develop a mass audience for serious music; others thought that it was impossible, and irresponsible, and that the attempt could only result in dilution and possibly, ultimately, destruction; listening in the wrong way was worse than not listening at all. Those who held that it was possible for a mass audience to be created usually welcomed the growth of recording; those who did not, or feared that music's power would be weakened by a surfeit of music, were antagonistic or dismissive or at least suspicious of gramophones and records. Those music-lovers who frequented the opera house and the concert hall and played chamber music and piano duet arrangements at home had never represented more than a very small minority of the population at large. But then men like Adorno never envisaged that a mass audience could ever appreciate the great masterworks of the central European tradition. He would have agreed with Schoenberg: 'It is not everyone's business to concern himself with difficult and profound things, just as these things are not thought of with everyone in mind', as the composer put it with regard to modern music on the radio in 1933.[37] The whole point of Schoenberg's Society for the Private Performance of Music which operated in Vienna between 1918 and 1922 was to remove new music from the public's gaze, from commercialization, from the dictates of fashion, and from the corrupting influence of market forces. And in England and on the continent many of the cultural arbiters of the 1930s campaigned against radio, film, newspapers, publicity in all forms, commercially-catered fiction, all offering 'satisfaction at the lowest level'. Schoenberg's attitudes reflect fears widespread among European intellectuals about the emergence of mass culture at the beginning of the twentieth century, and about the failure of universal education: 'in our headlong rush to educate everybody', T. S. Eliot was sure that 'we are lowering our standards . . . destroying our ancient edifices to make ready the ground upon which the barbarian nomads of the future will encamp in their mechanized caravans'.[38] Culture, the discerning appreciation of the arts and of literature, had always depended upon 'a very small minority', though F. R. Leavis did acknowledge that in the mid-twentieth century it was a larger one than formerly. 'Upon this minority depends our power of profiting by the finest human experience of the past; they keep alive the subtlest and most perishable parts of tradition.'[39] The Frankfurt theorists, Horkheimer, Adorno, Marcuse – though not Benjamin – shared the view that mass culture and the mass media, as developed under capitalism, were degrading civilization. And they blamed radio, cinema, newspapers, cheap books, and gramophones for the disappearance of the 'inner life'. Jazz, the art-form which was largely created and sustained and evolved through recording, the distinguished music historian Alfred Einstein described as 'the most abominable treason against all the music of Western civilization'.[40] The music appreciation movement, which was certainly responsible for greatly enlarging audiences for classical music after the First War, was held in contempt by a great many musicians, the 'music appreciation racket' as Virgil Thomson described it,[41] as being cultivated by most of its ardent devotees as a passport to social acceptability, as a means to the most superficial acquaintance with the most hackneyed and reactionary repertory played by a tiny handful of revered seers, the chosen performers, 'custodians of holy things', 'priests of beauty', 'guardians of spiritual themes', of whom Toscanini was the High Priest.[42]

At the time Adorno was working with the Princeton Radio Research Project, between 1938 and 1940, he wrote a critique of the NBC *Music Appreciation Hour*, a series of radio programmes with an accompanying *Teacher's Guide* booklet designed to develop a love of serious music in young people. Adorno was not impressed with this series. He considered the aim ludicrous anyway, to make difficult music painlessly accessible to a wide audience, and the programmes he thought gave no assistance in developing the ability to understand musical sense; on the contrary, they taught those who followed the series to listen in the most superficial way, they encouraged what he termed 'atomistic' listening, the spotting of themes, the recognizing of instrumental sounds as 'personalities'. He quoted from the *Teacher's Guide*: 'What can we do to get the most fun from what the radio fairy brings?' and commented:

> This is a compounded absurdity. The term fun, borrowed from the tritest spheres of everyday life, carries a touch of humor which, whatever its proper merits may be, is totally at variance with the serious music presented by the Hour. Moreover, a fairy is supposed to be a being from a higher, spiritual world, who may bring elation, happiness, anguish, everything but fun. Finally, the phrase links the fairy with radio, a technical tool which is essentially scientific, and by its very historical essence opposed to any 'aura' such as that suggested by the use of the fairy. . . . To get fun out of the slow movement of Beethoven's Hammerklavier Sonata or the C-sharp Minor Quartet . . . would be more difficult than simply to understand them.[43]

Such approaches, he thought, encouraged not enjoyment of the music itself but pleasure in the awareness that the listener knows about music. It allowed those who listened in this way to acquire a pseudo-cultural veneer of the most conventional type, the ability to exchange platitudinous half-truths about an art that in reality – in Adorno's version of reality – they had not begun to comprehend. But then there has always been an element of snobbery in the appreciation of art and culture in all societies; there was certainly an element of all this in the middle European upper-bourgeois culture from which Adorno himself emerged, a certain kind of knowledge of a selective general culture which corresponded to certain intellectual fashions and was of a piece with a code of behaviour and manners.[44]

Clear evidence that music could indeed only be appreciated by a select few was available, according to one music critic, when it was realized that this great increasing public interest in music that the ' "appreciation"-mongers' testified to was the result in the main of exposure to musical performances from mechanical contrivances: 'An enormous new public has undoubtedly come into music, but it is not approaching music in the old way. It is a very cheap, and, aesthetically, insensitive public, which seems quite content to eschew concerts, and to take its music from the gramophone and radio.'[45] In 1926 the critic Frank Howes was quite sure that radio listeners liked music just because of its novelty, they were simply wide-eyed with wonderment at the technology – because it was coming from Spain, or because the reception was much better than it was last year – or for even sillier reasons, because they heard someone cough. Listeners to the gramophone who said they enjoyed it were only pretending; 'aesthetic boredom always hovers close over the desiccated and condensed forms of music, because the human contacts are remote and precarious'.[46] Musical performance is of its essence communication and requires human presence and the interaction of players with an audience; 'proper' artistic pleasure, he thought, could never be obtained from radio or gramophone.

A great many of the ideas expressed about music appreciation, about mass culture, and about recordings, reflected the writers' views on innate musical ability. In an edition of *The Radio Times* in May 1933, 'Mr Alex Cohen, M.A., a violinist and chamber music player of high artistic and professional standing in the English Midlands', opposed attempts by the BBC to prepare listeners for music to be broadcast: 'We all either have something already within us to respond to the first intelligent reading we hear of a work or we have not; and if we lack this essential neither cold print nor warmer *viva voce* commentaries will of themselves supply the deficiency or enlarge our spiritual boundaries.'[47]

Even the editor of the *Music Bulletin* of the British Music Society, which organization existed to widen public interest in music, emphasized in 1926 that music, like all the arts, 'is essentially an aristocratic culture, and the present movement towards its democratization is fundamentally erroneous'.[48] And even one of the staff writers for *The Gramophone* could declare that 'the mob, flattered to the top of its bent, is spoiling music'.[49]

In 1930 a passionate music-lover turned on the musical profession for the ridicule and sarcasm which most of its members continued to pour on the gramophone, for the way most musicians had taken 'an almost malicious pleasure in watching [the] struggles and failures' of record companies,[50] and he rebuked them for their stubbornness in refusing to cooperate with the companies in enlarging the public for 'good' music. He was sure that those few who had demonstrated public support for recording over the past three decades had found that 'it involved a slight loss of caste among [their] peers':

You are like the heirs of a great heritage, a vast estate, a huge mansion – legislation by the people for the people, the march of events, the pressure of modern conditions threaten you. You have to surrender acre after acre; you are offered compensation. You can't get servants for your great house; you can't afford anything. What are you to do with all your traditions, your sensitiveness and pride, with even the thought of your own heir? It isn't easy. You can let everything go with a curse, snatch up the compensation money and turn your back on all that has made life worth living – and start again. Or you can return to your great house, close all the shutters, let the servants go, and eke out a miserable existence defiantly and proudly to the bitter end. . . . The third course is surely the best. It is to accept the situation and unselfishly with a high courage; to become a leader in the breaking up of your estate for the use of the public, to be yourself the guide and lecturer of the crowds who come to marvel at your pictures and furniture and gardens; yourself the historian of your great house and your great inheritance! With this never-flagging purpose in your heart, to ensure that as little damage as possible is done to a priceless inheritance, as much encouragement given to the enquiring and appreciative spirit, however humble, as it lies in your power to compass.[51]

Percy Scholes thought that antagonism towards mass culture derived from 'limited human sympathies'.[52] Those who were optimistic about the creation of mass audiences for serious music, those of wide human sympathies, could be found in very different educational and cultural settings. A schoolmaster teaching between the wars some of the most materially privileged boys in England was convinced 'that the native instinct exists in infancy in thousands of cases where it has never been suspected. It is the good gift of God, falling by the wayside, unrecognised and left to perish, or choked by the thorns of busy and quarrelsome homes. As with every other divine talent, the buried capital is not enough, the interest must be made by human care and industry. The flame must be fed; when once it is extinguished it cannot be rekindled. Therefore the responsibility lies with the parents in the first instance.'[53] The critic Frank Howes, though he denied that music could ever really be appreciated through a recording, thought that in the flesh any 'plain man' could appreciate true art; the 'plain man' had a 'highly developed sense of [musical] form which he exercises by the light of nature', provided his nature is sound; 'bad' harmony is 'insincere', 'superficial', 'inappropriate' harmony, and can be detected by the layman 'innocent' of musical knowledge just as the 'plain man' can detect such qualities in any other sphere.[54]

That American educationist from the Hartford Theological Seminary, Professor Pratt, held that those musicians who claimed, as he did, that the experience of music made men and women 'larger, higher, better' human beings in some sense, and that this benefit was due, 'not so much to an abnormal or entirely exceptional capacity in us that is non-existent in men generally, as to the enjoyment of special advantages and the development into full activity of powers that are at least potentially present in all men', had the obligation continually 'to revert to this question of the popularisation of music'.[55] If music could not become 'far more of a wide-working social force than hitherto . . . she is not worthy of the prodigious outlay of wealth and energy that has been lavished upon her'.[56]

Sir Richard Terry thought that the most vociferous condemnation of the gramophone came from vested interests, from 'music professors' and piano teachers who were alarmed at the falling off of pupils and so denounced 'canned music' as 'soulless and mechanical' and told the public that such contrivances could never replace the 'human touch'.[57] 'What is the pianoforte but a highly developed piece of mechanism?' he asked.[58] Far better to glimpse orchestral works by means of a recording than through the 'soulless medium' of a piano arrangement anyway. Pay no attention to these priggish academics and portentous highbrows who sniff at the gramophone: 'Don't suffer musical starvation, don't remain ignorant of Chopin's Ballades (*as a whole*), of Beethoven's Symphonies (*as a whole*), of Wagner's Operas (*as a whole*) because you can't (a) play them yourself, or (b) get Hamilton Harty with his Hallé orchestra to come to your town, or Bruno Walter and his Covent Garden company to your village to interpret them for you.'[59] Why should this be? Why should a man like Terry, the first organist of Westminster Cathedral and famous as a choir-trainer and as an unearther of a great amount of pre-Reformation English music, why should he particularly have been sure that there was indeed a mass audience for serious music and that the gramophone had a useful role in disseminating music when so many between the wars were unconvinced? Terry was a democrat and had a rare capacity for sympathy and empathy, and loved 'genuine' musical expression wherever he found it. He loved sea shanties from his childhood days living on the coast of Northumberland, and he became a collector and an authority. And he said he would rather any day go and hear *Champagne Charlie* or *Hi-tiddley-hi-ti*, or *They're All Very Fine and Large*, than the sloppy sentiment of Tosti's *Good-bye*, or the fustian of Stephen Adams's *Midshipmite*, or any other cerebrations of the Victorian drawing-room composers. He did not know whether he could 'admire them all' or believe in them in the sense that one admires or believes in a Beethoven symphony. 'But the songs', he thought, 'are at least human documents, and as such of profound interest.'[60] In the mid-1920s Terry travelled over England conducting for the *Daily Express* Community Singing Campaign. Conducting two thousand five hundred people singing themselves hoarse, his biographer tells us, he enjoyed to distraction, and the sound of massed singing always moved him to tears.[61]

T. S. Eliot wondered about the new fashion for community singing in the *Criterion* for June 1927, and the excitement generated when large numbers of people sing together; they sing, or rather bawl, he said, 'without much sense of tune or much knowledge of music', just as immense numbers of people today vote together, 'without using their reason and without enquiry. . . . It obviously cannot be explained by a new passion for Music . . . it should at present be suspect; it is very likely hostile to Art.'[62]

Muzak

Almost as soon as musicians became aware of recorded music in everyday life they warned against the insensitizing effects of too much music. Debussy feared in 1913 lest music be 'domesticated' through recording. 'Will it not bring to waste the mysterious force of an art which one might have thought indestructible?'[63] Schoenberg considered both the radio and the gramophone enemies of music, 'irresistibly on the march . . . opposition is a hopeless prospect'. They produced a 'boundless surfeit' which would wear music out.[64] Britten considered it 'one of the unhappiest results of the march of science and commerce' that Bach's St Matthew Passion, composed for performance on a particular day in the church's year, was now being used to provide a discreet accompaniment to the conversation of guests at a cocktail party.[65] To the generation who had discovered music before recordings, like the critic Neville Cardus, music in the second half of the century had become too familiar, had become less miraculous than it had once been.[66]

Certainly various kinds of mechanical music must have irritated people at times long before the invention of recorded sound. Princess Dorothea Lieven expressed her exasperation in 1820 in a letter to Prince Metternich at the dreadful barrel organs which went up and down London streets, one of which had stopped under her window, below the room in which she was attempting to compose a letter, fraying her nerves and driving her almost to tears. The existence of such contrivances she took as clear evidence that England was an unmusical country.[67] But in the second half of the twentieth century musicians and music-lovers fulminated against the constant barrage of recorded music that assaulted the ears in elevators, bars, taxis, supermarkets, and the usually more discreet aural tapestry provided in hospitals, prisons, and 'good' bookshops, Dvořák's *New World* Symphony while waiting on the phone, Orlando Gibbons in the dentist's chair, Mozart's Requiem and Strauss's Four Last Songs in a restaurant.[68] Records of songs like 'Rosa, we're going to Lodz, Lodz, Lodz', and 'Come into my arbour of love', and Czech folksongs, and records of Slezak and Caruso played over and over again in the evenings may have comforted Austrian soldiers in the trenches in 1915,[69] but no doubt some of the soldiers too were irritated and exasperated as Siegfried Sassoon was plagued beyond endurance as he lay in a ward in a convalescent home in England in 1917.[70] Even between the wars the portable gramophone was denounced by musicians as a curse; Eric Blom, who was the editor of the fifth edition of Grove's *Dictionary of Music and Musicians*, wrote in 1934 that if he had been a member of Parliament he would not have rested until he had succeeded in passing an act outlawing the manufacture of portable gramophones, and if he had been a voice on the Thames Conservancy he would have moved with all energy to ensure that 'every gramophone found on a riverboat . . . be confiscated at sight and sunk at hearing'.[71]

It's been estimated that in the urbanized industrialized environment of the West towards the end of the twentieth century perhaps six per cent of the acoustical environment is filled with the sounds of the natural world – of running water, of wind and of the sounds of animals – a quarter maybe with human sounds – of speech and laughter and live music-making – and more than two-thirds are technological sounds – sounds emanating from machines, traffic, incidental sounds, much of this 'technological' sound being noise, sound without a message, meaningless, irritating, boring sound we teach ourselves to shut out and try as much as we can to ignore. In the tribal communities of prehistory perhaps five per cent of the acoustic environment was composed of technological sounds – swords and ploughshares – and it may be imagined that the natural sounds which constituted possibly seventy per cent of the sounds that were heard had great significance and were often listened to with rapt attention.[72] In other words it's easy to conclude – at any rate many have concluded – that because the lives of so many today are filled with sounds that we teach ourselves to shut out and try as far as possible to ignore, we have become desensitized to sound and sound quality.

Muzak, the name which has come to be applied to all background music, is in fact the trade name of a company founded in New Jersey in 1934 which produces 'functional music as a tool of management in environmental situations',[73] chiefly for offices and factories, and it also manufactures recordings for use in stables to keep horses calm. In factories it aims to keep people calm and happy and to enhance the productivity of those engaged in repetitive occupations. The company emphasizes that the purpose of Muzak recordings is not to instil a love of music in those who hear its products, nor to improve listeners' minds, nor to elevate their thoughts, but simply to create certain psychological and physiological states, 'like a pretty painting or a room decoration'.[74] During the war the BBC broadcast their own version of Muzak, 'Music While You Work', not music to calm but music to 'invigorate' those on the factory floor, programmes of 'tuneful, rhythmic music for war-workers', introduced in June 1940, 'at the height of the "Go to it" period, when every minute counted more desperately than we knew'.[75] 'The American battleship *Alabama* was built to music', the *Radio Times* assured its readers. Musicians and music-lovers have been fierce in their denunciation of Muzak, 'the single most reprehensible and destructive phenomenon in the history of music', as it was described by the American composer Roger Reynolds.[76] Such use of music desensitized the listener, made it more difficult to sustain deep concentration on musical argument, blunted sensitivities to sound quality and subtleties in timbre, and made more difficult the discrimination between music as light diversion and profound utterance.

As early as 1888 the editor of *The Spectator* feared that all this delicate machinery for making visual and aural records was 'defeating the benefits conferred by oblivion', that in 'magnifying and embalming every little ripple of human energy' men would create piles of accumulated rubbish that would overwhelm coming generations, that all this wondrous scientific paraphernalia was giving 'artificial importance' to 'the pettiness' of human lives. 'We have a very strong belief that the scientific ingenuities of our day, acting under the imperious guidance of sensibilities which are as narrow as they are tender, will contrive to fill the world we leave behind us much too full of us for the free growth of our posterity; and that a time will come when it will be necessary to preach a sort of iconoclasm towards the pieties of ancestry in order to clear the way for anything like independent growth.'[77]

Many have agreed that the force and power of the masterpieces of the art music tradition of Western Europe are being destroyed through recordings, that a kind of cultural liquidation is taking place, that the half-hearing of fragments out of place and out of context and the endless repetitions of the greatest masterpieces were turning musical utterances whose effects were once grand and noble into the emptiest of clichés. But a few have suggested that this destruction of significances is desirable, that the weight of this magnificent tradition is suffocating, that an appreciation of many of the subtleties in rein-terpretations of the great works of the past presupposes a familiarity with the tradition which audiences can never again possess, since the tradition is now so fragmented: 'technology is disembowelling tradi-tional art', one has said. But, some have gone on to say, this is a process not to be feared. The 'bereavement . . . [will be] a relief . . . the creative powers formerly oppressed by tradition, by lingering pleasure, by social coercion, [will] regain their primitive strength'.[78]

New ways of experiencing music

What is not denied is that recordings have given listeners opportu-nities to browse, to sample, to investigate masses of music of all periods in the way that was possible with literature, in books, but was not pos-sible even to the most expert and erudite score-reader with music.[79] Recording has allowed the kind of intimacy to develop between listener and performer never previously possible; one listener has described the 'sense of human contact' present for him in the records of Caruso and Lotte Lehmann: 'we feel we know these people . . .'; 'I have this kind of fixation on the sound of Rosa Ponselle's voice and on Tito Schipa's lambent, loving pronunciation of the Italian language; on the chiaroscuro that Rachmaninoff brings to passage-work', and listening to 'a familiar record in fresh company', he thought, 'can revitalize the experience . . . providing a kind of fresh perspective through another's ears and responses'.[80] Leonard Bernstein once commented that a recording might not change, but the listener does.[81] Recordings have been used as aural icons to which a listener may return time and time again over many years, like a poem or a biblical text or a picture, sur-rounding the unchanging sounds with personal and ever-developing associations and memories. Clearly there is an air of unreality that sur-rounds listening to a symphony orchestra in a domestic setting but not to a solo pianist or a string quartet or one of Byrd's *Cantiones sacrae* written for performance by solo voices in a recusant's chapel after the Reformation; for such repertory private listening may represent a kind of ideal.

Recorded music has offered the chance to almost everyone of

experiencing musical sounds in ways only dreamt of by music-lovers in the past, and experienced by only a tiny handful of privileged men and women who could listen to music in their own homes. Montaigne's father thought it harmful to wrench a child from deep sleep and was able to employ a musician to ease his little son into consciousness with quiet instrumental music.[82] And Proust once summoned the Quatuor Capet to the Boulevard Haussmann to play just to himself Debussy's Quartet.[83] But even for a Proust or a Montaigne music could never be an entirely private affair, the auditor always being conscious of the musician's presence and of the need, or at least the expectation, of human interaction of some kind, even if the performer were a perfect stranger. 'Give me Books, fruit, french wine and fine whether [*sic*] and a little music out of doors, played by somebody I do not know',[84] said Keats whimsically, which was the most detached, the most impersonal, way he could imagine experiencing musical sounds. Today the magic of music unadulterated by humdrum human contact can be enjoyed by almost anyone at any time. Countless music-lovers have enthusiastically welcomed the opportunities recordings have offered them of experiencing music in new ways. A writer who disliked intensely the social decorum of the concert hall – the absurd spectacle of a violinist trussed up in a boiled shirt with sweat pouring off him – felt herself liberated when she could enjoy music by herself practically anywhere, when she could associate music with movement and with the colours and textures of landscape. A tape of a performance of an Allegro from a Mozart piano concerto lifted her spirits ever afterwards through its association for her with a fast car journey along a magnificent highway through the 'swashbuckling landscape of karst, sea and island' of Yugoslavia, from Istria to Montenegro. Mendelssohn's 'Italian' Symphony recalled for her the period of her life when she lived in an apartment above the Grand Canal in Venice where she had often played a recording of the work. The sounds would always conjure up for her the feelings of strutting self-confidence she imagined the composer himself experienced as he sailed down the Canal for the first time, on which occasion he felt, he said, like a prince coming into his inheritance.[85]

Teachers of musical appreciation and most reviewers of recordings up to the middle of the century (until perhaps the 1960s, the second decade of the LP) presented composers and works to prospective listeners. 'Even if Beethoven's B flat major Trio, let us say, were obtainable in a performance by the Archangels Gabriel, Michael and Raphael, it should still be bought for the sake of Beethoven', said one in 1934.[86] But by the end of the century the greatest musical master-pieces had been recorded again and again, if not by angels or archangels at least by all the greatest performing musicians of this world (and their performances given unearthly perfection through the wizardry of sound engineers) and any well-known work was always available on disc in multiple versions. In the introduction to their dis-cussion of Mozart recordings in *The Record Guide* published in 1951, the authors placed the composer in history, as a musical genius but 'personally unimpressive, feckless, a bad colleague', attempting in vain to cater for Viennese taste which always tended 'to frivolity'. They indi-cated the growth in appreciation of his music: in the middle of the nineteenth century he was generally considered a slight composer in comparison with Beethoven, charming but not profound; now he was recognized as a supreme master, and his reputation had never been higher. They attempted to encapsulate his essence: Mozart's was an art which combines 'elegance of manner and tenderness of heart', which 'smiles rather than laughs', its humour 'never far from melancholy', its nature 'truly aristocratic'. Introducing the piano con-certos, they emphasized the central position these occupy in Mozart's output, and they drew attention to C. M. Girdlestone's book giving an 'elaborate, detailed and most illuminating analysis of these works'. '[N]o fewer than sixteen of them' had been released on electri-cal coarse-groove discs in England and in 1951 there were recordings of twelve of them that could be purchased. In the record reviews of the 1990s there might be introductory remarks about the twentieth-century Norwegian composer Edvard Fliflet Bræin, or about William Dawson, the composer from Alabama who became Director of Music at the Tuskegee Institute, or Guillaume Bouzignac, 'the Charles Ives of the sixteenth century', but not about Mozart, or Bach, or Schubert, or Bruckner; about Boulez's *Pli selon pli*, maybe, but not about Beethoven's string quartets, at least for the kind of fairly sophisti-cated music-lovers for whom *The Penguin Guide to Compact Discs* was written.

Throughout the 1990s there were always at least six sets of record-ings of all the Mozart piano concertos generally available in England, and often more. Towards the end of the decade there were complete series by Perahia, Schiff, Barenboim, Brendel, Bilson, Ashkenazy,

Shelley, Jandó, Levin, and a good many other performances by other pianists of individual works or groups of concertos. In 1951 the critics limited themselves to a few words about individual interpretation – 'extremely musical', the keyboard technique of the conductor Bruno Walter was 'naturally less even than that of the best Mozartians' – and a few on the recordings: 'dry in tone and so badly balanced that the piano frequently drowns the orchestra', 'a little dry and unresonant', 'some of the woodwind details fail to stand out'.[87] And that was about that. But half a century later the critics would consider the interpretative style and power of each executant in great detail, the 'poetic insight and musical spontaneity' of one, the 'elegance and poise' of another, would draw attention to the lack of 'extrovert sparkle' in another: 'unfailingly elegant, but a little over-civilized . . . a faint hint of preciosity'. The playing of this pianist 'is hard to resist, even though it occasionally leads to over-exuberance and idiosyncrasies', in another the 'sensuous . . . is always tempered by spirituality'. The critics would make comparisons of sound quality arising from the different instruments used: on these particular discs, for example, 'a Bösendorfer piano and its relatively gentle, cleanly focused timbre has something of the precision of a fortepiano without any of the loss of colour which comes with a more modern instrument'.

The qualities of the recorded sound would also be closely analysed: there were comments on the 'full' sound of one of these Mozart sets, on the consistently 'beautiful' sound of another, with 'sweet strings and glowing woodwind', on the different perspectives accorded the piano in the different sets. Consistency in balance and sound quality were achieved in one set even though different Viennese locations were used in the making of the series, 'including the Mozarteum, the Grosser Saal of the Konzerthaus, the Viersen Festhalle, and the Millstatt Kirche'. The effects that distant microphone placing could have on the dramatic impact of particular passages in different works were recognized, enhancing the air of mystery to the opening of the D Minor Concerto K.466, and increasing the ethereal quality of the slow movement of the C major Concerto K.467. The critics noted whether the recording had had a digital original, which might increase the immediacy and 'presence' of the recording, and commented on the skills demonstrated in the remastering process: 'The strings now sound smooth and full (the previously noticed edginess has disappeared) and the balance gives no cause for complaint.' And their comments had to take into account the differences in cost, whether this was a 'full price', or 'mid-price' or 'budget' label.[88]

Performers listen to recordings

The possibilities that records offered for performers everywhere to listen to and to learn from the world's greatest artists were quickly recognized. In 1909 the text was published of 'The Herman Klein Phono-Vocal Method', a set of four books, one each for soprano, contralto, tenor and bass voices. The idea had been put forward by the American soprano Lilian Nordica, who thought that, since 'good singing was largely a matter of imitating good models', the gramophone could provide an invaluable pedagogical aid. She asked Herman Klein, an English singing teacher and writer and 'musical advisor' to the American Columbia Graphophone Company, if he would provide specific technical exercises for records. Klein, who was born in Norwich in 1856, had heard as a boy singers like Tietjens, Trebelli, Sims Reeves, Santley and Jenny Lind at the Norwich Festival and for four years as a young man had had lessons with Manuel Garcia, on whose 'Famous School' his 'Phono-Vocal Method' was based.[89] Various difficulties accompanied the recording of the forty double-sided discs and then, just as they were about to be launched in England, in 1912 or 1913, the Columbia factory burnt down and the stock of records and books was completely destroyed. After a replacement stock had been sent to England from New York in 1918 – the delay caused by war conditions – and these had suffered the same fate, another fire at the Columbia stores, Klein decided not to tempt fate further and gave up.[90] And nobody else took up the idea. But although he was an enthusaistic advocate of the gramophone as a teacher and guide for singers, Herman Klein recognized its dangers; in 1933 he auditioned a young man from whom there emerged now and then 'the unmistakable timbre of a really fine tenor voice'. He had never had lessons, he could not read music, but he had studied records by Caruso, the 'amplified' Caruso moreover, electrical reissues of the original acoustic recordings. And when he sang he inflated his chest, he let out 'a series of stentorian tones, which he sustained at high pressure, his face distorted by glaring eyes and dilated nostrils' in an effort to rival the volume of the recording.[91] This 'unsuspecting beginner' had committed 'the fatal error of mistaking the doctored article for the real thing'. For anyone to claim that a singing student just has to listen to the best singers on a record and go and do likewise is like the old conjurer who used to insist that he would let his audience into the secret of how it was done, and then after each mystifying trick would remark with a twinkle in his eye, 'And that's the way it's done!' Herman Klein was plainly irritated when the Gramophone Company issued a little book entitled *The Student of Singing* by Dawson Freer in 1931, simply a list of recommendations of electrical recordings from the HMV catalogue introduced with maxims of mind-numbing banality: 'The singer is the artistic middleman between the composer and the public', 'An ascetic attitude cannot produce an aesthetic result', 'Personality is paradoxical; it expresses individuality and, at the same time, it stands for the common humanity we all share'.[92]

And the conductor Henry Wood, who was himself a vocal coach, warned singers in 1924 of the dangers that the recorded Caruso could represent. A young tenor he knew had trained in London for five years and had become 'quite a refined, true and sympathetic singer'. And then after two years – during which time Sir Henry had not heard him at all – he came back and sang to him again. He was horrified at the change: the tone had become 'shouty, white, bleaty and very tight on the top notes'. It was his opinion that 'if you want to send a nice, pretty-toned little English voice to the devil – you will send it to Italy . . .'. Had he travelled through Europe? No, he'd stayed at home and had bought all Caruso's records and listened to some of them every day, modelling his style and tone on the records. 'And it was just in this that his ruin lay. . . .'[93]

Such use of recordings was probably rare with performers of classical music, although singers perhaps more than other re-creative artists experimented with sounds and styles discovered on discs. Learning performing styles and idioms through recorded performances was the way jazz developed, since the disc itself was the only source available. It's certainly hard to imagine classical performers using discs as did jazz musicians from the first. From the moment Louis Armstrong began releasing discs in the 1920s players everywhere began to incorporate elements of his idiosyncratic innovations into their own particular styles. The New Orleans trumpeter 'Red' Allen put the phonograph to much more technical and prosaic use: he learnt to become fluent in different keys by adjusting the old speed screw on the household's Victrola and playing along with the disc.[94] The jazz trumpeter Humphrey Lyttelton had one trumpet lesson and a book – he never learnt to read music – and otherwise learnt everything from the gramophone.[95] And the percussionist James Blades transcribed xylophone solos from records in the 1920s which he was still playing fifty years later.[96]

For most classical musicians right into the days of LPs, recordings were regarded as substitutes for musical experiences, to some a rather unfortunate economic necessity, and certainly not to be treated with the same kind of seriousness as a score or a manuscript. Musicians have continued to have a reputation for not being interested in listening to discs. 'It's not that I don't want a record player', Pierre Boulez once said, 'I don't need it . . . I prefer to read a score. . . . If you listen, you know, it can be just entertainment.'[97] The record producer Walter Legge was someone who clearly treated records with very great seriousness indeed and when he married Elisabeth Schwarzkopf he showed her how she might make creative use of performers' qualities through recordings in a way that would have been impossible otherwise. He set out 'to widen by recorded examples Schwarzkopf's imaginative concept of the possibilities of vocal sound', he said.

> Rosa Ponselle's vintage port and thick cream timbre and noble line; the Slavic brilliance of Nina Koshetz; a few phrases from Farrar's Carmen, whose insinuations were reflected in Schwarzkopf's 'Im Chambre séparée', one word only from Melba, 'Bada' in 'Donde lieta'; some Rethberg; and large doses of Meta Seinemeyer to show how essentially Teutonic voices can produce brilliant Italianate sound. Then Lehmann's all-embracing generosity, Schumann's charm and lightness, McCormack's incredible octave leap in 'Care selve', Frida Leider's dramatic tension – all these were nectar and ambrosia for Schwarzkopf's musical appetite. Instrumentalists too: Fritz Kreisler for the dark beauty of tone, his nobility and cavalier nonchalance; Schnabel for concentrated thinking over long musical periods, firmly rhythmical, seemingly oblivious to bar lines. From the analysis of what we found most admirable in these diverse models we made our own synthesis. . . .[98]

Such usage of recordings in the 1940s must have been exceptional.

More recently, though, performers have been freer in acknowledging the extent to which they have been inspired and influenced by recordings. As a young organist in the late 1940s and early 50s Peter Hurford was inspired in his own Bach performances by the broadcasts and recordings of Geraint Jones playing Bach on the organ at Steinkirchen in Germany built by Arp Schnitger in the 1680s, and on the Trinity organ at Ottobeuren built by Karl Joseph Riepp in the 1760s, by the instruments' clarity and transparency, by the way authentic sonorities revealed facets of the music which had been obscured on the nineteenth- and twentieth-century English organs on which he was accustomed to hearing this music played.[99] And he took hints from records of Pablo Casals – from the agogic accentuation in his performance of Bach's first suite for unaccompanied cello, from the way Casals gives life to the music by maintaining a regular pulse and yet within it impelling the music forward by skipping over the less important notes – and from Stokowski's success in projecting a singing line in his own sumptuous, unhistorical orchestral arrangements of chorale preludes.[100]

The lutenist and director of the Consort of Musicke, Anthony Rooley, exhorted the singers he worked with in Monteverdi to stimulate their imaginations about vocal possibilities by adventurous listening, by playing recordings of Buddhist Lama chanting – overtone singing, guttural throat singing – from Kyzyl in Tuva, and Indian classical music sung by the chanter Parween Sultana, and Little Richard, and Bobby McFerrin singing on the out-breath and in-breath.[101] Performers have usually professed rarely if ever to listen to their own recordings: 'Why should I?' said Frans Brüggen, the Dutch virtuoso recorder player.[102] It was simply one performance and next time, performers say, they would do it differently. The members of a string quartet were bewildered and irritated when they rehearsed the Dvořák Piano Quintet with a pianist who kept referring to a recording the string players had made several years previously with another pianist and reminding them of the details of that performance. He had evidently studied the recording imagining that points of interpretation would remain unchanged.[103] For some performers listening to their own recordings would be too often a disappointment, a reminder that intentions were never quite realized, and of mannerisms which a performer was certainly aware of but could do little to eradicate, even if he wished to.[104]

Perhaps this is just modesty, or false modesty; perhaps many do secretly listen to themselves more frequently than they acknowledge.

But certainly for performers, just as for everyone else, recordings have educated, have acquainted them with repertory that otherwise they would never have had the time or the opportunity to hear. The cellist Janos Starker, who at the height of his career would spend more than 250 days each year on tour, would listen to contemporary works that he might wish to learn himself, works which he would never be able to catch up with in live performances.[105] The LP gave young musicians the opportunity to become acquainted with the whole history of western music. As a student Frans Brüggen played Bach and Handel and Telemann and studied eighteenth-century musical treatises, but at the same time he listened avidly to Mahler, Bruckner and Wagner on records.[106]

Of course many musicians have remained suspicious of recordings. The critic Andrew Porter has met singers 'who grew indignant at the suggestion that they should seek instruction from old records: "I want to do my Norma, my Almaviva, my Carlo, not a copy of Rosa Ponselle's, Fernando De Lucia's, Battistini's."' He finds it '[s]trange and not sensible, the failure to realise that many great artists began by imitating the best of their predecessors and then, challenged and inspired by a full knowledge of what others had achieved, developed and refined a personal interpretation in the light of individual temperament and technique'. And he quotes the Italian soprano Renata Scotto: 'I make it a practice never to listen to recordings of roles which I am singing. The role must be completely my own. . . . I want to give the work everything that I have of my deep self.'[107] Andrew Porter evidently takes such defensiveness as a sign of an immature musical persona, an indication of a weak musical character, so to fear exposure to other interpretations. One record producer denied that mature experienced conductors at any rate are ever inhibited by the interpretations of others, even by the recordings of composers themselves; he had never seen, he claimed, an 'inhibited conductor'.[108] But certainly many performers have warned against modelling interpretations on recorded performances. Boulez agreed with Mahler that tradition is laziness and the business of the performer is first to dig deep into the score, to discover possibilities through the notation, not to be led into second-hand solutions by imitating the performances of others. What are most likely to be copied from a recording, in Boulez's opinion, are simply a performer's superficial mannerisms, not the essential character of a performer's art, which is unique anyway and therefore beyond imitation.[109]

That interpretations must be a 'natural outgrowth of the temperament' and the performer must learn the work, not another's interpretation of the work, is the view of André Previn, who only studies a recording if the work is new and of such notational complexity that it is difficult to obtain an impression of its musical substance in any other way.[110] Lotte Lehmann, born in 1880, was too busy as a young singer, she said, to listen to recordings, and never did so as an old lady, neither to the 'terrible' old ones, nor to modern LPs.[111] But some performers do admit to listening for pleasure: the American soprano Martina Arroyo would spend many evenings listening to recordings, modern ones, not old ones, and she loved listening to them; and André Previn listened for pleasure a lot, though never while evolving his own interpretation of a particular work. His four small children would listen to recordings of classical music for up to an hour before they went to sleep each night; to be deprived of this would be, he thought, their 'only genuine punishment'.[112]

Composers listen to recordings

At the turn of the century composers were only just beginning to take important constituent elements of their language and style and ethos from sources other than those demonstrated in the work of their immediate predecessors. Earlier composers had incorporated folk songs into their natural musical language, into the *lingua franca* of their time; now composers like Bartók and Vaughan Williams drew on folk songs to create new harmonies and counterpoints and rhythms and metres and to evolve formal procedures which they derived directly from the folk material itself. Holst and Vaughan Williams and Herbert Howells worked out compositional procedures from sixteenth-century English music and felt a close affinity with what they perceived to be its spirit. Debussy loved and drew creative inspiration from old composers – from Palestrina, Victoria and Lassus, Bach, and Couperin – and his imagination was also fed by the exotic music he heard at the 1889 Paris World Exhibition, at which he spent hours in the Dutch section listening to the 'inexhaustible combinations of ethereal, flashing timbres' of the Javanese gamelan.[113] But the gramophone immensely enlarged the amount and the range and character of music composers could hear. And it provided music in a way that allowed the music to be lived with, not just examined as a series of specimens but absorbed and assimilated through the most frequent exposure.

Michael Tippett was characteristically a twentieth-century composer in the stylistic fusion he attempted of widely and wildly different elements. In one of his earliest masterpieces, the *Concerto for Double String Orchestra*, completed in 1939, there are aspects of Handel's concerti grossi, the three-movement concertos of Bach and Vivaldi, Elgar and Vaughan Williams, and of the English tradition of writing for strings; there are formal elements – in the ternary forms and sonata-rondo schemes – that are Beethovenian in origin as well as motivic workings that derive from that composer; and there are idioms derived from English and Scottish folk song. Tippett exploits the expressive effects of false relations that he had found in Dowland and Weelkes and the independence of lines and the vitality of rhythm that he had experienced in English madrigals. But there are also Hindemithian touches in lines built round fourths; at this time he would often listen to the recording of Hindemith's String Trio no. 2 with the composer playing the viola and with Szymon Goldberg the violin and Emanuel Feuermann the cello.[114] And the false relations and the characteristic kinds of rhythmic anticipations of the piece can also be shown to derive from jazz. Jazz-derived too is the spirit, the kind of crazy dance movement that emerges from continuous attempts to subvert a regular pulse – strong accents just missing main beats, or extra accents added – an intoxicating kind of energy and exhilaration and buoyancy. And it is in recordings that he had experienced these qualities, in the recordings of Louis Armstrong and Bessie Smith. In the early 1930s Tippett would play over and over again Bessie Smith's 1925 recording of the *St Louis Blues*: jazz he loved not only for its rhythmic novelties but also for the 'virtuosity and humanity' of the best artists, and it seemed for him to carry with it a warning against the pretentiousness of high art. The Blues – which he regarded as a kind of twentieth-century archetypal musical form, like Purcellian ground basses for the seventeenth century – he loved especially, for their defiance and for the directness and power of their emotional impact.[115]

The Hungarian composer György Ligeti, born in Transylvania in 1923, was brought up in a household where the only musical instrument was the gramophone, and from that he devoured music.[116] The influences on his recent music, he told an interviewer in 1987, were mostly gleaned from records stumbled across by accident, 'Georgian folk music, music from fifteenth-century Italy and late fourteenth-century France; recent French music, particularly that of Claude Vivier and central African polyphonic music'.[117] The English composer Robin Holloway acknowledged that his experience as a choirboy in St Paul's Cathedral between 1952 and 1957 must have been crucial in forming him as a musician. But before that records on his parents' wind-up gramophone of the *Blue Danube* and Bach's *Italian Concerto* played by Landowska and the glockenspiel passages in *The Magic Flute* had lodged permanently in his mind, and certainly, as a child of the age of the mechanical reproduction of music, it was radio and records which provided him later with his musical awakenings, with those experiences which 'changed his ears', like the discovery through records of Debussy's *Jeux* and Schoenberg's *Erwartung*.[118]

In 1947 when he was three and with his mother away giving birth to his younger brother, the composer John Tavener played over and over and over again for comfort a record made in 1929 of 250 Manchester schoolchildren singing Purcell's 'Nymphs and shepherds', and his biographer suggests that this is early evidence of his enduring love for high and pure voices and for ritual and repetition, perhaps a defining moment.[119] In 1993 he encouraged singers wishing to perform his own music stylishly to listen to tapes of Father Dionysios Firfiris, the first Chanter of Protaton Mount Athos, who was in his nineties and 'a master of the great art of embellishing Byzantine music', and he suggested that cellists playing his music should listen to 'the instrumental music of the Middle East played on stringed instruments'. Through examination of other musical traditions he looked for an 'alchemical change' in performing techniques as well as in composition.[120]

When he was writing his Flute Concerto, completed in 1980, Nigel Osborne listened to recordings of flute playing from New Guinea, the Amazon basin, and Japan, and some of the sounds and techniques he heard in these recordings he adopted and transformed and they became, he said, 'an integral part of the inspiration and thrust of the work'.[121] Listening to the music of other cultures has had radical and far-reaching effects on other composers. In 1979 the English composer Giles Swayne was startled by a recording of African pygmy music, quiet, polyphonic, intimate, when he had imagined African music would all be loud, and out-of-doors in feel and effect. He listened to more music from Africa and in the end decided to go to the Gambia himself, and he made there his own recordings, twenty-seven hours in all, of music of the Jola people. This experience came at a time when he was feeling dissatisfaction with the complexities of contemporary European art music, and with the attitudes of musicians to their audiences, and with his place as a composer in what seemed to him an unreal and artificial world. The African experience caused him to change his attitude to the components of music and for a time his music became, as he described it, 'extremely simple, modal-based, without any harmony'. The sounds of the music and the understanding of the part music played in this African society was an exercise in, he said, cleansing his ear and cleansing his mind, and it enabled him to see a way forward, taught him new ways of manipulating notes, and a new way of regarding his vocation as a composer.[122]

Musicologists and historians don't listen to recordings

But if recordings have played such a crucial part in music in the twentieth century, why have they been so neglected by scholars and historians? In 1952 the American scholarly journal *The Musical Quarterly* began reviewing records, after 'frequent requests from many quarters', according to the editor.[123] This was in the journal's thirty-eighth year; it had grown up with the record industry but had hitherto paid no attention to recorded performances of the music whose scores and manuscripts and original performing conditions it discussed with such avidity. The record reviews in this publication, the editor explained, would not concern themselves with 'the execution of pizzicatos' or 'microphone placing', which could be read about in 'the average musical magazine or daily newspaper'. The scholars writing for this journal, 'who [knew] the scores' and did not 'merely listen to the records', were interested in 'the music (i.e. the "edition") that is being performed and the aesthetic and historical implications embodied in the performance, because the performance itself is ephemeral, whereas the work of art and the idea are permanent'.[124] So long as musicians and scholars held to the belief that a musical work really dealt with timeless realities, it made no sense to examine and analyse and dissect individual performances, each representing at best a partial interpretation, a different kind of failure to realize that meaning – whether an experience of the sublime or an understanding of Platonic truths or Gestalt principles – that was better approached by reference to the manuscript or printed score or even provisional sketches. One of the greatest of this century's pianists, Artur Schnabel, is supposed to have once said: 'Great music . . . is music that's better than it can be played.'

But the twentieth century has become increasingly reluctant to think about music in mystical or metaphysical or even theological terms. Great effort was formerly expended on attempting to discover what the creator – the author, painter, composer – was trying to convey through his work. Now in literary criticism, in art history, in aesthetics, a conviction has emerged that the meanings of works of art do not deal with timeless realities, nor are they exclusively the result of a creator's thought and conscious, or even unconscious intentions, but may be apprehended differently at different times, in different circumstances by different people. Meanings may always be in some sense partial or provisional but this doesn't imply that there's anything easy or straightforward about them. Which might suggest that the study of music in performance, of music in society, of the ways in which music has been used and the terms in which it has been discussed and pondered upon might long ago have seized the imagination of music historians. And yet this has not happened.

In 1971 the English music critic Martin Cooper explained in a broadcast talk that many musicologists write of music 'as an enclosed, self-contained world obeying its own laws; and they prefer to deny or disregard the influence of personal, social or economic factors which threaten the objective, scientific character of their work'. Whatever his private views on the desirability or otherwise of this state of affairs, he was not intending to criticize or to be provocative but to seek to define what he took to be the critic's task, the journalist's job, and to contrast it with the work of the academic musicologist, at least as those functions were carried out in the England of the 1970s. The 'musicologist proper', he thought, was concerned with 'the actual language of music and its historical development', he was 'the grammarian or philologist of the art, less interested in judgements of value than in the constatation and arrangement of facts'.[125] In 1980 a writer from within the academy, though one of a particularly idiosyncratic kind – his first book was *Music in Society*, a later series was entitled *Man and His Music*, and he had published a study of the Beatles, and was to write books on Bob Dylan and on 'Angels of the Night', popular female singers like Ethel Waters, Billie Holiday, Ella Fitzgerald, Joni Mitchell and Blossom Dearie, as well as on Bach and Beethoven – noted the same concerns of musicologists, who often 'deplored . . . any attempt to talk about music's "meanings" in other than technical terms'. Yet Wilfrid Mellers himself considered that 'description that goes no further than musical facts can never be more than a trivial occupation'.[126]

There have been many calls in the past twenty years to widen musicology's scope, exhortations to remember that the specialized techniques of musicological research must serve a greater purpose, namely the presentation of the works the scholar studies 'as living things',[127] but very little work on recorded music has been undertaken. Inevitably the research programmes of an institutionalized discipline change very slowly. It was not so surprising that gramophone records weren't reviewed in *The Musical Times* until 1921, but perhaps more surprising that they weren't reviewed in the journal *Early Music* until 1979. The launch of the journal in 1973 would have been impossible ten years earlier in the editor's opinion; then there were comparatively few musicians interested in the pre-Bach repertory and those that were interested tended to divide themselves up into specialists, into societies for recorder players, lutenists, or gamba-players, or into scholars and antiquarians. Now all had 'mysteriously changed'.[128] But there was no mystery about it. Radio and even more the long-playing record had created the enthusiasm for the pre-Bach repertory; it was recordings in effect that had created by the 1960s a growing early music army of performers and editors and commentators and it was recordings that were keeping the army on the march. And yet, for the first six years, *Early Music* contained no regular record reviews. When the editor announced their appearance he gave it as his opinion that the role of the record companies in the revival of early music had been 'seminal', but there were difficulties: the 'constant re-issues, the movement from one label to another of sections of a complete programme, the delays in British releases of many fine continental and American recordings' which made 'the scene more fluid and less well-defined than those of books and music'. All of which seem curiously lame reasons to be advanced by such a determined, energetic, and experienced editor.[129] The fact that reviews appeared no sooner was more likely indicative of deep-seated and unexamined attitudes towards records and recordings.

And although in 1985 Joseph Kerman described references to antagonisms between musicologist and performer as being based on 'old-fashioned stereotypes',[130] it's difficult not to guess that some of the reluctance of scholars to work in performance practice studies is indeed based on differences in character and temperament, on the continuing suspicion of the 'man of letters' for the instinctual artisan, as he may tend to regard him in his heart of hearts. And also some jealousy on his part for the performer's instrumental or vocal mastery or for the power some conductors appear to wield, and for the ringing applause which the lonely scholar will never enjoy. The foundation of *The Cambridge Opera Journal* in 1989 was greeted with cheers and relief by many scholars; here, at last, was 'a forum for serious opera scholarship unencumbered by advertising, opera trivia, and recording or production reviews'.[131]

Certainly the technological limitations of early recordings – up to the end of the shellac era, up to the 1950s – prevented them being given serious consideration by many musicians and cultural commentators. And antagonism or ambivalence towards mass culture was another element. But a further obvious reason why so little has been done to investigate discs and tapes is that there are very few large collections of sound recordings, and none of them are easy to use. Records are not accessible in the way books and musical scores are; great university and conservatoire libraries are not usually complemented by large and comprehensive sound archives. And then there's the absence of discographical control: sound recordings are notoriously difficult and time-consuming to catalogue. No large sound archive in the world has solved these problems. Computer catalogues and the possibilities of exchanging data may at last help to solve this.

Collections of recordings in Europe and North America

In 1954 Roland Gelatt regretted that no-one had yet 'seen fit to gather [the phonograph's] legacy together under one roof and make it available to the serious student (or even the curious layman)'. Until that happened – and he was sure that one day it would, 'given the will and the money' – 'the phonograph would remain an invention with a history but without a heritage'.[132] It cannot be said that sound archives have made a huge impact on the general public or even on the world of the professional musician or the historian or the scholar. With no traditions of scholarship in working with recordings, and with so few teaching organizations having privileged access to large collections, few scholars have been introduced to working with discs and tapes through their training as apprentice musicologists.

In some countries the deposit of sound recordings in a national archive or library is connected with purposes of copyright protection, as it is for example in Spain, Italy, Argentina, Brazil, and in the United States, where compulsory legal deposit of recordings was only granted in 1972. In a few others deposit is required for cultural purposes unconnected with copyright law, in Canada, for example, in Germany, in Greece, and in France. The French law on deposit has been in existence the longest, since 1925, and is one of the most far-reaching and includes 'all sound recordings offered to the public for sale, distribution or hire in France, including imported records'.[133] In Britain in 1951 the government set up a committee to consider revision of the Copyright Act. At the opening of the sessions at which legal deposit for sound recordings was to be discussed the chairman, the lawyer Lord Reading, remarked: 'What is the point of this? Anyone who wants to hear a record goes into a shop.' The suggestion was turned down. In 1977 when a government committee spent two years investigating deposit libraries in connection with copyright law, the chairman, the Honourable Mr Justice Whitford, gave it as his view that the whole field of sound and film archives certainly deserved further investigation by another committee that could 'assess the questions to be considered, namely the desirability and feasibility of setting up such archives', apparently ignorant of the fact that a national sound archive had existed in England for more than twenty years.[134] There is still no compulsory deposit for sound recordings in Great Britain.

Many of the earliest important collections of sound recordings were assembled by ethnologists and ethnomusicologists, who had early realized that the recording apparatus offered a means of preserving the languages and the music of purely oral cultures, that it would now be possible to capture the microtone intervals and irregular rhythms of folk musics that defied accurate registration by conventional notational means. The enthusiasm with which this new opportunity was seized by these turn-of-the-century psychologists, philologists and comparative musicologists derived in part from the youth of their disciplines. It was new, this enthusiasm for non-European cultures; interest had been growing throughout the nineteenth century, and marked a radical shift in historical understanding, a realization that cultures are many and varied, that civilizations and historical periods are each unique and each uniquely valuable for investigation, and a rejection of the conviction that reality is ordered by timeless, universal, unalterable laws. Probably the first to make field recordings was an ethnologist called J. Walter Fewkes who in March 1889 recorded songs and prayers and tales of the Passamaquody Indians in Maine, and he later recorded the Zuni and Hopi Pueblo Indians of Arizona; all these recordings were later deposited at the Peabody Institute in Baltimore. In Europe Béla Vikar collected Hungarian folk songs from 1898, and from 1904 there were others including Béla Bartók and Zóltan Kodály and László Lajtha, thousands of whose recordings were deposited in the Hungarian National Museum in Budapest; besides 280 cylinders of Hungarian folk music, Bartók himself made over 1,300 other cylinder recordings, of folk melodies from Eastern Europe, Slovakia, Ruthenia, Bulgaria, Rumania and Yugoslavia, and of Arabic folk music in the Biskra District in Algeria, and melodies from North Africa and Turkey. From 1906 Percy Grainger used a cylinder phonograph for collecting folk songs, the first in Lincolnshire where he recorded one of his best singers, Joseph Taylor, and the most famous one, since the Gramophone Company issued nine of his songs commercially in 1908.[135]

The first important collection of sound recordings was established in Vienna in 1899, the Vienna Phonogrammarchiv, the creation of a group of scholars at the Imperial Academy of Sciences, whose declared aims were to record European languages and dialects and also the languages of illiterate people for linguistic investigation, to record music – especially the music of 'primitive' peoples, in order to have a solid basis for comparative musicology ('vergleichende Musikwissenschaft') – and to record and collect so-called *Stimm-porträts* (voice portraits) of famous contemporaries. Later on the aims were enlarged to include medical recordings and wildlife sounds. Early field recordings organized by the Vienna Archive included expeditions to record the dialects of Yugoslavia and linguistic samples on the island of Lesbos; the anthropologist Rudolf Pöch took equipment from Vienna on his famous 1904–6 expedition to New Guinea; a project was started to record German dialects in Austria; a physician and amateur folklorist called Rudolf Trebitsch recorded the speech of European minorities like the Basques, the Bretons and the Welsh, Scottish and Irish populations, and as early as 1904 the zoologists Kreidl and Regen used recordings for their analysis of stridulating crickets.[136] And early 'voice-portraits' included Hugo von Hofmannsthal, Arthur Schnitzler and Ferdinand von Saar reading from their own works, and the voices of Franz Josef I, and Albert Einstein, and also Puccini.

The Berlin Phonogrammarchiv was established in 1904 from the collections of the Berlin Psychological Institute, and its director between 1906 and 1933 was Erich von Hornbostel, who published papers on Japanese, Turkish, Indian and American Indian music based on materials at the Phonogrammarchiv; his studies in comparative musicology derived from the approaches created for comparative linguistics. For such a scholar as Hornbostel the phonograph was a valuable piece of technology which aided and abetted a scientific enterprise; it made possible the analysis of specimens. In Paris too the establishment of a sound archive was the idea of a member of the Société d'Anthropologie, and the Musée Phonographique was established in 1900. The origins of the French national library of recordings lie in the suggestion of the record company Pathé Frères to the Académie de Paris in 1911 that they supply the necessary material and staff for the establishment of a sound laboratory for the preservation and study of languages and dialects. This became the Archives de la Parole; the appellation Phonthèque Nationale dates from 1938[137] and since 1977 the archive has been a department of the Bibliothèque Nationale.

The Archive of American Folk Song was established at the Library of Congress in 1928 and an Archive of Folk and Primitive Music was established at Columbia in 1936, which later transferred to Indiana University. The Victor Talking Machine Copyright Company had attempted to register a sound recording in the Library's Copyright Office in 1906 in order to determine the exact legal status of its products, but was refused registration, recorded sound being judged 'non-copyrightable matter'.[138] In 1923 a letter from a member of the legal department at Victor to Carl Engel, the Chief of the Music Division, made reference to 'Victor records becoming part of the archives of the National Library', of which plan both correspondents seem to have approved, but this only happened in 1925.[139]

By June of that year 412 Victor records had been donated together with an electrically driven Art-Victrola.[140] The selection was made by Carl Engel from catalogues and monthly bulletins supplied by Victor. Unfortunately no lists of acquisitions have been preserved, but from the correspondence it is clear that Engel had requested mainly 'Red Seals' – the label of the best-known classical artists, the 'celebrity' label – but also some jazz was requested and popular and folk music. The Company had offered to donate 400 discs, but with his order Engel writes: 'If you should feel inclined to increase your gift beyond this number, I would plead that you include a fair representation of the various samples of national and folk music of other nations (which are not listed in the main catalogue).'[141] And in November 1928 he was trying to trace a record he thought Congress should have, a number from the show *Luckee Girl*, 'Come, let's make whoopee'.[142] A new machine, an Orthophonic Victrola, was given on long-term loan to the Library in 1927, by which time it appears to have become established that the company would offer on a continuing basis selections of their discs made by Engel and his staff, and also themselves make suggestions of discs they thought particularly successful, either because of their technical quality or because they were selling in large quantities and therefore gave an indication of popular taste, records like Gene Austin's 'My blue heaven', an album of Victor Herbert melodies, and Jimmie Rodgers's 'Blue yodel'.[143] It is not clear just how much these discs were played; in 1928 Engel wrote to the company requesting a box of tungsten needles: 'The handsome machine is being put to quite a little use and is giving us a great deal of pleasure.' The gramophone was certainly used at meetings of learned societies and of the American Library Association, and E. H. Fellowes had used it when he lectured on English madrigals and church music the previous autumn. Occasionally, Engel told Victor, readers had been able 'to settle questions of tempo and interpretation by referring to the records'.[144]

By the 1990s the Library of Congress contained over 2,800,000 recordings, as well as more than 400,000 motion picture films and over 200,000 videos tapes.[145] The collections of western art music have been built up from the donations of record companies – from 1972 by means of the legal deposit legislation – and of donations by private collectors, composers, performers – including Geraldine Farrar, Rosa Ponselle and Serge Rachmaninoff – through limited purchases, and since 1940 through tapes of concerts organized by the Library in the Coolidge Auditorium, and through sessions in the recording studio. There are a number of collections of radio broadcast recordings including programmes of the American National Broadcasting Company, the Armed Forces Radio and Television Service, the Voice of America, and National Public Radio. And there are special collections such as the Berliner Collection, consisting of diaries, business papers, and recordings donated by the family of Emile Berliner, and numerous donations from private collectors such as a large collection of rare recordings made in Russia between the 1900s and the 1950s, including discs on the Beka, Ekstrafon, Favorite, Lirofon, Metropol, Orpheon, Sirena and Stella labels.

The Rodgers and Hammerstein Archives of Recorded Sound, part of the New York Public Library – until 1965, when it received an important gift from the Rodgers and Hammerstein Foundation, it was part of the Music Division – had its origins in gifts Columbia Records began making to the Library in the mid-1930s. Today the Archives hold more than 460,000 recordings, built up through the donations of record companies and broadcasting organizations and private individuals. Besides the commercial records there are Metropolitan Opera broadcasts from the 1930 to the 1990s, and there is the Toscanini Legacy, a gift of the Toscanini family including recordings of many live performances and rehearsals from 1926 to 1954, together with many smaller collections given by musicians, by the soprano Rosa Ponselle, by the pianist Rosalyn Tureck.[146]

But the few other large collections in America which include recordings of western art music are of much more recent date: the Archive of Recorded Sound at Stanford University, with more than 200,000 recordings of speech and music of all kinds, many of them of western classical music, was established in 1958;[147] the Collection of Historical Sound Recordings at Yale University was set up in 1961, on the initiative of two private record collectors, both of them graduates of Yale's Music School;[148] and the collections in the Syracuse University sound archive, the Belfer Audio Laboratory & Archive, established in 1963, numbered in 1999 more than 300,000 recordings in all formats, including cylinders, discs and magnetic tapes; one of its greatest strengths is the collection of late nineteenth- and early twentieth-century commercially released cylinders and phonodiscs. The Archive claims to be the third largest in the United States, and the largest collection held by a private institution in North America.

Britain's national archive of sound recordings

In the *London Evening News* for 22 March 1905 an anonymous writer suggested that the British Museum should create a collection of sound recordings of poets and statesmen, and of great preachers and orators, and of singers. An unnamed official of the Museum explained that since Parliament voted funds for the purchase only of books and manuscripts, the use of funds for the acquisition of gramophone records would almost certainly require new legislation. And Lord Avebury, a trustee of the Museum, pointed to an obvious problem, that records wear out, and that the most important, the ones that would be consulted the most frequently, would wear out fastest of all. The Gramophone Company were quick to respond – a reply was printed in the paper on the following day: they would be willing to deposit with the Museum metal masters rather than shellac pressings, though they would impose the condition that no matrix was to be used for the printing or pressing of new records until sixty years after the death of the speaker or singer. The Company suggested the formation of a committee nominated by the Trustees that would decide which of the recordings 'are worthy of being preserved in [the] institution', and offered to donate the records, to make them available 'free of all charges'. The first batch was given in 1906 and included recordings by Melba, Patti, Caruso and Tamagno, and there were further donations in 1907, 1908, 1909, 1911, 1921, 1921, 1929, 1932 and 1933; the recordings included the voices of royalty, statesmen and politicians, clerics, military men, Count Lev Tolstoy, the explorer Sir Ernest Shackelton, the actors Sir Herbert Beerbom Tree and Lewis Waller.

In December 1920 Lionel G. Guest offered the Museum a copy of his recording made by the new electrical process in Westminster Abbey the month before at the Burial of the Unknown Warrior;[149] it contained two hymns, 'Abide with me' to W. H. Monk's famous tune 'Eventide', and Rudyard Kipling's *Recessional* to John Bacchus Dykes's 'Melita', and it was put on sale at 4s. 6d. for the Abbey Restoration Fund. This was accepted, a pressing, not a matrix, and in the next three decades several dozen more shellac pressings were offered by various companies; a series of lectures entitled 'Twelve Famous Authors' by Dominion Gramophone Records, some of the Linguaphone Institute's language records, sets of Indian and Burmese dialect records, five recordings of that folk singer, Joseph Taylor, of Saxby All Saints in Lincolnshire, presented by Percy Grainger who had made them in 1906. When in October 1910 the committee had accepted recordings of Chaliapin and Tetrazzini and Melba, they turned down, 'for reasons of space', recordings of Arthur Bourchier and H. B. Irving's rendering of part of the 'great forte' of his father, Sir Henry, *The Bells*, the play with which he made his name as one of the greatest of all Victorian tragedians. And when Columbia offered them matrixes of their 'Lecture Series', two hundred double-sided twelve-inch discs of 'selected lectures and lecture courses given by scholars of all nations' – there was an 'Introduction to Vergil', and talks on 'The New Russia', and 'What is History' and 'Causes of the World War' – the committee felt able to accept only Sir Edmund Gosse's lecture on Thomas Hardy and Sir Johnston Forbes-Robertson's 'Shakespeare Recital', and of these, in fact, only a single matrix, the first quarter of each, since, as the committee explained, this would be sufficient for their purpose, 'which is merely to preserve an adequate record of the speaker's voice'. And since they already had an example of King George V, they also turned down an offer of a new recording the King made in 1928.[150]

So the British Museum Committee cannot be said to have displayed wholehearted enthusiasm for the new medium. It has been estimated that by 1925 probably 100,000 records had been issued all over the world; the British Museum held just a few dozen of them. No doubt it would have required a bold imagination in the 1900s to grasp the potential of recording techniques and to foresee the enormous impact records would have on music-making and music appreciation – and therefore the importance of these incunables, as it were, of recording history, these miserable scratchy recordings of operatic pot-boilers – when most serious musicians regarded the talking machine with contempt, and when records were sold in small shops in side streets, often bicycle shops, where discs and cylinders and needles lay side by side and jumbled up with spare wheels, pumps, cans of oil, repair outfits and Welsbach incandescent gas mantles.[151] Vespasiano da Bisticci tells us that the fifteenth-century Duke of Urbino had a superlatively good library, containing only manuscripts, since his beautifully illuminated parchment books would have been ashamed to share the shelves with printed books.[152] Perhaps in the 1900s the printed books of the British Museum would have been ashamed to share the shelves with little bits of shellac, with black discs made from the secretions of Indian tree insects.

One afternoon about 1930 a young music-lover called Patrick Saul went into the London gramophone shop in Cranbourn Street run by Mr Wilfrid Van Wyck and Mr W. Rimington and asked for Dohnányi's Violin Sonata in the arrangement by Lionel Tertis. To his amazement he was told that it was 'out of print', it was deleted. So he walked on to the British Museum determined to hear the recording at least, even if he couldn't buy it. He was told that there were no gramophone records at all at the British Museum. (Which was not quite true, but probably what nearly all the staff at the Museum imagined.) The realization that such performances seemed to be disappearing for ever was, Mr Saul said later, like a child hearing about death for the first time;[153] and he resolved to try and do something to prevent the deaths, or at least the disappearance, of these living performances. He made an appointment to see the director of the British Museum, but then, on being summoned into the presence of the great man, the teenager was seized with panic and rushed out of the building. He retired to a Lyons corner-shop to consider the situation further. A telephone call seemed altogether more appropriate, so the music-lover dialled the MUSeum number and harangued Sir George Hill for several minutes from the safety of a public call-box. Sir George agreed with him on the desirability of keeping a collection of gramophone records; he told his caller 'to go away now but come back when you are older and more experienced'.

After the war Patrick Saul attempted to discover what had been happening abroad; there were by then in existence a few big collections of recordings but the lack of enthusiasm of most cultural organizations in America and Europe for preserving recordings of classical music was more notable than any sustained endeavours to create archives of sound. This was merely a reflection of a general attitude; by the middle of the century it was no longer an eccentric thing to do, to collect records, but neither were records regarded as objects of great cultural significance. Patrick Saul managed to persuade the Association of Special Libraries and Information Bureaux to call a public conference to discover what interest there was in such a project. This was held in Church House, Westminster, in March 1948 and presided over by the President of the Royal Musical Association and the music critic of *The Times*, Frank Howes.[154] By this time, as he began to press publicly for the creation of a national collection of sound recordings, he was met with expressions of polite interest and gestures of support, but not with pledges of financial assistance. In the early 1950s Decca gave £200 and then, just as it seemed the attempt would fail, a Quaker trust in Birmingham gave £2,000. The philanthropist and patron of the arts Sir Robert Mayer guaranteed the rent and rates on a building owned by the British Museum in Russell Square and in 1955 the British Institute of Recorded Sound opened its doors to the public.[155] An appeal for public support through donations of discs – this was a time when music-lovers were replacing their collections of shellac discs with vinyl LPs – resulted in the acquisition of thousands of discs from private collectors including Percy Scholes.[156] When the Institute announced that its acquisitions policy would be to reject nothing 'on aesthetic grounds', that the director 'wanted everything', eyebrows were raised, apparently, 'in some quarters'. One of the governors of the Institute defended the decision: the aim was to be comprehensive, as the British Museum Library was comprehensive. 'We cannot tell just what will interest posterity; we ourselves should like to know the taste of the Ancient Greeks in light music as well as in Olympian hymns, and centuries hence theses may be written on the influence of Delius's harmony on the arrangements used by the Savoy Orpheans. The only safe rule is to be omnivorous.'[157] With the support of a group of musicians which included Sir Adrian Boult, Dame Myra Hess, Clifford Curzon, Denis Matthews and Yehudi Menuhin, the Institute approached the Treasury in 1960 and from 1961–2 until 1983 received an annual grant-in-aid from the government. In 1983 it became part of the British Library and became officially known as the National Sound Archive (NSA), and in 1997 it moved into the new British Library building at St Pancras. It is now one of the world's largest sound archives, with over a million discs and 170,000 tapes, and a growing collection of videos and laser-discs and television programmes.

Even though there is no legal deposit for recordings in Great Britain the National Sound Archive estimated that in the 1990s it was obtaining more than eighty per cent of recordings of classical music issued in Great Britain from donations by the record companies, and it bought discs from abroad as energetically as funds allowed, for new releases on such labels as the Swedish Sterling and Bis labels, the American New World and Composers Recordings and Lovely Music, the German Wergo and Preiser labels, the French Opus III and L'Empreinte Digitale, the Canadian Atma and Doremi, the Dutch Etcetera, releases like those of the Chicago Symphony Orchestra and New York Philharmonic archive recordings, the CDs and videos issued by the Stockhausen-Verlag in Kürten, the recordings released by the Contemporary Music Centre in Ireland, and the Anthologies of Australian Music on Disc series produced by the Canberra School of Music. The Archive's acquisitions policies are guided by the search for previously unrecorded repertory, for recordings by distinguished artists, and by the distinctiveness of interpretations. The Archive's collections of 78 rpm discs were built up largely from donations both by individuals and by organizations; in the 1950s there were important gifts from the Polish and Czechoslovakian governments and from the Oiseau-Lyre Company in Paris.[158] And donations have continued to be made. In 1997 a Dutch collector bequeathed a collection of about 6,000 78 rpm discs and LPs which filled some notable gaps in the Archive's holdings of continental discs issued before the First War. A particularly valuable collection came in 1978 from an American lawyer in Detroit – he had been a Rhodes scholar at Oxford in the 1920s – a collection of more than fifteen thousand 78s and LPs, which filled in a large number of gaps in the North American collections. In such large collections as these there were inevitably duplicates. But the Archive will always endeavour to acquire two copies of every disc for safety's sake and also for preservation purposes and with this donation from Detroit many duplicates had a special significance and value: a large number of early electrical HMV discs suffered from bad pressings, the result of either a deliberate experiment or the use of an impure mixture of shellac, paper and glue; this American collector had bought the performances on Victor, the American equivalent label, and these copies did not suffer from the same pressing fault. Important later donations from organizations included all the master-tapes held in the company archives by the Saga Record Company, Art and Sound Ltd, after the company ceased to trade.

The other main source for musical performances of classical music is the BBC. The NSA provides public access to all the recordings in the BBC's own Sound Archives – available otherwise only to BBC staff and other programme makers – and in addition it records off-air itself from BBC national networks – which it has been doing since the early 1960s – and occasionally from the independent station Classic FM, which began transmitting in 1992. In the 1990s the Archive was taping about two dozen classical music programmes each week from Radio 3, which total includes talks and features and documentary programmes about music and musicians as well as performances. This source complements all the commercially issued recordings and is particularly valuable for live performances and for new music. And each week two or three classical music programmes on TV were videoed in the 1990s, the intention being to complement the existing collections, not to usurp the role of the National Film Archive, which is the chief preserver of TV programmes in Great Britain. Among the programmes taken during the autumn of 1993, for example, were documentary programmes about Monserrat Caballé, and about the profession of conductor, *Everything you wanted to know about conductors but were afraid to ask*, a performance directed by Rostropovich of Britten's *War Requiem* in the Albert Hall, the UK première from Westminster Cathedral of Berlioz's *Messe solennelle*, a performance from the Vienna State Opera of Rossini's long-lost opera *Il viaggio a Reims* conducted by Claudio Abbado, the Welsh National Opera production of *Pelléas et Mélisande* conducted by Boulez, and the St Matthew Passion given by the Munich Bach Collegium and the Neubeuern Choral Society from the Romanesque church of Alpirsbach. Among the most notable donations of broadcast material were reel-to-reel tapes given by Voice of America, including recordings made in the 1950s and 1960s of live performances of the New York Philharmonic, Boston Symphony and Louisville Orchestras, and of Metropolitan Opera productions.

Numerous donations have been made through bequests or as gifts by musicians, or by the families or friends of composers or performing artists. The collection of Myra Hess material includes a tape of a recital of Bach, Schubert, Brahms and Scarlatti given in March 1949 at the University of Illinois at Urbana, and such live, 'unofficial' recordings can usefully complement the commercial 'official' disc recordings and also the broadcast material available at the NSA. And the BBC tapes of Hess include a talk on her teacher Tobias Matthay and a performance of Bach's Second English Suite, otherwise not recorded by her. Recordings donated of performances by another Matthay pupil, Harriet

Cohen, include performances on Hilversum Radio of Peter Racine Fricker's Piano Concerto, and of Bach chorale prelude arrangements and works by Turina and de Falla recorded for the Allies' troops on an ENSA disc in 1945. In 1996 the Archive received the private collection of recordings belonging to Shura Cherkassky, of his live performances from round the world, including concerts in Toronto, San Francisco, New York, Tokyo, Zurich, Sydney, Philadelphia and of his performances at home.

Recordings were presented to the Archive from the private collections of composers like John Ireland, Elisabeth Lutyens, Bernard Stevens, Bill Hopkins, Elizabeth Maconchy; there is a privately made recording of a rehearsal try-out of the revised version of Stravinsky's *Symphonies of wind instruments*, the composer conducting Hollywood film session musicians in the John Burroughs Junior High School Auditorium on 30 January 1948. A private collector donated a disc recording of the first performance of Britten's *Spring Symphony* in Amsterdam in 1949 with Jo Vincent, Kathleen Ferrier and Peter Pears which the Archive brought to the attention of Decca, who issued it as a commercial disc;[159] and in 1992, with the permission of the performers and the Wigmore Hall, the singer's agent gave a tape of the acclaimed first appearance in London of the Russian bass Sergei Leiferkus in October 1988. An English pupil of Olivier Messiaen donated an interview he recorded with the composer's widow when he was editing a book on the composer.

Organizations have made donations too: in the mid-1980s the National Youth Orchestra deposited its archive of recorded performances at public concerts from each year of its existence back to 1948. And the Sound Archive also holds a great number of test pressings, copies of 78 rpm recordings which were produced by a record company for the record producer and the players for their authorization or for the selection of alternative takes. The existence of a rejected take can sometimes throw light on performers' intentions: why was this take chosen in preference to that one? So, for example, the Archive holds a number of alternative takes for performances recorded during 1930s and 1940s sessions by Benno Moiseiwitsch, and from the 1944 and 1945 sessions for Benjamin Britten's *Serenade for tenor, horn and strings* with Peter Pears, Dennis Brain and the Boyd Neel String Orchestra and the composer conducting. Another such test pressing is of Harriet Cohen's performance of the C minor Prelude and Fugue from Book I of the Forty-Eight which she presented to Bernard Shaw and on which she inscribed: 'for G.B.S. – the nearest thing to a manuscript . . .'.[160]

The difficulties of working with recordings

Recordings are difficult to work with and to investigate; they are easily damaged and archives are reluctant to allow tapes and discs to be handled by researchers themselves. So recordings will usually be played back to listeners by staff, which is obviously inconvenient if the research requires the sampling of a large number of performances, though close individual supervision may sometimes be offered. But the provision of such services will be necessarily labour-intensive and therefore expensive. Copying material is difficult and time-consuming and so extremely expensive and copyrights will rule this out with certain categories of material.

But an even greater problem for the scholar is the absence of detailed and comprehensive catalogues of recordings. The title-page of a book will provide a title, an author's name, and a date and place of publication, and a descriptive catalogue entry using these elements can be easily drafted; the book can swiftly be uniquely identified. A catalogue entry for a piece of recorded music must document not only the work but also the performance. It may not be a straightforward task first to identify the work. A discographer described the kinds of difficulties that sometimes arose with the documentation of recordings from the 1930s: a disc of music for guitar indicates on the label 'Haydn: Trio'. But there are over two hundred trios by Haydn, each with three movements. It turned out that this Trio was none of these six hundred movements. It was in fact an arrangement of the Trio from the Minuet of the Symphony no. 96. On the other side of the disc was 'Mendelssohn: Song without words'. It turned out to be none of the Songs without words for piano, nor the piece so titled for cello and piano. It was in fact literally a song by Mendelssohn with the words left out, a song called 'Liedesplätzchen'.[161] Such unsophisticated description is much rarer today than it was in the 1930s, but inaccuracies or ambiguities of different kinds were not uncommon on LPs and on CDs: on the Waverly Consort's LP entitled 'Renaissance Christmas' the liner note refers to the familiar four-part version of Josquin's Ave Maria . . .

Virgo Serena, but in fact it is the six-voice one that is sung.[162] It may be desirable to document which edition of the music is being used by the performers, and the composer of the cadenza the soloist is playing, for example. The information with a disc, though, was not provided for the professional musician or the scholar but was part of the marketing of a product, of which of course meticulous and detailed information might have been a part but might not, might have repelled or intimidated a prospective purchaser, the record company may have thought; and standards of documentation have changed as audiences have changed and standards of sophistication and familiarity with repertory have increased. It will often be necessary for the cataloguer of recordings to have recourse to scores or thematic catalogues. Even when these are available, as they will be in national library collections, it is still time-consuming to consult them and to plan the work for these exigencies.

But the cataloguer must also give details of the performance: the date of the recording and location may be germane to a research topic, and whether it is a studio recording or live. So may the date of the harpsichord which the player is using and the builder's name be important to the researcher. If such details are given on documentation accompanying the disc they can quickly be added to a catalogue entry, though even today dates and locations are not invariably given even on first releases: Gimell never divulge recording dates on the recordings of the Tallis Scholars. Clearly many research tasks must be left for the individual researcher to undertake. But it is hardly satisfactory for a research collection to give no details or vague or ambiguous information about a performance date, for example, so that it is impossible to tell from the catalogue, when the same performers have recorded the same work on three different occasions, which of the nine labels and numbers on which it has appeared contains which performance.[163]

Such problems, however, can be extremely difficult and time-consuming to resolve. Sir Thomas Beecham recorded Haydn's Symphony no. 93 in D major with the Royal Philharmonic Society in the Kingsway Hall, in London, on 1 June 1950 and again with the same orchestra in the Salle Wagram in Paris on 4 October 1957. The 1950 recording was issued on 78 rpm discs with the numbers Columbia LX 1361, LX 1362 and LX 1363. But on LP it appeared at different times in different countries, in England as Columbia 33CX 1038, for example, and then as Philips NBL 5037; in the United States it appeared as ML 54374, in France as FCX 328, in Germany as WCX 1038, in Italy as QCX 10032. The 1957 recording appeared initially in Great Britain as HMV ALP 1624 – though it could also be bought as a box set of three discs when it was given the number SLS 846 (which may be the number that a scholar has traced and with which he is attempting to locate the recording) – and later appeared as HMV SXLP 30285; in North America it was issued at one time as Capitol SGCR 7127, but also, later, as Angel 36242/4; in Germany it appeared as Electrola 1C 137–50238/43; in Japan it was released as Tosh AA 7623. And so on. The British Library attempts to collect as many issues of such a performance as it can: its initial holding may have been a second-hand donated copy, and visual inspection cannot always reveal the true condition of a disc; some releases anyway may have been poor pressings; sleeve presentation, which is usually different on each release, is in itself often of great significance to the historian. But the sleeves of such discs rarely, for commercial reasons, give the date of the recording. So it may be unclear whether or not this particular disc is in fact a recording of the same performance as this other one. And after a purchasing decision has been made, still these ambiguities remain to be solved before a clear, unambiguous, useful catalogue entry can be created. Beecham's recordings fortunately were exhaustively researched and painstakingly documented in a work of the most thorough scholarship which appeared in 1979.[164] It's true that many CDs issued today give very full and accurate details about recordings, including locations and dates. But in the documentation of reissues of old material no record company will ever list all the earlier issue numbers that would make the recording's history plain.

Which in part explains why none of the world's major research libraries are able to provide scholars with the comprehensive and detailed catalogues of their holdings of sound recordings which they do, and are expected to do, with their collections of printed books and musical scores, and even manuscripts (which, though they may create many difficult problems of documentation, are nevertheless usually acquired at a steadier rate). In the 1990s the British Library acquired each year between 5,000 and 6,000 CDs of classical music through donation by UK record companies and through foreign purchase.

The Associated Audio Archives Committee of the Association for Recorded Sound Collections in North America organized the microfilming of the labels of all the 78 rpm discs in the collections in the Library of Congress, the New York Public Library, and Stanford, Syracuse and Yale universities. The exposed microfilm photography of the recordings was then projected on to large screens, and computer operators entered composer/author, performer, label name/issue number, matrix number, and holding institution sigla. The data was collated by computer, sorted by the categories listed in the preceding sentence and this information transferred to fiche and roll-film.[165] Those in-putting the data from the photographs were not discographically trained and so simply reproduced without enhancing or correcting the information given on the record label: so there are entries for Haydn's Symphony no. 101 in D major HW i/17 ('The Clock') on the completed fiche as 'Haydn: Symphony no. 4 in D major' or 'Symphony no. 101 in D major' or 'Symphony in D minor ("The Clock")'. Such limitations reduce the index's usefulness, but a more ambitious project would not have been realized because of the time and costs involved.[166]

To resolve ambiguities and to discover details about the history of a recording discographers will consult company catalogues and national listings like the *Gramophone* catalogues for the United Kingdom.[167] Sometimes it will be impossible to resolve problems without access to record company files; a few company archives are well organized and welcome researchers, but many have been neglected or destroyed, and at some discographers are assumed to be industrial espionage agents in disguise.[168]

The arcane knowledge necessary to interpret and understand the precise significances of the physical details of a gramophone record is very hard to acquire, scraps of information being hidden away in the obscure journals of record collectors and other enthusiasts or in impenetrable monographs published by specialized – but not university – presses. And yet much can hang on the understanding of, say, a matrix number, the sequence of numerals with letters sometimes, and sometimes also geometrical shapes engraved on the disc, often in the space in between the ending of the grooves and the label, numbers like 2–04755 CR 2265^I Δ[169] or 4646 Bb 2656^{II}.[170] The matrix number will usually also be printed on the label, which will carry the catalogue number as well. The numerical sequences of matrixes usually ran in chronological order; with HMV after 4 June 1914 *Bb* simply indicated a ten-inch disc recorded at Hayes in Middlesex. So a matrix number can often reveal the date and location of a recording, which would otherwise be difficult or impossible to discover. Before 4 June 1914 a *b*, say, would indicate that the recording 'expert', the producer, had been Fred Gaisberg, an *f* would have indicated his brother Will, an *h* would have meant Sinkler Derby; if the producer was Fred Gaisberg there might be a reference to the particular session in his memoirs.[171]

At the end of the matrix number a number or letter might indicate the take, as 'BVE 37455–6'; a full discographic entry might aim to list the number of all the takes, the date of each, the one selected for issue with the original catalogue number used, and to indicate whether the performer gave his authorization.[172] The opportunity to compare different takes – they may have been preserved in the company's archive or another library – may shed light on preferred interpretative detail. An R with HMV was for 'Relay' and indicated that a recording was made at one location and mastered at another, through the use of landlines or a mobile van. Additional letters after the take would show when a recording was made in duplicate, because of the unpredictability of the volume of sound, say, or because it would not be possible to repeat the performance and processing failure couldn't be risked. There might be a geometrical sign which would indicate the recording system used; this will allow a transfer engineer today to determine the frequency characteristics and enable him to recover the sound with a flat frequency response.[173] Certainly the matrix number can confirm authoritatively that a performance issued on a different number, a later reissue or a simultaneous issue in another country, is the same performance. No such marking exists on a long-playing record; the tape transfer number on an LP does not document an unedited recording session. But it can very occasionally serve to distinguish different recordings. In 1965 and 1966 Argo issued two different performances of Britten's *A Ceremony of Carols* by the choir of St John's College, Cambridge, directed by George Guest with the harpist Marisa Robles, although they both carried the same catalogue numbers, RG 440 the mono and ZRG 5440 the stereo version. The tape transfer numbers engraved in the vinyl and printed on the label – 2RG 2677–3L for the 1964 recording issued in 1965, 2RG 2865–4G for the 1966 recording – are the distinguishing indication.[174]

'The greatest masterpieces of man's creative genius will now repose, sheltered from death in these discs, heavy with spiritual secrets, that a three-year-old child can hold in his little hands', wrote Maurice Maeterlinck in the foreword to a programme of the Columbia Graphophone reception at the Théâtre des Champs-Elysées in 1928.[175] But the difficulties of locating recordings and of creating the right conditions under which research might be carried out are clearly formidable. Should the music historian devote time and energy to the study of tapes and discs? What insights might the scrutiny of recordings yield? What kinds of speculation about music does the examination of recorded performances provoke?

New views of musical history

Safford Cape and Pro Musica Antiqua recorded *El Grillo*, 'The Cricket', a frottola probably written by Josquin des Prez in the 1470s when he was working for Cardinal Sforza in Milan, and it was issued in 1953 as part of HMV's *History of Music in Sound*.[176] Safford Cape was born in Denver, Colorado, and moved to Brussels as a young man to study the piano and composition. But then he met a group of scholars and performers round the musicologist Charles van den Borren interested in early music. He married van den Borren's daughter, renounced his ambitions to be a composer and threw himself into performing the music of the thirteenth, fourteenth, fifteenth and early sixteenth centuries. 'There was no model from which I could draw inspiration. I was working in the dark', he once said.[177] The performance he directs of *El Grillo* is one unmistakably of the middle of the twentieth century. The sound and the articulation are clear, the projection gentle, unemphatic, and the overall effect polite, even perhaps genteel.

There was certainly an element of refinement in the music-making of Arnold Dolmetsch, who pioneered the performance of early music in England at the end of the nineteenth century, whose views and manner and tone were hugely and internationally influential for several decades. There was an exquisite, perhaps sometimes rather precious quality in the music-making of some of the early music pioneers, in those concerts at the Dolmetschs' house, 'Dowland', in the mid-1890s, where the concert-room, 'tinted a soft diaphanous green, was entirely illuminated by wax candles'.[178] There was an element of nostalgia in all this, a distaste for the speed and scale and noise of the late nineteenth century, for the squalor and emptiness of the lives of those who worked in factories. Dolmetsch moved in Pre-Raphaelite circles; he was a friend of Edward Burne-Jones and William Morris, who used to attend his concerts, and he was himself intimately bound up with the arts-and-crafts movement as a maker of instruments as well as a player. Arthur Symons dedicated a poem to Dolmetsch in which he speaks of 'a melancholy desire of ancient things'. And something of this quality long persisted among the practitioners of pre-baroque music. The scholar and keyboard player Erwin Bodky, a 1930s German emigré, wrote the programme-notes for the Society for Early Music in Cambridge, Massachusetts, in the early 1950s:

> Early Music was a highly aristocratic art and restraint governed even the display of emotion as well as the exhibition of technical virtuosity. This deprives concerts of Early Music of the atmosphere of electricity which, when present, is one of the finest experiences of the modern concert hall. Who seeks but this may stay away from our concert series. We want to take this opportunity, however, to thank our artists for the voluntary restraint in the display of their artistic capabilities which they exercise when recreating with us the atmosphere of equanimity, tranquility and noble entertainment which is the characteristic feature of Early Music.[79]

Clearly Bodky's attitude and the singing style of Pro Musica Antiqua reflect the dominating anti-Romantic tendencies in art and music of the times; whatever else these singers of Cape's may sound like, they don't sound as if they have ambitions to sing Donizetti or Verdi or Wagner.

Musica Reservata's performance of this little piece issued in 1975 belongs to a different world.[180] This new performing style emerged with the establishment of the group in 1960 when Pro Musica Antiqua's manner of performing was still well known and frequently heard. Musica Reservata's style is uncompromising, the tone forward, rather aggressive, uninflected, thrown at the listeners. What had happened? The long-playing record had happened, for one thing. New and bigger audiences had by now – in the 1960s – been created and there were new performing opportunities for musicians specializing in different early music repertoires, and wishing to make their mark, to establish their performing theories, to etch their sonorous image on the public's ear. Which Musica Reservata certainly did with a vengeance. There were no breakthroughs in the 1950s in our knowledge of Milanese singing timbres and styles in the fifteenth century; we knew as little in the 1960s as we did in the 1940s and as we know now, which is to say, practically nothing. Nor had Josquin scholarship suggested any radically new approaches.

The man steering Musica Reservata and guiding the creation of its distinctive sounds was the late Michael Morrow. What was he aiming for, and why? He was endeavouring, he explained, to identify the separate, defining elements of what might have constituted the techniques of medieval and Renaissance vocal styles, characteristic details of articulation, intonation, and vocal and instrumental colour. Language might give clues, he thought, and also the sounds of the surviving instruments, rebecs or lutes or crumhorns which might suggest complementary vocal timbres. Morrow attempted to set aside his singers' carefully nurtured twentieth-century musical instincts. To begin with he would not tell them what the texts were about lest they immediately fall back on conditioned reflexes and inject stereotyped feeling into their voices. He was particularly struck by folk singers from Yugoslavia and by the intonation of the male singers and was seized with a conviction that a thirteenth-century motet 'must have sounded something like that – perfect fourths and fifths, very wide major seconds and wide major thirds that really are dissonant – otherwise it will sound like nothing at all'.[181] He was galvanized by the style of a recording of a Portuguese passion play in which, as in the Middle Ages, scenes were mounted on a horse cart and took place in the open air. How had he heard this music, all this non-European folk music and art music? He heard it on the radio, on BBC broadcasts, particularly in the programmes made by A. L. Lloyd, and on the Folkways record label. Jantina Noorman, the singer whose idiosyncratic timbres and manner of delivery and rhythmic virtuosity came to characterize Musica Reservata, Michael Morrow first heard on a private recording – she was working with George Hunter at Illinois – and thought that here was something he could mould.[182]

But Michael Morrow admitted that much must remain speculative, that one medieval piece could be played in a dozen different ways and that it is simply impossible to judge which if any might approach the original sounds and performing style. What he looked for was 'intensity of conviction'[183] and he admired the ballad singers of the Balkans for the high seriousness with which these musicians regarded their art. His friends and collaborators noted the width and depth of his scholarship but were struck above all by his instinctive approach, by the absence of pedantry or archaeological exactitude with regard to the instruments he used; spirit and style of performance were everything.[184] And he himself did not hesitate to admit that a driving force was simply to create something different: 'My principal aim was not to have people singing like the BBC Singers.'[185] He didn't want university choral society sounds or indeed anything that smacked of Anglican church music. He was a maverick and an outsider, an Irishman in England, an autodidact, musically and in every other way; he regarded the conventional musical education of a conservative old English university as 'repellently orthodox',[186] one of his friends and collaborators guessed, one who had been so educated. One critic – he didn't like the singing of Musica Reservata – thought 'the whole idea' was to combat preciousness and the 'heigh-nonny-no school of dainty madrigal singers'.[187] It wasn't the whole idea but Michael Morrow certainly possessed a mischievous streak, he rather liked cocking a snook. His friends portray a driven personality. He spent most of his childhood in hospital and waged a lifelong battle with illness and disability. One of his friends described him as a visionary 'whose passion for early music appeared to sustain him . . . he loved it with a candour and innocence only possible in one for whom it was a consolation in every infirmity'.[188]

We hear an old recording and know immediately why particular performing characteristics strike us as odd or 'unmusical'. But it may be illuminating to attempt to answer the question: why wouldn't this pianist of 1919, or this tenor of 1930, or the members of this choir of 1911, have been so admiring perhaps of our own interpretations of this music? From this point of view, we begin to understand what an eminent ethnomusicologist means when he suggests that the recorded sound – the 'sonic content' of a performance – gives us perhaps ten per cent of the information about what is going on. It doesn't present us even with performance practice, it doesn't tell us how these sounds are made, or why they are being made, the context, the occasion, the precise significance of particular gestures.[189]

From the beginning of the twentieth century historians, journalists, critics and cathedral musicians themselves have been sure they can identify a style of singing peculiar to the fifty or so choirs that sing in English cathedrals. The 'essence' of the cathedral choir, said one twentieth-century authority, is 'the boy's voice', and its men are 'at their best when they blend with that clean white tone'.[190] The desired qualities must create impersonality; blend, balance, sweetness, smoothness are the crucial features. St George's Chapel, Windsor, has been at different times one of the most important choirs in setting standards and at establishing approved styles. It was certainly admired in the 1920s when the precentor at Windsor, E. H. Fellowes, the authority on Tudor church music, directed the choir. And yet that recording of Orlando Gibbons's *Hosanna to the Son of David* made in 1927 confounds expectations,[191] and is utterly unlike the kind of performance which is admired in the 1990s. How does it come about that a choir of a similar constitution to a modern counterpart and apparently holding very similar ideals should sound so different? Inevitably these early recordings mislead. Boys' voices were more difficult to record on both the acoustic and early electrical processes, and this is likely to be the main reason why the balance is always wrong, why the boys sound fainter and more distant than they should. Or than they actually did. Neither is the impersonality so much stressed by Terry and other authorities of the time a feature of these recordings. Rather is the listener today struck by the individuality, sometimes the rather unfortunate characterfulness, of the lower voices in these old recordings. This is evidently not because of the inadequacies or failings of the singers themselves. Fellowes emphasized that the lay clerks at Windsor in the years he directed the choir were the equal of any in England.[192] For the early electrical recordings a single microphone was placed a few feet above the singers' heads, and it was not possible to capture much sense of a building's acoustic until the development of the long-playing record. These were not performances produced for the microphone; the men phrase and articulate and project as they would have done for a congregation standing forty or fifty feet or more away from them. And Fellowes and Terry might well have wished their singers not to sustain the lines too smoothly, but to give the notes power and strength of attack, allowing the building to play its part in depersonalizing the voices with its resonance, which effect is simply not caught by the microphone of the time.

Some differences are not so difficult to explain: as a result of the introduction of new terms of employment and because of changed economic conditions, singing in a cathedral choir is not the full-time job it was in many of these choirs a century ago. In collegiate choirs lay clerks have been replaced partly or wholly by choral scholars, under graduate members of the college. So the average age of the men in the choirs is much lower. An advantage of this is that it has become possible to exclude voices that have deteriorated, have become looser and less focused, with a wide vibrato, and so to make a closer approach to currently held ideals concerning blend and balance.[193]

All musical performances since the 1920s have reflected the twentieth century's anti-Romantic and formalist aesthetics. It would certainly have been true that cathedral singers a hundred years ago were less indulgent over tempo changes (as we should now think) than solo singers or chamber musicians or orchestral players of the time. Fellowes did not have quite the reputation of his predecessor as conductor of the choir at Windsor, Parratt, as a strict 'classicist', but even so the very emphatic rallentandos he imposes in Gibbons's *Hosanna to the Son of David* may not have been excessive or eccentric to his own contemporaries. They simply belong to the stylistic world of Elgar. When in 1922 a cathedral organist drew attention to 'one of the most remarkable frailties of singers', namely 'the universal tendency to slacken the tempo when diminishing the tone, and to hurry it when making a crescendo',[194] he was merely reflecting a general tendency towards a greater fidelity to the letter of the score.

It is also not likely that excessive smoothness and unanimity in attack and polish in execution would have been considered particularly desirable, certainly by the lay clerks. To many of these early twentieth-century English church musicians the sentimentality and softness of Victorian church music was anathema. Mus Docs, Mus Bacs, English cathedral and collegiate organists of the time 'poured out beautifully correct and blameless harmonies', one of them lamented, 'nearly all devoid of virility'.[195] One of the qualities that men like Fellowes and Richard Terry emphasized in the English sixteenth-century music they rediscovered was its 'virility', the 'strong, virile music of our early English composers'.[196] In the introduction to the first of the *Tudor Church Music* volumes the editors drew attention to John Taverner's 'amazing vitality and virility'. Terry recalled his last meeting with his friend, the composer Philip Heseltine, and remembered him as 'healthy, tanned and exuberantly high-spirited ... virile and splendid'.[197] Effeminacy was a quality all these musicians recoiled from. In the 1890s – at least in the circles in which these cathedral musicians moved – 'Is he musical?' like 'Is he earnest?' was used as code for 'Is he homosexual?' It may not be fanciful to guess that aspects of the assertive, no-nonsense delivery of these early twentieth-century singers are deliberately cultivated.

In order to achieve the greatest possible accuracy and precision it is usual now for cathedral organists to direct the choir themselves most of the time, with an assistant accompanying. This was rare even after the Second War. Walter Parratt considered the conducting of the cathedral choir theatrical, 'unnecessary and unsightly'. Even if it were possible to obtain some extra expressive nuance with a conductor, he thought 'the loss of spontaneity' too great a sacrifice.[198]

So if we are to begin to understand these changes in timbre or in inflection or in tempo fluctuation or in matters of ensemble documented by recordings it may well be necessary to take into account economic and technological and aesthetic and psychological factors. The way such changes are commonly referred to in musical history: 'A new conception of beauty of playing was being formulated around this time . . .'[199] – this is the reason advanced by one writer for the stylistic changes in violin playing before the First World War – in fact reveals nothing about the process of change. In the twentieth century music has often been examined and thought about as 'organized sound'. But we may study it, not less truthfully or less accurately, as the meanings we ascribe to the sounds we hear. Recordings offer an opportunity to observe music being transformed; we hear sounds changing and new sounds being created, which may alert us to different meanings that are being attached to the music or to different ways in which music is being used. Recordings may assist the scholar by making the history of music much more difficult to write, by complicating the story. They provide no easy answers but may assist the formulations of questions which might produce fruitful investigations.

The historian working with sound recordings may start from a minute examination of the physical object itself. It may be necessary to interpret the matrix numbers in order to date the recorded performance, and to understand the studio procedures and the recording techniques of the time in order to take into account the ways in which these might have caused a performer to modify his performing style, or to distort what we can actually hear in the recording, just as historians have painstakingly investigated watermarks in order to establish the chronology of a composer's works, and searched and analysed the domestic archives of sixteenth-century cathedrals and private chapels to discover information on the payment of musicians that will indicate the performing forces employed in a particular repertory.

But he will be led on from the circumstances of the recording to try and recognize the meanings of precise musical gestures and the aesthetic values and intellectual doctrines that lie behind particular performing practices; he will wish to scrutinize the editions used in the recording, to try and glean something of the performer's attitude to the composer in question, and to form an impression of the player's views on the role of the interpreter from contemporary biographical sources, from concert programmes and interviews and reviews of recordings and live performances; he will attempt to understand the economic forces that led to this recording being made, to discover who wished to record this music and why and who listened to it under what circumstances. Historians of different kinds will certainly wish to submit recorded performances to the closest scrutiny and analysis. But the historian need not simply substitute the study of one object, the manuscript, the score, with another, the disc or tape. The study of recordings may give particular assistance to the scholar who wishes to write history by presenting musical activity as existing in many different dimensions, at many intersecting levels simultaneously, and in so doing to suggest in different ways the richness and the complexity of musical experience such as we ourselves know it always to be.

Bibliographical Note

The history of recorded music constitutes such a vast terrain that one-volume surveys of it are inevitably very different books. There are two recent studies. Michael Chanan's *Repeated Takes: a Short History of Recording and its Effects on Music* (London and New York, 1995) is a chronological history of the recording industry from Edison to the compact disc which treats jazz, pop and classical music, and examines topics such as disc jockeys, the gramophone as an item of domestic furniture, and the creative roles of record producers and engineers. *An International History of the Recording Industry* by Pekka Gronow and Ilpo Saunio, translated by Christopher Moseley (London and New York, 1998) – which appeared too late for me to profit from – is a chronological survey and treats popular music, jazz, classical music, folk music, and record production in Africa and India as well as in Europe and America. It contains a great deal of information on the record industry and commercial developments and includes a useful bibliography.

Roland Gelatt's *The Fabulous Phonograph: The Story of the Gramophone from Tin Foil to High Fidelity* (Philadelphia and New York, 1954; London, 1956) is indispensable, an intelligent, lucid and trustworthy account of classical music and recording up to the early days of the long-playing disc, which attempts to treat its subject from scientific, commercial and musical angles.

Oliver Read and Walter L. Welch's *From Tin Foil to Stereo: Evolution of the Phonograph* (second edition, Indianapolis, Kansas City and New York, 1976) contains valuable material that was omitted in the revision published as Walter L. Welch and Leah Brodbeck Stenzel Burt, *From*

Tinfoil to Stereo: The Acoustic Years of the Recording Industry (Gainsville, 1994). Both these books are concerned essentially with acoustic recording and principally with its technical and legal aspects, about which they provide a wealth of information. The first and second editions of the work especially present a strongly personal account full of unabashed biases; Edison is the authors' hero and his rivals or adversaries or those who, in the authors' opinion, have not paid sufficient homage to him receive short shrift.

The Guinness Book of Recorded Sound by Robert and Celia Dearling with Brian Rust (Enfield, 1984) contains much information that is merely curious or quirky, but much too that is important and interesting and otherwise difficult to track down.

Encyclopedia of Recorded Sound in America, edited by Guy A. Marco (London and New York, 1993), is not a list of recordings like R. D. Darrell's *The Gramophone Shop Encyclopedia of Recorded Music* or Clough and Cuming's *The World's Encyclopedia of Recorded Music* (see below) but a dictionary of terms relating to the history of recorded sound in the United States to 1970. Its limits are not strictly adhered to: there is considerable detail given about developments in Great Britain, for instance, and about developments since 1970, including digital recording techniques and the compact disc. There are valuable articles on certain record companies and labels, and on 'Woodwind Recordings' and 'Piano Recordings', particularly clear entries for 'Disc', 'Loudspeaker', and 'Microphone', for example, a valuable and exceptionally detailed account of 'Sonic Restoration of Historical Recordings', and a comprehensive list of 'Sound Recordings Periodicals'.

Andre Millard's *America on Record: A History of Recorded Sound* (Cambridge, 1995), which contains a useful bibliography, and William Howland Kenney's *Recorded Music in American Life: The Phonograph and Popular Memory 1890–1945* (New York and Oxford, 1999) are more restricted than their titles might imply, and classical music receives balanced scrutiny in neither of them.

Peter Copeland's *Sound Recordings* (London, 1991) is a short illuminating survey. In the *New Grove* dictionaries there are particularly useful entries for 'Sound Recording' and 'Discographies' in *The New Grove Dictionary of American Music* (London and New York, 1986). *The New Oxford Companion to Music*, edited by Denis Arnold (Oxford,

1983), contains an exceptionally clear historical survey by John Borwick under 'Recording and Reproduction'.

The Classical Long Playing Record: Design, Production, Reproduction – a comprehensive survey by Jaco van Witteloostuyn, translated by Antoon Hurkmans, Evelyn Kort-Van Kaam and Shawm Kreitzman (Rotterdam, 1997), contains a great many excellent reproductions of LP record sleeves.

A Note on the Recordings

There is no single authority, either published printed catalogue or database, which gives details of classical recordings from the whole of the century. A researcher may find sources for listings of recordings of his chosen subject, whether it be a Russian trumpeter, or a Spanish soprano, or a German conductor, or saxophone music, or Gregorian chant, in two important bibliographies of discographies: Michael H. Gray and Gerald D. Gibson, *Bibliography of Discographies, vol. 1: Classical Music 1925–1975* (New York and London, 1977); and Michael Gray, *Classical Music Discographies, 1976–1988: A Bibliography* (New York, Westport, Connecticut and London, 1989).

Some of the lists given by Gray and Gibson will be monographs like James Creighton's *Discopaedia of the Violin: 1889–1971* (Toronto, 1974), or James Methuen-Campbell's *Catalogue of Recordings by Classical Pianists: Volume 1 (Pianists born to 1872)* (Chipping Norton, 1984), some will be full historical and detailed listings in authoritative sources like *The Record Collector*, or *Recorded Sound*, but many, inevitably, will be half-page listings in review magazines of records 'currently available', of what could be bought in England in the summer of 1959, say.

Electrical 78 rpm discs are comprehensively documented in Francis F. Clough and G. J. Cuming's *The World's Encyclopedia of Recorded Music* (London, 1952; with *First Supplement*) (*Second Supplement*, 1953; *Third Supplement*, 1957). The editors state in the first edition: 'We have aimed at the inclusion of every record of permanent music issued since the advent of electrical recording up to April 1950, throughout the world. . . . No record issued between 1925 and 1950 has been omitted intentionally, except where we have had to exercise our discretion in curtailing slightly the most heavily-recorded operatic arias, piano pieces, and the like' (p. v). Details of 33⅓ rpm discs of 'composed "serious" music' are conveniently assembled in Kurtz Myers, *Index to Record Reviews: 1949–1977* (Boston, Mass., 1985), and Kurtz Myers, *Index to Record Reviews: 1978–1983* (Boston, Mass., 1985), nearly all the periodicals cited being English or American.

For CDs, GramoFile is a database with a Web site [http://www.gramofile.co.uk] of classical music reviews which have appeared in the monthly *Gramophone* magazine since March 1983. GramoFile is updated monthly. The database is also available as a CD-ROM.

Long-playing records and CDs may also be investigated by means of the national listings magazines which give details of discs during the period they were available for purchase. In the UK these have been the *Gramophone Long-Playing Classical Record Catalogue* (1953–1967) (tapes included from 1954); *Gramophone Classical Catalogue* (1977–96); *Gramophone Compact Disc Catalogue* (1983–90); and *R.E.D. Classical Catalogue* (1997–). There are the equivalent *Schwann-Opus* catalogues for the United States, *Diapason* for France, and *Bielefelder Katalog: Klassik* for Germany.

A very large number of acoustic recordings have been reissued on CD and so may be traced through modern listings and catalogues. There are few large and comprehensive listings for original acoustic material: Roberto Bauer's *The New Catalogue of Historical Records 1898–1908/09* (1947 edition, reprinted 1970) is one such; Julian Morton Moses' *Collectors' Guide to American Recordings: 1895–1925* (New York, 1936; 2nd edition 1949) is straightforward to consult and since a significant number of American recordings were of European origin, made by European affiliates of American record companies, its scope is wider than might at first appear. An important recent discography of acoustic recordings is Claude Graveley Arnold's *The Orchestra on Record 1896–1926: An Encyclopedia of Orchestral Recordings Made by the Acoustical Process* (Westport, Connecticut/London, 1997). *The Rigler-Deutsch Index* is a microfiche catalogue produced in 1985 of the acoustic and electrical coarse-groove discs in the five biggest North American sound archives including the collections in the New York Public Library, and the Library of Congress, Washington, D.C. The British Library holds a copy of this fiche catalogue.

Notes

The record numbers cited for commercial discs are those which recordings carried on their first release, or on first release in the UK where these were different from the country of origin numbers. '78 rpm' indicates a coarse-groove shellac disc but should be taken to indicate neither the proper speed of the disc (which may actually lie between about 70 and 84 rpm) nor the speed indicated on the label (which is not infrequently incorrect). 'Digital' indicates that the master recording was digitally encoded. BLNSA indicates the shelf-mark of a recording in the sound archive of the British Library.

I Making Recordings

1. Gregor Benko, 'The Incomparable Josef Hofmann', *International Piano Quarterly*, vol. 2, no. 7, Spring 1999, p. 12.
2. Abram Chasins, *Speaking of Pianists* (New York, 1958), pp. 22–6.
3. 'A selection of documents from the Josef Hofmann Archive' selected and annotated by Gregor Benko and Terry McNeill, a booklet accompanying *Josef Hofmann 1876–1957: The British Recordings*, International Piano Library 110 (12" 33⅓ rpm mono disc, New York, no date).
4. *The Musical Times*, vol. 30, no. 558, August 1889, p. 469.
5. See James Methuen-Campbell, *Catalogue of Recordings by Classical Pianists: Volume 1 (Pianists born to 1872)* (Chipping Norton, 1984), p. 8.
6. The original cylinders are preserved at the Edison National Historic Site, West Orange, New Jersey.
7. Robert Matthew Walker, 'The Recording of Johannes Brahms', *International Classical Record Collector*, vol. 2, no. 9, Summer 1997, pp. 24–7.
8. Ludwig Koch copied the cylinder, which was held in a Berlin museum and destroyed during the last war, and presented the acetate disc copy to the National Sound Archive in London; BLNSA 30B783 (12" double-sided 78 rpm acetate disc); the recording is included in 'Pupils of Clara Schumann': Pearl GEMM CDS 9904/9 (6 mono CDs).
9. For the history of the gramophone up to the coming of the long-playing disc see Roland Gelatt, *The Fabulous Phonograph* (London, 1956); see also Walter L. Welch and Leah Brodbeck Stenzel Burt, *From Tinfoil to Stereo: The Acoustic Years of the Recording Industry* (Gainsville, 1994).
10. See Claude Graveley Arnold, C.S.B., *The Orchestra on Record 1896–1926: An Encyclopedia of Orchestral Recordings Made by the Acoustical Process* (Westport, Connecticut/London, 1997), p. xvi.
11. William R. Moran, 'The Recorded Legacy of Enrico Caruso', in Enrico Caruso, Jr, and Andrew Farkas, *Enrico Caruso: My Father and My Family* (Portland, Oregon, 1990), pp. 608–9.
12. Jerrold Northrop Moore, *A Voice in Time: The Gramophone of Fred Gaisberg 1873–1951* (London, 1976), p. 72.
13. Editorial, 'Manliness in Music', *The Musical Times*, vol. 30, no. 558, August 1889, p. 460.

14. Joe Batten, *Joe Batten's Book: The Story of Sound Recording – Being the Memoirs of Joe Batten, Recording Manager* (London, 1956), p. 38.

15. Adrian Boult in a talk to the Oriana Society in Oxford in November 1909; reprinted in Jerrold Northrop Moore (ed.), *Music and Friends: Letters to Sir Adrian Boult* (London, 1979).

16. Both in an autograph in an album 'furnished to Company representatives throughout the world for the purpose of gathering testimonial advertising.... One of these representatives, and a personal friend of Edison, was one J. H. Block, who travelled to Russia in 1889–90, and again in 1894.' The album is now held at the Rodgers and Hammerstein Archives of Recorded Sound at the New York Public Library at Lincoln Center.

17. Fauré quoted by Jean-Michel Nectoux, 'Avant-Propos', *Gabriel Fauré – Discographie* (Paris, 1979), p. 10.

18. Debussy quoted in Arbie Orenstein, *Ravel: Man and Musician* (New York and London, 1975), p. 247.

19. A. M. Henderson, *Musical Memories* (Glasgow, 1938), p. 100.

20. Gramophone & Typewriter 03051 (12" single-sided acoustic 78 rpm disc).

21. Gramophone 053145 (12" single-sided acoustic 78 rpm disc).

22. Gramophone & Typewiter 53520 (12" single-sided acoustic 78 rpm disc).

23. HMV 43739 (10" single-sided acoustic 78 rpm disc).

24. Gramophone Monarch 05512 (12" single-sided acoustic 78 rpm disc).

25. HMV 05520–21 (2 12" single-sided acoustic 78 rpm discs).

26. Gramophone 08008 (12" single-sided acoustic 78 rpm discs).

27. Jerrold Northrop Moore, *Elgar on Record: The Composer and the Gramophone* (London, 1974), p. 6.

28. 12" double-sided electrical 78 rpm disc.

29. Josef Hofmann (piano); Brunswick 50044 (12" double-sided acoustic 78 rpm disc).

30. Chopin: *Scherzo no. 1 in B minor op. 20*, Josef Hofmann (piano); first released April 1926; issued on Nimbus NI 8803 (digital stereo CD) in 1995.

31. Grammophon 040784/91 (8 12" single-sided acoustic 78 rpm discs; released in England May–August 1914).

32. See Graveley Arnold, *The Orchestra on Record 1896–1926*, p. xviii.

33. Batten, *Joe Batten's Book*, p. 58.

34. 'P.P.', *The Gramophone*, vol. 2, no. 5, October 1924, pp. 176–7; details of cuts with reference to the Novello score are given in this review.

35. Ferruccio Busoni, *Letters to his Wife*, translated by Rosamond Ley (London, 1938), p. 287. (First published as *Briefe an seine Frau* (Erlenbach-Zürich/Leipzig, 1935).)

36. Rosa Ponselle, in John Harvith and Susan Edwards Harvith, *Edison, Musicians, and the Phonograph: A Century in Retrospect* (New York/Westport, Connecticut/London, 1987), p. 82.

37. Rosa Ponselle, ibid., p. 82.

38. Abram Chasins, ibid., p. 102.

39. Pacific PIZ 1561/4 (4 12" double-sided electrical 78 rpm discs).

40. Janos Starker in Harvith and Harvith, *Edison, Musicians, and the Phonograph*, p. 188.

41. Between 1901 and 1903 the Librarian at the Metropolitan Opera Company in New York made recordings during performances on an Edison 'Home' Phonograph which recorded two-minute wax cylinders. He recorded from the prompter's box, and later from a catwalk forty feet above the stage. Over a hundred of the cylinders have survived and these dim and distant fragments include recordings of the voices of Jean de Reszke and Milka Ternina, Lucienne Bréval and Emilio de Marchi that were otherwise not to be preserved; but there is value in the glimpses we are given of those others who did make recordings since they are shown on the operatic stage freed from the constraints and limitations of the studio. All the known playable recordings and fragments were issued in 1986: Rodgers and Hammerstein Archives of Recorded Sound set 001 (6 12" 33⅓ rpm mono discs and a 72-page booklet with texts, translations, and notes).

42. John Steane, *The Grand Tradition* (London, 2/1993), p. 7.

43. Gerald Moore, *Am I Too Loud? Memoirs of an Accompanist* (London, 1962), p. 60.

44. Percy Grainger, *Journal of the Folk-Song Society*, vol. III, no. 12, May 1908, quoted in John Bird, *Percy Grainger* (London, 1976), p. 107.

45. M. A. Rosanoff, 'Edison in his laboratory', *Harper's Magazine*, September 1932; quoted in Ronald W. Clark, *Edison: The Man who Made the Future* (London, 1977), p. 167.

46. Rosa Ponselle in Harvith and Harvith,

Edison, Musicians, and the Phonograph, pp. 80–1.

47. Rosa Ponselle, ibid., p. 81.
48. Northrop Moore, *A Voice in Time,* p. 99.
49. Fred Gaisberg, ibid., p. 121.
50. Mark Hambourg, *From Piano to Forte: A Thousand and One Notes* (London, 1931), pp. 288–9.
51. Sergei Rachmaninoff ('In an interview'), 'The Artist and the Gramophone', *The Gramophone,* vol. 8, no. 95, April 1931, p. 525; the recordings are listed in: Barrie Martyn, *Rachmaninoff: Composer, Pianist, Conductor* (Aldershot, 1990), pp. 453, 454.
52. Batten, *Joe Batten's Book,* p. 33.
53. Hambourg, *From Piano to Forte,* p. 288.
54. Moore, *Am I Too Loud?* p. 59.
55. Batten, *Joe Batten's Book,* p. 35.
56. Gramophone & Typewriter 7985 (12" double-sided acoustic 78 rpm disc); Guy A. Marco, 'Stroh Violin', *Encyclopedia of Recorded Sound in America* (New York and London, 1993).
57. Batten, *Joe Batten's Book,* p. 35.
58. Batten, *Joe Batten's Book,* pp. 35–6.
59. Herbert C. Ridout, 'Behind the needle – V: Looking over Forty Years of the Gramophone', *The Gramophone,* vol. 18, no. 210, November 1940, p. 131.
60. Gramophone 2–07920, 2–07918, 2–7922 (3 single-sided 12" acoustic 78 rpm discs; recorded 4 January 1915).
61. EMI Recording sheets, British Library microfilm; HMV D 963/6 (4 12" double-sided acoustic 78 rpm discs).
62. Northrop Moore, *A Voice in Time,* p. 19.
63. Batten, *Joe Batten's Book,* p. 58.
64. Imogen Holst, 'Recordings of Holst's Music', *Recorded Sound,* no. 59, July 1975, p. 440; this also contains Eric Hughes, 'The Music of Gustav Holst: A Discography', pp. 441–6.
65. See Larry Sitsky, compiler, *The Classical Reproducing Piano: A Catalogue-Index,* 2 vols (Westport, Connecticut/London, 1990); a list of pianists and of composers who made reproducing rolls is given under 'reproducing piano rolls' in Marco (ed.), *Encyclopedia of Recorded Sound in America.*
66. Delta issued Welte-Mignon recordings in 1964, which were reviewed by Stephen Plaistow, *The Gramophone,* vol. 42, no. 495, August 1964, pp. 104–5; Argo issued a selection from 'Ampico' piano rolls in 1966: see Denys Gueroult, 'The Ampico Rolls on Disc', *The Gramophone,* vol. 44, no. 518, July 1966, p. 54,

and for reviews *The Gramophone,* vol. 44, no. 517, June 1966, p. 31; *The Gramophone,* vol. 44, no. 518, July 1966, p. 80; and *The Gramophone,* vol. 44, no. 520, September 1966, pp. 181–2; Telefunken issued an anthology of a Welte-Mignon model O Steinway grand on LPs in 1971; these recordings were reissued in 1989: for a review of these and for an anthology issued on the Intercord label, see Lionel Salter, *Gramophone,* vol. 67, no. 798, November 1989, pp. 1015–16; L'Oiseau-Lyre issued a series in 1984 and 1985: see Lionel Salter, *Gramophone,* vol. 62, no. 739, December 1984, pp. 776, 781; Denis Condon has issued selections from his private collection of over 8,000 rolls, the latest in the early 1990s, and his disc 'Vladimir Horowitz: piano roll recordings', Condon Collection 690.07.009, was reviewed in *Gramophone,* vol. 71, no. 842, July 1993, pp. 96–7; track listings of eleven other Condon Collection CDs of piano rolls are given in the Gramophile CD-ROM under 'Condon Collection'; in 1995 Nimbus announced a series of between forty and fifty discs of recordings by some seventy pianists of 'Duo-Art' piano rolls transferred on a modern Steinway concert grand piano: Lionel Salter reviewed two of these, of rolls by Hofmann, Friedmann and Paderewski (Nimbus NI8802) and of rolls by Hofmann (Nimbus NI8803) in *Gramophone,* vol. 73, no. 871, December 1995, pp. 174, 176.

67. Catalogue: *Library of Welte-Mignon Music Records* (New York, 1927), p. 5 (Foreword).
68. Ibid., p. 9.
69. Ibid., p. 135.
70. Ibid., p. 121.
71. Ibid., p. 84.
72. Ibid., p. 150.
73. Abram Chasins in Harvith and Harvith, *Edison, Musicians, and the Phonograph,* pp. 97–103.
74. Max Wilcox, 'An Afternoon with Arthur Rubinstein', *Hi-Fidelity,* vol. 13, no. 7, July 1963, p. 28.
75. Arthur Rubinstein, *My Young Years* (New York, 1973), p. 31.
76. Harold Schonberg, 'From Leschetizky to Gabrilowitsch – Twenty pianists on Piano Rolls', *Hi-Fidelity,* vol. 14, no. 3, March 1964.
77. Gregor Benko, letter in *International Classical Record Collector,* vol. 2, no. 7, Winter 1996, p. 81; see also Cyril

Ehrlich, *The Piano: A History* (2/1990, Oxford), pp. 134–7.

78. *Moiseiwitsch: opinions on player piano rolls*; interviewed by Denys Gueroult on 26 October 1962; BBC Archives LP 28654 (12″ 33⅓ rpm mono disc).

79. J. F. Cooke, *Great Pianists on Piano Playing* (Philadelphia, 1913; reprinted 1976), pp. 201–2.

80. The Journal of the Pianola Institute, *The Pianola Journal*, 1987– (West Wickham, Kent), treats all aspects of the reproducing piano as well as the pianola.

81. Gelatt, *The Fabulous Phonograph*, p. 165.

82. For commercial reasons the record companies did not draw attention to discs made by the electrical process and did not distinguish between the electric and acoustic discs with different numbering systems; clear guidance on deducing from the label information whether a disc was recorded electrically is given in Boris Semeonoff, *Record Collecting: A Guide for Beginners* (London, 1949), pp. 3–8.

83. Stanley Chapple, 'In the Recording Studio', *The Gramophone*, vol. 6, no. 67, December 1928, pp. 289–91.

84. Victor Recording Book, entries for sessions on 10 April and 13 April 1929, British Library microfilm.

85. Sergei Rachmaninoff ('In an interview'), 'The Artist and the Gramophone', *The Gramophone*, vol. 8, no. 95, April 1931, pp. 525–6.

86. See 'Discography and list of reproducing piano rolls' in Barrie Martyn, *Rachmaninoff: Composer, Pianist, Conductor* (Aldershot, 1990), pp. 451–505.

87. Roy Henderson, recorded in February 1987: BLNSA Tape C90/88/02.

88. Gelatt, *The Fabulous Phonograph*, p. 175.

89. Ibid., p. 179.

90. H. T. Burnett reviewing 4,850 voices singing 'Adeste Fideles' (Columbia 50013–D; 12″ double-sided electrical 78 rpm disc; recorded in the Metropolitan Opera House, New York on 31 March 1925; issued in the UK in September 1925) in *The Gramophone*, vol. 3, no. 8, January 1926, p. 365; quoted in Gelatt, *The Fabulous Phonograph*, p. 177.

91. Comments in *The Gramophone* quoted ibid., p. 176.

92. Ernest Newman, *The Sunday Times*, 11 July 1926; quoted ibid., p. 178.

93. Fred W. Gaisberg, *Music on Record* (London, 1946), p. 172.

94. See for example: *The Gramophone*, vol. 5, no. 1, June 1927, Advertisements, pp.

ix–x, and *The Gramophone*, vol. 5, no. 10, March 1928, Advertisements, pp. xi–xii.

95. Gaisberg, *Music on Record*, p. 171.

96. Ibid., p. 164.

97. Decca K 1561/2 (2 12″ double-sided electrical 78 rpm discs).

98. Decca K 1175/6 (with Debussy's 'Prelude to *La Damoiselle Élue*'; 2 12″ double-sided electrical 78 rpm discs).

99. Decca K 1347/8 (2 12″ double-sided electrical 78 rpm discs).

100. Decca K 1388/92 (5 12″ double-sided electrical 78 rpm discs).

101. Edward Sackville-West and Desmond Shawe-Taylor, *The Record Guide* (London, 1951), p. 232; the Falla discs were Decca K 1158/60 (3 double-sided electrical 78 rpm discs).

102. John Culshaw, *Putting the Record Straight* (London, 1982), p. 133.

103. 'The Cassette Medium – Some Advantages and Disadvantages', in Edward Greenfield, Robert Layton and Ivan March (eds), *Penguin Cassette Guide* (Harmondsworth, 1979), pp. xi–xv.

104. See for example: Edward Greenfield, 'Quadraphonic Records – First Reviews', *The Gramophone*, vol. 50, no. 589, June 1972, p. 25; John Borwick, 'Quadraphonic Releases', *The Gramophone*, vol. 50, no. 599, April 1973, p. 1945.

105. John Culshaw, *Ring Resounding: The Recording in Stereo of* Der Ring des Nibelungen (London, 1967), p. 114.

106. *BPI Statistical Handbook 1995*, p. 21.

107. Sam Parkins in Harvith and Harvith, *Edison, Musicians, and the Phonograph*, p. 389.

108. Edward Greenfield, John Borwick, *Gramophone*, April 1979, p. 1774.

109. Kurt List, *Recorded High Fidelity* (New York, 1954), p. 13.

110. Eugene Ormandy in Harvith and Harvith, *Edison, Musicians, and the Phonograph*, p. 325, pp. 146–7.

111. Columbia M–33172/MQ–33172 (12″ 33⅓ rpm stereo/quad disc; released 1975).

112. Ray Moore in Harvith and Harvith, *Edison, Musicians, and the Phonograph*, p. 324.

113. Frank Ll. Harrison, *Music in Medieval Britain* (London, 1958/1963), p. 419.

114. Denis Stevens, *Early Music News*, March 1996, pp. 15–16.

115. Thomas Frost in Harvith and Harvith, *Edison, Musicians, and the Phonograph*, p. 370.

116. Thomas Frost, ibid., p. 370.

117. Gregor Piatigorsky in conversation with his accompanist, Ivor Newton; *Talking*

about Music 190; BBC Transcription Service disc 138127 [side number] (12" 33⅓ rpm mono disc).

118. Eugen Jochum, *The Gramophone*, vol. 50, no. 591, August 1972, p. 319.

119. George Szell, *The Gramophone*, vol. 48, no. 573, February 1971, p. 1291.

120. Jascha Horenstein, *The Gramophone*, vol. 48, no. 570, November 1970, p. 775.

121. David Soyer, the cellist of the Guarneri Quartet, in Harvith and Harvith, *Edison, Musicians, and the Phonograph*, pp. 257–8.

122. Moore, *Am I Too Loud?* p. 237.

123. Vladimir Ashkenazy in Harvith and Harvith, *Edison, Musicians, and the Phonograph*, p. 222.

124. Stephen Johnson, 'Berg and Beyond', *Gramophone*, vol. 70, no. 836, January 1993, p. 23.

125. André Previn in Harvith and Harvith, *Edison, Musicians, and the Phonograph*, pp. 211–12.

126. Alicia de Larrocha, ibid., p. 240.

127. Bernard Haitink, ibid., p. 235.

128. Pierre Boulez in Jean Vermeil, *Conversations with Boulez: Thoughts on Conducting*, translated by Camille Naish (Portland, Oregon, 1996), p. 107. (First published as *Conversations de Pierre Boulez sur la Direction d'Orchestre avec Jean Vermeil* (Paris, 1989).)

129. Jindrich Rohan in Harvith and Harvith, *Edison, Musicians, and the Phonograph*, pp. 175–7.

130. John Culshaw, 'The Outlook for Classical Music', *The Gramophone*, vol. 48, no. 574, March 1971, p. 1444.

131. Herman Klein, *The Gramophone*, vol. 10, no. 115, December 1932, p. 257.

132. HMV DA 1439 (10" double-sided electrical 78 rpm disc; matrix nos: OEA 2196–1; OEA 2197–1); *The Gramophone*, vol. 13, no. 150, November 1935, p. 239; Floris Juynboll and James Seddon, 'Elisabeth Schumann Discography', *The Record Collector*, vol. 33, nos 3/4/5, March 1988, p. 77.

133. Victor set M 1136 (11–9648/9: 2 12" electrical 78 rpm discs).

134. Decca MET/SET209/11 (3 12" 33⅓ rpm mono/stereo discs).

135. Culshaw, *Putting the Record Straight*, pp. 263–4.

136. Culshaw, *Ring Resounding*, pp. 155–6.

137. DG 2530 619 (12" 33⅓ rpm stereo disc).

138. Suvi Raj Grubb, *Music Makers on Record* (London, 1986), pp. 145–54; HMV set SLS 978 (4 12" 33⅓ rpm stereo discs).

139. It is very difficult to comprehend the extent to which a modern recording or broadcast interprets a performance since sound engineers rarely set out to capture sounds as they are actually experienced by those seated in a concert hall or opera house or church. A disc in the British Library of a service in York Minster in May 1997 sung by the Minster Choir and the choirs of Wakefield and Leeds Parish Churches does illuminate this, recording the confused aural impression received by a member of the congregation sitting in the nave: BLNSA call no.: 1CDR0000184.

140. Decca set MET252–3/SET 252–3 (2 12" 33⅓ rpm mono/stereo discs).

141. Edward Greenfield, 'Ten Years of Stereo', *The Gramophone*, vol. 46, no. 541, June 1968, p. 21.

142. Peter Evans, *The Music of Benjamin Britten* (London, 2/1989), p. 451.

143. Culshaw, *Ring Resounding*, pp. 95–6.

144. Ibid., pp. 190–1.

145. Ibid., p. 237.

146. Ibid., pp. 103–4.

147. Ibid., pp. 186–7.

148. Ibid., pp. 25–6.

149. Ernest Newman, *Wagner as Man and Artist* (London, 1914), p. 357, quoted as the frontispiece, ibid.

150. Ibid., pp. 22–3.

151. Otto Friedrich, *Glenn Gould: A Life and Variations* (London, 1990), p. 253.

152. Ibid., p. 254.

153. Glenn Gould, 'Music and Technology', Tim Page (ed.), *The Glenn Gould Reader* (London, 1987), pp. 353–4.

154. André Previn in Harvith and Harvith, *Edison, Musicians, and the Phonograph*, p. 212.

155. The fullest information about Gould's recordings is contained in Nancy Canning, *A Glenn Gould Catalog* (Westport, Connecticut/London, 1992).

156. Elisabeth Schwarzkopf, *On and Off the Record* (London, 1982), p. 238.

157. Culshaw, *Putting the Record Straight*, pp. 66–7.

158. Christopher Hogwood in James Badel, 'On Record: Christopher Hogwood', *Fanfare*, vol. 9, no. 2, November/December 1985, pp. 86–7.

159. Alexander Kipnis in Harvith and Harvith, *Edison, Musicians, and the Phonograph*, pp. 93–5.

160. Stanley Chapple, 'In the Recording Studio', *The Gramophone*, vol. 6, no. 67, December 1928, pp. 289–91.

161. Culshaw, *Ring Resounding*, pp. 26–7.

162. Abram Chasins in Harvith and Harvith,

Edison, Musicians, and the Phonograph, p. 103.

163. Thomas Frost, ibid., p. 364.

164. Culshaw, *Ring Resounding*, p. 92.

165. Thomas Frost in Harvith and Harvith, *Edison, Musicians, and the Phonograph*, p. 354.

166. Thomas Frost, ibid., p. 354.

167. David Wooldridge, *Charles Ives: A Portrait* (London, 1975), p. 330.

168. Charlie Gillett in H. Wiley Hitchcock (ed.), *The Phonograph and Our Musical Life: Proceedings of a Centennial Conference 7–10 December 1977*, I.S.A.M. Monographs: Number 14 (Institute for Studies in American Music, Department of Music, School of Performing Arts, Brooklyn College, City University of New York, New York, 1980), p. 51.

169. Thomas Frost in Harvith and Harvith, *Edison, Musicians, and the Phonograph*, p. 370; Ray Moore, ibid., pp. 327–8.

170. Stephen Johnson, 'Berg and Beyond', *Gramophone*, vol. 70, no. 836, January 1993, p. 23.

171. The early recordings of the favourite songs from *Floradora*, most of them made in 1900, have been reissued on Opal CD 9835 (mono CD; issued 1989).

172. Isabella Wallich in conversation with Jerrold Northrop Moore, 'Fred Gaisberg – Memories of my Uncle', *International Classical Record Collector*, vol. 2, no. 5, Summer 1996, pp. 51–9.

173. Gaisberg, *Music on Record*, p. 151.

174. Schwarzkopf, *On and Off the Record*, p. 16.

175. Ibid., p. 73.

176. Harvey Sachs, *Arthur Rubinstein: A Life* (London, 1996), p. 225.

177. Edward Greenfield, 'The Autocrat of the Turntable', in Schwarzkopf, *On and Off the Record*, p. 112.

178. Columbia 33CX 1858/SAX 2503 (12″ 33⅓ rpm mono/stereo disc); see Alan Sanders (comp.), *Walter Legge: A Discography* (Westport, Connecticut/ London, 1984), p. 380.

179. Edward Greenfield, 'The Autocrat of the Turntable', in Schwarzkopf, *On and Off the Record*, p. 109.

180. Isabella Wallich in *International Classical Record Collector*, Summer 1996, p. 54.

181. Schwarzkopf, *On and Off the Record*, pp. 16–18.

182. Ibid., p. 56.

183. Walter Legge in the Introduction to the Dover edition of Ernest Newman, *Hugo Wolf*, originally published in London in 1907 (New York, 1966), pp. xv–xvi.

184. Schwarzkopf, *On and Off the Record*, p. 86.

185. Ibid., p. 238.

186. Ibid., p. 87.

187. Ralph Vaughan Williams, 'A Musical Autobiography' (1950), in *National Music and Other Essays* (Oxford, 2/1987), p. 183.

188. Sanders (comp.), *Walter Legge: A Discography*.

189. Andrew Porter, quoted in Schwarzkopf, *On and Off the Record*, p. 5.

190. Culshaw, *Ring Resounding*, pp. 154–5.

191. Ibid., p. 89.

192. Ibid., pp. 22–6.

193. 'Goddard Lieberson talks to Alan Blyth', *Gramophone*, vol. 53, no. 626, July 1975, p. 161; John Culshaw, Obituary, *Gramophone*, vol. 55, no. 650, July 1977, pp. 161–2.

194. John Pfeiffer in Harvith and Harvith, *Edison, Musicians, and the Phonograph*, p. 341.

195. Thomas Frost, ibid., pp. 353–5.

196. Sam Parkins, ibid., p. 382.

197. For courses in England see: Laura Dollin (ed.), *Music Education Yearbook 1998/99* (London, 1998), pp. 423–7.

198. Marco (ed.), *Encyclopedia of Recorded Sound in America*.

199. Batten, *Joe Batten's Book*, p. 57.

200. Rosa Ponselle in Harvith and Harvith, *Edison, Musicians, and the Phonograph*, pp. 80–3.

201. Gaisberg, *Music on Record*, pp. 40–1.

202. John Denison in 'The Influence of the Record Industry on Musical Life Today', a symposium held at the British Institute of Recorded Sound (the National Sound Archive) on 22 February 1977: BLNSA Tapes P1141BW, T1505BW, M7010BW.

203. Busoni, *Letters to His Wife*, pp. 286, 287, 305.

204. Gaisberg, *Music on Record*, p. 174.

205. Batten, *Joe Batten's Book*, p. 36.

206. Percy Grainger, letter dated 14 May 1908 to Karen Holten in Kay Dreyfus (ed.), *The Farthest North of Humanness: Letters of Percy Grainger 1901–14* (London, 1985), p. 208.

207. Thomas Frost in Harvith and Harvith, *Edison, Musicians, and the Phonograph*, p. 360.

208. Walter Alcock, *The Rotunda*, vol. 3, no. 1, September 1929, pp. 21–3, quoted in *The Musical Times*, January 1996, p. 8; Walter Alcock (organ of Salisbury Cathedral): HMV C 1452 (12″ double-sided electrical 78 rpm disc; released March 1928).

209. Moore, *Am I Too Loud?* pp. 59–63.

210. Louis Kaufman in Harvith and Harvith, *Edison, Musicians, and the Phonograph*, pp. 111–12.

211. Jed Distler, 'Richter in Carnegie Hall', *International Classical Record Collector*, vol. 2, no. 7, Winter 1996, p. 38.

212. Arthur Grumiaux, *The Gramophone*, vol. 48, no. 572, January 1971, p. 1134.

213. Francis Poulenc in a letter to Madeleine Gray dated 7 June 1938 in Sidney Buckland (ed. and trans.), *Francis Poulenc: 'Echo and Source': Selected Correspondence 1915–1963* (London, 1991), p. 113.

214. Eugene Ormandy in Harvith and Harvith, *Edison, Musicians, and the Phonograph*, p. 149.

215. Jan Peerce, ibid., p. 135.

216. André Previn, ibid., pp. 209–10.

217. Francis Poulenc in a letter to Madeleine Gray dated 7 June 1938, in Buckland, *Francis Poulenc . . . Selected Correspondence*, p. 113.

218. Hambourg, *From Piano to Forte*, pp. 288–90.

219. Clifford Curzon, *The Gramophone*, vol. 48, no. 574, May 1971, pp. 1764, 1769.

220. Sergei Rachmaninoff ('In an interview'), 'The artist and the gramophone', *The Gramophone*, vol. 8, no. 95, April 1931, pp. 525–6.

221. HMV C 1379 (12″ double-sided electrical 78 rpm disc).

222. Gramophone Company recording books; British Library microfilm.

223. From notes by Nicholas Danby to Amphion PHI CD 132 (mono CD): *Guy Weitz: the complete recordings 1926–1931* (released 1995).

224. Martina Arroyo in Harvith and Harvith, *Edison, Musicians, and the Phonograph*, pp. 231–2.

225. Gaisberg, *Music on Record*, p. 155.

226. Pierre Boulez in Vermeil, *Conversations with Boulez*, p. 108.

227. *Moiseiwitsch: opinions on player piano rolls*; Moiseiwitsch interviewed by Denys Gueroult on 26 October 1962; BBC Archives LP 28654 (12″ 33⅓ rpm mono disc); the disc was HMV C 3209 (matrix no: 2EA 7664–1) (12″ double-sided electrical 78 rpm disc); see Bryan Crimp, *Benno Moiseiwitsch: An HMV Discography* (Hexham, 1990), p. 32.

228. Moore, *Am I Too Loud?* p. 237.

229. Ibid., p. 237.

230. Schwarzkopf, *On and Off the Record*, pp. 87–8.

231. David Soyer, Arnold Steinhardt, Michael Tree, members of the Guarneri Quartet,

232. Frans Brüggen, ibid., p. 204.

233. André Previn, ibid., pp. 211–12.

234. Jascha Horenstein, *The Gramophone*, vol. 48, no. 570, November 1970, p. 775.

235. Eugene Ormandy in Harvith and Harvith, *Edison, Musicians, and the Phonograph*, pp. 146–8.

236. Pierre Boulez in Vermeil, *Conversations with Boulez*, pp. 104–5.

237. Soyer, Steinhardt, Tree, of the Guarneri Quartet, in Harvith and Harvith, *Edison, Musicians, and the Phonograph*, p. 248.

238. Soyer of the Guarneri Quartet, ibid., p. 249.

239. Vox VBX 417/1–3 (3 12″ 33⅓ rpm mono discs).

240. 'Notes of a complete recording of Beethoven's piano works' [1966], in Alfred Brendel, *Musical Thoughts and Afterthoughts* (London, 1976), p. 15.

241. Alicia de Larrocha in Harvith and Harvith, *Edison, Musicians, and the Phonograph*, p. 241.

242. Alicia de Larrocha, ibid., p. 241.

243. Lotte Lehmann, ibid., p. 72.

244. Culshaw, *Putting the Record Straight*, pp. 94–5.

245. Dietrich Fischer-Dieskau, *The Gramophone*, vol. 48, no. 571, December 1970, p. 967.

246. Eugene Ormandy in Harvith and Harvith, *Edison, Musicians, and the Phonograph*, p. 147.

247. Vladimir Ashkenazy, ibid., p. 219.

248. Jasper Parrott with Vladimir Ashkenazy, *Beyond Frontiers* (London, 1984), pp. 139–40.

249. Walford Davies, 'Both Sides of the Microphone', *BBC Handbook 1929* (London, 1929), pp. 130–1.

250. Ibid., p. 131.

251. Alistair Cooke, *The Patient has the Floor* (London, 1986), p. 8.

252. Ibid., p. 9.

253. Hogwood, *Fanfare*, November/December 1985, pp. 90–1.

254. John Pfeiffer in Harvith and Harvith, *Edison, Musicians, and the Phonograph*, p. 344.

255. Martina Arroyo, ibid., pp. 225–6.

256. Lorin Maazel, *The Gramophone*, vol. 48, no. 574, March 1971, p. 1449.

257. Janos Starker in Harvith and Harvith, *Edison, Musicians, and the Phonograph*, p. 186.

258. Louis Kaufman, ibid., p. 115.

259. Neville Cardus in Robin Daniels, *Con-*

versations with Cardus (London, 1976), pp. 230–2.

260. Louis Kaufman in Harvith and Harvith, *Edison, Musicians, and the Phonograph*, pp. 117–20.

261. Pierre Boulez in Vermeil, *Conversations with Boulez*, p. 104.

262. Some of Boulez's own recordings reflect these trends in the number and placing of microphones; the disc of *Pli selon pli* released in 1969 (CBS 72770: 12″ 33⅓ rpm stereo disc, released in 1969) exemplifies the close-up sound characteristic of many labels at the time: compare, for example, the cello solo three bars before rehearsal number 9 on page 9 of *Don* (at 3′30″ in) with the same passage in the recording issued in 1983 (Erato set NUM 75050 (2 12″ 33⅓ rpm stereo discs)) (at 3′21″ in).

263. John Culshaw in Glenn Gould, 'The Prospects of Recording', *Hi-Fidelity*, vol. 16, no. 4, April 1966, p. 54.

264. Falk Schwarz and John Berrie, 'Sviatoslav Richter – a Discography', *Recorded Sound*, no. 84, July 1983, p. 7.

265. 'Talking to Brendel: Jeremy Siepmann' [1972], in Brendel, *Musical Thoughts and Afterthoughts*, p. 146.

266. 'A Case for Live Recordings' [1983], in Alfred Brendel, *Music Sounded Out* (London, 1990), p. 202.

267. Robert Cowan, *Gramophone*, February 1998, vol. 75, no. 898, pp. 60–4, reviewing 'Celibidache and the Munich Philharmonic Orchestra', EMI set CDS5 56517-2 (11 mono/stereo CDs).

268. Miha Pogacnik in Harvith and Harvith, *Edison, Musicians, and the Phonograph*, pp. 409–14.

269. 'Busking it till a Fairy Godmother Turns Up', Oliver Knussen interviewed by Stephen Johnson, *The Independent*, Independent Section Two, Friday 28 July 1995.

270. Culshaw, *Putting the Record Straight*, p. 143.

271. Eugene Ormandy in Harvith and Harvith, *Edison, Musicians, and the Phonograph*, p. 149.

272. Frans Brüggen, ibid., p. 205.

273. Bernard Haitink, ibid., p. 237.

II The Repertory Recorded

1. Thomas A. Edison, 'The Public is Very Primitive', *The Etude*, October 1923; quoted in Ronald W. Clark, *Edison: The Man who Made the Future* (London, 1977), p. 168.

2. *Schwann Opus Guide to Classical Music*, Spring 1998.

3. Ferdynand Zweig, *The Student in the Age of Anxiety: A Survey of Oxford and Manchester Students* (London, 1963), p. 27.

4. Joseph Kerman, *Musicology* (London, 1985), p. 25.

5. E. H. Fellowes, *Memoirs of an Amateur Musician* (London, 1946), p. 9.

6. Stephen Stratton, *Monthly Journal of the Incorporated Society of Musicians*, December 1888, quoted in Cyril Ehrlich, *The Music Profession in Britain since the Eighteenth Century: A Social History* (Oxford, 1985), p. 102.

7. Ralph Vaughan Williams, 'Gustav Holst: An Essay and a Note', *National Music and Other Essays* (Oxford, 2/1987), pp. 132–3.

8. Nan Dearmer, *The Life of Percy Dearmer* (London, 1940), p. 123.

9. 'Manliness in Music', *The Musical Times*, vol. 30, no. 558, August 1889, p. 460.

10. Ibid., p. 461.

11. Cyril Ehrlich, *The Music Profession in Britain*, p. 129.

12. Ibid., p. 105.

13. Cyril Ehrlich, *The Piano: A History* (Oxford, 2/1990), p. 135.

14. From an advertisement for the Rothermel-Brush Studio Model Pick-Up 'designed and engineered irrespective of cost for highest fidelity reproduction', *The Gramophone*, vol. 15, no. 169, June 1937, p. xiv.

15. From an advertisement for the 'H.M.V.' Model 801, Autoradiogram reproduced from a review in *The Gramophone*, May 1937, pp. 555–6.

16. Comments reproduced in an advertisement for Imhof's needles, *The Gramophone*, November 1937, p. vi.

17. Michael Flanders and Donald Swann, 'Reproduction' or 'Hi-fidelity', *At the Drop of a Hat*, recorded at the final performance at the Fortune Theatre, London, on 2 May 1959, Parlophone PCS 3001 (12″ 33⅓ rpm stereo disc).

18. Advertisement in *Gramophone* magazine, Awards issue, 1998, vol. 76, no. 907, p. 141: advertisement for a Hi-Fi Experience.

19. The *Encyclopedia* also listed the 'few acoustic records of unusual historical worth or artistic significance . . . and an occasional out-of-print disc . . . when the musical work itself is of considerable

worth and no other version is available';
R. D. Darrell (comp.), *The Gramophone
Shop Encyclopedia of Recorded Music*
(New York, 1936), p. vii.

20. Lawrence Gilman, 'Foreword', in
Darrell, *The Gramophone Shop Encyclopedia*, p. iv.

21. Ibid., p. iv.

22. Winthrop Sargeant, *Geniuses, Goddesses
and People* (New York, 1949), pp. 114–16.

23. George Dyson, 'The Future of Music',
address delivered at the Annual Confer-
ence of the Incorporated Society of
Musicians on Tuesday, 1 January 1935,
The Musical Times, vol. 76, no. 1104,
February 1935, p. 117.

24. C. H. H. Parry, *Studies of Great Composers* (London, 1886), p. 3.

25. Percy A. Scholes, *The Listener's Guide to
Music* (London, 10/1942), p. 77.

26. C. Henry Phillips, *The Singing Church*
(London, 1945), p. 73.

27. Gustave Chouquet in *Grove's Dictionary
of Music and Musicians*, First Edition, vol.
2 (1880), p. 173; reprinted up to the Fifth
Edition (1954), vol. 5, p. 424.

28. See J. A. Westrup, 'Purcell', *Grove*, Fifth
Edition (1954), vol. 6, p. 1009.

29. R. R. Terry, 'Musical Changes I have
seen in twenty-three years', [*London*]
Evening News, 19 March 1924.

30. Heinrich Schenker, *Harmony*, edited
by Oswald Jonas and translated by
Elisabeth Mann Borgese (Chicago,
1954), p. 69. (First published as *Neue
musikalische Theorien und Phantasien*, I:
Harmonielehre (Stuttgart, 1906).)

31. Parry, *Studies of Great Composers*, p. 360.

32. Ibid., pp. 103–4.

33. Edward Lockspeiser, *Debussy* (London,
5/1980), p. 241.

34. Alfred Einstein, *A Short History of Music*
(London, 1936), p. 124. (First published
as *Geschichte der Musik* (Leipzig/Berlin,
1918).)

35. Ibid., p. 178.

36. Parry, *Studies of Great Composers*, p. 373.

37. Ibid., p. 374.

38. Edward Sackville-West and Desmond Shawe-Taylor, *The Record Guide*
(London, 1951), p. 454.

39. Percy A. Scholes, *The Listener's Guide to
Music* (London, 1919), p. 76.

40. Einstein, *A Short History of Music*, p. 201.

41. Christopher Stone, 'The National
Gramophonic Society', *The Gramophone*,
vol. 12, no. 143, April 1935, p. 432.

42. Advertisement, *The Gramophone*, vol. 4,
no. 10, March 1927, p. 405.

43. Ibid., p. 405.

44. Gordon Bottomley, 'Concerning
Confidence', *The Gramophone*, vol. 4, no.
10, March 1927, p. 406.

45. Christopher Stone, 'The National
Gramophonic Society', *The Gramophone*,
vol. 12, no. 143, April 1935, p. 432.

46. Walter Legge in the introduction to the
Dover edition of *Hugo Wolf* by Ernest
Newman, originally published in
London in 1907 (New York, 1966), p. xvi.

47. Alan Sanders, *Gramophone*, vol. 58, no.
694, March 1981, p. 1177.

48. Compton Mackenzie, *The Gramophone*,
vol. 9, no. 102, November 1931, p. 203.

49. Roland Gelatt, *The Fabulous Phonograph*
(London, 1956), p. 199.

50. Desmond Shawe-Taylor, *The Gramophone*, vol. 12, no. 141, February 1935, p.
346.

51. But this series did not quite include the
complete works for solo piano; Brendel
seems to have been the first to have
done this with the final volume of the
sequence appearing in 1968: see Joan
Chissell, *The Gramophone*, vol. 46, no.
547, December 1968, p. 859.

52. Gelatt, *The Fabulous Phonograph*, p. 199.

53. Elisabeth Schwarzkopf, *On and Off the
Record* (London, 1982), pp. 95–6.

54. Donald Tovey and Geoffrey Parratt,
Walter Parratt: Master of the Music
(London, 1941), p. 25.

55. Gramophone 05512 (12″ single-sided
acoustic 78 rpm disc).

56. HMV D 576 (12″ double-sided acoustic
78 rpm disc).

57. Columbia L 1445 (12″ double-sided
acoustic 78 rpm disc; recorded in
London on 27 February 1922); see James
Methuen-Campbell, *Catalogue of Recordings by Classical Pianists: Volume 1 –
Pianists born to 1872* (Chipping Norton,
1984), p. 8.

58. Christopher Stone, *The Gramophone*, vol.
10, no. 118, March 1933, p. 409.

59. Reproduced on the sleeve of Chantry
ARC 1017 (12″ 33⅓ rpm mono disc),
issued in 1984 to mark the Diamond
Jubilee of the Haslemere Festival.

60. Darrell (comp.), *The Gramophone Shop
Encyclopedia*, p. 32.

61. Roger Smithson, *The Recordings of Edwin
Fischer* (London, 2/1990), pp. 20–1.

62. *The Gramophone*, vol. 11, no. 131, April
1934, p. 432.

63. *BBC Handbook 1928* (London, 1928), p.
87.

64. Ibid., p. 84.

65. Ibid., p. 99.

66. Ibid., p. 101.

67. César Saerchinger, *Artur Schnabel: A Biography* (London, 1957), p. 192.

68. 'Ariel', *The Musical Times*, vol. 68, no. 1013, 1927, p. 631.

69. Meirion and Susie Harries, *A Pilgrim Soul: The Life and Works of Elisabeth Lutyens* (London, 1989), p. 81.

70. Edwin Evans, 'Broadcasting and the Future of Music: Bridging the Gaps in Our Musical Experience', *The Radio Times*, 21 September 1928, p. 543.

71. *The Radio Times*, 28 September 1928, p. 607.

72. Waldo Selden Pratt, 'The Isolation of Music', *Proceedings of the Musical Association Twenty-First Session 1894–5*, p. 161.

73. H. G. Wells, *Fortnightly Review*, April 1903, quoted in Percy A. Scholes, *Music: The Child and the Masterpiece: A Comprehensive Handbook of Aims and Methods in all that is usually called 'Musical Appreciation'* (London, 1935), p. 13.

74. Quoted in Scholes, *Music: The Child and the Masterpiece*, pp. 17–18.

75. Percy A. Scholes, *Everybody's Guide to Broadcast Music* (London, 1925), p. 10.

76. Nicolas Slonimsky, *Baker's Biographical Dictionary*, Eighth Edition (New York, 1992), p. 1633.

77. W. R. Anderson, *The Musical Times*, vol. 99, no. 1387, September 1958, p. 501.

78. A. Machabey, entry ('Appendice') in *Encyclopédie de la Musique, Deuxième Partie: Technique – Esthétique – Pédagogie*, vol. 6 (Paris, 1931), p. 3887.

79. Percy A. Scholes, in entry 'Gramophone', *The Oxford Companion to Music* (10th ed., London, 1970), p. 420.

80. Percy A. Scholes, *The Columbia History of Music Through Ear and Eye: Period 1: To the Opening of the Seventeenth Century* (London, 1930), p. 12.

81. Quoted in Percy A. Scholes, *The Columbia History of Music Through Ear and Eye: Period III: From Bach's Sons to Beethoven* (London, 1932), p. 48.

82. Ibid., p. 48.

83. *The Gramophone*, vol. 12, no. 144, May 1935, p. 466.

84. Ibid., p. 466.

85. For the life and work of Louise Hanson-Dyer see Jim Davidson, *Lyrebird Rising: Louise Hanson-Dyer of L'Oiseau-Lyre: 1884–1962* (Melbourne, 1994).

86. Igor Stravinsky, *An Autobiography* (London, 1975), p. 152. (First published as *Chroniques de ma vie* (Paris, 1935); first published in English in 1936.)

87. Davidson, *Lyrebird Rising*, p. 455.

88. Ibid., pp. 466–7.

89. Ibid., p. 468.

90. Alec Robertson, *The Gramophone*, vol. 31, no. 361, June 1953, p. 3.

91. *The Gramophone*, vol. 38, no. 454, March 1961, pp. 474–5.

92. Alec Robertson, *The Gramophone*, June 1953, p. 4.

93. W. Barclay Squire, 'On an Early Sixteenth-century Ms. of English Music in the Library of Eton College', *Archaeologia*, vol. LVI, 1898, p. 102.

94. Alec Robertson, *The Gramophone*, January 1954, p. 301.

95. Edward Sackville-West and Desmond Shawe-Taylor, *The Record Guide* (revised edition, London, 1955), pp. 875, 889.

96. Lionel Salter, *The Gramophone*, vol. 32, no. 377, October 1954, p. 216.

97. Jeremy Noble reviewing vols II to VI on their appearance as LPs, *The Gramophone*, vol. 35, no. 415, December 1957, pp. 285–6.

98. Sackville-West and Shawe-Taylor, *The Record Guide* (revised edition, 1955), p. 885.

99. Ibid., p. 889.

100. Ibid., pp. 885–6.

101. Lionel Salter, *The Gramophone*, vol. 36, no. 431, April 1959, p. 536.

102. John Warrack, *The Gramophone*, vol. 36, no. 432, May 1959, p. 558.

103. Re-recordings in Volume II: *Early Medieval Music up to 1300*: side 3, 13–19; Re-recordings in Volume III: *Ars Nova and the Renaissance*: sides 1,2: 6–8; Re-recordings in Volume IV: *The Age of Humanism*: sides 1,2: 6,9; Jeremy Noble, *The Gramophone*, December 1957, p. 286.

104. 'The Music Boom', *The Economist*, 11 January 1947, p. 53.

105. Ibid., p. 53.

106. Robert Elkin (ed.), *A Career in Music* (London, 2/1960), p. 9.

107. *The PRS Bulletin*, August 1945, p. 96, quoted in Alan Peacock and Ronald Weir, *The Composer in the Market Place* (London, 1975), p. 101.

108. Sir William Haley, Director-General of the BBC, quoted in Humphrey Carpenter, *The Envy of the World: Fifty Years of the BBC Third Programme and Radio 3 1946–1996* (London, 1996), p. 9.

109. Carpenter, *The Envy of the World*, p. 9.

110. Desmond Shawe-Taylor, *New Statesman*, 5 October 1946, quoted in Carpenter, *The Envy of the World*, p. 35.

111. *Radio Times* schedules.

112. *Radio Times*, issue dated 30 October 1953.

113. See William Mann, 'Ten Years of LP: the Artistic Achievement', *The Gramophone*, vol. 38, no. 445, June 1960, p. 2.

114. See main entry 'Mahler' and entry in Supplement of Francis F. Clough and G. J. Cuming, *The World's Encyclopedia of Recorded Music* (London, 1952; with *First Supplement*); also J. F. Weber, *Mahler: Discography Series IX* (Utica, NY, 1971).

115. John Snashall, 'The Nixa/Pye story: part one', *International Classical Record Collector*, vol. 1, no. 1, May 1995, pp. 8–17.

116. Those American labels widely available in the UK at this time are listed in Sackville-West and Shawe-Taylor, *The Record Guide* (revised edition, 1955), pp. 19–23.

117. David Hall and Abner Levin, 'Record Manufacturers – a Panorama', *The Disc Book* (New York, 1955), pp. 15–35.

118. Graham Silcock, 'Seeking Haydn', *International Classical Record Collector*, vol. 3, no. 10, Autumn 1997, p. 39.

119. Desmond Shawe-Taylor, *The Observer*, 17 May 1953, quoted in Harley Usill, 'A History of Argo: problems of a specialist record company', *Recorded Sound*, no. 78, July 1980, pp. 32–3 (edited transcript of a talk given at the British Institute of Recorded Sound (National Sound Archive) on 23 May 1978; BLNSA Tape T2049).

120. Robert Angus, 'Urania: the Mystery Label that Keeps Coming Back', *International Classical Record Collector*, vol. 2, no. 6, Autumn 1996, pp. 18–19.

121. Ibid., p. 19.

122. Leslie Gerber, 'Classical LPs of Great Price', *International Classical Record Collector*, vol. 3, no. 12, Spring 1998, p. 36.

123. Silcock, *International Classical Record Collector*, Autumn 1997, p. 38.

124. Mark W. Kluge, 'Tales from the Vienna Studios', *International Classical Record Collector*, vol. 3, no. 11, Winter 1997, p. 62.

125. Ibid., p. 62.

126. Ibid., p. 62.

127. Ibid., p. 62.

128. H. C. Robbins Landon in Silcock, *International Classical Record Collector*, Autumn 1997, pp. 38–9.

129. Silcock, *International Classical Record Collector*, Autumn 1997, pp. 4–44.

130. A list of the Haydn Society LP records is given in Biba and Wyn Jones (eds), *Studies in Music History presented to H. C. Robbins Landon* (London and New York, 1996), p. 230.

131. Silcock, *International Classical Record Collector*, Autumn 1997, p. 44.

132. H. C. Robbins Landon, 'Haydn on record: I', *Early Music*, vol. 10, no. 3, July 1982, p. 351.

133. Ibid., p. 351.

134. Robert C. Marsh and Andrea McMahon, 'Discoveries for Haydn Seekers', *High Fidelity*, April 1972, pp. 75–8.

135. Robbins Landon, *Early Music*, July 1982, p. 352.

136. Usill, *Recorded Sound*, no. 78, pp. 32–3.

137. Robbins Landon, *Early Music*, July 1982, pp. 351–2.

138. Edward Greenfield, *The Gramophone*, vol. 48, no. 576, May 1971, p. 1779.

139. Compton Mackenzie, *The Gramophone*, vol. 32, no. 373, June 1954, p. 1.

140. Paul Johnson, 'Introduction: Britain 1900–1990', in Paul Johnson (ed.), *20th Century Britain: Economic, Social and Cultural Change* (London, 1994), p. 10.

141. Ralph W. Wood, 'The Future of Music-Making', *The Musical Times*, vol. 80, no. 1152, February 1939, p. 95.

142. Frank Howes, *The Borderland of Music and Psychology* (London, 1926), p. 37.

143. Robert and Celia Dearling with Brian Rust, *The Guinness Book of Recorded Sound* (Enfield, 1984), p. 53, p. 60.

144. Johnson (ed.), *20th Century Britain: Economic, Social and Cultural Change*, p. 256.

145. See Paul Campion and Rosy Runciman, *Glyndebourne Recorded: Sixty Years of Recordings 1934–1994* (London, 1994), pp. 9–10.

146. H. F. V. Little in *The Gramophone*, vol. 13, no. 152, January 1936, p. 331.

147. Spike Hughes, *A History of the Festival Opera* (London, 1965, third impression 1982), p. 51.

148. Gelatt, *The Fabulous Phonograph*, p. 223.

149. Ibid., p. 293.

150. *The Gramophone*, vol. 31, no. 366, November 1953, p. 202.

151. *BPI Year Book 1977* (London, 1977), p. 142.

152. *BPI Statistical Handbook 1996* (London, 1996), p. 16.

153. Dearling, Dearling and Rust, *The Guinness Book of Recorded Sound*, p. 202.

154. See Ivan March (ed.), *The Penguin Guide to Bargain Records* (Harmondsworth, 1966), pp. vii–x.

155. Stephen Plaistow reviewing Vox VBX 418/1–3 (3 12" 33⅓ rpm mono discs), recordings of Alfred Brendel playing Beethoven, *The Gramophone*, vol. 42, no. 493, June 1964, p. 12.

156. March, *The Penguin Guide to Bargain Records* (1965), p. 161.

157. Ibid., p. 114.

158. Guy Routh, *Occupation and Pay in Great Britain 1906–79* (London, 1980), pp. 166, 168.

159. Ferdynand Zweig, *The New Acquisitive Society* (Chichester and London, 1976), p. 24.

160. R. R. Terry, *On Music's Borders* (London, 1927), pp. 12–13.

161. Jacques Barzun, *Pleasures of Music: An Anthology of Writing about Music and Musicians* (London, 1952/1977), p. ix.

162. Ibid., p. ix.

163. George Steiner, 'The Retreat from the Word' [1961], *Language and Silence* (London, 1967), pp. 48–9.

164. E. H. Gombrich, 'The tradition of General Knowledge' (Oration delivered at the London School of Economics and Political Science on 8 December 1961), *Ideals and Idols: Essays on Values in History and in Art* (London, 1979), pp. 16–17.

165. Anthony Pollard, *The Gramophone*, December 1972, pp. 1119–20.

166. Full-page advertisement in *The Gramophone*, vol. 32, no. 378, November 1954, p. xix.

167. Ibid., p. xix.

168. Ibid., p. xix.

169. Richard Wagner, *Wagner on Conducting* [translated by Edward Dannreuther] (Leipzig, 1869; Dover edition 1989, a slightly corrected re-publication of *On Conducting (Über das Dirigiren): A Treatise on Style in the Execution of Classical Music*, originally published by William Reeves, London, in 1887), p. 8.

170. John Culshaw, *Ring Resounding: The Recording in Stereo of Der Ring des Nibelungen* (London, 1967), p. 16.

171. John Culshaw, *Putting the Record Straight* (London, 1982), pp. 140–1.

172. Fred W. Gaisberg, *Music on Record* (London, 1946), pp. 186–7.

173. Robert Baldock, *Pablo Casals* (London, 1992), p. 156.

174. Clifford Curzon, *The Gramophone*, vol. xlviii, no. 574, May 1971, p. 1764.

175. Kurt List, *Recorded High Fidelity* (New York, 1954), pp. 5–6.

176. Robbins Landon, *Early Music*, July 1982, p. 351.

177. James Badal, 'An Interview with Erich Leinsdorf', *Fanfare*, vol. 8, no. 1 (1984), p. 124.

178. Quoted in Howard Shanet, *Philharmonic: A History of New York's Orchestra* (New York, 1975), p. 277.

179. Archiv Produktion: Introduction to the 1963 Catalogue, p. 8.

180. Alec Robertson, *The Gramophone*, vol. 31, no. 361, June 1953, p. 3.

181. Alec Robertson, 'A New Age in Recorded Music', *The Musical Times*, vol. 94, no. 1323, May 1953, p. 209.

182. Meirion Bowen, 'Tributes to David Munrow', *Early Music*, vol. 4, no. 3, July 1976, p. 379.

183. 'David Munrow talks to Alan Blyth', *Gramophone*, vol. 52, no. 613, May 1974, p. 2009.

184. John Currie, 'Tributes to David Munrow', *Early Music*, vol. 4, no. 3, July 1976, p. 379.

185. Hugh Keyte, reviewing *Music of the Gothic Era* (DG Archiv Produktion set 2723 045 (3 33⅓ rpm stereo discs)), *Gramophone*, vol. 54, no. 642, November 1976, p. 862.

186. Alan Blyth, 'David Munrow', *Gramophone*, May 1974, p. 2010.

187. David Munrow Artist File, EMI Music Archive; reproduced in Peter Martland, *Since Records Began: EMI* (London, 1997), p. 292.

188. Bernard Levin, 'Farewell to a Friendly Pied Piper', *Taking Sides* (London, 1979), pp. 255–6 (originally in *The Times*, 18 May 1976).

189. Blyth, 'David Munrow', *Gramophone*, May 1974, p. 2009.

190. Christopher Monk, 'Tributes to David Munrow', *Early Music*, vol. 4, no. 3, July 1976, p. 379.

191. Pierre Boulez, 'Incipit' (1952), *Stocktakings from an Apprenticeship*, collected by Paule Thévenin and translated by Stephen Walsh (Oxford, 1991), p. 215. (First published as *Relevés d'apprenti* (Paris, 1966).)

192. Herbert Eimert, 'A change of focus', in Herbert Eimert and Karlheinz Stockhausen (eds), *Die Reihe: Anton Webern* (Bryn Mawr, Pennsylvania, 2/1959), p. 29. (First published in German in Vienna in 1955.)

193. Robert Craft, interview with Gwyn L. Williams for use in a five-programme series 'This Week's Composers: Schoenberg, Berg, and Webern' first broadcast on BBC Radio 3 between 29 September and 3 October 1997; BLNSA Tape C851.

194. Igor Stravinsky and Robert Craft, *Conversations with Igor Stravinsky* (London, 1959), p. 71.

195. Robert Craft, interview with Gwyn L. Williams; BLNSA Tape C851.

196. *Melos*, 24, no. 10 (October, 1957), pp. 304–5.

197. Jeremy Noble, *The Gramophone*, vol. 37, no. 439, December 1959, p. 306.
198. Ibid., p. 307.
199. Max Hinrichsen (ed.), 'The British Council and Music', *Hinrichsen's Musical Year Book 1949–50*, p. 204.
200. David Drew, *The Gramophone*, vol. 42, no. 500, January 1965, p. 322.
201. Ibid., p. 322.
202. William Glock, *Notes in Advance: An Autobiography in Music* (London, 1991), p. 58.
203. Ibid., p. 113.
204. Ibid., p. 115.
205. Ibid., p. 115.
206. Ibid., p. 114.
207. Nicholas Kenyon, *The BBC Symphony Orchestra 1930–1980* (London, 1981), p. 341.
208. William Glock quoted in Kenyon, *The BBC Symphony Orchestra 1930–1980*, pp. 305–6.
209. Glock, *Notes in Advance*, p. 115.
210. Nicolas Slonimsky, *Music since 1900* (London, 4/1971), p. 460.
211. Elliott Carter, 'Document of a Friendship with Charles Ives', Else Stone and Kurt Stone (comps), *The Writings of Elliott Carter* (Bloomington and London, 1977), p. 333.
212. David Hall, 'New Music Quarterly Recordings – a Discography', *Association for Recorded Sound Collections Journal*, vol. xvi, no. 1–2, 1984, p. 10.
213. Entry in Guy A. Marco (ed.), *Encyclopedia of Recorded Sound in America* (London and New York, 1993).
214. Entry for 'New Music Quarterly Recordings' in Marco (ed.), *Encyclopedia of Recorded Sound in America*.
215. Jed Distler, 'The Slonimsky Recordings', *International Classical Record Collector*, vol. 2, no. 6, Autumn 1996, pp. 32–7.
216. David Sachs, 'CRI at 30: Celebration and Challenge', *Fanfare*, vol. 8, no. 1 (1984), pp. 146–8.
217. Introduction to *NMC Recordings CD Catalogue 1994–5*.
218. Elisabeth Ostrow, 'A Note on New World Records, Recorded Anthology of American Music', in Charles Hamm, *Music in the New World* (New York, 1983), p. 693; the success of the projected 100 discs led to the continuation of the series on a commercial basis; the contents of the 12″ 33⅓ rpm stereo discs NW 201 to NW 316/317 are listed in Charles Hamm's book, pp. 695–703, and the latest catalogue is dated 1999.
219. Hans Heinz Stuckenschmidt, 'The Mechanization of Music', in *Pult und Taktstock*, no. 1 (1925), reprinted in Harry Haskell, *The Attentive Listener* (London and Boston, 1995), pp. 274–6.
220. Recorded by Georges Laurent and the Burgin Quartet on American Columbia 68186D in Columbia set M 191 (4 12″ double-sided electrical 78 rpm discs).
221. Stravinsky, *An Autobiography*, pp. 123–4; recorded by the composer on Columbia LF 139/40 (2 10″ double-sided electrical 78 rpm discs).
222. Herbert Eimert, 'What is electronic music', in Herbert Eimert and Karlheinz Stockhausen (eds), *Die Reihe I* (Bryn Mawr, Pennsylvania, 1958), p. 4. (First published in German in Vienna in 1955.)
223. DGG LP17243 (12″ 33⅓ rpm mono disc).
224. Nonesuch H–71250 (12″ 33⅓ rpm stereo disc).
225. Nonesuch H–71223 (12″ 33⅓ rpm stereo disc).
226. Nonesuch H–71231 (12″ 33⅓ rpm stereo disc).
227. Nonesuch H–71174 (12″ 33⅓ rpm stereo disc).
228. Nonesuch H–71208 (12″ 33⅓ rpm stereo disc).
229. Nonesuch H–71225 (12″ 33⅓ rpm stereo disc).
230. Liner-notes for Nonesuch H–71225 (12″ 33⅓ rpm stereo disc).
231. Alexander Goehr, 'An Orchid in the Land of Technology', Lecture 2 of the 1987 Reith Lectures: 'The Survival of the Symphony', *The Listener*, 26 November 1987, p. 18.
232. Ibid., p. 18.
233. Herbert Eimert, 'What is Electronic Music', *Die Reihe I*, p. 10.
234. William Brooks, 'The Americas, 1945–70', in Robert P. Morgan (ed.), *Music and Society: Modern Times – From World War I to the present* (Englewood Cliffs, New Jersey, 1993), p. 311.
235. Aaron Copland, *Music and Imagination* (Cambridge, Mass./London, 1952), p. 109.
236. Ibid., pp. 109–10.
237. Pierre Boulez, *Pierre Boulez: Conversations with Célestin Deliège* (London, 1976), p. 77.
238. Copland, *Music and Imagination*, p. 109.
239. Michael Tippett, 'A Composer and His Public', *Moving into Aquarius* (St Albans, 2/1974), p. 100.
240. Michael Tippett, 'Desert Island Discs', BBC Radio 4, 5 January 1985: BLNSA Tape T7465BW.
241. See Edward Greenfield, Robert Layton

and Ivan March, *The Penguin Guide to Compact Discs* (Harmondsworth, 1990), pp. viii–ix.

242. Nick Kimberley, 'Biddulph', *BBC Music Magazine*, October 1995, p. 15.

243. John Culshaw, *Putting the Record Straight* (London, 1982), pp. 144–5.

244. Ibid., p. 146.

245. *EMI Classics 1995 International Compact Disc Catalogue*.

246. Robert Cowan, 'Sound and Vision: the Loner's Guide', *The Independent*, 2 April 1997.

247. Garry Booth, 'The Eclectic Edge', *BBC Music Magazine*, July 1994, p. 13.

248. Nick Kimberley, 'More than a Mere Caprice', *BBC Music Magazine*, April 1995, p. 16.

249. Ibid., p. 16.

250. C. H. H. Parry, *Johann Sebastian Bach: The Story of the Development of a Great Personality* (London, 1909/1934), pp. 548–9.

251. Carpenter, *The Envy of the World*, p. 46.

252. Ton Koopman, 'Recording Bach's Early Cantatas', *Early Music*, vol. 24, no. 4, November 1996, pp. 605–19 (first three volumes are vol. 1: Erato 4509–98536–2 (3 digital stereo CDs); vol. 2: Erato 0630–12598–2 (3 digital stereo CDs); vol. 3: Erato 0630–14336–2 (3 digital stereo CDs).

253. See Leon Botstein, 'Music, Technology, and the Public', *The Musical Quarterly*, vol. 78, no. 2, Summer 1994, pp. 181–8.

254. John Drummond, in Carpenter, *The Envy of the World*, p. 336.

255. Leonard Bernstein, *The Joy of Music* (London, 1959/1974 ed.), p. 151.

III Changes in Performing Styles Recorded

1. Landon Ronald, *Variations on a Personal Theme* (London, 1922), pp. 103–4.

2. John Harvith and Susan Edwards Harvith, *Edison, Musicians, and the Phonograph: A Century in Retrospect* (New York, Westport, Connecticut, London, 1987), pp. 93–5.

3. HMV set SLS 1435843 (3 12-inch 33⅓ rpm digital stereo discs; recorded at live performances at La Scala during December 1982).

4. HMV D 1281/2 (2 12″ double-sided

electrical 78 rpm discs); see E. A. Hughes and A. E. Cooban, 'Violet Gordon Woodhouse: a Discography', *Recorded Sound*, no. 41, January 1971, pp. 727–9.

5. HMV D 2014/5 (2 12″ electrical 78 rpm discs).

6. Robert Philip, *Early Recordings and Musical Style: Changing Tastes in Instrumental Performance 1900–1950* (Cambridge, 1992), pp. 160–3.

7. HMV DB 1259/61 (3 12″ electrical 78 rpm discs).

8. Menahem Pressler quoted in Nicholas Delbanco, *The Beaux Arts Trio* (London, 1985), p. 174.

9. Ibid., p. 174.

10. Grammophon 040784/91 (8 12″ single-sided acoustic 78 rpm discs; released in England May–August 1914).

11. Archiv 439 900–2 (digital stereo CD; recorded at a live performance in March 1994).

12. John Steane, *The Grand Tradition* (London, 2/1993), pp. 599–600.

13. Ibid., p. 600.

14. See, for example, Robert Philip, 'The Recordings of Edward Elgar (1857–1934): Authenticity and Performance Practice', *Early Music*, vol. 12, no. 4, November 1984, pp. 481–9; John Milsom, 'Organ Music I', in Peter Hill (ed.), *The Messiaen Companion* (London, 1995), pp. 51–71; László Somfai, 'The Significance of Bartók's Own Recordings', *Béla Bartók: Composition, Concepts, and Autograph Sources* (Berkeley, 1996), pp. 279–95.

15. Philip, 'The Recordings of Edward Elgar', *Early Music*, November 1984, p. 485.

16. HMV C 2085 (12″ double-sided electrical 78 rpm disc).

17. HMV CSD 1595 (12″ 33⅓ rpm stereo disc).

18. RCA set LRL2 5120 (2 12″ 33⅓ rpm stereo discs).

19. EMI CDC 7 54412 2 (digital stereo CD).

20. ARGO ZRG 528 (12″ 33⅓ rpm stereo disc).

21. See Henry Pleasants, 'Tracking Down the Oldest Singing Voice', *Recorded Sound*, 85, January 1984, pp. 12–16.

22. Will Crutchfield, 'The Nineteenth Century: Voices', in Howard Mayer Brown and Stanley Sadie (eds), *Performance Practice: Music after 1600* (London, 1989), pp. 452–5.

23. Will Crutchfield, 'Vocal Ornamentation in Verdi: the Phonographic Evidence',

19th-Century Music, vol. vii, no. 1, Summer 1983, p. 18.

24. James Methuen-Campbell, *Chopin Playing from the Composer to the Present Day* (London, 1981), p. 71.

25. Runolfur Thordarson, 'Discography: Works by Liszt Played by his Pupils', *Journal of the American Liszt Society*, vol. 31, January–June 1992, pp. 47–55.

26. H. C. Deacon, *Grove's Dictionary of Music and Musicians*, first edition (London, 1890), vol. 4, p. 260.

27. H. C. Colles, *Grove's Dictionary of Music and Musicians*, third edition (London, 1928), vol. 5, p. 494.

28. James Methuen-Campbell, 'Chopin in Performance', in Jim Samson (ed.), *The Cambridge Companion to Chopin* (Cambridge, 1992), pp. 191–2.

29. Bernard D. Sherman, 'Tempos and Proportions in Brahms: Period Evidence', *Early Music*, vol. 25, no. 3, August 1997, p. 464.

30. Richard Taruskin, *Text and Act: Essays on Music and Performance* (Oxford, 1995), pp. 133–5.

31. Sherman, 'Tempos and Proportions in Brahms', *Early Music*, August 1997, p. 464.

32. Robert Philip, *Early Recordings and Musical Style*, p. 212.

33. Flesch, *Memoirs*, p. 50, quoted in Philip, *Early Recordings and Musical Style*, p. 160.

34. HMV ASD 2783 (12″ 33⅓ rpm stereo disc).

35. Virgin Classics VC 7 59319 2 (digital stereo CD).

36. HMV DB 2588 (12″ double-sided electrical 78 rpm disc).

37. DGG set 104962–5 (4 12″ 33⅓ rpm stereo discs).

38. L'Oiseau Lyre 421 333–2 (digital stereo CD).

39. G. S. R. Kitson Clark, 'The Romantic Element – 1830–1850', in J. H. Plumb (ed.), *Studies in Social History: A Tribute to G. M. Trevelyan* (London, 1955), pp. 228–9.

40. A. H. Fox Strangways, *Grove's Dictionary of Music and Musicians*, third edition (1928), vol. 4, p. 465.

41. Philip, 'The Recordings of Edward Elgar', *Early Music*, November 1984, p. 484.

42. Jerrold Northrop Moore, *Elgar on Record* (London, 1974), p. 195.

43. Richard Wagner, *Wagner on Conducting* [translated by Edward Dannreuther] (Leipzig, 1869; Dover edition 1989, a slightly corrected re-publication of *On Conducting (Über das Dirigiren): A Treatise on Style in the Execution of Classical Music*, originally published by William Reeves, London, in 1887), p. 49.

44. Daniel Koury, *Orchestral Performance Practices in the Nineteenth Century: Size, Proportions, and Seating* (Ann Arbor, 1986), p. 74.

45. Nicholas Cook, *Beethoven: Symphony no. 9* (Cambridge, 1993), pp. 49–51.

46. Anton Seidl, quoted ibid., p. 50.

47. Henry Smart, quoted ibid., p. 50.

48. Ernest Walker, 'An Orchestra of the Past', *Free Thought and The Musician* (London, 1946), p. 141.

49. Ibid., p. 142.

50. Ibid., pp. 141–2.

51. Ibid., p. 142.

52. Ernest Walker, 'Some Questions of Tempo', ibid., pp. 134–5.

53. Fred Gaisberg, *Music on Record* (London, 1946), p. 227.

54. Ignacy Jan Paderewski, 'Tempo Rubato', originally written for *Success in Music and How it is Won* by Henry T. Finck (New York, 1909); reprinted in Ronald Stevenson, *The Paderewski Paradox* (Lincoln, 1992), p. 26.

55. Quoted in Stevenson, *The Paderewski Paradox*, p. 44.

56. Charles Tournemire, *César Franck* (Paris, 1931), p. 50.

57. Ibid., pp. 49–50.

58. Gerald Abraham, *The Tradition of Western Music* (Berkeley, 1974), p. 3.

59. András Schiff in Hilary Finch, 'Still Life with Colourful Piano', an interview with András Schiff, *The Times*, August 7 1997.

60. Ibid.

61. Taruskin, *Text and Act*, p. 188.

62. Philip, *Early Recordings and Musical Style*, p. 92.

63. Columbia 4211 (10″ double-sided electrical 78 rpm disc; issued 1927).

64. W. Somerset Maugham, *The Summing Up* (London, 1938), p. 119.

65. Walford Davies, 'About Church Music', *The Musical Times*, vol. 73, no. 1072, June 1932, p. 505.

66. Ibid., p. 505.

67. Walter Legge in William Mann, 'Ten Years of LP: The Artistic Achievement', *The Gramophone*, vol. 38, no. 445, June 1960, p. 5.

68. Ibid., p. 5.

69. Thomas Frost in Harvith and Harvith, *Edison, Musicians, and the Phonograph*, p. 355.

70. Decca SXDL 7593 (12″ 33⅓ rpm digital stereo disc).

71. Erato 4509–92887–2 (digital stereo CD).

72. Olympia set OCD 289 (2 digital stereo CDs).

73. Philip, *Early Recordings and Musical Style*, p. 92.

74. Sir Henry Wood, *The Gentle Art of Singing* (London, 1927), p. 87.

75. HMV DB 970/4 (5 double-sided electrical 78 rpm discs).

76. HMV D 1154/7 (4 12″ double-sided electrical 78 rpm discs).

77. HMV ALP 1998/ASD 548 (12″ 33⅓ rpm mono/stereo disc).

78. Lorin Maazel, *The Gramophone*, vol. 48, no. 574, March 1971, p. 1449.

79. David Hamilton in H. Wiley Hitchcock (ed.), *The Phonograph and Our Musical Life: Proceedings of a Centennial Conference 7–10 December 1977*, I.S.A.M. Monographs: Number 14 (Institute for Studies in American Music, Department of Music, School of Performing Arts, Brooklyn College, City University of New York, New York, 1980), pp. 69–70.

80. Hans Keller, 'Furtwängler 1886–1954: an Appreciation', *Opera*, February 1955; reprinted in *Opera*, April 1986, p. 383.

81. Alfred Brendel, 'A Case for Live Recordings' [1983], in *Music Sounded Out* (London, 1990), pp. 200–1.

82. Christopher Hogwood in James Badel, 'On Record: Christopher Hogwood', *Fanfare*, vol. 9, no. 2, November/December 1985, p. 90.

83. Joseph Horowitz, *Conversations with Arrau* (2/1992, New York), p. 92.

84. Alan Blyth, *Gramophone*, vol. 58, no. 694, March 1981, p. 1223.

85. Basil Tschaikov in *The Evolution of the Symphony Orchestra: History, Problems and Agenda* (the report of a conference sponsored by the Wheatland Foundation held in Jerusalem in December 1986) (London, 1990), p. 13.

86. Brendel, *Music Sounded Out*, p. 206.

87. Ibid., p. 207.

88. Barry Millington, reviewing recitals of Beethoven violin sonatas at the Barbican Hall in London in October 1998, *The Times*, 21 October 1998.

89. Herbert Read, *English Prose Style* (London, 2/1952), p. 173.

90. Alfred Einstein, *A Short History of Music* (London, 1936), p. 200. (First published as *Geschichte der Musik* (Leipzig/Berlin, 1918).)

91. *Conversations with Arrau*, by Joseph Horowitz (New York, 2/1992), pp. 111–12.

92. Edwin Fischer, *Beethoven's Pianoforte Sonatas: A Guide for Students and Amateurs*, translated by Stanley Godman with the collaboration of Paul Hamburger (London, 1959), p. 94. (First published as *Ludwig van Beethovens Klaviersonaten: Ein Begleiter für Studierende und Liebhaber* (Wiesbaden, 1956).)

93. Ibid., p. 68.

94. Alfred Brendel, 'Werktreue – an Afterthought', in *Musical Thoughts and Afterthoughts* (London, 1976), p. 27.

95. Quoted in Ian Kemp, *Hindemith* (London, 1970), p. 7.

96. Hermann Scherchen, *Handbook of Conducting* (London, 1933), pp. 27–8.

97. Wanda Landowska, 'Bach's Keyboard Instruments', in *Landowska on Music*, collected, edited and translated by Denise Restout assisted by Robert Hawkins (London, 1965), p. 149.

98. Telefunken AZ6 42935 (12″ 33⅓ rpm digital stereo disc).

99. Edward T. Cone, *Musical Form and Musical Performance* (New York, 1968), p. 59; see Taruskin, *Text and Act*, in which this passage by Edward T. Cone is quoted at page 115.

100. Arnold Dolmetsch, *The Interpretation of the Music of the XVIIth and XVIIIth Centuries Revealed by Contemporary Evidence* (London, 1915), p. 284.

101. Ibid., pp. 6–7.

102. Arnold Schoenberg, 'Today's Manner of Performing Classical Music: 1948', *Style and Idea: Selected writings of Arnold Schoenberg*, edited by Leonard Stein and translated by Leo Black (London, 1975), p. 320.

103. Darius Milhaud, 'French Music since the War', in *Études*, 1927; quoted in Percy A. Scholes, *The Columbia History of Music Through Ear and Eye: Period V: The Twentieth Century* (London, 1938), p. 65.

104. Erik Satie, postscript to 'Choral Hypocrite', no. 1 of *Choses vues à droite et à gauche (sans lunettes)* for violin and piano.

105. Cyril Scott, *My Years of Indiscretion* (London, 1924), p. 100.

106. Eric Walter White, *Stravinsky: The Composer and his Works* (London, 1966, 2/1979), p. 80.

107. Arthur Schopenhauer, *Die Welt als Wille und Vorstellung*, vol. 2, p. 307, lines 29–31, in *Sämtliche Werke*, ed. Arthur

Hübscher, 2nd ed. (Wiesbaden, 1946–50).

108. Igor Stravinsky, *Poetics of Music in Form of Six Lessons* (bilingual edition, Cambridge, Mass., 1970), p. 49. (First published as *Poétique musicale* (Cambridge, Mass., 1942; first published in English in 1947).)

109. Arthur Honegger, *I am a Composer*, translated by Wilson O. Clough in collaboration with Allan Arthur Willman (London, 1966), p. 79. (First published as *Je suis compositeur* (Paris, 1951).)

110. Igor Stravinsky, *An Autobiography* (London, 1975), p. 118. (First published as *Chroniques de ma vie* (Paris, 1935); first published in English in 1936.)

111. Ibid., p. 118.

112. Manfred Bukofzer, *Music in the Baroque Era* (London, 1948), pp. xiii–xiv.

113. Alexander Goehr, 'A Letter to Pierre Boulez', *Finding the Key: Selected Writings of Alexander Goehr* (London, 1998), pp. 5–6.

114. Ibid., p. 19.

115. From the introduction to a performance of Boulez's *Structures*, Book I; BBC Third Programme, 18 March 1957; BBC Sound Archives LP 23936 (12" 33⅓ rpm mono disc); the final sentence is a quotation from a letter to John Cage: see *The Boulez-Cage Correspondence*, edited by Jean-Jacques Nattiez, translated and edited by Robert Samuels (London, 1993), pp. 102–3. (First published as *Pierre Boulez/John Cage: Correspondance et documents* (Winterthur, Switzerland, 1990).)

116. Roger Smalley, 'Some Aspects of the Changing Relationship between Composer and Performer in Contemporary Music', *Proceedings of the Royal Musical Association*, no. 96, 1969–70, p. 75.

117. Stephen Pruslin, 'Maxwell Davies's Second Taverner Fantasia', *Tempo*, no. 73, Summer 1965, p. 2.

118. For styles in flute-playing during the first half of the century see Philip, *Early Recordings and Musical Style*, pp. 110–18.

119. Jack Brymer, *Clarinet* (London, 1990), pp. 204–5.

120. Phyllis Rose, *Jazz Cleopatra: Josephine Baker in Her Time* (London, 1990), p. 21.

121. Norman C. Nelson, 'King of the Clarinet: Reginald Kell remembered', *International Classical Record Collector*, vol. 4, no. 16, Spring 1999, pp. 36–46; two of Kell's most famous and characteristic recorded performances are of Brahms's Clarinet Quintet in B minor op. 115 with the Busch Quartet (HMV DB 3383/6 (4 12" double-sided electrical 78 rpm discs; issued in 1938)) and Mozart's Clarinet Quintet K.581 with the Philharmonia Quartet (Columbia DX 1187/90 (4 12" double-sided electrical 78 rpm discs; issued in 1945).)

122. Brymer, *Clarinet*, pp. 204–8.

123. Philip, *Early Recordings and Musical Style*, p. 210.

124. Carl Flesch, *The Art of Violin Playing*, translated by F. H. Martens (New York, 1924–30), I, p. 40. (First published as *Die Kunst des Violinspiels* (2 vols, Berlin, 1923–8).)

125. Nelson, 'King of the Clarinet: Reginald Kell remembered', *International Classical Record Collector*, Spring 1999, pp. 36, 38.

126. Leon Goossens in Leon Goossens and Edwin Roxburgh, *Oboe* (London, 1977), p. 87.

127. Northrop Moore, *Elgar on Record*, p. 194.

128. Sir Michael Tippett in *Alfred Deller (1912–1979)*, BBC Radio 3, May 14 1980, BLNSA Tape T3087BW.

129. Alfred Deller in Michael and Mollie Hardwick, *Alfred Deller: A Singularity of Voice* (London and New York, 1980), p. 94.

130. Tippett in *Alfred Deller (1912–1979)*, BLNSA Tape T3087BW.

131. James Bowman in Michael Church, 'Living the High Life', *The Independent*, 5 March 1999.

132. Sir David Willcocks in talk: 'The choir of King's College, Cambridge', BBC Transcription Service disc 134648 [side number] (12" 33⅓ rpm mono disc; issued 1974).

133. George Guest in an interview with Bernard Keefe, BBC Radio 3, 12 December 1991, BLNSA Tape B8899.

134. Victoria, *O Domine Jesu*, in *The History of Music in Sound*, vol. IV, side 6: HMV HMS 34 (12" double-sided electrical 78 rpm disc).

135. Decca LW 5070 (10" 33⅓ rpm mono disc).

136. Peter Phillips, 'The golden age regained, 2', *Early Music*, vol. 8, no. 2, April 1980, p. 181.

137. From the programme leaflet for a concert of music by Sheppard sung by the Clerkes at St John's, Smith Square, London, on 7 December 1986, quoted in Timothy Day, *A Discography of Tudor Church Music* (London, 1989), p. 36.

138. David Fallows, *Gramophone*, vol. 56, no. 672, May 1979, p. 1926, reviewing Argo ZRG 897 (12" 33⅓ rpm stereo disc).

139. Bowman can be heard as a soloist at this time singing with the choir of New College, in Gibbons's *See, see, the word is incarnate* and in Byrd's *Lullaby, my sweet little baby* on Abbey 652 (12″ 33⅓ rpm stereo disc; issued 1968); the way in which his voice could suffuse an ensemble is heard strikingly on Abbey 603/S603 (12″ 33⅓ rpm mono/stereo disc).

140. A list of commercial recordings and tapes of broadcasts given by the Clerkes of Oxenford is given in Day, *A Discography of Tudor Church Music*, pp. 295–6.

141. They were given their fullest treatment in David Wulstan, 'A High Clear Voice', *Tudor Music* (London, 1985), pp. 192–249.

142. Roger Bowers, 'The Performing Pitch of English Fifteenth-Century Church Polyphony', *Early Music*, vol. 8, no. 1, January 1980, p. 25.

143. Roger Bowers, on Latin Church Polyphony in England, c.1500–58, *Journal of the Royal Musical Association*, vol. 112, part 1, 1987, p. 46, footnote 20.

144. Ibid., p. 53, footnote 36.

145. Ibid., p. 48, footnote 24.

146. Ibid., p. 48, footnote 23.

147. See Day, *A Discography of Tudor Church Music*.

148. Gustav Leonhardt, 'One Should Not Make a Rule', in Bernard D. Sherman, *Inside Early Music: Conversations with Performers* (New York, Oxford, 1997), pp. 203–4.

149. The Early Music Consort of London/David Munrow, *The Art of Courtly Love*, EMI set BOX 86301 (3-disc set SLS 863 (3 12″ 33⅓ rpm stereo discs).)

150. All the above are from *The Mirror of Narcissus: Songs by Guillaume de Machaut (1300–1377)*, Gothic Voices with Emma Kirkby (soprano), Christopher Page (director), Hyperion A66087 (12″ 33⅓ rpm stereo disc; recorded 7,8 April 1983).

151. Most of these ideas about performances of Machaut are Christopher Page's and were presented by him in a lecture with recorded illustrations given at the National Sound Archive on 16 October 1984: BLNSA Tape T8791W; a recent discography is in Lawrence Earp, *Guillaume de Machaut: A Guide to Research* (New York and London, 1995), pp. 389–445.

152. David Munrow on p. 10 of the booklet accompanying *The Art of Courtly Love*,

153. EMI BOX 86301, set SLS 863 (3 12″ 33⅓ rpm stereo discs).

153. David Munrow, *Instruments of the Middle Ages and Renaissance* (London, 1976), p. 5.

154. Rudolf von Ficker, 'Polyphonic Music of the Gothic Period', *The Musical Quarterly*, vol. 15, no. 4, October 1929, p. 505.

155. Desmond Shawe-Taylor, *The Record Guide* (revised edition) (London, 1955), p. 873.

156. Martin Cooper, *The Listener*, April 26 1951, p. 684.

157. Harry Haskell, *The Early Music Revival: A History* (London, 1/1988), pp. 109–11.

158. Gustave Reese, *Music in the Middle Ages* (New York, 1940), p. 353.

159. Liner note on *Ah Sweet Lady: The Romance of Medieval France*, New York Pro Musica, John White, Decca DL 79431 (12″ 33⅓ rpm stereo disc; released 1967).

160. Johan Huizinga, *The Waning of the Middle Ages* (Harmondsworth, 1990), p. 257. (First published as *Herfsttif der Middeleeuwen* (Haarlem, 1919; first English edition 1924).)

161. Christopher Page, 'The English *a cappella* Renaissance', *Early Music*, vol. 21, no. 3, August 1993, p. 454.

162. See Thomas Binkley, 'Zur Aufführungspraxis der einstimmigen Musik des Mittelalters – ein Werkstattbericht', *Basler Jahrbuch für Historische Musikpraxis* I (1977), pp. 19–76; a list of Binkley's recordings is given on p. 76.

163. Telefunken Das Alte Werk AW6 41275 (12″ 33⅓ rpm stereo disc; issued 1975).

164. Otto Klemperer, in Peter Heyworth (ed.), *Conversations with Klemperer* (London, 1973), p. 76.

165. Igor Stravinsky and Robert Craft, *Themes and Conclusions* (London, 1972), p. 95.

166. Igor Stravinsky, 'Foreword', in Herbert Eimert and Karlheinz Stockhausen (eds), *Die Reihe: Anton Webern* (Bryn Mawr, Pennsylvania, 2/1959), p. vii. (First published in German in Vienna in 1955.)

167. Igor Stravinsky and Robert Craft, *Conversations with Igor Stravinsky* (London, 1959), p. 128.

168. György Ligeti, *György Ligeti in Conversation* (London, 1983), pp. 18–20.

169. Ibid., pp. 18–20.

170. Ibid., p. 20.

171. Ernst Laaff, 'Vom Beginn des 20. Jahrhunderts bis zur Gegenwart', in entry under 'Deutschland', *Die Musik in*

Geschichte und Gegenwart, vol. 3 (Basel, 1954), pp. 343ff.

172. Philips set L 09414–7L (4 12″ 33⅓ rpm mono discs).

173. Jeremy Noble, *The Gramophone*, vol. 37, no. 439, December 1959, p. 307.

174. Véga C 30 A 66 (12″ 33⅓ rpm mono disc).

175. Véga C 30 I 120 (12″ 33⅓ rpm mono disc).

176. Wilfrid Mellers, *Caliban Reborn* (London, 1968), p. 108.

177. Pierre Boulez, *Conversations with Célestin Deliège* (London, 1976), p. 79. (First published as *Par Volonté et par Hasard: Entretiens avec Célestin Deliège* (Paris, 1975).)

178. Pierre Boulez in Stephen Plaistow, 'Boulez at 70', *Gramophone*, vol. 72, no. 862, March 1995, p. 14.

179. Walter Kolneder, *Anton Webern: An Introduction to His Works* (London, 1968), p. 194.

180. Decca K904 (12″ double-sided electrical 78 rpm disc).

181. Letter to Reich dated 9 December 1939, quoted in Hans Moldenhauer in collaboration with Rosaleen Moldenhauer, *Anton von Webern: A Chronicle of His Life and Work* (London, 1978), p. 519.

182. Peter Stadlen, 'Serialism Reconsidered', *The Score*, February 1958, p. 12.

183. Ibid., p. 12.

184. Ibid., p. 13: a recording exists of Stadlen's performance of the Variations at the Darmstadt Summer School in 1948: BLNSA Tape M5645.

185. Hartmann, quoted in Moldenhauer, *Anton von Webern*, p. 542.

186. Hermann Scherchen, *Handbook of Conducting* (London, 1933), pp. 29, 31.

187. Ibid., p. 94; The British Library holds a tape of a radio broadcast of a performance of the cantata *Das Augenlicht* directed by Hermann Scherchen (Bavarian Radio Chorus and Orchestra, BBC Radio 3, 7 July 1967; BLNSA Tape M875W).

188. Otto Klemperer, in Peter Heyworth (ed.), *Conversations with Klemperer* (London, 1973), p. 76.

189. Edward Steuermann, quoted in Moldenhauer, *Anton Webern*, p. 460.

190. Peter Stadlen, 'Serialism Reconsidered', *The Score*, February 1958, p. 14.

191. Pierre Boulez, 'Proposals' (1948), *Stocktakings from an Apprenticeship*, collected by Paule Thévenin, translated by Stephen Walsh (London, 1991), p. 54. (First published as *Relevés d'apprenti* (Paris, 1966).)

192. Jonathan Harvey, 'Reflection after Composition', *Tempo*, no. 140, March 1982, p. 4.

193. Jonathan Harvey, *New Sounds, New Personalities: British Composers of the 1980s in Conversation with Paul Griffiths* (London, 1985), p. 52.

194. Jonathan Harvey, 'New Directions: A Manifesto', *Soundings*, no. 11, Winter 1983–4, p. 4.

195. Pierre Boulez, 'The Vestal Virgin and the Fire-Stealer: Memory, Creation and Authenticity', *Early Music*, vol. 18, no. 3, August 1990, p. 357.

196. H. C. Colles in *The Times*, 4 March 1929; reproduced in Jerrold Northrop Moore, *Edward Elgar: A Creative Life* (London, 1987), p. 779.

197. J. R. Schultz (trans.), 'An Unpublished Letter of Mozart', *Harmonicon*, 3 (1825), pp. 198–200.

198. Schlösser's account of the meeting with Beethoven is translated in Elliot Forbes (ed.), *Thayer's Life of Beethoven* (Princeton: Princeton University Press, 1964), p. 851; for the authoritative discussion of the authenticity of these two sources, see Maynard Solomon, 'Beethoven's Creative Process: A Two-Part Invention', in Solomon, *Beethoven Essays* (Cambridge, Mass.: Harvard University Press, 1988), pp. 126–38.

199. Busoni, *Sketch of a New Aesthetic of Music*, reprinted in *Three Classics in the Aesthetics of Music: Debussy, Busoni, and Ives* (Dover/1962), p. 84. (First published as *Entwurf einer neuen Ästhetik der Tonkunst* (Trieste, 1907); first published in English in 1911.)

200. Aaron Copland, *Music and Imagination* (Cambridge, Mass./London, 1952), p. 50.

201. See Nicholas Cook, *Music: A Very Short Introduction* (Oxford, 1998), pp. 65–70.

202. Letter dated 25 August 1945 from John Ireland to Sir Adrian Boult who had conducted a performance of Ireland's *These things shall be*; quoted in *Music and Friends: Letters to Adrian Boult*, ed. Jerrold Northrop Moore (London, 1979), p. 147.

203. Terry Coleman, 'Pierre de Résistance', *Guardian*, 13 January 1989.

204. Marguerite Long, *At the Piano with Ravel*, translated by Olive Senior-Ellis (London, 1973), p. 59. (First published as *Au piano avec Ravel* (Paris, 1971).)

205. Vera Stravinsky and Robert Craft, *Stravinsky in Pictures and Documents* (London, 1978), p. 281.

206. E. W. Galkin, *A History of Orchestral Conducting: In Theory and Practice* (New York, 1988), p. 583.

207. Letter dated 25 August 1945 from John Ireland to Sir Adrian Boult, quoted in Northrop Moore (ed.), *Music and Friends*, p. 147.

208. Northrop Moore (ed.), *Music and Friends*, p. 121.

209. R. Vaughan Williams, 'The letter and the spirit', *National Music and Other Essays* (Oxford, 2/1987), p. 124.

210. David Woolridge, *Conductor's World* (London, 1970), p. xi.

211. Quoted in Fanny Davies, 'Some personal recollections of Brahms as pianist and interpreter' (1905), *Cobbett's Cyclopedic Survey of Chamber Music* (London, 1929), p. 184.

212. S. Avins (ed.), *Johannes Brahms: Life and Letters*, translated by J. Eisinger and S. Avins, (Oxford, 1997), letter 433. Avins dates the letter January 1884.

213. Quoted in David Woolridge, *Conductor's World* (London, 1970), p. 109.

214. Quoted in John Bird, *Percy Grainger* (London, 1976), p. 117.

215. Maurice Dumesnil, 'Coaching with Debussy', *The Piano Teacher*, 5 (Evanston, USA), September/October 1962, part 1, quoted in Roger Nichols, *Debussy Remembered* (London, 1992), p. 161.

216. André Marchal and Felix Aprahamian (speakers), 'Interpreting César Franck', recorded at the British Institute of Recorded Sound, 38 Russell Square, London, on 15 October 1962; BLNSA Tape NP361.

217. BBC Radio 3, 4 November 1970; BLNSA Tape NP1625.

218. Milsom, *The Messiaen Companion*, p. 58.

219. Copland, *Music and Imagination*, pp. 49–50.

220. The fullest discography of Stravinsky's own recordings is Philip Stuart, *Igor Stravinsky: The Composer in the Recording Studio* (Westport, Connecticut/London, 1991).

221. Béla Bartók, 'A gépzene' (Machine Music), in *Szép Szo*, 1937 (Budapest), quoted in booklet accompanying box set of discs *Bartók at the Piano* – Hungaroton LPX 12326/33 (8 12" 33⅓ rpm mono discs).

222. Alan Walker (ed.), *Franz Liszt: the Man and His Music* (London, 1970), p. 28.

223. Carl Bamberger (ed.), *The Conductor's Art* (New York, 1965), p. 195.

224. Alfred Brendel, 'Liszt misunderstood' [1961], in *Musical Thoughts and Afterthoughts* (London, 1976), p. 81.

225. Part of the profile of the pianist provided in the programme book for a recital on 8 July 1961 at the Royal Festival Hall, London.

226. Neuhaus, ibid.

227. 'Notes of a Complete Recording of Beethoven's Piano Works' [1966], in Alfred Brendel, *Musical Thoughts and Afterthoughts*, p. 25.

228. Mstislav Rostropovich, 'Dear Ben', in Anthony Gishford (ed.), *Tribute to Benjamin Britten on his Fiftieth Birthday* (London, 1963), p. 17.

229. Claudio Arrau, in Joseph Horowitz, *Conversations with Arrau*, 2/1992 (New York), pp. 171–2.

230. Richard Morrison, *The Times*, 15 August 1998, p. 17.

231. Roger Norrington on pp. 30, 31 of the booklet accompanying EMI set CDC 7 49852 2; 6 digital stereo CDs, set released 1989; see Taruskin, *Text and Act*, pp. 230–4.

232. Pierre Boulez in Jean Vermeil, *Conversations with Boulez: Thoughts on Conducting*, translated by Camille Naish (Portland, Oregon, 1996), p. 63. (First published as *Conversations de Pierre Boulez sur la direction d'orchestre avec Jean Vermeil* (Paris, 1989).)

233. Aaron Copland, *Music and Imagination* (Cambridge, Mass/London, 1952), pp. 49–50.

234. Wanda Landowska, 'Tradition in the Interpretation of Music of the Past', in *Landowska on Music*, collected, edited and translated by Denise Restout assisted by Robert Hawkins (London, 1965), p. 96.

235. A. C. Boult, 'Casals as Conductor', *Music & Letters*, 4 (1923), p. 150.

236. Quoted in Horowitz, *Conversations with Arrau*, pp. 87–8.

237. G. F. Hartlaub, 'Zynismus als Kunstrichtung?' *Fragen an die Kunst: Studien zu Grenzproblemen* (Stuttgart, no date), p. 39; quoted in Stephen Hinton, 'Germany, 1918–45', in Robert P. Morgan (ed.), *Music and Society: Modern Times – From World War I to the Present* (Englewood Cliffs, New Jersey, 1993), p. 94.

238. Stravinsky, *Poetics*, p. 165.

239. Edward Elgar in a letter dated 16 April 1924 to Alice Stuart Wortley, in Jerrold Northrop Moore, *Edward Elgar: The Windflower: Letters to Alice Caroline Stuart Wortley and Her Family* (Oxford, 1989), p. 290.

240. Tournemire, *César Franck*, p. 8.

241. John Willett, *Art and Politics in the*

Weimar Period (New York: Pantheon, 1978), pp. 112, 161.

242. Quoted in Peter Heyworth, *Otto Klemperer: His Life and Times: Volume 1, 1885–1933* (Cambridge, 1983), p. 127.

243. Wilhelm Kemp in the *Blätter der Bücherstube*, no date (Wiesbaden), quoted in Peter Heyworth, *Otto Klemperer: Volume 1*, p. 127.

244. Lazare Saminsky, *Music of Our Day* (New York, 1932), pp. 299–300.

245. W. R. Anderson, reviewing Columbia LX35/8 (4 12" double-sided electrical 78 rpm discs), *The Gramophone*, vol. 8, no. 87, August 1930, p. 128.

246. 'C.J.', *The Gramophone*, vol. 6, no. 70, March 1929, p. 445.

247. 'Discus', *The Musical Times*, vol. 70, no. 1034, April 1929, p. 327.

248. Lionel Salter reviewing Biddulph LHW023 (mono CD), *Gramophone*, vol. 73, no. 866, July 1995, p. 132.

249. *Landowska on Music*, p. 356.

250. Bird, *Percy Grainger*, p. 118.

251. Ibid., p. 117.

252. Percy Grainger, recorded 16 May 1908; Pearl GEMM CD 9933 (mono CD).

253. Percy Grainger (piano), Hollywood Bowl Symphony Orchestra, Leopold Stokowski (conductor): International Piano Library IPA 508 (12" 33⅓ rpm mono disc; recorded 15 July 1945).

254. Percy Grainger (piano), Aarhus Municipal Orchestra, Per Drier (conductor):Vanguard VRS–1098 (12" 33⅓ rpm mono disc; recorded 25 February 1957). Grainger also made a piano roll of the Concerto with his own reduction of the orchestral part (Duo Art roll number 6475/79/85; issued in 1921), and this has been recorded by an orchestra with the piano roll orchestral reduction blocked out: Sydney Symphony Orchestra conducted by John Hopkins (RCA RL 10168 (12" 33⅓ rpm stereo disc; released 1978)). Grainger's roll was given a performance in this form by the BBC Symphony Orchestra conducted by Andrew Davis at a Henry Wood Promenade Concert in the Royal Albert Hall, London, on 17 September 1988 (BLNSA Tape B3245).

255. Hogwood, *Fanfare*, November/December 1985, pp. 88–9.

256. Mitsuko Uchida, *Schwann Opus*, Fall 1994, p. 10.

257. Mstislav Rostropovich, *The Daily Telegraph*, 29 May 1995.

258. Boulez in Plaistow, 'Boulez at 70', *Gramophone*, March 1995, p. 12.

259. See E. H. Gombrich, 'The Logic of Vanity Fair: Alternatives to Historicism in the Study of Fashions, Style and Taste', *Ideals and Idols: Essays on Values in History and in Art* (London, 1979), pp. 60–92.

260. Josef Hofmann, *Piano Playing with Piano Questions Answered* (Dover edition, 1976, with an introduction by Gregor Benko), p. xix. (First published in New York in 1909.)

261. William H. Youngren, 'Vocal Violin', *The Atlantic*, November 1992, pp. 144–8, quoted in Sherman, *Inside Early Music*, p. 207.

262. Brendel, *Music Sounded Out*, p. 221.

IV Listening to Recordings

1. *Gramophone* magazine, Awards issue 1998, vol. 76, no. 907, p. 1.

2. Christopher Fox and Philip Clark in Christopher Fox, 'Bridging the Gap: to Plug In or Not to Plug In?' *Society for the Promotion of New Music: New Notes*, November 1998, p. 1.

3. Yo-Yo Ma in an interview with Hilary Finch, 'More Strings to Ma's Bow', *The Times*, 10 May 1994.

4. Schweizerische Radio- und Fernsehgesellschaft: *Musik und Publikum* (Deutsche Schweiz). *Studie der Abteilung Forschungsdienst* (photocopy) (Bern, SRG 1979), quoted in Kurt Blaukopf, *Musical Life in a Changing Society*, translated by David Marinelli (1992, Portland, Oregon), p. 207. (First published as *Musik im Wandel der Gesellschaft* (Munich, 1982).)

5. *BPI Statistical Handbook 1995*, p. 62.

6. *BPI Yearbook 1976*, p. 55.

7. *BPI Statistical Handbook 1995*, p. 27.

8. Ralph Vaughan Williams, 'A Musical Autobiography', in *National Music and Other Essays* (Oxford, 2/1987), p. 183.

9. Geoffrey Skelton, *Paul Hindemith: The Man Behind the Music* (London, 1975), pp. 85–6.

10. Ibid., p. 95.

11. Quoted in Percy A. Scholes, *The Child and the Masterpiece* (Oxford, 1935), p. 40.

12. Dr Charles Burney, 'Essay on Musical Criticism', *A General History of Music from the Earliest Ages to the Present Period (1789)*, 4 vols (1776–89); 2-volume edition, ed. Frank Mercer (London, 1935), II, p. 7.

13. Quoted in Carl Dahlhaus, *The Idea of Absolute Music*, translated by Roger Lustig (Chicago/London, 1989), p. 3. (First published as *Die Idee der absoluten Musik* (Kassel, 1978).)

14. Peter Gay, 'The Art of Listening', *The Naked Heart: The Bourgeois Experience, Victoria to Freud* (London, 1995), p. 14.

15. Ralph W. Wood, 'The Future of Music-Making', *The Musical Times*, vol. 80, no. 1152, February 1939, pp. 94–5.

16. Theodor W. Adorno, 'Analytical Study of the NBC Music Appreciation Hour', a manuscript found in the Paul F. Lazarsfeld papers at Columbia University and one of four studies Adorno wrote in English between 1938 and 1941 under the aegis of the Princeton Radio Research Project, published for the first time in *The Musical Quarterly*, vol. 78, no. 2, Summer 1994, p. 330.

17. Heinrich Schenker, *Free Composition*, edited and translated by Ernst Oster (New York, 1979), p. 28. (First published as *Neue musikalische Theorien und Phantasien, III: Der freie Satz* (Vienna, 1935).)

18. Adorno, 'Analytical Study of the NBC Music Appreciation Hour', *The Musical Quarterly*, Summer 1994, p. 356.

19. Schenker, *Free Composition*, p. 160.

20. Theodor W. Adorno, *Prisms*, translated by Samuel and Shierry Weber (Cambridge, Mass., 1967), pp. 149–50. (First published as *Prismen*, 1967.)

21. Schenker, *Free Composition*, p. 27.

22. Arnold Schoenberg, 'Art and the Moving Pictures: 1940', *Style and Idea: Selected writings of Arnold Schoenberg*, edited by Leonard Stein and translated by Leo Black (London, 1975), pp. 155–6.

23. Eric Blom, 'An Essay on Performance and Listening', in A. L. Bacharach (ed.), *The Musical Companion* (London, 1934), p. 703.

24. E. H. Gombrich, *A Lifelong Interest: Conversations on Art and Science with Didier Eribon* (London, 1993), p. 16.

25. Hans Gál (ed.), *The Musician's World: Great Composers in their Letters* (published in 1978 as *The Musician's World: Letters of the Great Composers*) (London, 1965), p. 82.

26. James H. Johnson, *Listening in Paris: A Cultural History* (Berkeley, Los Angeles/London, 1995), p. 76.

27. Frederic Harrison, *Memories and Thoughts* (New York, 1896), pp. 299–302.

28. Richard Schickel, *The World of Carnegie Hall* (New York, 1960), p. 46.

29. Hugo Wolf, *Musikalische Kritiken*, edited by R. Batka and H. Werner (Leipzig, 1911), p. 228.

30. Quoted in Edward Lippman, *A History of Musical Aesthetics* (Lincoln, Nebraska/London, 1992) pp. 242–3.

31. Gay, *The Naked Heart*, p. 31.

32. Ibid., p. 33: reproduced in Gay following p. 116; and also in Nicholas Cook, *Music: A Very Short Introduction* (Oxford, 1998), p. 20.

33. Heinrich Schenker, *Harmony*, edited by Oswald Jonas and translated by Elisabeth Mann Borgese (Chicago, 1954), p. 60. (First published as *Neue musikalische Theorien und Phantasien, I: Harmonielehre* (Stuttgart, 1906).)

34. Schoenberg, 'Criteria for the Evaluation of Music', *Style and Idea*, pp. 133–6.

35. Igor Stravinsky and Robert Craft, *Expositions and Developments* (London, 1962/1981), pp. 147–8.

36. Pierre Boulez in an interview, Terry Coleman, 'Pierre de Résistance', *Guardian*, 13 January 1989.

37. Schoenberg, 'Modern Music on the Radio: 1933', *Style and Idea*, pp. 151–2.

38. T. S. Eliot, *Christianity and Culture* (New York, 1968), p. 185.

39. F. R. Leavis, *Mass Civilisation and Minority Culture* (Cambridge, 1930), p. 5.

40. Alfred Einstein, *A Short History of Music* (London, 1936), p. 200. (First published as *Geschichte der Musik* (Leipzig/Berlin, 1918).)

41. Virgil Thomson quoted in Joseph Horowitz, *The Post-Classical Predicament: Essays on Music and Society* (Boston, Mass., 1995), p. 11.

42. See Joseph Horowitz, *Understanding Toscanini* (London, 1987), p. 122.

43. Adorno, 'Analytical Study of the NBC Music Appreciation Hour', *The Musical Quarterly*, vol. 78, no. 2, Summer 1994, pp. 355–6.

44. See, for example, Gombrich, *A Lifelong Interest*, pp. 26–7.

45. Francis Toye, *Morning Post*, 18 November 1926, quoted in Scholes, *The Child and the Masterpiece*, p. 56.

46. Frank Howes, *The Borderland of Music and Psychology* (London, 1926), pp. 36–7.

47. Quoted in Scholes, *The Child and the Masterpiece*, p. 37.

48. Quoted ibid., p. 70.

49. W. R. Anderson, *The Gramophone*, vol. 11, no. 122, July 1933, p. 56; quoted in Scholes, *The Child and the Masterpiece*, p. 73.

50. Christopher Stone, 'Musicians and

Mechanical Music', *The Gramophone*, vol. 7, no. 81, February 1930, p. 423.

51. Ibid., p. 421.

52. Scholes, *The Child and the Masterpiece*, p. 72.

53. A. B. Ramsey, one-time Master of the Lower School, Eton College, quoted in Scholes, *The Child and the Masterpiece*, p. 46.

54. Howes, *The Borderland of Music And Psychology*, pp. 231–2.

55. Waldo Selden Pratt, 'The Isolation of Music', a paper given in London on 16 July 1895, *Proceedings of the Musical Association Twenty-First Session 1894–95*, p. 161.

56. Ibid., p. 161.

57. R. R. Terry, 'Canned Music', *Voodooism in Music* (London, 1934), p. 41.

58. Ibid., pp. 46–7.

59. Ibid., p. 47.

60. R. R. Terry, 'Music-hall Songs', *On Music's Borders* (London, 1927), p. 170.

61. Hilda Andrews, *Westminster Retrospect* (London, 1948), p. 166.

62. T. S. Eliot, *The Monthly Criterion*, vol. V, no. III, June 1927, p. 286.

63. *Debussy on Music*, collected and introduced by François Lesure, and translated and edited by Richard Langham Smith (London, 1977), p. 288.

64. Schoenberg, 'The Radio: Reply to a Questionnaire [July 31, 1930]', *Style and Idea*, p. 147.

65. Benjamin Britten, *On Receiving the First Aspen Award 1964* (London, 1964), p. 17.

66. Neville Cardus in Robin Daniels, *Conversations with Cardus* (London, 1976), p. 232.

67. Princess Dorothea Lieven, *Private Letters to Prince Metternich*, translated and edited by Peter Quennell and Dilys Powell (London, 1937), pp. 49–50.

68. Nicholas Spice, 'Hubbub', a review of *Repeated Takes: A Short History of Recording and its Effects on Music* by Michael Chanan (1995) and of *Elevator Music: A Surreal History of Muzak, Easy Listening and Other Mood Song* (1995), in *London Review of Books*, 6 July 1995, p. 3.

69. Robert Musil, 'Diaries' (translated from *Tagebücher*, Reinbek bei Hamburg, Rowohlt Verlag, 1955, by David McDuff), Newcastle upon Tyne, *Stand*, vol. 21, no. 2, 1980; quoted in Jon Glover and Jon Silkin (eds), *The Penguin Book of First World War Prose* (Harmondsworth, 1990), p. 96.

70. Robert Graves, *Goodbye to All That* (Harmondsworth, rev. ed./1957), p. 268.

71. Blom in A. L. Bacharach (ed.), *The Musical Companion*, p. 705.

72. R. Murray Schafer quoted in Kurt Blaukopf, *Musical Life in a Changing Society*, translated by David Marinelli (1992, Portland, Oregon), pp. 186–7. (First published as *Musik im Wandel der Gesellschaft* (1982, Munich).)

73. Jane Jarvis in H. Wiley Hitchcock (ed.), *The Phonograph and Our Musical Life: Proceedings of a Centennial Conference 7–10 December 1977*, I.S.A.M. Monographs: Number 14 (Institute for Studies in American Music, Department of Music, School of Performing Arts, Brooklyn College, City University of New York, New York, 1980), p. 13.

74. Ibid., p. 16.

75. *Radio Times*, programmes for 20–26 June 1943, p. 1.

76. Roger Reynolds, in Wiley Hitchcock (ed.), *The Phonograph and Our Musical Life*, p. 16.

77. 'What will Come of the Phonograph?' *The Spectator*, 30 June 1888, p. 881.

78. Jacques Barzun, *The Use and Abuse of Art* (The A. W. Mellon Lectures in the Fine Arts, 1973, The National Gallery of Art, Washington, D.C.) (Princeton/London, 1974), pp. 144–7.

79. Joseph Kerman, *Musicology* (London, 1985), p. 25.

80. David Hamilton in Wiley Hitchcock (ed.), *The Phonograph and Our Musical Life*, pp. 68–9.

81. Quoted in John Harvith and Susan Edwards Harvith, *Edison, Musicians, and the Phonograph: A Century in Retrospect* (New York, Westport, Connecticut, London, 1987), p. 269.

82. Michel de Montaigne, 'On the Rearing of Children' (1588), *Essais*, ed. J-V. Leclerc (4 vols, Paris, 1925), vol. 1: Book 1, chapter xxv, p. 186.

83. George D. Painter, *Marcel Proust* (Harmondsworth, one-volume ed./1983), p. 561.

84. John Keats, letter to Fanny Keats, 28 August 1819, in H. E. Rollins (ed.), *Letters of John Keats* (Cambridge, Mass., 1958), vol. 2, p. 149.

85. Jan Morris, 'On Music', *Pleasures of a Tangled Life* (London, 1989), pp. 32–4.

86. Blom in A. L. Bacharach (ed.), *The Musical Companion*, pp. 703–4.

87. See Edward Sackville-West and Desmond Shawe-Taylor, *The Record Guide* (London, 1951), pp. 378–85.

88. See Ivan March, Edward Greenfield and Robert Layton, *The Penguin Guide to*

Compact Discs (London, 1996), pp. 823–36.

89. William R. Moran (ed.), *Herman Klein and The Gramophone* (Portland, Oregon, 1990), p. 2.

90. Herman Klein, 'The Story of my "Phono-Vocal" Adventure', *The Gramophone*, vol. 8, no. 87, August 1930, pp. 123–4; Herman Klein, 'The Story of my "Phono-Vocal" Adventure', *The Gramophone*, vol. 8, no. 88, September 1930, pp. 171–2; reprinted in William R. Moran (ed.), *Herman Klein and The Gramophone* (Portland, Oregon, 1990), pp. 301–4.

91. Herman Klein, 'The Penalties of Exaggeration', *The Gramophone*, vol. 11, no. 124, September 1933, p. 130; reprinted in Moran (n. 90), p. 377.

92. Herman Klein, 'How to Imitate Good Records', *The Gramophone*, vol. 8, no. 94, March 1931, pp. 481–2; reprinted in Moran, pp. 315–16.

93. Sir Henry Wood, *The Influence of the Gramophone on Musical Culture*, paper read at the Fourteenth Annual Convention of the British Music Industries, Folkestone, May 1924 (London, 1924), p. 10.

94. Martin Williams in Wiley Hitchcock (ed.), *The Phonograph and Our Musical Life*, pp. 43–4.

95. Humphrey Lyttelton, *I Play as I Please* (1954), pp. 15–16, 34.

96. James Blades, *Drum Roll* (1977), p. 95.

97. Pierre Boulez in Coleman, 'Pierre de Résistance', *Guardian*, 13 January 1989.

98. Walter Legge, quoted in Elisabeth Schwarzkopf, *On and Off the Record* (London, 1982), p. 144.

99. See 'A tribute to Geraint Jones 1917–1998: historic BBC and HNV recordings 1949–1955' (Amphion PHI CD 148; released 1998 (mono CD)).

100. Peter Hurford in a lecture given at the Royal College of Organists, Kensington Gore, London, on 1 October 1985; the recorded illustrations together with the text of the lecture are preserved at the British Library: BLNSA Tape C941.

101. Anthony Rooley interviewed by George Pratt in 'Spirit of the Age', BBC Radio 3, 2 July 1994, BLNSA Tape H3562.

102. Frans Brüggen in Harvith and Harvith, *Edison, Musicians, and the Phonograph*, p. 203.

103. David Soyer, cellist of the Guarneri Quartet, ibid., p. 265.

104. Vladimir Ashkenazy, ibid., p. 222.

105. Janos Starker, ibid., p. 188.

106. Frans Brüggen, ibid., p. 205.

107. Andrew Porter in 'Visions Beatific', a *New Yorker* review dated 10 January 1977, reprinted in *Music of Three Seasons: 1974–1977* (London, 1979), p. 479.

108. Goddard Lieberson in Glenn Gould, 'The Prospects of Recording', *Hi-Fidelity*, vol. 16, no. 4, April 1966, p. 57.

109. Pierre Boulez in Robert Cowan, 'Pierre Boulez: History in the Present Tense', *CD Review*, December 1990, p. 23.

110. André Previn in Harvith and Harvith, *Edison, Musicians, and the Phonograph*, p. 215.

111. Lotte Lehmann, ibid., pp. 75–6.

112. André Previn, ibid., p. 215–16.

113. Robert Godet quoted in Edward Lockspeiser, *Debussy: His Life and Mind*, vol. 1 (London, 2/1966), p. 113.

114. Columbia LX 311/3 (3 12″ electrical 78 rpm discs); Ian Kemp, *Tippett: The Composer and His Music* (London, 1984), p. 70.

115. Kemp, *Tippett*, pp. 147–8, 439; Meirion Bowen, sleeve note to *Concerto for double string orchestra* in Virgin Classics VC 7 90701-1 (12″ 33⅓ rpm stereo disc).

116. György Ligeti, in the booklet accompanying *György Ligeti Edition vol. 3: Works for Piano*, Sony SK 62 (digital stereo CD).

117. Nicholas Kenyon, 'Back to the Future', *The Observer*, 7 June 1987.

118. Paul Griffiths, *New Sounds, New Personalities: British Composers of the 1980s* (London, 1985), p. 113; 'Music that Changed Me', *BBC Music Magazine*, October 1993, p. 122.

119. Geoffrey Haydon, *John Tavener: Glimpses of Paradise* (London, 1995), p. 15.

120. John Tavener talking to Malcolm Crowthers, *The Musical Times*, vol. 135, no. 1811, January 1994, p. 13.

121. From a programme note by the composer, Universal Edition.

122. Giles Swayne, BBC World Service, 10 April 1987: BLNSA Tape T9189.

123. Paul Henry Lang, *The Musical Quarterly*, vol. 40, no. 3, July 1954, p. 384.

124. Ibid., p. 385.

125. Martin Cooper, 'The Critic's Task', *Judgements of Value* (Oxford, New York, 1988), p. 5.

126. Wilfrid Mellers, *Bach and the Dance of God* (London, 1980), p. vii.

127. Denis Arnold, quoting Egon Wellesz's article in *Grove's Dictionary of Music and Musicians* (5th ed., 1954), in Edward Olleson, 'The Profession of Musical Scholarship', *Modern Musical Scholarship* (Stocksfield, 1978), p. 13; see also, for

example: Friedrich Blume, 'Musical Scholarship Today', in Barry S. Brook, Edward O. D. Downes, and Sherman Van Solkema (eds), *Perspectives in Musicology* (New York, 1972), pp. 15–31; Claude V. Palisca, 'Reflections on Musical Scholarship in the 1960s', in D. Kern Holoman and Claude V. Palisca (eds), *Musicology in the 1980s: Methods, Goals, Opportunities* (New York, 1982), pp. 15–30; and for hints on the specific opportunities that recordings might offer see Joseph Kerman, *Musicology* (London, 1985), pp. 24–5.

128. J. M. Thomson, *Early Music*, vol. 1, no. 1, January 1973, p. 1.

129. J. M. Thomson, *Early Music*, vol. 7, no. 3, July 1979, p. 306.

130. Joseph Kerman, *Musicology* (London, 1985), p. 203.

131. Deborah Coclanis, *Notes*, vol. 46, no. 2, December 1989, p. 411.

132. Ronald Gelatt, *The Fabulous Phonograph* (New York, 1954, 1955), pp. 303–4.

133. Gillian Davies, 'Compulsory Deposit of Sound Recordings', *Recorded Sound*, no. 62, April 1976, p. 519.

134. *Copyright and Designs Law: Report of the Committee to consider the Law on Copyright and Designs* (Chairman: The Honourable Mr Justice Whitford, 'The Whitford Report', presented to Parliament in March 1977) (London, HMSO, Cmnd 6732), p. 209.

135. John Bird, *Percy Grainger* (London, 1976), p. 111.

136. Dietrich Schüller, 'The Vienna Phonogrammarchiv 1899–1981', *Recorded Sound*, no. 81, January 1982, pp. 33–9.

137. Roger Decollogne, 'La Phonothèque Nationale', in Henry F. J. Currall (ed.), *Gramophone Record Libraries: Their Organisation and Practice* (London, 2/1970), p. 268.

138. James R. Smart, 'Carl Engel and the Library of Congress's first acquisitions of recordings', *Journal of the Association for Recorded Sound Collections*, vol. 15, nos 2–3, p. 7.

139. Ibid., p. 10.

140. Ibid., p. 11.

141. Ibid., p. 11.

142. Ibid., p. 14.

143. Ibid., pp. 13–14.

144. Ibid., p. 18.

145. Unattributed article, 'The Library of Congress', *The Record Collector*, vol. 39, no. 2, April/May/June 1994, p. 148.

146. 'The New York Library for the Performing Arts: The Rodgers and Hammerstein Archives of Recorded Sound' publicity leaflet, not dated, available 1997; see also David Hall, 'The Rodgers and Hammerstein Archives of Recorded Sound', *Journal of the Association for Recorded Sound Collections*, vol. 6, no. 2, 1974, pp. 17–31.

147. William R. Moran, 'Stanford Archive of Recorded Sound', *The Record Collector*, vol. 41, no. 3, September 1996, pp. 189–90.

148. Linda Blair, 'The Yale Collection of Historical Sound Recordings', *Journal of the Association for Recorded Sound Collections*, vol. 20, no. 2, Fall 1989, pp. 167–76.

149. Memorial Record, Columbia Graphophone Co. Ltd; BLNSA 9TL0000447 (12″ double-sided, electric 78 rpm disc).

150. Peter Copeland, 'The British Museum Collection', *The Historic Record*, no. 28, July 1993, pp. 12–14.

151. Joe Batten, *Joe Batten's Book: The Story of Sound Recording* (London, 1956), p. 32.

152. Vespasiano da Bisticci, 'Federigo, Duke of Urbino', in *The Vespasiano Memoirs: Lives of Illustrious Men of the XVth Century*, translated by William George and Emily Waters (London, 1926), p. 104.

153. Patrick Saul, BBC World Service, 10 April 1987 (BLNSA Tape T9189).

154. Patrick Saul, 'A Brief Note on Archives of Sound Recordings', *The Journal of Documentation*, vol. 4, no. 2, September 1948, p. 87.

155. Patrick Saul, 'The British Institute of Recorded Sound', in Currall (ed.), *Gramophone Record Libraries: Their Organisation and Practice*, pp. 222–3.

156. Ibid., p. 222.

157. Desmond Shawe-Taylor, *The Gramophone*, vol. 33, no. 389, October 1955, pp. 171–3.

158. Trevor Fisher, 'The British Institute of Recorded Sound', *Tempo*, no. 45, Autumn 1957, pp. 24–7.

159. Decca Historic 4400632 (mono CD; released 1994).

160. BLNSA 9TL0000746.

161. Geoffrey Cuming, 'Problems of Record Cataloguing', *Recorded Sound*, vol. 1, no. 4, Autumn 1961, p. 119.

162. CBS/Columbia M 34554 (released 1977).

163. Among the most valuable recent writings on discography are: Martin Elste, 'Evaluating discographies of classical music', in *IASA Phonographic Bulletin*, no. 54, July 1989, pp. 64–77 (which contains a bibliography of 'literature on the methods of discography'); Michael

H. Gray, 'Discography: Discipline and Musical Ally', published simultaneously in *Music Reference Services Quarterly*, vol. 2, no. 3/4, 1993, pp. 319–25; and in Richard D. Green (ed.), *Foundations in Music Bibliography* (1993), pp. 319–25; Guy A. Marco, 'Bibliographic and Bibliothecal Considerations for Discographers', *ARSC Journal*, vol. 25, no. 1, Spring 1994, pp. 1–8; Jerome F. Weber, 'Formulating guidelines for discographies to be published in the *ARSC Journal*', *ARSC Journal*, vol. 28, no. 2, Summer 1997, pp. 198–208.

164. Michael H. Gray, *Beecham: A Centenary Discography* (London, 1979).

165. *The Rigler-Deutsch Index – A National Union Catalogue of Sound Recordings – Part I: An Index to the 78 rpm Sound Recordings in the Association for Recorded Sound Collections/Associated Audio Archives member Libraries*: a listing of the coarse-groove discs held at the following North American sound archives: Rogers and Hammerstein Archives of Recorded Sound of the New York Public Library, New York City; Syracuse University Audio Archives, Syracuse, New York; Yale University Audio Archives, New Haven, Connecticut; Recorded Sound Collection, Library of Congress, Washington, D.C.; and the Stanford University Archive of Recorded Sound, Stanford, California [1985].

166. Elwood McKee, 'ARSC/AAA: Fifteen Years of Cooperative Research', *Journal of the Association for Recorded Sound Collections*, vol. 20, no. 1, Spring 1989, pp. 3–13.

167. *Gramophone Long-Playing Classical Record Catalogue* (1953–1967) (tapes included from 1954); *Gramophone Classical Catalogue* (1977–96); *Gramophone Compact Disc Catalogue* (1983–90); and *R.E.D. Classical Catalogue* (1997–), the *Schwann-Opus* catalogues for the United States, *Diapason* for France, and *Bielefelder Katalog: Klassik* for Germany; for details of electrical 78 rpm discs there are R. D. Darrell's *The Gramophone Shop Encyclopaedia of Recorded Music* (New York, 1936; 2nd ed., 1942; 3rd ed., 1948) and *The Gramophone Shop, Inc.: Record Supplements* (New York, 1937–53), and also Francis F. Clough and G. J. Cuming, *The World's Encyclopedia of Recorded Music* (London, 1952; with *First Supplement*) [(*Second Supplement*, 1953; *Third Supplement*, 1957)]; for details of 33⅓ rpm discs there are Kurtz Myers, *Index to*

Record Reviews: 1949–1977 (Boston, Mass., 1985), and Kurtz Myers, *Index to Record Reviews: 1978–1983* (Boston, Mass., 1985).

168. Michael Gray, 'Discography: Discipline and Musical Ally', *Music Reference Services Quarterly*, vol. 2, nos 3/4, p. 320.

169. HMV C 1740 (12″ double-sided electrical 78 rpm disc issued in 1929).

170. HMV 305 (10″ double-sided acoustic 78 rpm disc issued in 1924).

171. Brian Rust, 'Dates of Records', *The Gramophone*, vol. 49, no. 581, October 1971, p. 613.

172. See for example: Barrie Martyn, *Rachmaninoff: Composer, Pianist, Conductor* (Aldershot, 1990), pp. 451–97.

173. Peter Copeland, 'Why Matrix Numbers?' *The Historic Record*, no. 7, March 1988, p. 10.

174. J. F. Weber, *Discography Series xvi: Benjamin Britten* (Utica, New York, 1975), p. 25.

175. Reprinted in Denis Stevens, *Musicology: A Practical Guide* (London, 1980), p. 70.

176. HMV HMS 28 (12″ double-sided electrical 78 rpm disc).

177. Bernard Gagnepain, 'Safford Cape et le "Miracle" Pro Musica Antiqua', *Revue Belge de Musicologie*, 34–5 (1980–1), pp. 204–19.

178. Mabel Dolmetsch, *Personal Recollections of Arnold Dolmetsch* (London, 1958), pp. 17–18.

179. Helen S. Slosberg, Mary V. Ullman and Isabel K. Whiting (eds), *Erwin Bodky: A Memorial Tribute* (Waltham, Mass., 1965), p. 141, quoted in Harry Haskell, *The Early Music Revival: A History* (London, 1988), p. 178.

180. Musica Reservata (director Michael Morrow)/Andrew Parrott; Argo ZRG 793 (12″ 33⅓ rpm stereo disc; issued 1975).

181. Michael Morrow (in an interview with J. M. Thomson), 'Early Music Ensembles I: Musica Reservata', *Early Music*, vol. 4, no. 4, October 1976, p. 515.

182. Ibid., p. 517.

183. Michael Morrow, 'Musical Performance and Authenticity', *Early Music*, vol. 6, no. 2, April 1978, p. 237.

184. John Southcott in 'Michael Morrow, 1929–94', *Early Music*, vol. 22, no. 3, August 1994, p. 538.

185. Michael Morrow (in an interview with J. M. Thomson), *Early Music*, October 1976, p. 517.

186. David Fallows in 'Michael Morrow, 1929–94', *Early Music*, August 1994, p. 538.

187. Denis Arnold, *Gramophone*, vol. 46, no. 550, March 1969, p. 1316.
188. Christopher Page in 'Michael Morrow, 1929–94', *Early Music*, August 1994, p. 539.
189. William P. Malm in Harvith and Harvith, *Edison, Musicians, and the Phonograph*, p. 274.
190. George Dyson, 'Of Organs and Organists', *The Musical Times*, vol. 93, no. 1317, November 1952, p. 492.
191. Columbia 4211 (10″ double-sided electrical 78 rpm disc; recorded 8 July 1927): see p. 156.
192. E. H. Fellowes, *Memoirs of an Amateur Musician* (London, 1946), p. 94.
193. See Peter Phillips, 'The Golden Age Regained – 1', *Early Music*, vol. 8, no. 1, January 1980, pp. 3–16; Peter Phillips, 'The Golden age Regained – 2', *Early Music*, vol. 8, no. 2, April 1980, pp. 180–98.
194. Charles H. Moody, *The Choir-Boy in the Making* (London, 1922), pp. 27–8.
195. Terry, 'The Obsession of the Hymn-tune', *On Music's Borders*, p. 202.
196. R. R. Terry, 'A Question of Idiom', *On Music's Borders*, p. 188.
197. R. R. Terry in Cecil Gray, *Peter Warlock* (London, 1934), p. 273.
198. Donald Tovey and Geoffrey Parratt, *Walter Parratt: Master of Music* (London, 1941), p. 67.
199. Margaret Campbell, 'Symbol of an Epoch: Fritz Kreisler', *The Great Violinists* (London, 1980), p. 117.

Index

Machaut, Guillaume de   82, 115, 120, 165;
    Douce dame jolie, different performances
    compared   174–8
McFerrin, Bobby   223
Mackenzie, Sir Alexander Campbell   137
Mackenzie, Compton   71
Maconchy, Elizabeth   91, 243
madrigals, English   74, 226, 235; madrigal
    singers   253
Maeterlinck, Maurice   248
Magdalen College, Oxford, the choir of
    170–3
magnetic tape   20–21; tape editing   23, 26,
    156; tape 'hiss'   21
Magnetophon tape recorders   96
Mahler, Gustav   5, 15, 93, 97, 101, 138, 139,
    140, 192, 224
Mahout, Albert   188
Malipiero, Gian Francesco   94, 95
Mallarmé, Stéphane   64
Manguin, Henri   140
Manns, August   1, 153–4
Marais, Marin   81
Marchal, André   188
'Marching through Georgia'   2
Marcuse, Herbert   207
Marenzio, Luca   82, 92
Markevitch, Igor   134, 137
Marquet, Albert   140
Marriner, Neville   84
Marty, Adolf   188
Märzendorfer, Ernst   100
Mascagni, Pietro   3, 203 (*Cavalleria
    rusticana*)
Massart, J. L.   168
mass audiences for classical music: the
    creation of: by radio in the 1920s and
    1930s   73–6; by war-time National Gallery
    concerts   88; by the BBC Third
    Programme   89–92; by the BBC in the
    1960s   120–2; opinions on the possibility
    of   206–13
Massenet, Jules   42
masterpiece, nineteenth-and twentieth-
    century concepts of the musical   64–7
Mathias, George   148
Matisse, Henri   139
Matrix (record label)   135
matrix numbers   247–8, 255
Matthay, Tobias   242
Matthews, Denis   240
Mattins, 1924 recording of music for   12
Maurel, Victor   148
Maxwell Davies, Sir Peter   119, 140
Mayer, Sir Robert   240
Medtner Society   71
Méhul, Etienne-Nicolas   85
Melba, Nellie   4, 39, 131, 222, 237, 238
Melbourne Conservatorium of Music   83
Mellers, Wilfrid   180, 230

Mendelssohn, Felix   3, 17, 18, 50, 66, 69, 75,
    92, 95, 101, 144, 152, 217, 244
Mengelberg, Willem   193
Menuhin, Yehudi   135, 240
Mercury (record label)   122
Messiaen, Olivier   101, 119, 121, 135, 163,
    188, 243
Metropol (record label)   236
Metropolitan Opera House, New York   1, 3,
    46, 54, 236, 242
Metternich, Prince   213
Mewton-Wood, Noel   89
Meyerbeer, Giacomo   3 (*Le Prophète*), 203
    (*The Prophet*)
Michalowski, Aleksander   148
Michelangeli, Arturo Benedetti   113
microgroove disc: *see* LP
microphones, numbers and placing of
    23–6, 219
Mikuli, Karol   148
Milhaud, Darius   13, 91, 95, 97, 161, 163,
    193
Minneapolis Symphony Orchestra   93; and
    Chorus   24
Minstrel Boy, The   4
Mitchell, Joni   230
Mitropoulos, Dimitri   93
'mixing' techniques   23–6, 28–9
Moeck, Hermann   176
Moeran, E. J.   119
Mohawk minstrels   205
Moiseiwitsch, Benno   50, 243; on piano rolls
    15
monaural sound (mono)   20
Monk, W. H.   237
mono: *see* monaural sound
Montserrat Abbey   86, 170
Montaigne, Michel Eyquiem de   217
Monteux, Pierre   134
Monteverdi, Claudio   63, 82, 91, 94, 101,
    110, 114, 223
Montmartre, a mistress in   60
Montpellier Codex   84
Moore, Douglas   122
Moore, Gerald   10, 47, 48, 50
Morandi, Giovanni   137
Morkov, A.   137
Morley, Thomas   82
Morley College Choir   90
Morris, William   249
Morrow, Michael   251–2
Moscheles, Ignaz   153
Moser, Andreas: *Violinschule* (with J.
    Joachim)   148
Moore, Ray   25
Moussorgsky   74, 137
Moussorgsky, Modest Petrovich   74
Mozarabic liturgical chant   86
Mozart, Wolfgang Amadeus   3, 6, 18, 29
    (*Don Giovanni*), 43, 63, 66, 68, 69, 75, 84,